Reclaiming San Francisco

History, Politics, Culture

A CITY LIGHTS ANTHOLOGY

Edited by
James Brook, Chris Carlsson, and Nancy J. Peters

CITY LIGHTS BOOKS
SAN FRANCISCO, CALIFORNIA

Cover photograph: Courtesy the Bancroft Library. Carville, cable car graveyard at Lincoln Way and the Great Highway, c. 1900. After the 1906 earthquake, refugees converted the cars into living quarters, and for a brief time Carville was a thriving community.

Cover design: Nigel French, Small World Productions

Typography: Typesetting Etc.

Cataloging-in-Publication Data

Reclaiming San Francisco: History, Politics, Culture
A CITY LIGHTS ANTHOLOGY
Edited by James Brook, Chris Carlsson, and Nancy J. Peters.
p.   cm.
ISBN: 0-87286-335-2
1. San Francisco (Calif.)—History. 2. San Francisco (Calif.)—Politics and government.
3. San Francisco (Calif.)—Social life and customs. 4. Arts—California—San Francisco—History.
I. Brook, James. II. Carlsson, Chris, 1957-   . III. Peters, Nancy J. (Nancy Joyce)   IV. City Lights Books.
F869.S357R43   1998   97-22799
979.4'61—dc21
CIP

City Lights Books are available to bookstores through our primary distributor:
Subterranean Company. P. O. Box 160, 265 S. 5th St., Monroe, OR 97456.
541-847-5274. Toll-free orders 800-274-7826. FAX 541-847-6018.
Our books are also available through library jobbers and regional distributors.
For personal orders and catalogs, please write to
City Lights Books, 261 Columbus Avenue, San Francisco, CA 94133.
http://www.citylights.com

CITY LIGHTS BOOKS are edited by Lawrence Ferlinghetti and Nancy J. Peters and published at the City Lights Bookstore, 261 Columbus Avenue, San Francisco, CA 94133.

Contents

Preface

The true problem for historians is to succeed in expressing the complexity of reality, even if this involves using descriptive techniques and forms of reasoning which are more intrinsically self-questioning and less assertive than any used before.

—Giovanni Levi, "On Microhistory"

THROUGHOUT THE BRIEF HISTORY of San Francisco the official story of the city has been one of progress, development, and growth, leavened with enough "preservation" of architecture, views, and amenities to make it more livable than most cities—and more attractive to investors and the heads of major corporations. The Chamber of Commerce, the Planning Commission, the Redevelopment Agency, the Port Commission, the Convention and Visitors Bureau, and the plethora of "citizens groups" that are really corporate fronts have been all too successful in controlling San Francisco's image, the makeup of its population, its position in the regional, state, national, and global economies, and the shape of its land and skyline. With antecedents in the nineteenth-century vigilante associations that did the bidding of the business elite, the modern structures of corporate and bureaucratic power continue to dominate according to the same principles: make a lot of money and screw the poor.

Reclaiming San Francisco is an anthology of fresh appraisals of the contrarian spirit of the city—a spirit "resistant to authority or control." Like a lot of cities in America and the world, San Francisco is undergoing tremendous changes as a result of global shifts of power and capital. But San Franciscans are unusually ready to challenge the corporate agenda for their city. This collection is part of that challenge.

The more than two dozen contributors include historians, geographers, poets, novelists, artists, art historians, photographers, journalists, citizen activists, an architect, and an anthropologist. They are a diverse group: African American, Chinese American, Filipino American, Latino, white (a category that conceals a multitude of national origins), male, female, gay, straight, older, younger, comfortably well off, and flat broke, according to our informal census. They have no program in common, but all care passionately for the city that private interests are shaping for private gain. For the contributors, "reclaiming" is a synonym for *restoration* and *criticism*. They want San Francisco to be more San Francisco and less like the city of office towers, chain stores, theme parks, and privatized public services and property that appears to be its immediate fate.

Because of its turn-of-the-century look and its compact size, dictated by its location on the tip of a peninsula, San Francisco has often been called a "European" city. In reality it is very American and modern—and at the same time it is unlike any other American city. When the poet Kenneth Rexroth first settled here in the late 1920s he found it a cultural backwater, but an open and congenial one, as he notes in *An Autobiographical Novel* (New York: New Directions 1991):

> San Francisco was not just a wide-open town. It is the only city in the United States which was not settled overland by the spreading puritan tradition. . . . It had been settled mostly, in spite of all the romances of the overland migration, by gamblers, prostitutes, rascals, and fortune seekers who came across the Isthmus and around the Horn. They had their faults, but they were not influenced by Cotton Mather. . . . The ocean was at the end of the streetcar line. Down the peninsula and across the Golden Gate the Coast Range was still a wilderness, and the High Sierras were a short day's trip away. More important, nobody cared what you did as long as you didn't commit any gross public crimes.

The unbridled nature of the immigrant population—rich and poor alike—did indeed add to the attractiveness of the city as a place to live (if not to look at: in the nineteenth century San Francisco was known for its ugliness). Beginning with the Gold Rush, people came to San Francisco from all over the world to strike it rich, to start anew, to live freer. In addition to the "rascals" that Rexroth describes, immigrants included Chinese and other Asian laborers, and refugees from the failed European revolutions of 1848.

A restive, nonconformist, and enterprising population of diverse nationality, ethnicity, and religious and political persuasion rapidly transformed a Mexican and Anglo outpost into a bustling city. It's not that everyone got along famously, but in a rich and expanding city many differences were easily tolerated. There was, however, a singular exception. The whites and those who would be white—Yankees, Southerners, Germans, French, Irish, Italians, Basques—constructed their identity in part through hatred of the Chinese, who were long excluded from civic life and subject to discriminatory immigration laws. White hegemony would eventually be challenged with African American immigration during World War II, followed by increasing numbers of Central Americans, Chinese, and Southeast Asians beginning in the 1970s.

Immigrants—with their different ways of life and different languages—no longer added an exotic air to a white city: they were becoming the city. Ill-tempered remarks about "political correctness" aside, new identities have been forged, and they are every bit as authentic and strong as such earlier ones as "Irish" or "working class." Significantly, recent immigrants have brought a renewed interest in urban living to San Francisco, and their experiences of the city have altered the way all experience life here.

Whether adventurer, misfit, or refugee from another city, country, or distant war, people come to San Francisco for a better life. The California Dream started here, with the Gold Rush, and expectations have always been high and continue to be so. If prospectors didn't strike it rich in the gold fields, they could command high wages working construction in town or stevedoring. Rough equality was in the air, and there was no lack of personal freedom.

The fondest dreams of the business class, on the other hand, have been nightmares for many of the people affected. True, for much of San Francisco's history there's been broad consensus that improvements to infrastructure are beneficial to the city as well as to those pocketing the profits. Paving the streets—demanded at the turn of the century by bicyclists!—electrification, public transit, tunnels, and building the Civic Center were generally popular with voters and elite decision makers, even when there was contention over particular projects or over how the spoils were to be shared. Business made money on the spot and prepared the way for future investment. When business was doing well, organized labor could claim higher wages; and improvements to infrastructure often made life easier for the average citizen. Enthusiasm for the Golden Gate and Bay Bridges was general, for instance.

But consensus began to break down at the end of World War II. While the business–organized labor partnership was even more solid (thanks to the New Deal and wartime cooperation), the average citizen wasn't automatically convinced of the benefits of progress. If elite planners thought the future of the city was at stake, so did the citizen activists who emerged starting in the 1950s to oppose the elite agenda for San Francisco.

Those with a popular vision of the city have scored many successes: the freeways were stopped in mid-course, some destroyed housing was replaced, restrictions were imposed on office buildings (though *after* the 1980s construction boom), and a weak version of rent control was imposed. But business did, in fact, get its way most of the time, partly because the local bourgeoisie thinks more strategically and is better organized than its factionalized, single-issue oppositions. The local bourgeoisie also has a clearer understanding of its position in the regional, state, national, and global economies—and what it takes to survive in these environments.

Downtown has always looked for room to grow and space to order. It's not "market forces" but planning-plus-market-forces that has created a more vertical downtown—serviced by the Bay Area Rapid Transit (BART) lines that bring office workers in from the East Bay suburbs. A similar configuration of forces has enabled downtown interests to extend to the South of Market. The Yerba Buena Center, with its art museums and other attractions, anchors further development down to China Basin: a new sports stadium, the loft spaces of Multimedia Gulch, and the high-end cafés and night spots catering to professionals. Farther south is the site of the Mission Bay project, where a new "city within a city" will soon arise, anchored by a University of California medical research campus. Office buildings and biotech labs will combine with dormitories for professionals, parks, and entertainment facilities to create a neo-neighborhood based on real estate speculation and giveaways of public property and funds.

The Civic Center is being redesigned and rebuilt. Its current showpiece is the New Main Library, which is a professedly high-tech "library of the future"— and a test case of the "public-private partnership" model of funding. But the new building has little room for books amid ramps that lead nowhere and already obsolete computer terminals that provide limited access to a butchered collection.

Other targets of development include the Presidio, an army base that has passed under the control of a trust charged with making the new national park profitable within fifteen years. Probable uses are luxury housing, entertainment, office space, and some nonprofit window-dressing, which will only increase the value of the land for private exploitation.

Recently, the state legislature granted Mayor Willie Brown, longtime friend of development interests, the power to appoint a committee to sell off rights to Treasure Island, a former navy base. Rumors are rampant that Treasure Island is slated to be a theme park—with a little space set aside for a new women's jail and a tiny enclave of "affordable housing." The waterfront, though mandated for maritime uses, is also set to be turned into a profitable strip extending from touristic Fisherman's Wharf down to the previously abandoned—and recently rediscovered as "historic"—shipyards off Potrero Hill.

With a narrow vote in spring 1997 Willie Brown & Co. won approval to build a stadium-and-mall complex to replace Candlestick Park, whose bonds were only recently paid off. Marred by many irregularities, including enthusiastic balloting by the dead, the vote on the stadium proposal was brought out by promises of jobs to the black community at Bayview–Hunters Point. Many believe that these jobs will never appear and that the stadium complex could spell the beginning of urban renewal—once known as "Negro removal"—for the area.

Meanwhile, environmental justice advocates, bringing to light shocking cancer rate statistics in the same neighborhood, have fended off a recent attempt to place a third power plant there. Other urban activists are also pressing forward. There are over one hundred community gardens thriving in publicly owned open spaces in every corner of San Francisco. Neighbors are working to restore native plant species on almost every hilltop; from San Bruno Mountain to the Presidio citizens are campaigning to protect the remnants of original habitat. Bicycle advocates, bolstered by the monthly show of force from Critical Mass, are pushing for traffic calming and bike- and pedestrian-priority streets all over town.

San Francisco is at a crossroads: its shape for the coming century is being determined now. Indications point to the fabrication of a very different place, with less of the openness that once characterized the city. A city of mostly "middle-class professionals" loses vitality and authenticity, and the skyrocketing price of housing contributes to a homogeneous population. The city's new architecture tends to look like an "artist's rendering" even after it's built, right down to the ornamental shrubbery and security lighting. In accord with the logic of commodification, these piles rapidly go from "brand new" to rundown without ever having seemed lived in. It's as if San Francisco were becoming a shopping mall with an urban theme. . . .

Nonetheless, San Francisco has not been entirely transformed into an image of itself. The city is not reducible to postcard views, tourist attractions, great restaurants, and multiplex cinemas. San Francisco remains contradictory, conflictual, multiple, various, diverse; fortunately for the life of the city, the contrarian spirit arises after every setback. By taking a look back at some of San Francisco's pasts, by casting colder eyes on its current state, and by glancing ahead to its possible future, we hope that *Reclaiming San Francisco* will encourage local contrarians to redouble their efforts toward making the city a better place to live in. With them, we believe that the dystopia of marketing and finance isn't the only vision of San Francisco that stands a chance of being realized. We hope, too, that readers in other towns around the country will appreciate the particulars of the history and struggles of San Francisco—while gaining fresh insight into the lives of their own cities, inevitably caught in the same vortex of power and resistance.

—*JB, CC & NJP*
San Francisco, November 1997

An Appetite for the City

by Richard A. Walker

SAN FRANCISCO IS RENOWNED as a beautiful, vibrant, livable city. But it was not always so: nineteenth-century San Francisco was excoriated as a wood yard of unusual extent and, later, as a scene of vulgar display by the newly rich. And it would be less admirable today were it not for an extraordinary popular upheaval against the wrecking ball and new construction. Nowhere else in America was such opposition as successful as in postwar San Francisco, and this revolt conserved much of what makes the city livable. I want to retell that story as one of pitched battle over civic space, a war of position between the titans of capital Downtown and people from many neighborhoods and many walks of urban life. But more than that I want to tell it as a struggle for the soul of the city, in which an unlikely configuration of people from many points on the social compass came to defend the city they lived in and loved from destruction by the forces of progress.

Such opposition is not what one would expect in a country in which "progress" is the watchword. Not in a country always profoundly ill at ease with cities, whose urban landscapes have been pulled down and built over without a second thought. Not in a state with impeccable Republican credentials for most of its history, and not at a time when urban renewal and suburban flight gutted city cores from San Jose to San Diego. Not even in San Francisco, whose present image as a comely dowager belies its history as the cannibal city of the nineteenth-century West, devouring the resources of the Pacific Coast and its own little peninsula with aggressive callousness. How did this rapacious polis become more civilized over time?

Such cultivated urbanity is founded on political economy and political culture more than on natural scenery and urban design. It does not arise naturally from affluence or maturity. Consider the eagerness with which the local burghers tried to pull down the city after World War II. A politics of resistance and preservation

Market Street (c. 1940)

Reclaiming San Francisco

derives from a vision of the city as a good place, informed by an aesthetics of urbanism and a sense of popular entitlement to urban spaces. Moreover, it must be driven by a civil society breathing life into oppositional words, having the political capacity to take on the powerful, and providing the armies of the night to rebuild the everyday city again and again out of the fragments of stone and memory lying all about.

Saving the City

A simple political geography of San Francisco places downtown business at the center, a hodge-podge of neighborhoods east of Twin Peaks as the heart of opposition, and the outer realms as conservative minions of order. The business class, led by the biggest banks, industrial corporations, and property owners, initiated the battle for the city after World War II by their plans to expand the Downtown through better transit, clearance of nearby areas, and more and taller buildings. They were met on every side by popular revolt. Although the city's core was recast dramatically over the next thirty years, resistance nevertheless achieved a great deal. Skyscrapers were prevented from going west and north, saving Chinatown, North Beach, Telegraph Hill, and the old retail district. The Tenderloin is still alive with hotels and poor working people. Freeways were stopped before they could desecrate the northern waterfront and Golden Gate Park. The Ferry Building still stands. Many fine old commercial buildings were saved, and thousands of Victorian houses have been restored. Meanwhile, a cosmopolitan throng continues to occupy city neighborhoods: Africans, Chinese, Filipinos, Vietnamese, queers, residual hippies, punks, and poets. The living city lives on, even through hard times.

Downtown Expansion: Property and Progress

From the Depression through the fifties, decaying urban cores were a national obsession. San Francisco business leaders in particular suffered from intense vertigo induced by a metropolis spinning outward like a red giant, threatening to leave a dwarf city behind. This spurred coordinated action through bodies such as the Public Utilities Commission, the Regional Plan Association and the Bay Area Council. A plan for a Bay Area Rapid Transit (BART) system was drawn up by Bechtel Corporation to keep commuters flowing downtown. This was conceived in 1942 and built in the 1960s. The 1940s also saw the first designs for a freeway network, spurred by national planning for a national defense highway system. The California Department of Highways went to work right after the war, and freeway madness hit full speed with passage of the 1956 Federal Highway

Act. Freeways were soon marching up from the Peninsula, around the waterfront, and behind the Civic Center. Freeway off-ramps led directly into all the principal redevelopment zones. New bridges were envisioned across the northern and central bay. Obsolete forms of transit, like cable cars and trolleys, were destined for the scrap heap.

Urban renewal legislation passed by Congress in 1949 and 1954 gave cities the power to assemble land, clear it of offending uses, and finance redevelopment. San Francisco, like all big cities, established a Redevelopment Agency to spearhead its efforts. Justin Herman directed that agency aggressively for many years, backed by the San Francisco Planning and Urban Renewal Association (a citizens group), and later the Convention and Visitors Bureau (arm of the hotel and tourism industry).

The first renewal plan targeted the Western Addition, an area of dense rental housing occupied by former wartime shipyard workers, many of them black. The Agency aimed to rid the city of over two square miles of Victorian houses, replacing them with thirty-three ten-story slabs to lure middle-class suburbanites back to the city. One planner put it succinctly: "Nothing short of a clean sweep and a new start can make the district a genuinely good place in which to live." The project began by ramming through the Geary Expressway and clearing old Japantown for a retail complex; then it headed south on both sides of Fillmore. Four thousand people were rousted out in the late 1950s and over 13,000 in the 1960s. Over 1,000 Victorian houses were clear cut, eliminating ten percent of the city's total stock.

Along the northern edge of Downtown lay the produce district, eyed for renewal. The Blythe-Zellerbach Committee, formed in 1956, drew up the Golden Gateway project (including the Embarcadero Center, to be built with Rockefeller and Mellon money). The Montgomery Block, the city's oldest building and bohemian haunt, was cleared in 1959. Cyril Magnin, port commissioner and later president of the Chamber of Commerce, had the city buy back its port from the state in 1959, then offered a grand design for hotels and offices along the Embarcadero. Chinatown was targeted and Portsmouth Square was torn up for a parking garage. Manilatown, a stretch of Kearny Street known for its many Filipino residents and shops, was slated for demolition.

South of Market an assault was planned on Skid Row. In 1954, Ben Swig, the biggest hotel owner in San Francisco, laid out a nine-block Yerba Buena project as a combination convention center, stadium, hotel, and park. The area was a jumble of single-room-occupancy hotels built after 1906, replete with eateries and entertainments for the poor; occupants were overwhelmingly single, retired white men, blacks, and Filipinos who had worked as dockers, sailors, and day laborers. For years, San Francisco had the highest proportion of hotel housing of any city in the United States.

Urban renewal was only the prelude to the property boom that followed from 1960 to the recession of 1973–1975. The planners need not have worried, after all. Soon Downtown was bristling with new skyscrapers. Any number of buildings could be cited as flash points for opposition to Manhattanization: Bank of America's Darth Vader hat, Transamerica's pyramid, new hotels around Union Square, or a proposed US Steel tower flanking the Ferry Building. After 1975 a new boom came clad in postmodern finishes and Downtown surged across Market Street until halted by the recession of 1985–1986. Twenty-five-million square feet of new office space were added, doubling the size of the corporate heart of San Francisco. More hotels went up, and dozens of cheap residential hotels in the Tenderloin were converted for upscale uses.

The tragedy is not that Downtown grew and San Francisco was physically transformed; rather, it is the way in which thousands of ordinary people and urban places the size of a small city were cleared away with the rubble. In the symbolic contest for space, the victims shrink to insignificance. The class and race hatred behind the Downtown master vision should not be underestimated. The ruling elite sought to level the waterfront haunts of longshoremen who had brought the city to its knees in 1934, to drive blacks out of the Fillmore, to sweep aside the aging and discarded workers from their last redoubts south of Market Street, and to be rid of eyesores such as Manilatown. Crowds, dense quarters, and the commingling of classes and races have always provoked a chill of horror in the heart of the local bourgeoisie.

Downtown Encircled: Resistance on Many Fronts

As soon as the grand design for Downtown was put into motion, San Francisco was shaken by popular revolt. The first volleys were fired from the northern flanks of Telegraph and Russian Hills by well-to-do (but often bohemian) residents worried about their bay views. Frida Klussman put her foot down over the removal of the cable cars as early as 1947, winning them National Landmark Status in 1964. Then came the Freeway Revolt in 1955, triggered by the advancing Western Freeway that was to run through Golden Gate Park. The Supervisors stood up to the state highway department in 1959, and San Francisco became the first city to stop the freeway mania. Next, apartment buildings on the northern waterfront were killed by shipping magnate William Matson Roth and his friends, and Ghiradelli's shuttered chocolate factory was resurrected as a cozy shopping plaza, becoming the model for such conversions around the world.

Organized under the Western Addition Community Organization and several African American churches, the people of the Fillmore fought against the bulldozers and for replacement housing. They won the first court injunction in the country against an urban renewal project in 1968, and local Congressman Philip Burton pushed through a law requiring compensatory housing. After that the southern tier of the clearance area was filled with public and subsidized housing for the poor. The African American neighborhood was not eliminated, and it eventually reoccupied a large part of the redeveloped housing (but the wretchedness of the ghetto dwellers also produced the People's Temple and its mass execution at the hand of Jim Jones). The project was a dismal failure in attracting investment, and huge swathes of land lay barren for twenty years.

The historic preservation movement was born of this rebellion. A taste for Victorian houses was produced not so much by revulsion at modernist aesthetics as from distaste for the modern wrecking ball. A City Landmarks Commission was established in 1968 and the Foundation for San Francisco's Architectural Heritage in 1971. Political alliances made for strange bedfellows, with the Junior League of San Francisco working hand in hand with African American groups, gay activists, and gentrifiers. As a consequence, the political significance of architectural preservation in San Francisco was more radical than the commercial heritage industry that swept the country in the 1980s.

Meanwhile, as the familiar skyline disappeared behind an archipelago of towers, the high-rise revolt erupted. Enter Alvin Duskin, who had fought off Lamarr Hunt's mad scheme to place a giant Apollo spacecraft on Alcatraz as atonement for the 1969 Native American occupation. Duskin wanted a drastic height limit on buildings, and his ballot initiatives of 1971 and 1972 gathered support from a broad coalition of preservationists, hillside dwellers, environmentalists, anti-redevelopment groups, and political progressives. Though defeated, they spurred city officials, led by Planning Director Allan Jacobs, to write a new Downtown plan, with a line drawn at Kearny and Clay Streets to stop Downtown's northward and westward march. This was too late to save the International Hotel, bought for a high-rise by Hong Kong investors but defended from the wrecking ball by thousands of angry demonstrators, before finally being torn down in 1978.

An elderly cohort of workers in the South of Market, living out their days on meager pensions and vilified as winos, were similarly being forced out by the Redevelopment Agency. But the old men drew on their experience in organized labor, forming the opposition group Tenants and Owners in Opposition to Redevelopment, under George Woolf, former president of the Alaska Cannery Workers Union, and Peter Mendelssohn, former seaman and Communist Party organizer. By a series of lawsuits, they were able to extract new housing projects for the poor and elderly. Protracted opposition led to the collapse of the project by 1975, to be replaced by a stripped-down version. Ground was broken for a convention center in 1979, yet two huge city blocks lay barren for another decade.

Discontent with the rule of Downtown and with the transformation of San Francisco also surfaced in residential neighborhoods such as the Haight, the Castro, and Noe Valley. Activists began pushing an electoral reform plan that pivoted on district elections of the Board of Supervisors, picking up the support of gays, hippies, African Americans, Asians, and the progressive white middle class. The key figure in the revolt of the neighborhoods was Harvey Milk, the man most responsible for turning the Gay Awakening into a political movement. The return of district elections allowed Milk to take a seat on the Board of Supervisors in 1977 as the country's first openly homosexual elected official.

Electoral reform mobilization converged with the efforts of the anti-high-rise and anti-renewal forces to unseat Mayor Joe Alioto, leader of the pro-growth coalition. They also dovetailed with the political aspirations of George Moscone and the liberal Democratic machine of Phil Burton. The building boom went bust between 1973 and 1975, throwing the developers into disarray and giving opposition forces a precious opening. Moscone beat out John Barbagelata for mayor in 1975, on a promise to return control to the neighborhoods and end high-rise construction. Moscone did not keep his promise, though he did appoint some valuable mavericks, such as Sue Bierman, to the Planning and Landmarks Commissions. Neither Moscone nor Milk was allowed to finish his work. Both were assassinated in 1978 by Supervisor Dan White, a reactionary ex-cop and Marine, who represented a white working class suspicious of a changing civic landscape and the lone remaining spokesman for Downtown interests on the Board.

In the Tenderloin another grassroots mobilization took shape in the early eighties, led by Brad Paul of the North of Market Planning Coalition, Cecil Williams of Glide Memorial Church, and Leroy Looper of the Cadillac Hotel. Encroachment from Union Square, building conversions, and rising rents were forcing out the elderly residents. But opponents were able to win rent and conversion controls that held the property owners at bay, while nonprofits and churches began upgrading buildings for the poor.

As the property market heated up again, anti-high-rise activists forced votes on height limits in 1979 and 1983. These initiatives narrowly lost, but officials were again forced to respond, with Planning Director Dean Macris's Downtown Plan. This new plan altered very little, holding the line in the Financial District (where property values and landmarked buildings prevented most building anyway) and giving its blessing to construction south of Market. Activists responded with Proposition M, a more severe containment measure, which finally triumphed in 1986. The battle over Downtown catapulted liberal Art Agnos, another Burton prodigy, into the Mayor's office, but he promptly lost supporters by backing unsuccessful ballot issues for a new baseball park and an end run around Prop M by the gigantic Mission Bay project. The building boom was exhausted all the same, terminated by economic crisis.

Roots of Urban Resistance

The contrariness of San Franciscans to the annihilation of their city has been exceptional, as has the success of antidevelopment politics. Simple defense of living space and neighborhoods against the wrecking ball has played its part, to be sure, and so have the organizing efforts of dedicated radicals and the peculiarities of local political structures. But these visible parts of civic resistance need roots and soil to grow in, and here San Francisco demonstrated for a time a most favorable economic, political, and cultural substratum.

Under the Economic Volcano

Economics undergirds so much, and it is hard to escape San Francisco's legacy of wealth. Cities have been wellsprings of modernization and modern life because of their capacity to siphon wealth from many corners of the land (and overseas), concentrating and multiplying it in a narrow space. California has, moreover, been one of the greatest engines of economic growth in the world over the last fifty years. While Los Angeles outgrew its northern rival before World War II, the Bay Area has been singularly favored by the wars in the Pacific, its financial complex, and the growth of electronics.

That prosperity erected new pyramids downtown, but also helped generate opposition to the business vision of civic progress. It brought many new residents to the city in the first place, as California's booming economy generated millions of jobs and supported a large public sector. This magnetic field of opportunity drew everyone from ex-GIs enrolling at the Art Institute in the 1940s to computer hackers in Multimedia Gulch in the 1990s. It called up people of every class, from the professionals in the Marina district to immigrant workers in the Mission. It provided a cushion for those who did not come for economic reasons, whether beats, students, hippies or gays, and allowed them the freedom to create subcultures that reinvigorated the city. The mass character of those bohemian elements was unprecedented, and can only be explained by the economic liberation of the young. The civic surplus even supported many of those who explicitly opposed redevelopment, whether businessmen like Duskin, bohemians like Lawrence Ferlinghetti, or gay activists like Milk.

Prosperity worked its magic more effectively as long as rents remained low enough to allow artists, refugees, and those outside the mainstream to survive, if not prosper, in the inner city. The long slump in central-city investment due to depression, war, and suburbanization had left property markets relatively untouched for two decades. The confluence of economic growth without property speculation through the 1950s was ideal for nurturing the countercultures that mushroomed in San Francisco. Conversely, the heating up of real estate in the seventies and eighties drove out many of the marginals; as old commercial space disappeared, the affluent crowded into gentrifying neighborhoods, and mortgage markets overflowed with easy credit.

A Republic in Miniature

American leftists are prone to beg the question of the origins of urban protest by reference to grassroots movements and to reject any class analysis of such upheavals. Others refer vaguely to the middle-class character of the antigrowth movement. Neither interpretation will do. In San Francisco the balance of classes has tripped up the business elite in their efforts to command the civic skyline. The Downtown capitalists do not rule the roost in so clear-cut a fashion as in other cities. This weakness (relative, to be sure) is sometimes attributed to schisms such as those between the Spreckels and DeYoungs or Giannini and the Anglo-Saxons of Montgomery Street, but there is little evidence for a falling out in the postwar era within San Francisco, when the real fight was with the East and South Bay. Instead, difficulties came from below, and from three different directions.

To begin with, San Francisco has a curiously skewed class distribution because of its role as a commercial, financial, and corporate center as well as a government and public service node that is heavy on administration, education, medicine, and foundations. The division of labor tips toward upper-level managers, professionals, and technical workers, including doctors, lawyers, journalists, accountants, computer programmers, and administrators. This makes the city's class structure bulge in the middle. Add to this the skilled workers who keep business and the city running through supporting roles in printing, electrical, office machines, carpentry, technical writing, and the like, and the working class skews upward as well, with wages well above the national average.

At the same time, the workers of San Francisco have historically been well organized and able to hold their own against the bully-bosses, through union militancy and political activism. Racial exclusion reinforced working-class strength and the sense of rough equality among European Americans of diverse backgrounds. At the end of World War II, San Francisco was a union town and working-class leaders were powers to be reckoned with. Although key unions cut a deal with big business and Mayor Alioto to support Downtown building, many workers still carried memories of militancy and class hatreds in their trouser pockets. This is manifest in the old Filipino, white, and black longshoremen, and sailors fighting against the destruction of their hotels. Worker empowerment and good wages fueled class struggles rather than dousing them, brought alliances between skilled and unskilled male workers, and blurred the edges between the working and middle classes.

Finally, rapid growth and personal mobility have had a permanently destabilizing effect on the class system, top to bottom. The massive influx of people into California, and rapid turnover at all levels, has frequently meant that class allegiances are poorly formed, with individualism in the ascendant. Moreover, a certain wage and rank mobility and the rapid formation of new businesses by aspiring people of skill (from Esprit to *Wired*) has reinforced individualist aspirations. The effect has been to strengthen the middle-class outlook of San Francisco, a further petty bourgeoisification at the expense of both ends of the class spectrum. Curiously, this has not made San Franciscans less but, instead, more liberal, and even libertarian, in the face of power plays by big business. This contrasts with Los Angeles which, with a similar class structure, has always been more conservative.

Lifelines of Liberality

Politics is more than the geometry of class forces, and the liberal bent of San Francisco's citizenry cannot be explained by the mere presence of a working-class or petty bourgeois bloc among the electorate (nor by race, in the white postwar era). Electoral politics have been so progressive that they have won San Francisco the moniker "Left Coast City," making it a liberal island in a sea of California Republicanism. Voting patterns have a clear geography, with the east of Twin Peaks tilting consistently to the left (with its own political microgeography based on race, class, and sexual orientation). Worse for the business interests, the east side has been the part most impacted by development.

Behind this liberalism lies a political culture forged out of the class standoff between capital and labor in the early twentieth century. That political culture includes high voter turnout, political clubs, freewheeling initiatives, and weak mayors. Capital could not vanquish labor from the political landscape of the city, so it has had to go through progressive Republicans such as Sunny Jim Rolph and Warren Christopher or pro-growth Democrats such as Joe Alioto and Willie Brown to get its business done without mobilizing class opposition. At the same time, a liberal Democratic party apparatus could be stitched together that owed little to capital, as was done by Harvey Milk's Gay Democratic Club, and Phil Burton, who became a civic, state, and national power from the 1950s to the 1980s.

Part of the aims and accomplishments of this political culture has been to dispose middle-class people toward organized labor and to weaken their allegiance to the burghers of Pacific Heights. This sort of position is rarely rationalized in terms of class, but rather as libertarian independence from all power blocs and sympathy toward the oppressed. As a result, any number of transgressive political bridges were constructed in the postwar era across conventional boundaries of class and race formation. Harvey Milk organized gay men across the class spectrum, turning personal liberation into political power. Burton got his start by uniting Chinatown and white workers of the hotel districts, then brought in middle- and upper-class liberals from the eastern half of the city. Civil Rights activists and the Burton machine forged alliances between African Americans protesting black removal and white liberals opposing Downtown expansion. Meanwhile, the beats and hippies contributed by their rebellious race-mixing and incorporation of black culture into their practical critique of the oppressions of bourgeois expression and repression.

A Taste for the City

Neither can politics stand alone as an explanation for widespread opposition to the spatial incursions of the Downtown. The protagonists of urban preservation were inspired by more than distaste for capitalist power plays, particularly since so many of them were (petty) bourgeois in background or aspiration. Nor were they simply defending hearth and home. People rallied to protect urban life as they knew it. The everyday urbanity of San Francisco is undergirded by a webbing of popular culture and public vitality that sustains the city; the wellsprings of affection for urban life flow from many quarters. All opponents of redevelopment, of whatever origin or neighborhood, had experiences of urbanism to draw on and visions of civic space as a public good. These experiences inspired people and got their backs up against the destruction of San Francisco (often after drawing them to the city in the first place). Such urbanity is rarely taken into consideration by leftists, even proponents of the postmodern turn. Yet the density, commingling and variety of the city, and inhabitants' ordinary encounters with the urban world, have real effects on consciousness and action.

It helps that San Francisco had a rich cosmopolitan tradition to begin with. The city was the urban oasis of the West in the nineteenth century. The Victorian makeover of the last quarter of the century rebuilt the city as a stage set of middle-class rowhouse respectability and upper-class pomposity, but left the vast redoubt of the working class lying South of Market, and the public secrets of the Barbary Coast and the waterfront on full display. After half the city was erased in the catastrophe of 1906, San Francisco was rebuilt along radically new, vertical lines. The central districts were reconstructed at a much higher density as hotels and apartments. Thousands of multiple housing units were purpose-built for businessmen, saleswomen, clerks, longshoremen, and the whole gamut of the urban labor force. These were, moreover, intentionally done in a modern style, with the latest improvements, as an explicit alternative to the suburban house; these were meant to be homes for urban living. This was the high tide of dense urbanism, full of pedestrian life, bright lights, and popular entertainments along the Great White Ways such as Market, Mission, and Fillmore. Many San Franciscans still occupied this urbane space after World War II, long after it had been junked in favor of the suburban model for American cities.

The rebellion against Downtown was not fought by denizens of the past but by the city's postwar occupants, many of whom were new arrivals. At the very moment when most Americans were fleeing the central cities, others fled in droves to San Francisco to escape dystopian suburbs and to create their own utopias. This was urban renewal of a different stripe. It brought African Americans into the Fillmore district during the war, along with the first gays discharged from the military. Next came former GIs who had seen the city in passage from Toledo to Guam and had fallen in love with it. The pioneering beats drifted in after the war, finding refuge in North Beach and the Fillmore; they were joined by growing numbers of alienated white youths in the 1950s. Students came from around the country, swelling the ranks of those cutting ties to bourgeois domesticity.

After the beats established San Francisco as the countercultural capital of postwar America and student rebellion heated up in Berkeley, the Bay Area became a new sort of urban oasis. Hippies overran the Haight, a district on the decline (bordering the Fillmore), with spacious Victorians and cheap rents. Gays flocked to the queer Mecca of the Castro district in the 1970s (the Castro was another working-class neighborhood emptying out). Gay liberation jump-started the yuppie era and its celebration of personal indulgence among the well-paid middle classes spawned by Downtown's office revolution.

For the beats, hippies, gays, and yuppies the city itself was an object of celebration as well as a place of liberation. More than housing, it promised tolerance, promiscuous mixing, cheek-by-jowl density, public life, and a landscape to delight the eye. The beats fit easily into North Beach's Italian community, with its traditions of anarchism, café chatter, and public display. Beat sculptors used the rubble of building demolitions for their found art. Lawrence Ferlinghetti, a founder of City Lights Bookstore, was a protester at the razing of the Montgomery Block. A local judge refused to censor Allen Ginsberg's *Howl*. Hippies painted up the Victorians of the Haight, held their Be-ins at neighboring Golden Gate Park, and listened to rock in the nearby Fillmore Auditorium. Urban space served as a critical resource for the flowering of gay life, providing collective self-affirmation and protection in the face of a hostile world. Few people outside the police department gave a damn about enforcing heterosexuality. Gays pioneered the improvement of Victorian housing and the South of Market, and they were leaders in the preservation movement. Yuppies had good, city-based jobs and bought city homes to go with them. They sought the kind of urbane culture they had witnessed on student travels to Europe and Latin America, and took to gentrifying Victorian and Edwardian neighborhoods with a vengeance.

Contrary Spirits

Along with the spirit of urbanism, San Franciscans, particularly intellectuals, have moved in counterflow to mainstream ideas of modernity. Despite living at a crossroads of American capitalism, where money, commerce, industry, and commodities bray from every corner, they developed a critical distance from the sirens of modernism and modernization. In short, they never bought wholeheartedly into the ideology of progress. This was by no means true of nineteenth-century San Francisco, the Las Vegas of its time. Over the years, the lust for money-making at the cost of land and landscape had been blunted.

The first meek turning away came as San Francisco's second generation bourgeoisie sought to erase its ragtag origins in the mining districts and create a semblance of civilized urbanism modeled after eastern cities. San Francisco's burghers eschewed the sinewy modernism of Chicago in favor of Victorian fiddle-faddle (though such buildings were thoroughly modern in construction). A second turning away came at the end of the century, when third-generation burghers rejected Victoriania but also refused the modernism of Prairie or Bauhaus for the historicism of the Shingle, Renaissance, and Mediterranean styles. More generally, they fell under the sway of the Arts and Crafts movement; nowhere was the radical romanticism of William Morris embraced more fervently than in California. So dominant was the cultivated rusticity propagated by Bernard Maybeck that modernism finally came to the Bay Area in the 1930s clad in redwood and rough-hewn planks suitable to the regional myth of the naturalized city. Contrast this with Los Angeles, which abandoned historicism in favor of high modernism in the 1920s, and never looked back.

The leading contrarian of the Progressive era was John Muir, a mechanic and naturalist turned rustic bohemian and transcendental mystic, whose crusading zeal and savvy propaganda for the mountains of California launched the American environmental movement. The most popular writer of the time was Jack London, and Frank Norris was not far behind. Both made nature the backdrop for their greatest novels, while pushing the critical reach of literary realism to the limits of respectability. And both, despite their contrasting social origins, were thoroughly imbued with the petty bourgeois streak of independence and self-righteousness of their home city. Journalists Lincoln Steffens and Upton Sinclair were cut of the same cloth, one moving east and the other west in the course of their careers.

The New Deal era found San Francisco at the head of labor upheavals with the General Strike of 1934 and the cultural turn toward social realism in painting, photography, and literature, another flux of contrary modernism. Diego Rivera spent his first years in the United States working here, where he left a host of local acolytes. Dorothea Lange, Paul Strand, and the f64 movement redefined photography both in subject matter and in art. Ansel Adams broke away to follow Muir's vision of pristine nature. Contrarian writers nurtured in isolation around the region between the wars included Robinson Jeffers, Henry Miller, and Eugene O'Neill.

After the war, San Francisco was propelled from cultural Hill Station to the global focal point for a generation of youth rebellion and countercultural experimentation. Many beat writers were restless New Yorkers drawn to San Francisco because their sort of ragged poesy and vagabondage was irresponsible, even deplorable, in New York's literary and political hothouse. San Francisco offered the right combination of urbanity and obscurity to ferret away New York's mantle as the cultural capital of modernity, and to begin in a marginalized, noncommercial, anarchistic way to stumble toward postmodernism. When realism gave way to abstraction in the visual arts, San Francisco leapt on the boat from New York in the glory years of abstract expressionism at the Art Institute in the late forties. But the counterflow of local culture twisted back into a figurative turn in the 1950s and, in the hands of Bruce Conner, Wally Hedrick, and Jess, shifted constructivism toward the political art of the 1960s. Musically, black jazz briefly merged with white poetics; then the Bay Area sound of Dave Brubeck went off on its own iconoclastic tangent.

The Beat Generation slid easily into the rebellious sixties, with politics and counterculture in closer dialogue in the Bay Area than anywhere else. Rock was the voice of the new generation and San Francisco's Fillmore Auditorium the launching pad for its most innovative bands, such as Big Brother and Jefferson Airplane, or the black-white combustibles of Sly and the Family Stone and Tower of Power. The most enduring were those epigones of laid-back licks, the Grateful

Dead. Psychedelic poster art was a kind of *Jugendstil* gone mad, while clothing took a lurch back to Victoriana. A familiar strand of the counterculture was an affection for nature, running from Kenneth Rexroth, the key intellectual bridging the 1930s and 1950s, to Gary Snyder, beat poet and Zen master of bioregionalism today. Disaffected hippies and students took to the countryside by the end of the sixties, seeking a rural utopia after their urban one had failed.

Gays were largely white and middle class and had more disposable income than earlier countercultures; nonetheless, they were social pariahs. They elevated the joyful abandon of civic sinning to a level not seen since the closing of the Barbary Coast. Gay liberation exceeded even the beats and hippies in its flouting of social convention and confirmed San Francisco's reputation as a refuge from small-minded America. On the other hand, the counterculture's rejection of consumer culture was swamped by the hedonistic rush of gay pleasure-seeking (not without contradiction: hedonism fell afoul of the AIDS epidemic and consumerism split the well-heeled from poor gays and lesbians).

As the eighties dawned, the San Francisco counterculture had achieved an unexpected degree of mainstream acceptance. The yuppie consumer culture carried some of the spirit of refusal against American domestic rectitude, ushering in the "latte leisure class," as well as gay sensibilities in architecture, dress, and the arts. The yuppies' affluence and consumerism eroded the radical basis of urban culture, but distinguished the Bay Area's petty bourgeoisie as a world-historical force in the realm of consumption: nouvelle cuisine, hot tubs, wines, personal computers, the Nature Company, backpacking gear, New Age music, Esprit and Gap clothes, and more spewed from this fount of liberatory self-indulgence.

The beats, hippies, and gays represented a very ungenteel sort of bohemianism that was more confrontational, more political, and more bizarre than ever before in this country. Rexroth, Ginsberg, and the rest showed a ferocious independence and spiritual refusal to follow orthodox parties, preferring a left anarchism that is a touchstone of San Francisco's political culture. The New Bohemianism was absolutely critical in forming the political consciousness and urbane outlook of the Bay Area, moving the middle class decisively to the left of the American mainstream, celebrating the frightful asymmetries of urbanity and re-igniting a radical romanticism that went far beyond the aesthetics of Arts and Crafts, the mystical environmentalism of John Muir, or the manly socialism of Jack London.

What Next?

San Franciscans can be justly proud of their record of opposition to the bulldozer of progress, but such resistance has decided limits. Downtown expansion was contained on the north and west, only to cross Market Street and trigger the radical transformation of the South of Market to Mission Bay. Property speculation fell into the doldrums for a decade after 1985, but has picked up again. Downtown's growth is limited more by the property cycle than by social protest. As the city's economy went into the tank in the worst depression in fifty years, job loss (30,000 in San Francisco) laid waste thousands of lives. Political conditions around the state and the country have deteriorated, as the triumphant demagogues of the right put the screws to urban Democrats, the intelligentsia, working people, immigrants, and the poor. Even in San Francisco, bourgeois reaction is out of the closet, where popular struggles had locked it up for half a century, and the ruling class is more interested in sweeping the streets of the homeless and cutting wages than in meeting the needs of the people.

Meanwhile, the wellsprings of opposition have been drying up. The left is worn out, gays have been preoccupied with AIDS, yuppie exuberance is gone. High rents put the squeeze on the counterculture, and outcast youth today are more likely to be homeless than bohemian. Wages and union strength have eroded, and the working class has been recomposed as largely foreign-born Asian and Latin peoples who face greater obstacles than their white predecessors, and whose political and organizational presence is just awakening. At the same time, the skilled hotshots of computing, multimedia, and brokerage are more inclined toward monetary payoffs and expensive cars than to the public duties and pleasures of civic life. A fine and noble epoch is over and done with much as the Gold Rush era of libertine opportunity faded away in its time. San Francisco has not sunk as far as the rest of America (Dole got only 17 percent of the vote in 1996), but the survival of the city as a decent place to live is by no means assured.

References

THE BEST TREATMENT of the planned expansion of downtown and the battle to save the city from redevelopment is Chester Hartman, *The Transformation of San Francisco* (Totowa, NJ: Rowman & Allenheld, 1984). Other valuable sources are Bruce Brugmann and Greggar Sletteland, eds., *The Ultimate Highrise: San Francisco's Mad Rush Toward the Sky* (San Francisco: Bay Guardian Books, 1971), John Mollenkopf, "The Postwar Politics of Urban Development," *Politics and Society* (1975) 5:247–95, and *The Contested City* (Princeton, NJ: Princeton University Press, 1983), and Gray Brechin, "Progress in San Francisco: It Could Have Been Worse," *San Francisco Magazine* (Oct. 1983) pp. 58–63). For the view of the city planners, see Mel Scott, *Western Addition District: An Exploration of the Possibilities of Replanning and Rebuilding One of San Francisco's Largest Blighted Districts* (San Francisco: Department of City Planning, 1947) and *The San Francisco Bay Area: A Metropolis in Perspective* (Berkeley: University of California Press, 1959), and Allan Jacobs, *Making City Planning Work* (Chicago: American Society of Planning Officials, 1978). The freeway revolt has not been fully researched yet, but see Kathy Johnson, "The San Francisco Freeway

Revolt" (unpublished manuscript, Geography Department, University of California, Berkeley, 1996). On the origins of BART, see Seymour Adler, *The Political Economy of Transit in the San Francisco Bay Area, 1945–63* (doctoral dissertation, Department of City and Regional Planning, University of California, Berkeley, 1980) and J. Allen Whitt, *Urban Elites and Mass Transportation: The Dialectics of Power* (Princeton: Princeton University Press, 1982).

REDEVELOPMENT AND FREEWAYS typically targeted industrial and working-class areas, which are described in Paul Groth, *Living Downtown: The History of Residential Hotels in the United States* (Berkeley: University of California Press, 1994) and Richard Walker, "Landscape and City Life: Four Ecologies of Residence in the San Francisco Bay Area," *Ecumene* (1995) 2/1: pp. 33–64, and "Industry Builds the City: the Suburbanization of Industry in the San Francisco Bay Area, 1850–1940," *Journal of Historical Geography* (forthcoming). The fight to save the city sparked a new interest in its architectural heritage, such as Roger Olmsted and T. H. Watkins, *Here Today: San Francisco's Architectural Heritage* (San Francisco: Chronicle Books, 1969), Judith Waldhorn and Sally Woodbridge, *Victoria's Legacy* (San Francisco: 101 Productions, 1978), and Michael Corbett, *Splendid Survivors: San Francisco's Downtown Architectural Heritage* (San Francisco: California Living Books, 1979). For more background on local building styles, see David Gebhard, "The Bay Tradition in Architecture," *Art in America* (1964) 52: pp. 60–63, L. Freudenheim and E. Sussman *Building with Nature: Roots of the San Francisco Bay Region Tradition* (Santa Barbara: Peregrine Smith, 1974), and Richard Longstreth, *On the Edge of the World: Four Architects in San Francisco at the Turn of the Century* (Cambridge: MIT Press, 1983).

THE ECONOMIC DEVELOPMENT of San Francisco since World War II has not been well studied, but see Richard Walker, "Another Round of Globalization in San Francisco," *Urban Geography* (1996) 17/1: pp. 60–94, Paul Rhode, "The Nash Thesis Revisited: An Economic Historian's View," *Pacific Historical Review* (1994) 63/1, pp. 363–92, Richard Walker and the Bay Area Study Group, "The Playground of US Capitalism? The Political Economy of the San Francisco Bay Area in the 1980s," in Mike Davis, et al., eds., *Fire in the Hearth* (London: Verso, 1990) pp. 3–82. On the downside of economic prosperity, see Richard Walker, "California Rages Against the Dying of the Light," *New Left Review* (1995) No. 209, pp. 42–74 and Sandra Smith and Richard Walker, "California or Bust: the Property Boom of the 1980s" (unpublished manuscript, Department of Geography, UC Berkeley, 1997).

THE BEST CASE FOR THE PECULIARITY of San Francisco's petit bourgeois class structure is still Carey McWilliams, *California: The Great Exception* (New York: A. A. Wyn, 1949). I make the same argument for recent years in Walker et al., "The Playground of US Capitalism?" This view is rejected, I should add, by Peter Decker, *Fortunes and Failures: White-Collar Mobility in 19th Century San Francisco* (Cambridge: Harvard University Press, 1978) and Gray Brechin, *Imperial San Francisco: Urban Power, Earthly Ruin* (Berkeley: University of California Press, forthcoming), who argue for the dominance of the big bourgeoisie. The fine social history by William Issel and Robert Cherny, *San Francisco, 1865–1932: Politics, Power, and Urban Development* (Berkeley: University of California Press, 1986) stands somewhere in the middle.

EVERYONE AGREES, HOWEVER, that the city has been politically progressive (liberal to left) during most of the postwar era. This is well documented in Richard DeLeon, *Left Coast City: Progressive Politics in San Francisco, 1975–1991* (Lawrence: University of Kansas Press, 1992), and backed up by John Jacobs, *A Rage for Justice: The Passion and Politics of Phillip Burton* (Berkeley: University of California Press, 1995). The historical antecedents of this political tilt are presented by Philip Ethington, *The Public City: The Political Construction of Urban Life in San Francisco, 1850–1900* (New York: Cambridge University Press, 1994), and Bill Issel, "Business Power and Political Culture in San Francisco, 1900–1940," *Journal of Urban History* (1989) 16(1), pp. 52–77 and "New Deal and Wartime Origins of Postwar Urban Economic Policy: The San Francisco Case" (unpublished manuscript, Department of History, San Francisco State University, 1995). This is corroborated by Roger Lotchin, "World War II and Urban California: City Planning and the Transformation Hypothesis," *Pacific Historical Review* (1993) 62/2: pp. 143–71.

ONE FOUNDATION FOR THIS LIBERALITY is undoubtedly the strong labor movement of the past, which is well treated by McWilliams but in more detail by Issel and Cherny, and Michael Kazin, "The Great Exception Revisited: Organized Labor and Politics in San Francisco and Los Angeles, 1870–1940," *Pacific Historical Review* (1986) 55: pp. xxxx, and *Barons of Labor: The San Francisco Building Trades and Union Power in the Progressive Era* (Urbana & Chicago: University of Illinois Press, 1987), and David Selvin, *A Terrible Anger: The 1934 Waterfront and General Strikes in San Francisco* (Detroit: Wayne State University Press, 1996). Kazin and Selvin understand the curious class makeup and outlook of San Francisco workers, who were mostly skilled and highly independent.

ANOTHER WELL-REHEARSED THEME is the cosmopolitan character of the city, and its free-wheeling, tolerant, and even libertine ways of life. See, for example, Herbert Asbury, *The Barbary Coast: An Informal History of the San Francisco Underworld* (New York: Alfred Knopf, 1933), John Findlay, *People of Chance: Gambling in American Society from Jamestown to Las Vegas* (New York: Oxford University Press, 1986), Paul Groth, *Living Downtown,* Irena Narell, *Our City: The Jews of San Francisco* (San Diego: Howell-North Books, 1981), and Glenna Matthews, "Forging a Cosmopolitan Civic Culture: the Regional Consciousness of San Francisco and Northern California," in Michael Steiner and David Wrobel, eds., *Many Wests: Essays in Regional Consciousness* (Lawrence: University of Kansas Press, in press).

SAN FRANCISCO HAS A LONG BOHEMIAN TRADITION of wayward intellectuals and iconoclastic artists going back to the Gold Rush. This is surveyed by Frances Walker, *San Francisco's Literary Frontier* (New York: Alfred Knopf, 1939), Oscar Lewis, *Bay Window Bohemia: An Account of the Brilliant Artistic World of Gaslit San Francisco* (Garden City, NJ: Doubleday, 1956), and Lawrence Ferlinghetti and Nancy Peters, *Literary San Francisco: A Pictorial History from its Beginnings to the Present Day* (San Francisco: City Lights Books, 1980). The intellectual counterculture stole the national spotlight with the coming of the beats in the 1950s. On that era, see Jerry Kamstra, *Stand Naked and Cool Them: North Beach and the Bohemian Dream, 1950–1980* (San Francisco: Peeramid Press, 1981), Michael Davidson, *The San Francisco Renaissance: Poetics and Community at Mid-Century* (New York: Cambridge University Press, 1989), Rebecca Solnit, *Secret Exhibitions: Six California Artists* of the Cold War Era (San Francisco: City Lights Books, 1991), Richard Candida Smith, Utopia and Dissent: Art, Poetry and Politics in California (Berkeley: University of California Press, 1995), and Linda Hamalian, A Life of Kenneth Rexroth (New York: W. W. Norton, 1991).

BY THE END OF THE BEAT ERA, the counterculture had become a mass movement, led by hippies, as described by Sherri Cavan, Hippies of the Haight (St Louis: New Critics Press, 1972), and Charles Perry, The Haight-Ashbury: A History (New York: Random House, 1984), and was joined by the political high tide of the civil rights movement, student rebellion, antiwar actions, and the rest of the sixties. The latter history has not been adequately told for the Bay Area, but see Max Heirich, The Spiral of Conflict: Berkeley, 1964 (New York: Columbia University Press, 1971), Gene Marine, The Black Panthers (New York: Signet Books, 1969), and Albert Fortunate Eagle, Alcatraz, Alcatraz: The Indian Occupation of 1969–71 (Berkeley: Heyday Books, 1992). The best treatment of the sixties in the Bay Area is by an Australian, Anthony Ashbolt, in Tear Down the Walls: Sixties Radicalism and the Politics of Space in the San Francisco Bay Area (doctoral dissertation, Australian National University, 1989).

ON THE GAY REVOLUTION, see Allan Bérubé, Coming Out Under Fire: The History of Gay Men and Women in World War Two (New York: The Free Press, 1990), Manuel Castells and Karen Murphy, "Cultural Identity and Urban Structure: The Spatial Organization of San Francisco's Gay Community," Urban Affairs Review (1982) 22: pp. 237–59, Randy Shilts, The Mayor of Castro Street: The Life and Times of Harvey Milk (New York: St. Martin's Press, 1982), Mike Weiss, Double Play: The San Francisco City Hall Killings (Reading, MA: Addison-Wesley, 1982), and Susan Stryker and Jim Van Buskirk, Gay by the Bay: A History of Queer Culture in the San Francisco Bay Area (San Francisco: Chronicle Books, 1996).

ONE HAS TO BE CAREFUL not to romanticize a social order that was accompanied by vicious racism. On this see Alexander Saxton, The Indispensable Enemy: Labor and the Anti-Chinese Movement in California (Berkeley: University of California Press, 1971), Susan Craddock, "Sewers and Scapegoats: Spatial Metaphors of Smallpox in Nineteenth Century San Francisco," Social Science and Medicine (1995) 41/7: pp. 957–68, Albert Broussard, Black San Francisco: The Struggle for Racial Equality in the West, 1900–1954 (Lawrence: University of Kansas Press, 1993), and Kazin, Barons of Labor. The civil rights movement was relatively strong in the Bay Area; however, there is little documentation on this.

Going Public: The San Francisco Civic Center

Conversations and Photographs; An Essay by Susan Schwartzenberg

As I leave my apartment, I pass a window in the curve of the hallway where I see the very tip of the spire of City Hall. Through a tunnel of windows I see a pair of feet and a constantly flickering television in the room of a neighboring building. For a moment, in my mind, the world of the private spectacle and the center of city government commingle.

I'm new to this neighborhood; in fact the neighborhood is in the process of renewing itself. The 1989 Loma Prieta earthquake damaged many buildings, and caused the local freeway system to be demolished. This 65-block section of San Francisco, which has at its heart the Civic Center, is in the process of rebuilding and re-thinking itself as a place to live, work, and visit.

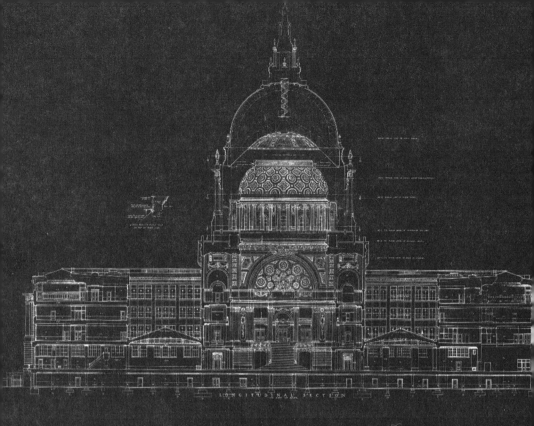

A walk through the neighborhood is accompanied by the sounds of jackhammers, wrecking balls, traffic jams, and distant voices on construction sites. The government and cultural buildings were built in 1915 in the Beaux Arts style, and are almost all currently undergoing seismic upgrades and massive renovation. The Civic Center is surrounded by residential neighborhoods representing an amazing array of cultural and economic "difference." In fact the Civic Center embodies the homeless situation, with its central plaza sometimes referred to as a camp. The plaza is the largest open space within this conglomerate of neighborhoods, and is a focus of current debate on the design and use of public space in cities at the turn of the century.

" The first 'city hall,' before 1840 was an office in a house, or the back room of a hotel which was moved around a lot because of fires and political corruption. By 1869, after a severe earthquake and with a constant influx of people, anyone with a stake in the future of San Francisco wanted to build a spectacular metropolis. So of course they needed a grand city hall.

The new city hall was designed as a complex of buildings to be built on a triangular park, the former site of an old cemetery. The state appropriated the land and auctioned off portions of the property—the scheme was to raise a million and a half dollars for construction costs, and get it built in three years. Construction began in 1870, was finished 27 years later, in 1897, and cost six million dollars. Just nine years later it was all but destroyed by the earthquake and fire of 1906.

It was a nineteenth-century thing; you give a contract to friends, or friends of friends. With seven chief architects, over twenty-seven years there was ineptitude after ineptitude. The materials were compromised; even the cast bricks were rumored to be shoddy. Fireplaces were built and later heating systems were installed. There were major sewage problems, the place was said to stink all the time. The floors didn't match up, chimneys didn't draw so the rooms were smokey, it was a mess. . . .

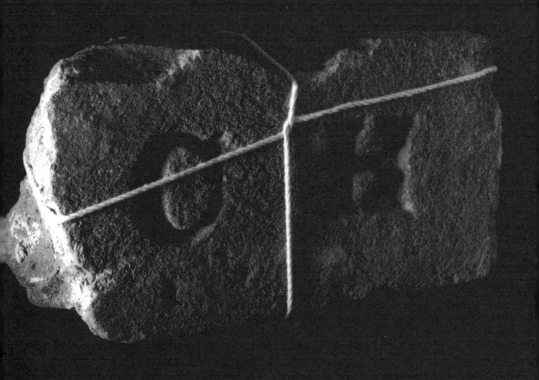

The design was a Second Empire, French-style emerging in the 1860s in Paris when the monarchy was restored and Napoleon III was in power. Ironically, in 1871 during the Paris Commune, which was in part a rebellion against the monarchy, much of Paris burned. So oddly, this was the architectural style, the democratic ideal adopted for government buildings throughout America. . . .

The property which had been sold to raise money remained empty for years and became sort of impromptu demonstration areas—I don't think they had a strong sense of 'public space' at that time. So these lots became the forerunner of the plaza, I guess you could say. They were called the sand lots where workers would congregate and often marches started from there, until of course they plopped the Pioneer monument in the middle. . . ."
—San Francisco City Planner

"I study evolutionary theory, as well as human evolution, and the morphological characteristics of human bone—what it goes through—through time and a lifetime.

It was the southeast corner of the Civic Center, the site of the old City Hall where the new library was built. But in the 1840s the entire area was the Yerba Buena cemetery—the city's first graveyard. Supposedly, they had moved the bodies in the 1850s, but it was suspected that some remains might still be found —so when they began the excavation for the library I was called to be on site in case there was an exhumation.

We found no whole skeletons but some rib and fibula fragments. We found a lot of hand and finger bones, and teeth—things that slip through the cracks. Every day we would comb through the sand, the wind would blow all night and you'd return and see new exposed bones. We found most of it just north of an incredible brick sewer—a piece of the old infrastructure still underneath the city. Around it we found a lot of Chinese coins, pipes, and jewelry bits, so I assume it was built by Chinese labor.

The artifacts were found in the foundation, you don't know what happened. A lot of the things were
personal items. Maybe they
belonged to the people
who worked at
City Hall. . . .

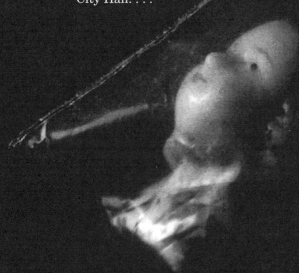

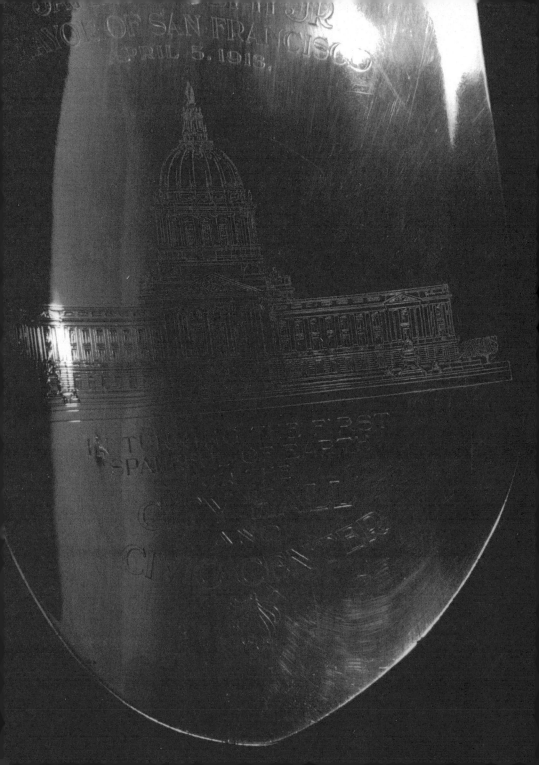

The artifacts could have been dropped by passersby, or maybe it was just stuff thrown in with the rubble. It was like public remnants, things that fell out of people's pockets. There were combs, a little shaving knife, bottles, beer cans, utensils, a little makeup tin, and coins.

It was garbage, really, but from all different eras.

The wedding ring was probably the oldest thing we found. It was inscribed and I know it was from the finger of someone who had been buried there. I was sifting through the sand and this gold thing fell out into my hand—and it had an inscription in it. You know it's an incredible feeling to be holding something—you want to be telepathic, you feel there is still something attached to it.

It was a large and very eerie site. In the afternoon the winds would come up—you're in this pit with the noise of the city all around you, and it becomes quiet for you, you're isolated. No one can get at you —you're walking around, alone in the past."
—Physical Anthropologist

Civic Center Plaza:
Meeting at the American Institute of Architects, Fall 1996

The discussion for today is on the Civic Center. We have an overview and detail information from the Department of City Planning. We have a proposal for an International, Cultural, Ecology Park. We would like feedback on the proposal and I know there is going to be a very interesting discussion of the issues—the city's plans for a redesign of the Civic Center.

"The city was allowed $700 million to repair public buildings damaged by the 1989 earthquake, and to build new buildings. We wanted to make sure that the new spaces would be publicly accessible and as fully utilized as possible both day and night. We looked at the traditional civic center, the Daniel Burnham/Cahill plan—now considered an historic district. The Civic Center has expanded. Our goal is to knit together a cohesive set of discreet neighborhoods—to functionally link them together via a cultural corridor along Market Street to the theater district, Yerba Buena Center, and downtown. Our recommendation is for physical improvements.

The area needs increased lighting to remove the shadows these monumental Beaux Arts buildings leave—they were built to be awesome and to humble you. At night people sleep there and sometimes-they jump out at you. The patrons of the cultural facilities are frightened. So we developed an 18-month strategic plan with 14 physical improvements: increasing the amperage of the streetlights, wall lights on the buildings, land-scaping, intensifying the parking garages, a lighting plan from the garages to major destinations.

Fundamental principle number one: we are going to close the area to street traffic. We have an important view and ceremonial access from Market Street to City Hall. And even though we haven't had political demonstrations for a while—being that we are a relatively apathetic society—there was a time when hundreds of thousands of people would stream up from Market Street and congregate in Civic Center Plaza. A place for the city collective to come together and voice itself. The plaza is also the main local open space for the adjacent neighborhoods, particularly the Tenderloin."

—San Francisco City Planner

"The idea is to create a Living Library. We are looking at a rich site, from the cultural and educational institutions, to the government itself. The Beaux Arts design could be a structural framework—four themed gardens in the four quadrants of the park. One could be a Government, Law and Justice garden—an opportunity to bring the meaning and content of the government outside. We could do this by symbolic plantings, lectures, demonstrations, and research institutes, through visual and performed artworks and through state-of-the-art communications technologies. This could not only bring the insides of these institutions outside, but could link to other parts of the city, making the Civic Center the true heart of our city. The gardens could also relate to diverse cultural groups: we are Hispanics and African Americans, we are Koreans and Chinese, we are Vietnamese, we are an international city.

I am suggesting a social weaving, an overlay integrated into the Beaux Arts design to bring life for the present and the future."
—Environmental Planner

"The real problem with a lot of planning is that it's not married to an economic development strategy—an economic engine. This could be an entertainment/recreation center. Microsoft is very interested in using new cinema space to demonstrate new applications of its software during the day when the cinema is in low utilization. Of course, they would have to install desk space behind the seats. There could be a book outlet run by the library in cooperation with a large book retailer, a shop connected to the Asian Art Museum, and then lots and lots of food. This would bring people on weekends and at night when the employees aren't there—making it safe, and diluting the encamped homeless." —Architect

"Do you want a Pac Bell plaza or something?" —Architect

"Not living in the city, I'm not immersed in the civic life of San Francisco. I'm here to keep current. What I don't hear is what exactly you want to do. What is the driving program or purpose? I hear confusion, a lot of gathering of objectives. One thing that struck me is that this location is right on the edge of the Tenderloin. There is a great population that could use this space. I also heard the words, 'to dilute the homeless population.' This struck me—because I believe these people would rather be strengthened and encouraged, and empowered rather than diluted. Can that happen here? Do you want it to happen?" —Architect

"Whether I agree with this politically or not—we are talking about a civic space! Which should fundamentally be kept a civic space! I'm concerned that it might be parceled up and filled with little things to appeal to the different constituencies by giving them each a plot of land. It's not good urban design. To me this is not civic, it seems more of a community garden than a real Civic Center Plaza!" —Architect

"It already is being parceled out. We have a quiet zone for the library, and another quadrant is a children's play area. Unfortunately, with the incivility today of adults toward children this area needs to be fenced off. So we've lost two quadrants of the park. It is my job to keep as much open space as possible for public gatherings, marches, rallies, parades, fiestas, whatever. We must have this ceremonial gathering place, that's what the Civic Center is and that's what the master plan says it should be." — San Francisco City Planner

"There is only one great open space in San Francisco and that's Golden Gate Park. And with the market-based nature of American culture—people go where there is some place to do what they want to do. My concern is that we will create a space and nobody will go there. And it will remain exactly what it is now. A windblown place where people who have to go, will. I think we are talking about a new observation, a century after we created this place in the image of Jeffersonian Democracy and the City Beautiful. In another version, in another vision that has some relevance to the 21st century. I think children have relevance, the Tenderloin does, and all the adjacent neighborhoods. This is a design problem—a sort of meeting of things in a knuckle. And the solution isn't a Beaux Arts plaza with some playgrounds." —Architect

"I've read the documents and the only policy I can see is to restore the 1915 plan. But that would just be rearranging the pattern of the homeless people and the benches. We have a Beaux Arts design based on a French model brought to the United States—and it's based on a whole way of living—not just congregating, but thinking and interacting. And this is directly related to the kind of discourse people have in public spaces. The root of the question we should be asking is, what is the nature of political life in America? I mean what is a Civic Center for the 21st century?" —Architect

Conversations on citizenship, architecture, and public life, at Civic Center Plaza, United Nations Plaza and Farmer's Market, October 1996

"A citizen? A person that has rights to travel and to be able to look and enjoy the scenery—freedom. I guess citizens are all the people, human, yeah, all people. I went to school here, I grew up here. I might be a little biased as opposed to someone who just started livin' here from some other places. I am at home here. I guess these buildings represent the rules, the policies, the ordinances, the resolutions. All of that has to be OK'd here. So it kind of stands for the boss. The-government-of-the-makers-of-the-rules-that-surrounds-us. Is that OK?"

Correction fluid

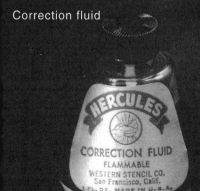

Telephone

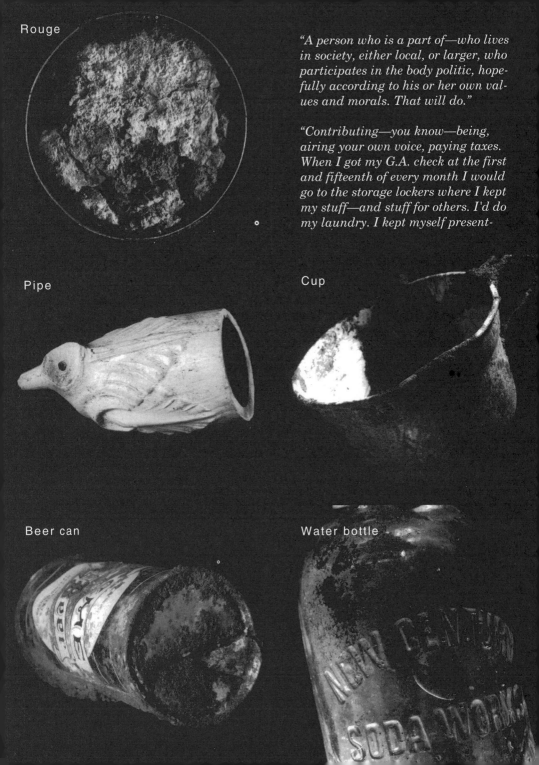

Rouge

Pipe

Cup

Beer can

Water bottle

"A person who is a part of—who lives in society, either local, or larger, who participates in the body politic, hopefully according to his or her own values and morals. That will do."

"Contributing—you know—being, airing your own voice, paying taxes. When I got my G.A. check at the first and fifteenth of every month I would go to the storage lockers where I kept my stuff—and stuff for others. I'd do my laundry. I kept myself presentable—when I got re-employed I was still livin' on the street, I'd get up, take my alarm, ditch my sleeping bag, and go to work. Same thing day after day, get up survive, go eat—Glide, St. Anthony's— than go to sleep and start all over again. One day you wake up and think, what's the point? I work at a sex club. That's what got me off the street. I have a wonderful paying job. I afford $825 a month by myself. Imagine going from homeless to that—sometimes I would come back to this camp in tears over my life—the drama. I was takin' from—and it's good to be givin' back. If grass can grow through the cracks in the sidewalks —we can get out of the cracks too."

"These buildings are about the rights of citizens, but I guess they don't tell you who isn't one. No, the world shouldn't have a rubber-stamp architectural model for government. Of course not, but I like this building, and I like the style. When people come together as a community, there are obligations and benefits. The Greeks defined citizens as those who could vote—was that it? I guess there are more definitions, but in simple

Comb

terms just a member of a community. As I defined a citizen, I am one yes, I live in the community. I mean, you could look at the building and say it's ridiculous to spend money renovating brick and morter when there are people—living human beings in need. On the other hand, when you go to Washington, D.C., and you see the great landmarks—there never was a good time to build them. There have always been people in need."

"I don't want to sound conservative, you've got people who live in the city, so I'm talking about families, you've got people who work in the city, and then you have the tourist, and that covers it."

"This plaza helps the people around here to go out sometimes. These old buildings are nice, it's something monumental, you know it's historical. It gives you the feeling that this is not a new country only, it's an old country too. Citizen? Is a person who serves his country first, and enjoy what that country should give him after serving, you know? Not taking only, mutual relation, you know? So this should be the relation: giving and taking, not taking only. Actually, I'm going to apply for citizenship, so I like it, as much as I give, I'll take. I've been here three years, I'm from Egypt."

"A lot of people come through here, everything, legal, and illegal things can be found, so it's a hub. I guess citizenship would be a sense of belonging, maybe. I vote, so I can bitch."

"To get to know your neighbor, not to become real close friends, but to say hello at the bus stop. Planting flowers

on my sidewalk and tending them.
Yeah, I have a garden. Am I achieving
my goals of citizenship? I'm taking
over my section of the sidewalk."

"Some of this is good, and some's
bad—how to explain—I don't like tall
buildings, I live in a building with five
floors, I don't think it's good, I'm not a
citizen, I really have no idea what it
means. I come here for study in economics. After graduation I must
decide, if I stay or go. I am not sure at
this moment."

"They're dreaming for California you
know, not only the weather, it's the
style of living—and for the first time
in America, it's a more easy life—but it
can't be, it's only first impression. But
in this plaza, I like how these people
are living together in their first meeting. It's the best here for me. But it is
only my experience you know."

Imagery
Historic photographs and artifacts from the
History Room of the San Francisco Public
Library and City Hall collection.

1. Blimp over City Hall, c. 1915
2. Blueprint, c. 1913, City Hall Collection
3. Map, S.F. Planning Department
4. City Hall brick, c. 1870
5. Face of Liberty statue, c. 1870's
6. Old City Hall, c. 1890's
7. Doll's head, artifact c. 1900
8. Silver shovel, artifact, c. 1910
9. Wedding ring, artifact, c. 1840's
10. Civic Center Plaza, c. 1930's
11. Civic Center Plaza, 1945
12. Naturalization, 1943
13. Correction Fluid c. 1940
14. Telephone, c. 1940
15. Compact with rouge, undated
16. Pipe, undated
17. Tin cup, c. 1860–1906
18. Acme beer can, 1935–1950
19. New Century Soda Works, 1904–1910
20. Comb fragment, c. 1915
21. Employees Hall of Records, c. 1920,

Contributors
American Institute of Architects
Department of City Planning
S.F. Public Library
Susana Montana
Evan S. Rose
Larry L. McDonald
Bonnie Sherk
Donna M. Garaventa
Deborah Harkins
Mary Hanni
Pat Ackre
Susan Goldstein
Marina McDougall
Zane Vella
Marc Treib
Christina L. Wallace
Bonnie Ng
Vincent Marsh
Boyd Stevens
Philip Henry
Robert Jacobvitz
*Unidentified people in Civic Center,
    U.N. Plaza and Farmer's Market*

Weeds
A Talk at the Library

by Nicholson Baker

I THOUGHT, WHEN I WAS ASKED BY Melissa Riley and the Librarian's Guild to be a part of tonight's festivities, that I was just going to be arguing for the preservation of the public card catalog for this library, which still exists, intact, in the Old Main building, on the second floor—although the City Librarian doesn't want you to know that, for reasons I now think I understand. I was going to try to convince you, if you needed convincing, of the card catalog's value as a historical artifact, which, despite its flaws (and all indexes and search tools have flaws), is able to tell us possibly interesting things, like for instance what was in the library as of 1991, the date when it was officially "frozen" (to use the term librarians use)—that is, when it was no longer updated, though it was still available to the public. I was going to point out that the card catalog holds the organizing intelligence of several generations of librarians, and that it still is, though out of date and inaccurate in its inventory of the current library, nonetheless superior to the on-line catalog for certain kinds of research. It offers an alternative route into the stacks, and since in this new library, over half the stacks are closed to the public, and therefore unbrowsable, we need all the alternate routes that we can possibly have.

I was going to ask you to entertain the notion that since it is a piece of the intellectual history of San Francisco, the card catalog should be moved from the old library building to the empty space near the San Francisco History Room, above us on the sixth floor, since the history room is where several earlier catalogs of the San Francisco Public Library, those of the 1880s and that of 1909, are now preserved. There is space for it up there, and the wooden "binding," if you will, of this million-page manuscript, is itself a thing of intricately carved beauty. There is no reason to auction it off. The card catalog is a potential tourist attraction, a place for benefactors and well-wishers to pause and think for a moment about this institution's distinguished past.

That was what I was going to say. Then I started talking to the people who work in this building. They are disappointed and demoralized. They feel that they have been lied to. And I think they have been lied to. And as a result, librarians, technicians, pages, and other staff members in this building who would not ordinarily have volunteered their opinions and stories to an outsider like me are now doing so, even though they worry about reprisals and ask me not to identify them in any way. This is a group of smart, funny, learned, brave but apprehensive people. They are apprehensive—and to tell you the truth, I am apprehensive—about the City Librarian, Mr. Ken Dowlin, who came here in 1987, and who has been responsible, since the earthquake, I believe, for the destruction of—not twenty thousand books, not fifty thousand books, not a hundred thousand books, not a hundred and fifty thousand books, but the destruction of, the systematic removal to a landfill of—at least *two hundred thousand library books*, more library books than were destroyed in the so-called Ham and Eggs fire that burned nearly everything in the collection in 1906.

That can't be, can it? Surely I'm exaggerating? Let's start with the recent move. In the first months of this year, the Main Library was supposed to transfer its contents from an old building that was too small to a new building that was much bigger. All the consultants, and the Friends of the Library, and the Library Foundation, the Commission, and, most important, the voters, had reached a rare and ecstatic state of consensus over the fact that the old library building couldn't

The much-heralded atrium at the New Main. But where are the books?

hold what it was being asked to hold and that more space was urgently needed. So the city built a new building. It's an enormous building on the outside. And inside, as well, everywhere you walk you can enjoy expanses of wall-to-wall carpeting and vistas of distant gift shops and teen centers and sweeping stairways and uninterrupted sight-lines in almost every direction. Throw back your head, and you stare upward through a towering void that extends to a conical cornea of whitened glass hundreds of feet above you. One of the architects, James Ingo Freed, is on record as saying that he caught his passion for space exploration from Mies van der Rohe. "I've been involved with it ever since," he told the *Chronicle*, "layering it, bridging it, carving out monumental atriums, as in the library, so people can experience space, move through it and, most of all, enjoy it." And Mr. Dowlin, the City Librarian, is also an admirer of space—not only physical space but what he has called the "neogeography" that is created by virtual communities formed of individuals who are far away from each other physically.

But space, from the point of view of an existing collection of books, means something quite different from floor space, or atrium space, or even magnetic sectors on a file server or megahertzes of bandwidth in a telecommunications cable, all of which this library has in relative abundance. Space, to a book, means shelves; shelves of a certain height and width. Unfortunately, several people seem to have made basic mistakes of arithmetic when they were estimating the number of shelving units that they would have to install in this new building. And they did not consult the librarians who would be responsible for individual areas of the transposed collection. You can get up to seven shelves on one shelving unit, so long as the books are uniformly under eleven inches tall. But books aren't uniform, and if you measure the available shelf space in a new building in linear feet, and don't take into account the variable height of books, you are going to have a problem. But that seems to be what happened. Every librarian I have talked to, every technician, every page, everybody, even when they disagree about other things, agrees on this point: the departments of this library were promised at least enough shelf space to hold their existing collections. And yet they did not get it. They have, with the possible exception of Business and Technology, less shelf-space than they had before. The true horror of this state of affairs only began to dawn on the staff late in 1995, when individual librarians began mapping potential book arrangements prior to the move. Tape measures came out, calculators were turned on, rules of thumb were invoked. Suddenly it was clear. The collection in the Old Main Library was not going to fit in the New Main Library. Something had to be done. And something was done. The collection was attacked. It was thoughtlessly and hastily reduced in volume. It was "weeded."

Now, "weeding" is a term of art in librarianship, and it is a necessary part of what librarians do. If you have five copies of an old edition of Samuelson's *Economics*, or of Booth Tarkington's *The Man from Indiana*, your librarianly duty is to reduce the number, so that there will be space for other books. The library sells them or gives them away, or even throws them away, if nobody wants them, so as not to be choked by the foliage of what was once heavily in demand but is no longer. But beyond these self-evident cases, weeding a great public library such as San Francisco's takes time and careful thought. You have to assess the worthiness or worthlessness of your weed from several perspectives. If it's a little out of your primary area of knowledge, you have to look it up in standard bibliographies. You have to check the record in the catalog and consider what other books are in the library on the same subject. If the catalog says that there is a duplicate copy some-where in the system, you have to verify that that duplicate copy is actually on the shelf and is in good shape, since a book can be missing or stolen and listed as still owned. You have to keep in mind the historical tradition of your library, its known strengths and weaknesses, its imagined future. If the book under your eye is an old edition of something that has been republished, you have to ask yourself whether that old edition has some special merit, something about its annotation, or the eminence of its editor, or the historical flavor of its presentation, that the new one may lack. All this and more comes in to play when an astute librarian goes about weeding his or her collection. And even then there are differences of opinion, of course. To quote from a book called *Garden Friends and Foes*, by Richard Headstrom, "If you were asked to prepare a list of weeds and compare it with one prepared by someone else, they would probably not be in complete agreement."

But what has gone on at the San Francisco Public Library over the last year was not weeding. It was a hate-crime directed at the past. I found *Garden Friends and Foes* in a room near the shipping and receiving entrance in the Old Main Library. It's called the Discard Room and it is still in use. You walk down a slope, through a Dickensian stone arch, you cross the inner courtyard of the old build-ing, and arrive finally at a windowless, high-ceilinged room, measuring maybe ten by twelve feet. It's not a beautiful part of the world. Stenciled on the wall, sever-al times, in red, are warnings to stack discards neatly. This is the room through which over two hundred thousand books passed. Every Tuesday, for years, until this past January, in fact, a Department of Public Works truck drove down to that room, a flatbed truck with wooden sides of the kind they use to pick up brush and old washing machines and bulk refuse, and two, sometimes three men threw the books, which were tied with string in bundles of eight or ten, into the back of the truck. Sometimes the truck held other things, like an old chair, or a carpet pad,

At the back of the old Main Library, June 1995. A Department of Public Works truck and its load are bound for the landfill.

and sometimes it just held books. It's not a simple matter to estimate the capacity of such a truck, but I think I can safely say that it could not hold more than twenty-five-hundred bundled volumes. When it was loaded the truck drove the books to one of the DPW's own landfills and dumped them there. This happened week after week, month after month, year after year. But things got especially bad this past winter, when the Chief of the Main Library, Kathy Page, panicking, it seems, at the fearsome magnitude of the miscalculation—put out a euphemistic call to all stations: weed. The crew arriving from the DPW would crack open the door of the discard room and close it fast, afraid that an eight-foot-high pile of books would collapse on them.

Some of what was in that room came from the branch libraries. In the summer they were sent a surge of new books bought with Proposition E money, for which they had to find space. At the branches, if one book comes in, one old book has to go out. Many books were pulled and sent back to the Main Library, where they awaited the DPW truck in the discard room. The trucks came twice a week in the summer.

But this book, *Garden Friends and Foes,* isn't from one of the branches. It's from the Main Library's circulating collection. According to the on-line catalog, there are now no copies of this book on the shelf here. There are no duplicates of it at UC Berkeley, or at Stanford, or at UCLA, or at Davis. There are copies of a number of Headstrom's other books in this collection—he has written about spiders, lizards, birds, insects, and even a *Complete Field Guide to Nests in the United States*—but this sole copy of his work on weeds was weeded. Why? Because the weeders, as they are called, were told to weed based on condition. The spine of this book, you will notice, is torn, therefore it had to go, since the preservation department, which might once have rebound such a book, is understaffed.

Here's another weeded book I found in the discard room when I snuck down alone the other day: *Rivers of North America,* by Israel C. Russell, published in 1907. It gives a complete chemical analysis of a water sample taken from a hydrant in Los Angeles on September 8, 1878, along with similar results for other samples from the Hudson, the Cumberland Reservoir, the Mohawk River, and the Rio Grande. It turns out that water from a Sacramento hydrant has less sulfuric acid, measured in parts per thousand, than the hydrant water from LA. Why is this book a weed?

There is a record for *Rivers of North America* in the on-line catalog, but there is no actual location information linked to it: instead there is this: "Ask librarian for holdings information." I have seen this sentence so often by now that it has come to have a somewhat sinister flavor. Some of the books that say it are reference books, which are incompletely inventoried. There's nothing wrong with that. We can expect some confusion after a move this huge. But if you ask a librarian at one of the public desks for holdings information about a book like *Rivers of North America*, as the on-line catalog tells you to do, you will inevitably, in my experience, get one answer: the book is gone. It's lost or stolen, they often say. That's what they believe. That's what they've been told. The record is still in the computer, they suggest, because records sit around in there for a while, but eventually it'll be purged. The automation department confirms that "Ask librarian for holdings information" means the book is gone from the library.

Now, I hasten to say that many of the books in the discard room that I have personally checked do have duplicates on the shelves, or at least have later editions of the same work. But here are some other books I found the other day that either have no record on line at all, or say "Ask librarian for holdings information," code for "I have been purged." There is *Crumbling Idols*, by Hamlin Garland, *Homing with the Birds*, by Gene Stratton-Porter, *Principles of Physical Geography*, by F. J Monkhouse, *The Earth Upsets*, by Chase Osborn, *The Book of Natural Wonders*, by Ellison Hawks, *The Handbook for the Woman Driver*, by Charlotte Montgomery, which devotes a whole chapter to "Clothes and Beauty En Route." ("Dark glasses are a *must*.") It was published in 1955 and last checked out in August of 1987. It isn't in this library system now. *Studies of Abnormal Behavior in the Rat*. And here, *The Way to Study Birds*.

The mix in the discard room changes from week to week, as the weeders proceed through the general collection, vainly endeavoring to make it fit into a place of shelter that is, partly as a result of the arithmetical deficiencies of the space planners and partly by design, much too small. Bird books were objects of special attention recently. And yet I would like to say again there are books that should be thrown out, or recycled, or given away. Mr. Dowlin himself offered a defensible theory of discarding to a questioner at a meeting in 1992. He said, "We have many books where we may buy two hundred copies of that book because there are thousands of people who want to read it. It makes no sense to keep all two hundred copies for the rest of our life. So at the time that the usage of that particular book drops, we will retain one, two, five, whatever the appropriate number is." Except for the inflated figure of two hundred, which is off by a factor of ten, that is a fair description of what went on before Mr. Dowlin took command. Before the earthquake, the volume of junked books going into trucks was relatively small. Here, for instance, is a classic discard candidate: the *1983 Arco Civil Service Exam Book for Sanitation Workers*. I found it in the discard room last week, under ten books about ethics. There are twenty copies of this book in the library system now; nobody is going to miss this one. Question 67 on page 90 of *Sanitation Workers*, by the way, asks you to choose the last phrase of the following jumbled sentence: "the book / the top shelf / of the bookcase / wanted was on / which she." The answer is "of the bookcase." "The book that she wanted was on the top shelf of the bookcase." *It wasn't in the back of a DPW truck.*

Aggressively "weeded" books awaiting transportation

The good news is that as of this past January, no more books have been dumped. On January 9, the *Chronicle*'s Andy Ross published a story headlined "SF Library Tossing Thousands of Books" and a picture of the discard room. "The ongoing crime was so apparent by then," one observer told me. "The blood was seeping under the door." Since that scandal, which was quickly contained with several half truths about "dilapidated or multiple copies," no book, to my knowledge, has been thrown away. Instead, representatives of charitable groups are invited to tour a large room in the basement of the Old Main Library, where the books are neatly arranged on shelves, sorted into fiction, nonfiction, large print, and children's books. It's a model program, though understaffed, and the people who tend to it deserve our gratitude. Today, in fact, all day long, about sixty charitable groups, chosen on the basis of need, browsed through something like twenty thousand books, taking whatever they could use.

If it is going to be the policy of a library's senior administration to dismantle the contents of its old collection, to throw out last copies of old bird books and geography books, for example, then this Adopt-a-Book program, in which texts go to schools, and prisons, and rural libraries here in California or in Armenia, or in villages in South Africa, is exactly what we would want to see happen. Some village somewhere is going to be getting a copy of *Birds in the Garden and How to Attract Them*, by Margaret McKenny, which I noticed on the shelf of the Adopt-a-Book collection. Still, if you are a citizen, rich or poor, who lives in the Bay Area, and who looks to the public library as a place where you might learn how to attract birds, or learn how people once thought you ought to go about attracting birds, or what birds people once held to be worth attracting, and if you therefore attempt to see a copy of this book from the library's own collection, and you "Ask librarian for holdings information," you aren't going to find it on the shelves.

Still, one part of the crime has been stopped. This library's fresh discards will continue their lives in readable form, and not make up a layer in the ultimate closed stack, the sanitary landfill. What is maddening, though, is how late we were in stopping it. For in addition to the regular pickups, there was an earlier period of massive book-dumping, during Ken Dowlin's reign, and nobody outside the library knew about it, and the staff couldn't stop it. In October of 1989, there was an earthquake. "The earthquake," one librarian told me, "was the best thing that ever happened to Ken Dowlin." Mr. Dowlin himself said, in a speech at the Annual Conference of the American Library Association in 1992, "I can tell you what happens when you get an earthquake that puts five hundred thousand books on the floor. It's a perfect opportunity to rearrange them."

Rearrange them he did. He merged the old Literature and History department and folded it in with most of Science, despite staff protestations and petitions, creating a large catchall category that is now called General Collections and Humanities and is on the third floor of this building. He put cell biology, tree books, sports, Elizabethan poetry, cookery, model trains, and pets all in the same group, I believe, because they represented to him the old-fashioned library of knowledge, with its space-intensive storage needs, its vexingly long-lived book collection. If he collapsed three or four departments into one, they would necessarily take up less mental room and could be budgeted accordingly. Following the earthquake, Mr. Dowlin kept the library closed for two and a half months in order to complete this reorganization, even though his staff told him that they were prepared to open much earlier. Meanwhile large numbers of books were moving all over the place. The ones that had never been entered into the computer were taken to a room in the north wing, on the third floor, and every department was asked to go through these NOFs, as they were called, which stands for "not on file," and make decisions about whether they ought to be kept or withdrawn. (Withdrawn, by the way, is a confusing word: it means, withdrawn from circulation; thrown away or sold or given away.) For a brief time post-earthquake, according to one eye-witness, the DPW trucks were leaving with loads of books every day. A branch information memo, dated December 7, 1989, advised: "There will be no discard pick-ups until the discard room at the Main Library can be cleared. It is so full it has become a fire hazard." Here again, what happened cannot properly be described as weeding, unless one can be imagined weeding at the helm of a bulldozer. After much discarding and transferring to remote storage, the remaining NOF books sat in boxes in what came to be known as the Deselection Chamber. They sat there for about five years, totally inaccessible, as the boxes sagged and collapsed, and the bindings within gave way. It is my belief that Mr. Dowlin wanted them to be injured, so that when they were eventually inventoried, they would have to be tossed out based on their condition. Also, if you keep a book out of circulation, you can claim that nobody wants it, because nobody has taken it out.

He could have had them reshelved, of course, but he didn't. I don't think he wanted them in his library. He had already signaled his intention before the earthquake, when he told a reporter for the *Bay Guardian* that he planned to clean out what he called the "Augean stables" of the library. King Augeus, remember, had a problem with a backlog of ox-dung, and Hercules cleverly managed this situation by redirecting the flow of a convenient river. Mr. Dowlin envisions himself, with fetching modesty, as the Hercules of the Electronic Library, and one of his first labors was to redirect the river of federal earthquake money in order to cleanse the dun-colored books from his stalls. The damage to the stacks was not structural; nonetheless Mr. Dowlin made the most of it. The FEMA, or Federal Emergency Management Agency, grant application that he prepared requested money for sensible things like physical repairs to the stacks, rebinding, and fixing a gas line. But he also solicited FEMA money for (and I'm quoting the minutes of a Library Commission meeting here) "staff costs for reconfiguring the Main Library," which was part of his reorganizational blueprint and was unrelated to earthquake damage. And he asked FEMA for a new computer system, ostensibly to track earthquake-dislocated books as they were moved here and there. FEMA eventually obliged with a large sum. The card catalog was frozen in 1991, and the library got an expensive new computer system some months later. While the budget for automation swelled, money for the low-tech job of collection maintenance—that is, book repair—stayed flat or dropped. Some books were probably repaired and rebound with FEMA money; many more were simply thrown away.

So this is how the people I talked to arrived at a figure of two hundred thousand books withdrawn from the library in the years between 1989 and 1996. There was a big discard after the earthquake, and another huge one before the move, and a steady flow, both from the branches and from the Main, every month in between. Mr. Dowlin's own figures support this estimate. In his speeches, he used to talk about a Main Library collection of over 1.2 million books. Once he said it was 1.5 million books. Now, on the information sheet called "Fast Facts about the New Main," the number of books in the collection is given as 1 million. That pesky .2 is gone. And this, you will remember, is after a large purchase of new books for the Main Library funded with Proposition E money, most of which are shelved in the First Stop section on the first floor. Two hundred thousand books destroyed is a conservative figure. Some librarians here believe that the real number is closer to three hundred thousand. That landfill is thinking some beautiful thoughts.

From one point of view, destruction on such a scale makes perfect sense. To a manager who has no personal interest in old books, no conception of why anyone would want to spend his or her life reading and thinking about them—to a manager who believes in the pipeline model of information, and who expects databases and Internet access to replace large numbers of monographs in the library of the future, an easy first step to take, even before you buy a database or a CD-ROM jukebox, even before you have digitized one paragraph of text, or designed one Web page, or had lunch with one multiplexer salesman, is simply to reduce the number of old books you own. You've accomplished something; like an urban renewalist of thirty years ago who had a vision of a transformed city and began by tearing down a neighborhood, you take the first step. The fewer old books you have to scan and catalog and store, the easier it is to live up to the impossible promises you had to make to city officials who gave you the money to buy all the hardware and software you asked for. Mr. Dowlin isn't much of a reader, but he isn't stupid, and when he put his hard hat on and toured the jostled stacks in October of 1989, he felt, I believe, the happy calm of a man who knew that the earthquake was his ticket into the twenty-first century.

He has been telling us all along what he's been doing, it's just that we haven't quite understood him. In August of 1992, he introduced the concept of "leveled access" in the humanities to the San Francisco Planning Commission. "Leveled access" involves offering the public, in Mr. Dowlin's words, "a large, generally accessible collection that is designed essentially to be current material—if you will, a mass selection." He has throttled the book budget in math, biology, and literature, while spending far too much money on computer hardware, but he is famous for that, and people with similar enthusiasms are being hired by library boards all over the country. A library director who observed Mr. Dowlin in Colorado told me: "Ken Dowlin for me was a symbol of what not to do. The collection suffered under him." The unfair but widely circulated verdict on his tenure at the Pikes Peak Library System in Colorado Springs was: "Not one book was bought under Ken Dowlin." So not enough books were bought. But what we didn't quite grasp, what is so bewildering and unthinkable, is that, aside from his almost commonplace habit of wasting money on technology, which we all do from time to time, he wanted to damage, to downsize, what had been achieved, at considerable expense, by his predecessors. The staff understood, though. On December 6, 1989, William Ramirez, who was then Chief of the Main Library, wrote a memo for the file describing staff concerns over the events that followed the earthquake. Staff members, he wrote, "believe that current and planned actions will: Decimate the collection [through] weeding, discarding materials from the collections—both circulating and reference which make this library unique." The staff believes that these actions will, Mr. Ramirez went on, "move us in the direction of changing this library from a strong, reference, research resource and service center to an undistinguished 'popular library.'" That was in 1989. Mr. Dowlin, who spent six years in the Marine Corps before a part-time job at the wheel of a bookmobile diverted his interest toward library administration, was predictably unfazed by William Ramirez's report. He has stuck to his plan and he has stuck to his post. It is now 1996, and the books we pay him to protect are still leaving the shelves.

Fortunately for us, many of his employees continue to resist him. When asked to sort books into those that circulated within the past two years and those that circulated less frequently, they did not sort. When asked to weed, they have not weeded. They have saved thousands of books on the sly, for the public, without any supervisor's knowledge—sequestering them in boxes in unvisited areas, quietly transferring them from one department to another, and hiding them in their lockers. They reintroduce these books when the danger has passed. We owe them our thanks. But this is no way for a major urban library to be functioning.

It's especially important now to see Mr. Dowlin's intentions clearly, because of the existence of a place called Brooks Hall. Brooks Hall is a huge underground area that stretches below Fulton, between Larkin and Hyde. In ancient times, computer conventions were held there, but it has fallen into decay, and now the library rents it, I'm told, month to month. They have to rent it, because this building is full. It is full to the point of impaction. Book trucks from Golden Gate Dollie Rental line the walls in the staff areas and crowd the paging stations. The press releases told us there would be room for another million books, but that is laughable. The library, as presently configured, is full. What is interesting, though, is that in Brooks Hall—which has a wood-paneled sort of name but is in fact a gigantic, dusty hole in the ground that I have visited on my own several times by walking down the ramp past the loading dock about fifty feet from this room—in Brooks Hall there are at least seven shelf-miles of books. Almost all the periodicals before 1985, which wasn't so long ago, are stored there. To get them, you have to put in a request and wait twenty-four hours. Just the printout of Brooks Hall periodicals, which you can ask to see at any paging station, goes on for a hundred and eighteen pages, with fifty periodical titles listed on every page. There are four miles of magazines and scholarly journals down there. It's an astounding sight. I don't believe that Ken Dowlin wants to own the majority of those periodicals. He can't throw them out just yet, but they don't accord with his bizarre conviction that this must no longer be a research library. The administration will wait six months, or a year, and then order the teams to weed Brooks Hall once more.

But that's not all there is down in Brooks. The entire McComas science fiction collection, including unbound copies of *Amazing Stories* going back to 1929, for example, is there; and the locked-case collection that used to be in History and Social Sciences in the old building—valuable eighteenth- and nineteenth-century books of engravings of moths and birds; *Bligh's Voyages to the South Seas*, Sir Arthur Evans's multivolume archeological study of the Palace of Knossos; a fine tome called *British Trees* by Rex Vicat Cole, and another called *Hardy and Half-Hardy Plants*. This is a book-dealers' paradise, sitting out in the squalor of a storage area, near carpet remnants and construction debris. Some of the Brooks books are in the on-line catalog, and some are not. Some correctly say "Brooks Hall," some say "Ask librarian for holdings information," some say "Your search for Hardy and Half Hardy Plants did not locate any titles in the database." None of this precious material, needless to say, is being properly overseen by the impressive closed-circuit surveillance system that inhabits gray ceiling bubbles in the staff halls of the Main Library building. Last week I was in Brooks for two hours. Nobody asked who I was when I walked down the ramp. I took nothing, for these aren't discards yet.

In addition to the books on the shelf in Brooks, there are, by my count, twenty-seven pallets of collapsing book boxes and big crates of music scores. Many of the book boxes say NOF in big letters, for they are some of the very books that sat inaccessibly in the Deselection Chamber in the Old Main ever since the earthquake. I opened a box and saw Italian poetry, German bibliography, and a Russian language encyclopedia. Nobody is going to encounter any of these books on the shelf, because they aren't on a shelf, they're in a box, and nobody is allowed into Brooks Hall, anyway: even the staff is discouraged from going down there. Almost all the titles I wrote down and checked later against the on-line catalog are not in the on-line catalog. Only the old card catalog knows that they exist as part of the San Francisco Library. Mr. Dowlin is waiting—he knows he has to wear down resistance. He is confident, I think, that he will eventually unload this overstock.

But let's do the arithmetic for a second. There were, according to the press release, 19.4 miles of stacks in the Old Main, and thirty-two miles of stacks in the New Main. But we know that isn't true, because the Old Main doesn't fit into the New Main. So we know that there are probably less than, say, twenty miles of stacks in the New Main. And there are at least seven miles of books in Brooks Hall, plus the ten thousand or so NOF books that are being shamefully mistreated on pallets. So conservatively, one-third of the Main Library's surviving collection, even after weeding and reweeding, is stored right now in rented space under the street, outside the confines of a building that this City Librarian designed and built at a cost of a $135 million.

What happened, I believe, is that Mr. Dowlin intentionally designed the new building to be too small for the existing collection, in order to force an inventory reduction, but he wasn't aware that there were also serious flaws in the estimates that his henchpeople were giving him. Otherwise, there is simply no rational explanation for the enormity, the insanity, of Brooks Hall.

But even the books that made it into the climate-controlled safety of the New Main Library building are in some cases being injured by the technology that has been installed to handle them physically. In the old library, returned books slid down a chute into the old sorting room in plastic bins, like the containers that hold bags of groceries at some supermarkets. It was a simple, durable system. In the new library, there is a motorized conveyor belt, which you may be able to hear humming away right now if you listen carefully, since it's installed only a few feet from this room. There's nothing intrinsically wrong with a motorized conveyor belt, of course. But the books go down the chute one at a time, rather than loosely packed in bins, and when they jam, they get hurt. It's as if you sent your clothes down to the luggage handlers in the airport without putting them in a suitcase. Many books, some say hundreds, have been torn and injured this way. Someone has taped up a postcard of a pained-looking Ezra Pound right over the opening out of which the books slide. And the sorting room itself, besides being understaffed, has no installed shelving. The old sorting room could hold tens of thousands of books on shelves. In the new, smaller sorting room, book handlers take what pours off the conveyor belt and fling it, as if they were dealing cards, into one of several huge mounds on the floor. I looked in last week and saw a sign taped to the wall that said "800s," which in the Dewey system means books of literature, and under it was an enormous spreading berm of books. This time, I was gently and politely reprimanded by a security guard for being in a staff-only area.

No page or librarian or technician, as far as I have been able to determine, was ever asked what they would want or need in a new sorting room. The sorting room has a contempt for books built into it. As one staff member told me: "This is not a good book building. There's not enough room for books, there's not enough staff to get the books back on the shelves, there's not enough staff to check the books out—however it happened, it's an absolute disaster. Books are being destroyed when they're returned."

But now, we have to turn for a moment from books back to the card catalog. I have repeatedly asked to see it, and I have gotten no response. At the last Library Commission meeting, on May 21, I gave Mr. Dowlin a letter formally requesting the right to inspect the card catalog under section 6250 of the Public Records Act, which is California's equivalent of the Federal Freedom of Information Act. The San Francisco Library pledges itself, when you dial up its computer, to the "free and equal access to information to all citizens." Why is it that Mr. Dowlin is afraid of letting me access the information on the card catalog? There could not be a more public document than this one. It is very strange that I would have to resort to a legal request in order to touch what millions of fingers have already touched. Nobody's privacy is threatened; no matters of state security are involved. I'm beginning to think that Mr. Dowlin doesn't want anyone to see the card catalog not because he knows that I know that there are cards in it for books that aren't yet in the on-line system, but because it is our only clue as to what was in the library before some of the weeding. If Mr. Dowlin has committed a crime against knowledge and against public property, that card catalog is the evidence. Take a representative number of drawers in the catalog, look up the call numbers for several thousand cards, make allowances for theft and loss by patrons, and you will some idea at least of what was flushed from the Augean stables since 1990. You might not be able to determine all the books that were thrown out just after the earthquake, and you won't find out how many branch books were tossed, since branch books aren't listed in the main card catalog. But you will know more than you know now about what happened at the Main Library. That's why the plan is to dump the cards and put the cabinets up for public auction. It's evidence.

Luckily, though, some of the evidence, some of the card catalog, is plastered to the wall on three floors of this building, and some of what is on the wall is reproduced on postcards for sale in the Friend's Gift Shop, thanks to the public art project created by Ann Chamberlain and Ann Hamilton. In the little postcard pack, which is, incidentally, the fastest selling item in the Gift Shop, because people like card catalogs, and are willing to spend money to touch facsimiles of them—in this card catalog pack, you will come upon the card for a biography of Anatole France, by G. M. Brandes. It isn't in the library any more. I asked the technical services department whether all the cards they supplied to the artists represented records that as of the time they were handed over were in the on-line catalog. They said they were. (The cards for the art project, by the way, were taken from the shelf list, not the card catalog.) Another postcard, also from the public art project, is for a German edition of Walter Benjamin's letters, edited by Gershom Scholem. The on-line record has been purged. Here's one: a book by Doris Miles Disney, called *Next of Kin*. The book is gone. Here's a Modern Library edition of Faulkner's *Sanctuary*. Gone. *Korea: Its People and Culture*. Gone.

Out of twenty-seven cards in the postcard packet, eight, possibly nine, represent books that you can't get any more anywhere in this library system, books that have likely been discarded since the art project began: four or five represent titles that are gone, and another four represent particular editions of titles that are gone. One card is what is called an "analytic": a helpful sublisting of a play that is still owned but isn't given a separate title entry on line. Eight out of a pool of twenty-seven books gone: thirty percent. Obviously this is an unscientific sampling, but then Mr. Dowlin is standing in the way of any science I might want to do. If I'm wrong, if all the staff members who, in supplying me with their best estimates of the number of books that were destroyed, are wrong, then the card catalog could exonerate Mr. Dowlin. It will be his friend. On the other hand, if any administrators are foolish enough to order people up those stairs to the catalog room in the old building to throw the cards out, after I have made a formal request under the Public Records Act to see them—and I suggest that everyone here make a similar request—it will constitute, to my mind, the admission of guilt.

Garden Friends and Foes is a good book title to close on. This is still an excellent research library. I have found things here that I never found at Stanford or UC Berkeley. It is worth all of our efforts to rescue it. What we have to do is a little aggressive weeding of our own; we need to rid our public commons of one particularly stubborn and invasive piece of vegetation. Let us weed. Thank you.

AUTHOR'S NOTE: This is the full, uncorrected text of a talk delivered on May 30, 1996, at the Koret Auditorium of the San Francisco Public Library. Some of it was later incorporated, with many adjustments, into an article that appeared in the October 14, 1996, *New Yorker*. Since the version given here represents the original verbatim text, I have allowed several factual errors to stand. They are: the date of one of the old surviving book-form catalogs is 1901, not 1909; the atrium is not "hundreds" of feet high, it is 86; the number of linear miles of shelving in Brooks Hall as of May 1996 was probably six, according to a librarian's re-measurement, not "at least seven"; the library was borrowing the space in Brooks, not renting it; and *Korea: Its People and Culture* was not a last copy. Also, the catalog cards glued to the wall in the new building were taken from departmental catalogs as well as the shelf list; none of the cards, however, came from the main card catalog. And Booth Tarkington's book is called *The Gentleman from Indiana*, not *The Man from Indiana*. All other factual assertions in the original talk were, as far as I can tell, correct. The City Librarian resigned in January 1997.

About That Blood in the Scuppers

by Georgia Smith

I.

DOWN ON CALIFORNIA STREET, in San Francisco's financial district, stands the old stone eminence of the Merchants Exchange Building, a gray granite island among high-rises of glass and steel. The building went up in 1903, promptly went down in the 1906 quake, and was stubbornly put back up in 1909. Enter this postquake expression of mercantile will—you'll pass between two stolid, segmented columns surmounted by scrolls—and cross the lobby. Just beyond, there's a spacious, gorgeous room occupied, at this writing, by a closed bank branch.

This was originally the trading hall of the Chamber of Commerce's marine department, and the room retains the discreet opulence of its era: gold-leaf coffered ceiling, massive oak paneling, marble columns. A skylight illumines arched alcoves where specially commissioned murals depict the source of all this confident prosperity: shipping, which made San Francisco possible.

At the center of the main wall, high above the absent tellers' heads, a particularly beautiful panel shows a three-masted sailing ship being tugged toward us. A warm sunset gilds the water, the sails, the sky, the Marin hills, and the distant Golden Gate, unbridged: W. A. Coulter made the picture in 1909. Its title, *Arrived All Well*, refers to the note chalked on the board in this trading hall when a ship had come safely into port.

If you look closely you can see, ranged along the yardarms that branch out from the ship's main mast, more than a hundred dizzying feet above the deck, tiny men furling the heavy canvas sails after months of sea and wind. Their view of San Francisco must be very pretty in the late-day light.

The ship in the painting is real: it's the *W. F. Babcock,* built in Maine in 1882 and named after a prominent San Francisco shipping merchant. Its first captain was James F. Murphy—alias "Shotgun Murphy," a hotdog navigator who rose to command very young. The serenity of the painted scene is impeached somewhat by a contemporary note about him:

> When coming out of 'Frisco, bound for Liverpool one voyage, finding everything unusually quiet and peaceful at the start, he called his mates aft and addressed them as follows:

> "What's the matter aboard this here ship? Have I got a couple of old women for mates? Here, we've been out of 'Frisco more 'n a week and I ain't seen any blood running in the scuppers yet." (Lubbock 1929)

It's just an anecdote and anyway the gaudy image of human blood running along the gutters that drain an enormous sailing ship is the kind of buccaneer prose that doesn't invite belief these days—and thus a layer of history disappears. To retrieve it, you have to haunt used-book stores, craning your neck after titles like *Ships and Men, Fenceless Meadows,* and *Blood on the Deck*—unfashionable volumes, full of inconsistent details and outlandish adventures.

A sailor's view of pre-quake San Francisco was unique, and he paid for it in a different coin than today's Golden Gate Transit ferry customers, who traverse the postmodern maritime scene each morning. The sailor was part of an industrial work force, but his workplace, a square-rigged ship, was a singular object of great beauty, crafted and run with enormous skill, much of it his. His official twelve-hour day was typical of the industrial revolution, but a ship needs manning on weekends, too; storms mock the time clock; and the work itself is of a kind unrelated to any factory job, unpredictable, in locations exotic or hellish but in any case, remote.

In the plush Beaux Arts interior of the trading room (designed by the San Francisco élite's star architect, Julia Morgan) the crewmen are nearly invisible, just dots in a frame. Even so, the painting crystallizes two views: the sailor's view of shore and the landsman's return regard. These perspectives met in the thin strip of San Francisco—almost entirely destroyed in the 1906 earthquake and fire—that was its waterfront.

Anyone who remembers the original Hunan restaurant down on Kearny Street—with its sputtering flame-licked woks, its windows opaque with steam and those spicy, enticing dishes costing almost nothing—might experience a flash of recognition at this view from a ship's apprentice at the turn of the century:

> If an apprentice knew his way about in 'Frisco he could do a good deal with a dollar in those days. Down on Third Street was a little eating-house where for

W. A. Coulter, *Arrived All Well* (1909)

fifteen cents you could get soup, fish, meat and a slice of pie. A feed every night of the week and ten cents left over! It was not a very high-class eating-house, of course. Cockroaches crawled over the floor, walls and tables. But then cockroaches crawled about the half-decks, too! Then, too, there was that place that every apprentice who was ever in 'Frisco will remember—Clark's on Kearney Street. "Clark's bakery." You'd see dozens of apprentices there of a Saturday night, for ten cents would buy you a big cup of first-rate coffee and a whopping big doughnut, cream puff, slice of pie, or snail. Put down your dime, go to the long counter and help yourself. But Clark's burned up in the big fire after the earthquake, and Kearney Street is altogether different to-day. (Adams 1975)

The old Hunan went in the 1989 earthquake, and Kearny Street is different today, again.

Anecdotal moments like these are a whiff of the familiar: eating, drinking, smelling salt air or fetid garbage—they come across as pretty much "the same" in the past as today. For a moment, it's as if we experience an instant of history directly. That "as if" is of course deceptive; historians labor long and faithful hours to avoid reliance on the "merely" anecdotal in its apparent, but not always transparent, context.

Sometimes there's no choice: much of the waterfront's past is revealed only in anecdotes, by which I mean accounts that make a particular moment vivid by telling a funny story (or an outrageous or a grotesque one), or by revealing an evocative detail, or by indulging in an emotional outburst. One afternoon in the 1890s, Hiram Bailey and his friend Ben (neither one a sailor) went into a dive down on the waterfront:

> Looking round we found ourselves in a rather coarse, and certainly common Battery Point saloon, kept by one "Calico Jim," a Chilean as I subsequently learned. (This same gentleman some years later shanghaied six San Francisco policemen sent to arrest him; and was eventually relentlessly followed and shot dead by one of them on the streets of Callao in Chile, South America.)

> We were about to return outside, not liking the general atmosphere of the place, when a tallish, high-cheeked, square-jawed adder-eyed, raw type of man arrested us with his silvery-toned voice—

> "Say, yoo two, ef yer want a lonesome conversassy, jest vamoos inter thet er room there." (He indicated a door at the opposite end.) "Yoo'll sure be all possum in there . . . out of the bar-room heat and thet. . . . Jest ring fur yer poisons."

> We sat down in that chair-spangled fatal room. Really it proved refreshingly cool; and through the window overlooking the harbour I noticed in the fading evening light several large and graceful sailing-ships: some deeply laden and at rest as if cut in cameo, whilst others, quite light, with their yards already "cock-billed," were evidently preparing to proceed immediately up the Sacramento River to Crocket or Port Costa to obtain their grain cargoes for Europe. (Bailey 1934)

Did someone really dupe (or dope) six cops, all at once, put them on a ship, and get away with it? Was the man who spoke to Bailey really high-cheeked, square-jawed, *and* adder-eyed? A rich vein of unreliable history is mined by guys sitting around getting drunk, telling each other lies—which are, however, slathered onto a base of truth. Calico Jim figures in shanghaiing lore, and though his authenticity is disputed, his profession was real: he was a crimp, one who made a living by delivering men—via persuasion, trickery, or force—to sailing ships in need of crew.

Bailey, still in the bar:

> Over our drinks, I conveyed to Ben casually—for Ben knew nothing of sea-life, and I but a little more—that it was common talk about the harbour that the Benares had put to sea with two clergymen, three bar-tenders, four agricultural labourers—all shanghaied. . . .

> "But what is the meaning of 'shanghaied'?" inquired my companion, looking puzzled.

I was about to explain in detail when Ben turned and ordered from Calico Jim a small bottle of whiskey. "A little of it does your nerves good," he added to me. "No whisky like Old Country whisky." I manfully agreed, as I closely examined the sealing of the cork. "New untouched bottle, no dope in this," I remarked to Ben intelligently and with the air of knowing a thing or two. I was eighteen.

The man in pulling the cork and joining in our conversation butted the matter of shanghaiing clean out of my mind. Calico Jim, who now sat at the same table with us, brought his glass and very suavely invited himself to join in our conversation. He gave us indeed from a special bottle a good "swig"—"The best" he said, complimentarily.

Though it is a long time ago now, I can still remember a strange but pleasant sort of drowsy feeling stealing over me whilst taking that "swig" and there is still silhouetted upon my mind that scoundrel's evil face intently watching me. It never occurred to me why.

Of course, their whiskey was drugged. Bailey says that he and his pal woke the next day to a kick in the stomach and orders to heave hard, and they labored at sea for months.

The history of the waterfront is buried under an encrustation of such local "lore," and it demonstrates the power of anecdotes to perpetuate, and trivialize, a given version of history. Go look at the sign outside Shanghai Kelly's bar at the corner of Broadway and Polk Street, and you'll see the result of the trivialization process: a goopy caricature of a paunchy man with a sort of truncheon (maybe a blackjack, or maybe a rubber bath toy) who looks as if he might spank you.

There was a real James "Shanghai" Kelly, who kept a boarding house (variously reported to be on Pacific or Broadway) and who later ran the Boston House at the corner of Davis and Chambers streets. He's highly mythologized: they say his saloon had three trapdoors through which unconscious sailors—whether drugged or knocked on the head—were dumped and then spirited away to waiting ships. They say that Chinatown cigar makers made up special brands for him, laced with opium, to give to unsuspecting Sailor Jack. They say he shipped out corpses and even, once, a cigar-store Indian. (A competitor, Nikko the Lapp, who was a runner for the shanghaier Miss Piggott, supposedly specialized in sewing rats into a dead man's clothing, then dumping the corpse in a bag and delivering it to a ship as a "dead-drunk" sailor; the rats made it twitch in a reasonably lifelike manner. So they say.)

They say Shanghai Kelly was himself shanghaied by fellow-crimp Johnny "Shanghai Chicken" Devine, and that Kelly was shot down in Peru, just as Calico Jim was supposedly shot down in Callao, or, in some versions, Valparaiso.

The most elaborate Shanghai Kelly anecdote runs like this: three ships lay anchored in the bay waiting for crews, and Kelly decided to make a pile of money by getting crews for all three. He chartered a paddle-wheeler to throw a birthday bash for himself, and issued a blanket invitation along the waterfront. Ninety people packed the steamer. Then:

> Kelly, the story went, first ordered the boat south toward Alviso. But as the merrymakers drained the barrels of booze and grew more intoxicated, the steamer turned around and headed out the Golden Gate into the Pacific Ocean. By that time, the partygoers were in a stupor, drugged by the liquor's knock-out potions.

Kelly hoisted the drugged parties over the side onto each of the three waiting ships. On his way back to town—what extraordinary luck!—

> By coincidence, a ship, the Yankee Blade, had wrecked shortly before and it was believed Kelly picked up some of the shipwrecked survivors. In the excitement when the boat returned to dock, no one questioned what had become of his original revelers. (Pickelhaupt 1996)

This story has been carefully discredited by Bill Pickelhaupt in his thoroughly researched book, *Shanghaied in San Francisco*. The ships involved were apparently not in, or even near, San Francisco at the time the events were supposed to have taken place; in fact, Pickelhaupt finds that the Yankee Blade wreck was 300 miles south, off Point Conception.

But shanghaiing—drugging a man and then kidnapping him to work on a ship—was real. It was commonplace. A nineteenth-century sailor's experience of San Francisco generally involved the process of being kicked back out to sea again.

There were good reasons for this. If ships needed crews they would pay so-called "blood money" for the necessary men. Certain voyages were difficult to staff even when men were available: for example, the run from San Francisco to Shanghai, China, was unloved because it was difficult to get a return trip; usually you had to ship all the way around the world to make it home to San Francisco, which could easily take more than a year. It was this phenomenon that gave birth to the nickname "shanghaier" to denote the crimps of San Francisco.

Blood money (which, though outlawed partway through the century, continued to be paid when necessary) was just part of what the crimps were after. Sailors were allowed two months' advance on their wages before a trip, to pay off debts and to outfit themselves for the trip. The sailor wasn't given the money: he might abscond. His creditors got it directly from the ship. This was the taproot of the shanghaiing system. According to a former seaman:

> When sailors were scarce, the boarding-house master who supplied the ships with crews had recourse to the shanghaiing of any man who would sit and drink with him. Friends of the boarding-house master signed the ship's articles for the

proposed victim, giving the man's name, if they knew it; but sometimes a man would wake up at sea and find himself with a new name. After the ship had sailed the boarding-house master would collect the advance made out in his favour for "board and lodgings and clothing supplied." The game was very profitable. . . . (Farmer n.d.)

Sometimes the captain got a kickback from the crimps:

[T]he Pitcairn's cargo was discharged, her skipper secured a new charter, and two days before sailing he and the shipping-master said something to each other over a table in the Fair Winds saloon, where the shipping-master had his little private room. Here it was that he invited skippers to help him solve simple mathematical problems—easy, they consisted of subtracting something from something and dividing by two. (Sonnichsen 1903)

A sailor's wages could thus be shared by a fair number of people, excluding only the sailor himself.

The 1897 U.S. Supreme Court decision in *Robertson v. Baldwin* lays bare the foundations on which such a system could exist. The court excluded civilian sailors on merchant ships from the 13th Amendment's protection against involuntary servitude, with the extraordinary rationale that "Seamen are . . . deficient in that full and intelligent responsibility for their acts that is accredited to ordinary adults," and therefore must be protected from themselves "in the same sense in which minors and wards are entitled to the protection of their parents and guardians." (Quoted in Pickelhaupt 1996)

The Rev. James Fell founded the Seamen's Institute, a social center and safe haven for sailors in San Francisco during the 1890s. In a report to the British Government on the situation of merchant seamen in San Francisco, Fell rails against the institutionalized abuse of sailors. When he tells an anecdote, he's convincing partly because he's so prissily cautious in his presentation. It's too bad he never named names:

One afternoon the large ship ———— came into the bay, after being at sea for months. The crew, of course, knew nothing about the scarcity of sailors on shore, and the ships waiting in the bay for men. The crimps, as usual, boarded the ship, and extraordinary tales of the lucrative jobs on shore just waiting for men to fill them were told, the usual drinks flew round, and some of the men went with them. . . . The next morning, at 10 a.m., the writer was talking to the second officer of the ship which was waiting for men in the bay, and he remarked, "We've got our men; they're off the ———— , which came in yesterday afternoon." He was asked, "Are they drunk?" and the answer was, "Yes, violent; we've got 'em locked up." Then he was asked, "What time did they come on board?" and he said "Nine o'clock."

Now, the British Consul's office where men sign articles on British ships closes at 3 p.m. and opens at 10 a.m. Even if these men did get ashore by 2:30 p.m., which was impossible, it is ridiculous to think that, fresh from a six months' voyage, they would go within half an hour of landing and sign articles on another long-voyage ship going [on] a four or five months' trip. We all know that, easily taken in as sailors are, they would never do that. They were on board the ———— by 9 a.m. in a drunken state, and the Consul's office did not open till 10 a.m. Who, then, signed the articles, and their two months' advance away? On this and kindred subjects being mentioned to a shipping authority, his reply was that it was best not to mention these things, as they had to be done in busy times. (Fell 1899)

In W. A. Coulter's painting of the *W. F. Babcock*, an insignificant-looking rowboat is pulling away from the ship. The patriarch of San Francisco's Crowley Maritime started his business among these boats, which carried runners from grocers, tailors, boarding houses, and chandleries—all trying to get the ship's business, or its men. This is the one clue in the picture to San Francisco's system of bartenders and pimps and runners and crimps, who ran the waterfront so effectively that police and political authorities were often dependent upon, related to, or were themselves part of the shanghaiing trade.

Arrived All Well (detail)

II.

Sailing memoirs are not about life on shore: they're about ships and the sea. They aren't usually indexed, and finding their stories of San Francisco entails swimming through texts that are 95 percent about wind, ballast, the crack of a shattered mast, maggotty food, splendid beauty, and ghastly pain. They're pretty good. The writing is unprofessional (with notable exceptions, like Richard Henry Dana), and the book in hand is usually the only one the author wrote. At the time of his experiences he probably didn't plan to write anything. The "reporting" is heretical—lengthy conversations that took place twenty or thirty years before the writing are quoted with ease. But the writer usually has no agenda except to tell a good story, and his big-fish exaggerations are of a recognizable species. Once you've read a few of these books, their common references, descriptions, and assumptions begin to form a background against which others can be calibrated. The sailor who arrived in San Francisco Bay after four to six months at sea comes into perspective.

Ships from Europe or the East Coast faced Cape Horn on the way to San Francisco. If winds were unfavorable—and on the trip from east to west they prevail the wrong way—a ship could flounder there, the deck under layers of ice, the rigging frozen into thick, glassy rods, food and fresh water running low, the overpowering wind heaving the ship back and forth, for weeks:

> Morning came, and a Horn hurricane; and it snowed—a cold, white horror. Night came again, and the hurricane and snow. Life-lines were frozen hard, so that it hurt a man with torn hands to grasp them, and a sob would be driven down his throat by the yelling Horn winds. A topsail blew to ribbons, and up we went to lash its ragged ribbons on the spar; and came down again, choking for a chance to breathe in that great wind.
>
> The sea lifted her head and roared across the deck, waist deep in the darkness.
>
> Morning came, and the hurricane and snow.
>
> Clegg went to the bridge and shouted to the mate—close in his ear—
>
> "Five hands missing, sir."
>
> And the mate said—
>
> "All right."

What else could he say? (Adams 1923)

The *W. F. Babcock* sailed around the Horn many times. And although this ship was beautifully crafted, a flaw made the passage a purgatorial proposition:

> The *W. F. Babcock* had one peculiarity, which gained her the nickname of the "Balky Babcock." Sometimes in heavy weather she would get into the trough of a sea and refuse to move, and nothing her captain or mates could do in the way of sail handling or steering could make her resume her course until she chose. Her balking trick was most often exercised when off the pitch of the Horn, and it sometimes happened when she had a fair wind, to the great annoyance of her officers. (Lubbock 1929)

On one run from Baltimore to San Francisco (at around the time Coulter made his painting), the *W. F. Babcock* fought continuous gales for three months to reach the Cape, where it was battered by even heavier weather: "for 20 days in one stretch, the ship was unmanageable due to the rigging being encased in ice. Both topsail yards on the mainmast and the cross jack yard were carried away." By the time they reached San Francisco, the crew had been at sea 172 days. (Matthews 1930)

A sailor's memoir that mentions San Francisco usually mentions crew members jumping ship there. In 1850, before the Barbary Coast had become an organized racket, a Massachusetts sailor named John Whidden arrived in the gold-crazy encampment that was trying to become a city:

> Sighting the Farralones, a cluster of small, rocky islands, in the morning, we took a pilot on board, and entering the Golden Gate, we passed up the bay. . . .

> Although our crew had shipped to discharge the cargo, all hands except the captain and mate went ashore the following morning, landing at Clark's Point. (Whidden 1908)

He ran into a friend, who was staying in "a shanty built of rough boards and canvas, with a sign over the door bearing the name of one of the swell hotels of New York City, 'Delmonico's.'" Whidden checked in, too:

> The terms were $50 per week, plenty to eat if one was not too fastidious, and a good bunk to sleep in; what more would one wish? Of course the bar made it a little noisy, and a free fight, now and then, made everything exciting and lively. Although about every man carried a revolver, or some weapon, they were seldom resorted to. Each man knew his opponent was armed, and the drawing of a knife or gun was the signal for a battle to the death, or at least severe wounding. Men would hesitate before being killed or perhaps permanently disabled for any small quarrel, and generally settled the matter with fists. (Whidden 1908)

A well-worn waterfront anecdote helps color in the picture of fighting in early San Francisco. On June 13, 1868, Johnny Devine, the low-life crimp nicknamed "the Shanghai Chicken," was on a drunk with another shanghaier, Johnny Nyland. They were going around town beating up sailors for the hell of it. Eventually they took over the bar at Billy Maitland's boarding house on Battery Street. At this point they were in possession of a chef's knife. Maitland was asleep upstairs but awoke and came down:

> He was an expert all-hands-in fighter, and in a jiffy he had whipped the long knife from Devine's grasp. As the Chicken tried to retrieve it Maitland brought the keen-edged instrument down across Devine's wrist, slicing his left hand clean off. Maitland had already kicked Nyland out into the street and now he repeated the performance with the mutilated Chicken. Once out in the street Devine screamed, "Maitland, you dirty bastard, chuck me fin out!" and Maitland did just that. Then the two vanquished heroes staggered to a drug-store on Pacific Street, and just before he collapsed the Chicken ordered a quack called "Doc" Simpson to "stick me fin on again."

> Eventually the Chicken was taken to hospital, being given, sometime later, a hook in place of his fist. (Hugill 1968)

Sailors deserted relentlessly in San Francisco, right through the century, and often in circumstances absurdly unfavorable to themselves. British ships (frequently a majority in the bay) signed up seamen for a round trip, with wages paid only on the return to England. A man who left at the halfway mark forfeited all his wages. Yet leave they did, by the hundreds.

This phenomenon was welcomed by many captains, who saved a lot of money for the ship owners if their crews deserted. It became standard practice to make conditions in port intolerable, so the sailors would leave. One dirty trick was to deny them shore leave when they were tied up at a wharf for weeks. San Francisco dumped its refuse and its sewage at these wharves, gradually filling in the bay. In addition to a stunning smell, typhoid and other illnesses wafted along the waterfront. Coulter's *Babcock* painting is discreetly faithful to this fact: he places a bit of garbage—a discarded cask—in the center foreground.

One large ship, arriving in the 1890s, anticipated a long layover in the bay. The captain refused to advance the crew any pocket money, so they were literally penniless in port. He also refused to sign up a tailor (from whom sailors might borrow, at high interest, against their wages: the tailor could put the loans down as clothing expenses and get the money from the ship).

Meanwhile, a crimp offered the crew $25 each to desert. The men were owed far more than that in wages, and they refused, holding firm for weeks. The crimp finally lost patience:

> It was Sunday, and the sailors were lying in their bunks or strolling about the decks when he of the rings and watch-chain came down. . . . It was of no avail. The men were obdurate and told him he might as well go over the side of the ship, and that he was at liberty to dwell in a warm place.

> This was too much! It was insult added to injury. To refuse 25 dollars! a sailor! what had the world come to? The boarding-master lost his temper, his rocker became deranged. The philanthropist departed and the tiger took his place. In his wrath at being foiled for a month and altogether, he did the worst thing he could have done under the circumstances: he produced a paper, which he showed to the sailors; on this paper were written down the names of every man in the forecastle, and opposite each name was the amount owing to each man and also the amount he—the boarding-master—was to get for every man he lured out of the ship, and told them the "job" had been put into his hands to get the men out of the ship. (Fell 1899)

When John Whidden returned to the bay in the 1860s he had advanced from sailor to captain, and this visit was quite different. (He didn't desert, for starters.) At the dock, he found himself across from the ship *Guiding Star*, which a Captain Small had brought from Boston:

> In the evening I went on board to make Captain Small a social call, and when, after passing a very pleasant hour, he invited me to spend the night with him, I

accepted, and he gave me his stateroom, taking a spare room for himself.

Retiring about eleven o'clock, and pulling off my boots, I disrobed and turned in, sleeping soundly until morning, when I arose, and proceeding to dress, found nothing left of my boots but the soles and straps. All outside of these resembled a piece of brown tissue paper perforated with tiny holes. On asking Captain Small about it, he explained that he meant to have told me to put everything, including my boots, in the basket at the head of the bed, but he forgot it! The cockroaches had eaten them in the night, and the captain's forgetfulness cost me a new pair of boots. However, he was good enough to loan me a pair to put on. (Whidden 1908)

III.

Today's blocks of sleaze along Broadway and Columbus Avenue are the rebuilt remnants of a prototourist district where miners and sailors were intended to be fleeced. The sailor's salient characteristic, for these purposes, was that he spent almost all his time at sea. He knew about that. Shore life was unfamiliar, unrhythmic, and—on the San Francisco waterfront with its trumped-up diversions—unnatural. The area stretched up from the water's edge, expanding as the city grew and prospered:

Red-light houses were to be found in Grant Avenue, Market Street, Clay Street, Pacific Street, Washington Street, North Broadway, Stockton Street, Sacramento Street, the Waterfront, Kearney Street, Powell Street, Montgomery Street, Commercial Street, and Morton Street, as well as down many a side crack, cul-de-sac and alley. . . . Some of these brothels had fantastic signs above their doorways, signs such as Madame Lucy's Ye Olde Whore Shoppe in Sacramento Street; and Madame Lazarene's great red, iron rooster with a red light in its beak, and a sign-board in its talons, displaying the gilded name of the house, the Sign of the Red Rooster. In the hall, however, she had a smaller cock-a-doodle with another board bearing the title by which the place was usually known: At the Sign of the Red Cock. (Hugill 1968)

Barkers were already in place, hawking the girls and the acts inside: in the early years there was Oofty-Goofty, who daubed himself in tar and did a wild man act (yelling "oofty-goofty!"). And Big Bertha, a "so-called soprano," who let herself be lashed to a donkey for an act called "Mazeppa's ride." There were "waiter girls" in fanny-grazing skirts and deep-cut necklines and no underwear: "Such an omission was widely advertised, on little bits of pasteboard passed around among visiting sailors."

Such descriptions are easy to find: they're the traditional costumes in which the Barbary Coast has been handed down to us. A sailor's point of view is missing here; he's just part of the waterfront cliché.

Bill Adams sailed into the bay from England, an apprentice on the Silberhorn, when he was about twenty years old. It was 1899:

> The 'Frisco waterfront was lovely in those days. Why, you could walk for blocks beneath the long jib-booms of clippers stretched across the street. You'd see their figureheads. A dragon, one ship had, its red maw open and its white fangs showing. And some had knights and warriors, with spears and swords, and shields. And many ships had women for their figureheads. Ours was the fairest figurehead of all. A white-robed woman with her white breast bare. One arm outstretched, a finger pointing to the far away. And in her other hand she held a long silver horn to her lips, about to blow on it. (Adams 1975)

This is the same waterfront that variously stank of sewage and roiled with shanghaiers. Anecdotal memoirs, though limited by their point of view, retain the corollary virtue of preserving more moods than one.

Adams and his shipmates headed up to the Barbary Coast:

> The others wandered on ahead of me and Paddy, and we were all alone. Then a window opened, and a soft voice spoke. Soft scent was on the air.

> "Come on, Bill," said Paddy.

> So we went in. One girl was there alone. She kissed me first, then Paddy. Her gown was of pale gold. Her hair was golden. Her eyes were ocean blue. Her slender arms were bare. Her hands were soft. Oh, very. And that neat little room, with carpet and with cushions, with pale pink wall paper, dim-lit by a warm roseate little lamp, was, ah, so different to our cramped half-deck with its rusty stains, and cockroaches, and our old oilskins hanging everywhere. She took our fingers in her soft scenty hands and looked at our cracked palms; our scars from cold Cape Horn.

> She said, "You poor dear boys."

> And then she kissed my palms.

> "Minnie will kiss your hurts away, and you'll forget," she said.

> By and by, I went out to the street. Dim street, with far-spaced, rosy little lights. Paddy came later.

> "She was all right, Bill, wasn't she?" he said.

IV.

The precise scenario of the Shotgun Murphy anecdote, cited at the beginning of this article, may have improved in the retelling, but the punch line is probably accurate. So-called "discipline" on commercial American sailing ships in the nineteenth century was violent and unrestrained. Seawater sloshing over the deck, mixed with blood from a sailor clubbed senseless, might easily run red streams down the scuppers.

There are hundreds of accounts of abusive treatment, and they're discouragingly consistent: men worked to exhaustion, sleep-deprived, taunted about their "rights"; sick and injured men beaten for not working properly; men strung up on the rigging or shackled in a rat-infested "lazarette," a ship's closet-sized version of a cell. This is a typical story:

> The *Crusader* sailed from New York on October 22, 1872 under the firm hand (fist) of Captain Lewis. One of the crew was Seifert Nelson, an ignorant but strong and healthy Norwegian. To pass the time away, Mate Henry began to work him over. . . . [H]e was slung over the bows in the teeth of a howling snowstorm off Cape Horn. At the very water's edge he was required to scrape rust off the chains. . . .
>
> [H]e was soon forced to parade back and forth on the deck as a ludicrous "lookout," carrying on his shoulder an unloaded musket. When he could not obey orders fast enough, the captain had him stripped stark naked and forced another sailor, named Grant, to rub him down with ashes and canvas [a technique for stripping paint off wood]. When the *Crusader* docked on the Embarcadero, Nelson . . . was carried to the Marine Hospital but soon passed away. (Dillon 1961)

Crews had scant legal recourse. In the above case, the captain and mate drew fines of $100 and $300, respectively. Most abuses went unreported, for sailors knew it was almost impossible to get satisfaction, even if they got a rare conviction:

> One of the most flagrant cases of babying the sadistic brutes called buckos was the case of a mate McCausland, alias McCortland, who arrived in the Bay in 1868 or 1869 from Boston. He had dreamed up new humiliations and tortures which he carried out on the ship's boys. For one thing, he forced them to eat large chunks of tobacco washed down with water. He had his own crude but cruel version of the Chinese water torture, forcing men to sit on the deck and drink and drink until their stomachs were distended. Then, when it seemed they would burst, he would force them to carry heavy planks about the deck, willy-nilly. . . .
>
> Arrested in San Francisco, he drew eighteen months in the state prison at San Quentin but Warden Holden took pity on the beached bucko. He placed him in command of his yacht and soon gave him all but complete freedom. When he was not busy taking the Warden's or Governor's lady friends on a bay cruise, he would loaf the days away at the saloons which sprang up just outside the gates of the penitentiary at Point San Quentin. (Dillon 1961)

Richard Henry Dana (whose sailing days, chronicled in *Two Years Before The Mast*, preceded a legal career) wrote a scathing commentary on a case in which officers who tortured and killed crew members were let off lightly because the judge discounted the sailors' testimony as a matter of course, assuming it to be unreliable. Dana queried bitterly, "Ought their character, as seamen, so to taint their evidence, that though the jury may believe them, and bring the party in guilty, yet the penalty must be reduced to almost a nominal matter?" ("Cruelty to Seamen—Case of Nichols and Couch," *American Jurist and Law Magazine*, v. 4, October 1839)

In the closing decades of the nineteenth century, the Coast Seamen's Union newspaper published a catalog of shipboard brutality called the "Red Record." Shotgun Murphy was cited in 1893: "He was accused of making no attempt to save a man who fell overboard from the royal yard. The ship was being heavily pressed on a wind under topgallant sails, and the captain's answer was that the weather was too bad for him to lower a boat." (Lubbock 1929) Robert J. Graham, captain of the *W. F. Babcock* for most of the 1890s, was notorious in the "Record": he was noted once for breaking the teeth of some of his men, another time because he had "pummeled a sailor on the head with a pair of handcuffs, ranting 'You lime-juice son of a bitch, take that, and that, and that!'" (Dillon 1961)

The "Red Record" was derided by newspapers of the day for being lurid and sensational. Sailors' rights were won only as they gradually lost importance: as sailing ships became obsolete.

Arrived All Well is a painting—and an expression—that portrays a ship but scarcely indicates a crew. The artist, W. A. Coulter, was born in Ireland and went to sea at the age of thirteen. He was a self-taught painter who knew every rope, wire, chain, sail, and knot on a ship. (In later years, when he lived in Sausalito, Coulter would decorate his daughter's dresses with fancy knotwork.) All but one of the paintings that decorate the marine trading hall are his: five of the six large panels and eight smaller medallions that dot the upper walls.

The fire that followed the 1906 earthquake destroyed many Coulter paintings that hung on the walls of merchants and magnates who prized the technically accurate renderings. This accuracy is lost on the uninitiated, but the story of the crew is not so arcane. It didn't burn and it need not be lost. Stories by real sailors still haunt the bookstores, shelved sometimes under "history" and sometimes under "fiction," and sometimes in that oddly inclusive category, "nautical." Dismissing these stories as "mere" anecdotes, indistinguishable from the clichéd mythology of the Barbary Coast, telescopes the sailor down to a postcard persona—daubs of paint in a fancy frame.

References

Adams, Bill. 1923. *Fenceless Meadows*. New York: Frederick A. Stokes.

———. 1975. *Ships and Memories*, Brighton: Teredo Books.

Bailey, Hiram P. 1934. *Shanghaied Out of 'Frisco in the 'Nineties*. 2nd ed. London: Heath Cranton.

Dillon, Richard H. 1961. *Shanghaiing Days*. New York: Coward-McCann.

Farmer, H. F. n.d. *The Log of a Shellback, A Narrative of Life and Adventure Before the Mast in the 'Nineties*. London: Newnes.

Fell, Rev. James. 1899. *British Merchant Seamen in San Francisco, 1892–1898*. London: Edward Arnold.

Gowland, Gladys M. O. 1959. *Master of the Moving Sea; The Life of Captain Peter John Riber Mathieson, from His Anecdotes, Manuscripts, Notes, Stories, and Detailed Records*. Flagstaff: J. F. Colton.

Hugill, Stan. 1967. *Sailortown*. New York: E. P. Dutton.

Le Scal, Yves. 1967. *The Great Days of the Cape Horners*. Translated by Len Ortzen. New York: New American Library.

Lubbock, Basil. 1929. *The Down Easters*, Boston: Charles E. Lauriat.

Matthews, Frederick C. 1930. *American Merchant Ships 1850–1900*. Salem, Mass.: Marine Research Society.

McLaren, Jack. 1933. *Blood on the Deck; The True Record of the Author's Strange Experiences in a Deep-sea Sailing-ship*. London: George G. Harrap.

Pickelhaupt, Bill. 1996. *Shanghaied in San Francisco*. San Francisco: Flyblister Press.

Robinsdon, Elizabeth Muir. 1981. *W. A. Coulter, Marine Artist*. Sausalito: James V. Coulter & the Sausalito Historical Society.

Sonnichsen, Albert, Able Seaman. 1903. *Deep Sea Vagabonds*. New York: McClure, Phillips.

Whidden, John D. 1908. *Ocean Life in the Old Sailing-Ship Days; from Forecastle to Quarter-Deck*. Boston: Little, Brown.

The Progress Club
1934 and Class Memory

by Chris Carlsson

The piecards [paid union officials] took the hiring hall away from us by putting goons like "Johnny Loudmouth" in control of job dispatching. His specialty is to intimidate the guys up in age. It's a way of destroying memory. We don't write our history. Those guys are it.
> —Hector Soromenho

THE STRATEGIES USED SINCE the 1934 General Strike to overcome San Francisco's working class have wrought profound changes in work, technology, and daily life. This process has been sold as "progress"—as in "you can't stop it"—and has enjoyed explosive success on a global scale during the post–World War II growth of the world market. Progress conveniently masks changes in social arrangements, making them appear as "natural" results of technical and market rationality, rather than the self-serving moves of a powerful elite.

Progress unifies capitalist planners around shared values and assumptions, as if they were in the same social club (which they often are, literally, as well). Progress is also an ideological "club"—in the sense of "blunt instrument"—wielded against recalcitrant workers and uncooperative communities to ridicule opposition to corporate development plans. Progress as ideology has assured that all changes are both for our own good and, in any case, inevitable. Meanwhile, the forces behind progress have broken and rewoven the texture of human life at work and at home repeatedly over decades.

Progress brings modernized machinery; to accommodate new machines, work habits and production processes have been radically changed, reducing the human labor component of most jobs and making it easier to shift work from one place to another. These changes in turn have eliminated elaborate relationships based on shared cultures and artisanal knowledge. This kind of progress has also undermined organizations (like industrial unions) that grew during earlier moments in history (when there were different jobs and business structures, and the fight between workers and owners led to unions as a compromise).

A growing self-awareness and a working-class talent for wildcat strikes in the late 1930s shook San Francisco's controlling class to the core. The elite responded with a decades-long process to regain the upper hand in the balance of power. The forces unleashed by the Depression-era upheavals on the waterfront made San Francisco's local class struggle a crucial staging area for reshaping ruling-class response. Ultimately, this long-term counteroffensive changed life, both at work and at home. What began as an effort to circumvent organized workers in San Francisco by regionalizing the local economy became a model for the globalization that has swept the world in the past quarter-century. San Francisco has been an important test site for our society's most advanced techniques for improving and extending the control of capitalism.

Confronted by the full arsenal of ruling-class power over the last six decades, San Francisco's once-vaunted labor movement at the end of the twentieth century has been reduced to whispering where it once roared. The local outcome of this old dance with capital is a restructured city economy. The once dominant waterfront is dead, replaced by a predominantly low-wage, non-union economy based on tourism, entertainment, shopping, eating, and financial and medical services. The working class, rarely identified as such anymore, is fragmented along racial and status lines, and increasingly stratified at work. New categories of white-collar technicians and professionals, while still wage workers, are far removed from the gritty industrial working class of mid-century and earlier. Another third of the working population is consigned to drift from temporary job to temporary job, under constant pressure to improve and diversify their personal skills to offer prospective employers maximum flexibility.

Accelerated residential transience within and between urban centers has further fractured and atomized workers, largely destroying the long-term institutions and facilities that help city dwellers discover each other and enliven real communities. In today's San Francisco thousands of homeless people eke out survival amid remarkable material abundance, while most of us work and shop in an invisible but "normal" isolation. Communities based on ethnic or national origins, neighborhoods, or occupations have been dispersed and worn down by several decades of urban redevelopment and economic modernization. San Francisco has a much different working population in the 1990s, doing different work, than it had half a century ago, with people living in much more expensive housing for shorter durations.

The exhilarating grassroots working-class culture that discovered itself in the strikes and organizing campaigns of the 1930s has been unmade and erased in the following half a century. How did 100-percent unionization of restaurants in 1941 (a union card in the window practically required to get steady customers) become the low-wage, temporary, non-union cappuccino bars, taquerías, pizzerias, chain stores, and dessert boutiques of today? How come no one thinks there *is* a working class, let alone that *they are in it?*! Our basic ability to see our lives as a collective rather than individual predicament has practically disappeared. How did this all happen?

When the Workers Rose

The 1920s was the decade of the "American Plan" in San Francisco, with the open shop and untrammeled business power calling the shots across the city's economy. The well-financed Industrial Association, an entity formed to carry out a coordinated labor strategy among San Francisco's largest companies, relentlessly fought every attempt by workers to regain lost wages, shorten working days (to eight hours), and organize independently.

Shipping magnate Robert Dollar (Dollar Lines, beneficiary of over $20 million in annual federal subsidies during the late 1920s to handle mail across the Pacific Ocean) illustrated the hardball tactics that propelled owners into the driver's seat. Speaking to a National Association of Manufacturers meeting in New York in 1923, Dollar described a recalcitrant judge who refused to jail locked-out maritime workers in 1919:

> We told him that because of his reluctance to prosecute we had found it necessary to form a vigilance committee and if the serious conditions along the waterfront did not stop at once, our first official act would be [to] take him and string him up to a telephone pole. . . . I can see that official yet. He could not believe we really meant it, so he said to me, "Mr. Dollar, do you mean that?" I answered, "I was never more earnest in my life." My reply brought him to time [sic] and he at once promised to cooperate with us and he did. . . . (ILWU 1963)

It took many years, but by 1933 waterfront workers were again organizing independently. The June 1933 National Industrial Recovery Act provided workers "the right to organize and bargain collectively through representatives of their own choosing." Longshoremen quickly deserted the company union known as the "Blue Book" and rejoined the International Longshoremen's Association (ILA). The new union militants held a convention in San Francisco in February 1934 for all the International Longshoremen's Association longshoremen along the West Coast. The workers met for ten days but excluded paid union officials as delegates. They resolved that no agreement could be valid unless approved by a rank-and-file vote. They demanded union recognition, union-controlled hiring halls to

"Bloody Thursday," July 5, 1934. A day of rioting along the waterfront and Rincon Hill resulted in two killed and hundreds injured.

replace the humiliating "shape-up" (in which workers had to submit to nepotistic and corrupt bosses every morning to seek work), a raise in pay, a thirty-hour week, and a coast-wide agreement covering all U.S. ports. They also called for a waterfront confederation of all marine workers, including teamsters; rank-and-file gang committees to handle grievances instead of business agents; and opposition to arbitration, since it always led to defeat. They also sought to prevent the use of new technology ("labor-saving devices") such as four-wheel wagons and the use of jitneys to pull two wagons at once. The shippers refused to negotiate, and in May 1934 the strike that would engender so many changes began.

Local business leaders failed to grasp the shifting balance of power that such a large, cross-occupation and well-organized rank-and-file strike could produce. William H. Crocker, grandson of the original "Big Four" railroad baron, said during the General Strike:

> This strike is the best thing that ever happened to San Francisco. It's costing us money, certainly. We have lost millions on the waterfront in the last few months. But it's a good investment, a marvelous investment. It's solving the labor problem for years to come, perhaps forever.... Mark my words. When this nonsense is out of the way and the men have been driven back to their jobs, we won't have to worry about them any more. They'll have learned their lesson.

Not only do I believe we'll never have another general strike but I don't think we'll have a strike of any kind in San Francisco during this generation. Labor is licked. (Nelson 1988)

Certain that brute force could win, as it had during the previous decade, San Francisco's Industrial Association decided to force the issue after strikers had closed the port for two months. On July 3, 1934, using strikebreakers and the San Francisco Police Department, they forcibly moved cargo from the strikebound port to warehouses a few blocks inland. Violent confrontations between thousands of strikers and police exploded along the southeastern slopes of Rincon Hill and the waterfront. After a holiday truce, July 5, 1934, became memorialized as "Bloody Thursday" when two men died and scores were hospitalized in daylong skirmishes and hand-to-hand combat all over the waterfront. The brutality of the police shocked the city and the country.

A silent funeral procession of over 40,000 filled Market Street a few days later, and by July 13 a General Strike was spontaneously unfolding in San Francisco and around the Bay Area. The Central Labor Council, which had denounced the maritime strike leaders as communists in late May, scrambled to head off the General Strike by creating a Strike Strategy Committee, an effort characterized by activist Sam Darcy as an effort "to kill the strike, not to organize it." (Brecher 1972)

At 8 a.m. on Monday, July 16, the San Francisco General Strike officially began, affecting around 150,000 workers around the Bay. But it had already been rolling along for a few days by then. Between July 11 and 14, over 30,000 workers went out on strike, including teamsters, butchers, laundry workers, and more; by July 12 twenty-one unions had voted to strike, most of them unanimously.

The General Strike began to weaken almost as soon as it officially began. The National Guard occupied the waterfront and violent attacks by vigilantes (off-duty police and hired thugs, coordinated by the Industrial Association) occurred all over San Francisco. The conservative Strike Committee authorized so many workers to go on working that they dramatically undercut the movement. On the very first day, they allowed municipal carmen (running the streetcars) to return to work, ostensibly because their civil service status might be jeopardized. The chairman of the Labor Council and the Strike Committee was Edward Vandeleur, who was also president of the Municipal Carmen and had opposed the strike from the beginning. The ferryboatmen, the printing trades, electricians, and telephone and telegraph workers were never brought in on the strike. Typographical workers and reporters continued to work on newspapers that spewed forth antistrike propaganda. Labor Council leaders even went so far as to issue a work permit to striking sheet-metal workers to return to their jobs in order to repair bullet-riddled police cars.

Martial law. 2,500 National Guardsmen occupied
San Francisco's waterfront during the General Strike.

President Franklin Roosevelt stayed officially aloof from the strike, his Labor
Secretary Frances Perkins cabling him that the General Strike Committee of
Twenty-Five "represents conservative leadership." On July 19 the General Strike
Committee narrowly voted to end the strike. On July 20, the Teamsters voted to
return to work, fearing that the Mayor's Committee of 500 and the Industrial
Association would put strikebreakers on all the trucks in San Francisco and leave
the Teamsters without any jobs. This was the end for the Longshoremen and
Seamen's strikes along the waterfront. By July 31, they ended their strikes and
accepted federal arbitration, which ultimately led to partial victories on wages and
hours, but the key issue of union control over hiring halls was settled with a formu-
la that allowed for joint management of hiring halls with the shipping companies.
Since the unions got to pick the dispatchers, they enjoyed control in fact if not by
contract. The 1934 General Strike put a lethal dagger into the heart of fifteen years

of "American Plan" propaganda (the 1920s' version of anti-union, anticommunist, pro-American patriotism) and open shop conditions.

A Sleeping Giant Stirs

Daily life changed dramatically after 1934. In spite of a desultory and ambiguous conclusion to the 1934 upheaval, it still led to an extended period of worker activism, unionization, and a profound shift in power relations in most of the city's workplaces, creating and reinforcing a broad sense of camaraderie and solidarity among the working class. Crocker's gloating claim that the strike would "lick labor" and end all strikes could not have been more wrong. Workers across most occupations discovered the power of strikes, and by the late 1930s unions were becoming entrenched in most parts of San Francisco's economy.

Strikes among different workers peaked in different years after the middle of the decade as the following chart (California 1940) shows (these numbers are for all of California):

INDUSTRY	YEAR	WORKERS	LOST DAYS
machinists	1936	1,661	19,091
textiles	1936	5,938	83,513
lumber	1936	1,814	137,954
transport/commun.	1936	29,131	1,122,659
paper/printing	1937	427	45,424
transport equipment	1937	15,264	230,703
domestic service	1937	8,333	341,392
trade	1938	8,206	328,214
iron and steel workers	1938	2,555	31,348

Each year between 1927 and 1933 saw fewer than ten strikes in the Bay Area, but after the 42 strikes involving over 100,000 workers in 1934, the rest of the 1930s saw an average of over 60 strikes per year, involving about 25,000 workers annually for about a half-million lost work days per year.

On San Francisco's contentious waterfront the longshoremen gained practical control over the allocation of work. Worker-elected dispatchers rendered individual employers irrelevant by establishing a remarkably egalitarian "low-man-out-first" system to share the available work. (This system, which equalized opportunity to work but not necessarily income, was developed by longshoremen in San Pedro and copied by the San Francisco local. (Weir, interview with author, 1997)) Moreover, the daily rhythm of the "four-on, four-off," along with numerous restrictive work rules spread the work out even further while maintaining a pace of work set by the longshoremen themselves. Offshore unions of sailors and others gained complete control of their own hiring hall after the violent waterfront strike of 1936.

The ILWU itself pursued an organizing strategy it called the "March Inland." Warehouse workers were ready to join. Joe Lynch told interviewer Harvey Schwartz:

> You had commercial warehouses strung along the waterfront from the Hyde Street pier over to Islais Creek; then you had cold storage warehouses; behind those you had mills, feed, flour, and grain; behind those you had grocery—big grocery, with 1500 people—and that's the way they organized. Gee, it was terrific. Then came hardware, paper, and the patent drug industry, and the coffee, tea, and spice in '37. Liquor and wine came in '38. Then it was a mopping up operation after that. By World War II, the union had under contract, either wholly or partially organized, 46 different industries in warehouse, distribution, production and processing. (Schwartz 1995b)

Another worker, Brother Hackett, told Schwartz:

> After the 1936–37 strike everybody organized. You went around the neighborhood on your lunch hour, found somebody havin' lunch, and started talkin' to 'em. If they didn't belong to a union, you asked 'em what wages they were getting. When you found out how little they were being paid, you'd say, "We just joined the Warehouse Union and went out on strike for a lousy couple of months, and doubled our salary." The guy'd say, "Just lead me to it." See, there was a tremendous surge then. We had a meeting every week. There was always fifteen, fifty, or a hundred to two hundred people being sworn in. The people were just waiting in the weeds for somebody to hit them with a stick. It was just like a great awakening or a crusade. (Schwartz 1995a)

With the ILWU setting the example, unionization of workers in other industries continued through the 1930s. The culinary union made rapid gains during this period. Waitresses Local 48 organized first in restaurants patronized by union clientele, spread its drives to restaurants outside working-class neighborhoods, swept up cafeteria, drugstore, and tea-room waitresses, and then included waitresses employed in the large downtown hotels and department stores. By 1941, waitresses in San Francisco had achieved almost complete organization of their trade, and Local 48 became the largest waitress local in the country.

Culinary organizers credited the new climate of solidarity:

> There is a much better spirit of cooperation than formerly and the Culinary Workers have profited from it. We are indebted to the Maritime Unions and . . . in fact all the unions pull with us whenever we go to them with our troubles, thus our brothers did not give their lives for nothing. (Cobble 1991)

Workers enthusiastically took more power in worksites all over town, utilizing innovative tactics from sitdowns and occupations to costumed picket lines, theatrical demonstrations, and clever grassroots informational campaigns. After enduring hundreds of short wildcat strikes during the 1930s, employers naturally began to look at the bigger picture. How could the chokehold of organized labor be bypassed, if not defeated? The foundations for a capitalist counterattack had already been laid, even as workers took more daily control than they'd ever had before.

The Owners Regroup

Most workers flocked to the new CIO industrial unions, but less well remembered is the extent to which employers, too, saw an answer to a restive and increasingly assertive working class in the new unions. A number of large U.S. companies, including General Electric and U.S. Steel, embraced the new centralized unions of the CIO to control unruly industrial workers. The romantic lens through which leftist historians have viewed the 1930s has underplayed the conflicting forms of working-class organization that fought each other in that tumultuous decade. Rank-and-file democratic structures created by strikers were generally dismantled as they entered the new industrial unions, and power was transferred from the shop floor to the union offices.

> From 1937 through the 1950s, when organization among San Francisco restaurants remained close to 100 percent, *many employers willingly complied with this system of union-sponsored industry stabilization and cooperation.* Employers who failed to recognize the good business sense of unionization . . . faced increasing pressure through the [labor] council's "We Don't Patronize" list. Few employers could withstand the business losses of withdrawn union patronage when approximately one-fifth of San Francisco's entire population belonged to a labor organization. (Cobble 1991; emphasis added)

In *The Turbulent Years*, Depression labor historian Irving Bernstein recounts how in 1937 San Francisco's "leading businessmen formed the Committee of Forty-Three, hoping to persuade the unions to join in a program to stabilize labor relations." Though labor refused at first, the Committee soon became the Employers' Council, whose purpose was "the recognition and exercise of the right of the employers to bargain collectively." (Zerzan 1977) The stabilization offered by union contracts inspired most San Francisco business owners in 1938 to join the San Francisco Employers' Council, which promoted industry-wide, multi-employer bargaining. By 1948, the single-employer contract had become the exception, with over 75 percent of all union workers falling under "master" industry-wide contracts. (Selvin 1967) But a stable, adversarial union still makes demands and puts some constraints on the power of business owners. With the benefit of a half-century of hindsight, we can see that the pragmatic accommodation with unions was not a permanent change but a temporary tactic to gain time for a much grander strategy.

Ruling-class planning in San Francisco faced an entrenched, self-confident, smart, historically savvy working class in pre–World War II San Francisco. World War II spurred cataclysmic changes worldwide, and war mobilization in San Francisco promoted a regionalization of industry and an influx of new workers, altering forever the composition and residential distribution of the area's working class. Regional planning, underway since the 1920s, combined with New Deal infrastructural investments to cross the bay with new bridges and surround the region with new highways. In regionalizing the Bay Area economy, planners moved shipping to Oakland, heavy industry to the north and to the East Bay, while high-tech industries grew around university enclaves and military bases. Regionalization was pursued for its perceived economic benefits, but its purpose in the heated battle for the control of work was clear to some.

In 1948, at a Commonwealth Club debate, a San Francisco banker said:

> Labor developments in the last decade may well be the chief contributing factor in speeding regional dispersion of industry. . . . Large aggregations of labor in one [central city] plant are more subject to outside disrupting influences, and have less happy relations with management, than in smaller [suburban] plants. (Mollenkopf 1983)

Postwar economic planning expanded the logic of regionalization to globalization, under U.S. domination. San Francisco's role was to be a corporate headquarters, overseeing a far-flung network of production and distribution. This was well underway soon after World War II, further encouraging the deindustrialization of the city. For example, banking employment in San Francisco during the 1950s more than doubled, while maritime work fell by 25 percent. (Mollenkopf 1983) Blue-collar, unionized work was under calculated assault as the logical companion of much larger dynamics in the marketplace.

Racial tensions were exacerbated by thousands of newly laid-off black shipyard workers, many of whom had come to the Fillmore and Hunters Point (as well as Oakland and Richmond in the East Bay and Marin City in Marin County) during the war, and now competed with white workers for unionized industrial jobs.

After the strike wave of 1946 (the largest in U.S. history until then, with over two million workers taking part) President Truman and the Democrats in Congress joined with the Republican majority to attack the workers' movement. The 1947 Taft-Hartley Act constricted the legal space in which unions had flourished, outlawing effective tactics used by workers to gain power in negotiations and on the job, including secondary picketing, which can spread strikes across the boundaries of occupation and industry. Taft-Hartley also mandated that union leaders sign declarations that they were not communists. Cold War hysteria swept the union movement, driving the most radical and militant workers underground if not out of work.

The "1934 men" along San Francisco's waterfront were subjected to unrelenting red baiting, most visibly in the multiple prosecutions and attempted deportations of ILWU president Harry Bridges, because of his always-denied and oft-alleged communism. (Party membership notwithstanding, he was a close follower of the political line of the Communist Party of the USA, which was in turn a close follower of Stalin's Soviet Union.) The coercive mistrust and paranoia produced by the anti-Communist crusade of the 1950s eroded much working class spontaneity. The powerful nationalism of World War II and then Cold War America was mobilized against suspected radicals and assorted malcontents and deviants. In the case of San Francisco's waterfront, a quasi-militarization that had started during World War II was reinforced and stepped up by an August 1950 Congressional mandate to use the Coast Guard to screen out "security risks" on the docks and ships. Men who appealed their abrupt firing were shown no evidence incriminating them. The Coast Guard would simply insist, "you tell us why you think you've been classified a security risk." (Larrowe 1972)

Automating Intimidation

> *Containerization is the technological underpinning of the global economy. You can bet your sweet ass that if all them transmissions was being hand-handled and put on a pallet board and sent ashore, rather than 20 tons of transmissions in a goddamned container box, transmissions'd still be built in Detroit. The container has been the physical means of exploiting cheap labor throughout the world.*

—Herb Mills, former ILWU Local 10 official (Mills 1996)

The longshoremen under Harry Bridges stood at the radical edge of unionism in 1934. Waterfront workers maintained a work culture that was powerfully resistant to speedups and increased exploitation for twenty-five years. But after that period, affectionately remembered as "the golden age," Bridges and his colleagues began to accept the "inevitability" of capitalist modernization. By the late 1950s, the emergence of new technologies associated with the conversion to trucking and highways (that is, containers) threatened control over work by the unionized workers.

Longshoring was once a complicated job requiring great coordination and cooperation among agile, quick-thinking crews of strong men. The job changed from day to day, from dock to dock, ship to ship, and cargo to cargo. It took many finely developed skills to quickly load and unload a ship before the widespread adoption of containers. A list of typical cargoes, each packed for shipping in its own way, gives an idea of the variety facing the pre-automated longshoreman, and when you add the hundreds of different ships of all shapes and sizes, the complexity and variety increases proportionally. Typically, cargo consisted of

> differing sized crates and packages of varying weights shipped by small manufacturers. . . . Larger crated shipments of such variously sized and weighted items as machines and machine parts, furniture, glassware, dishes and ceramics, sports equipment, clothing, and relatively exotic or "specialty" food products; still larger and variously packaged shipments of all sorts of food—from 25 pound boxes of Norwegian sardines through 100 pound barrels of Greek olives—were common. So, too, were shipments of wines, beer, liquor, cheeses, teas, coconut and tapioca, tropical fruits, candy, cookies, and specialty desserts, plus a wide variety of canned goods. A host of industrial products—from ingots of copper, through sheet and bar steel, pipe and rails, to steel pellets, corrugated metals, and fencing—were standard. The number of sacked or bagged goods was legend: cement, flour, wheat, barley, coffee, and all sorts of nuts and dried fruit. Then, too, there were the offensive sacked cargoes which were worked at a penalty rate of pay, e.g. animal bones and meat scraps, blood and bone meal, fish meal, coal, lime, phosphates and nitrates, lamp black and soda ash. Baled goods were also common—cotton, rubber, rags, gunnies, jute, pulp and paper. Deck loads of lumber and/or logs, or creosoted pilings, utility poles, or railway ties, of farm and construction equipment and all sorts of commercial vehicles were almost always worked. (Mills 1976)

With the advent of the container, all that variety was buried in an endless stream of twenty-ton boxes.

In 1960, the famous Mechanization and Modernization Agreement between the ILWU and the Pacific Maritime Association accelerated the process of capitalist restructuring that killed San Francisco's commercial port and radically reshaped San Francisco's economy. The ILWU reaffirmed the traditional U.S. trade union bargain: money (raises, pensions, bonuses) in exchange for control over work—its organization, its purpose, its use of technology. The owners got the long-sought power to change the structure of work and, by co-opting the longshoremen, to lay the essential foundation for the globalization of production.

> In one fell swoop, the detailed work rules built up over twenty-five years of work stoppages, "quickie" strikes, hours of negotiations and scores of arbitration decisions were discarded. Gone were the double handling of cargo, the job "witnesses"—men who performed no work but only watched, manning scales, first place of rest, and so on. The employer was free to install any machines or methods he chose. The work, however, must be safe. The work of the individual longshoremen could not be made more "onerous." (Selvin 1967)

Slingload weights increased and became derisively know as "Bridges Loads."

(Weir 1967) The M&M Agreement also contractually reinforced the old categories of worker seniority, officially denoting a three-tier hierarchy: "A" and "B" and "casual."

> The B men are a permanent and regular section of the work force who get the pick of the dirtiest and heaviest jobs that are left over after the A, or union, men have taken their pick. After the B men, casuals hired on a daily basis get their turn at the remainders. The casuals get none of the regular fringe benefits. . . . [The B men] pay a pro-rata share of the hiring hall's operating expenses, but have no vote . . . they sit in a segregated section of the [union] meeting hall's balcony. . . . (Weir 1967)

Stan Weir organized a group of eighty-two B men who were briefly upgraded to A status (fulfilling a long-standing union promise to them) but were abruptly kicked back down to B status the very next day after the personal intervention of union president Harry Bridges. It's a long, tangled, and much-disputed tale, but Weir argues that the real lesson of this saga was to strike fear into the A men, demonstrating that their brothers, sons, and friends were subject to the capricious whims of the union leadership if they wanted a steady union job on the waterfront. (Weir 1997) The solidity of a waterfront job was only as good as one's loyalty to the Bridges regime. (It should be noted that some loyal ILWU stalwarts vehemently deny this version of events and insist that Stan Weir is all wrong.)

> In 1963, in collusion with the employers [Bridges] led the Kafkaesque purge that expelled 82 [B men] from the waterfront jobs they had held for 4 years. (Over 80% of the 82 are Negroes.) They were tried in secret. The charges against them were not revealed. Their number, but not their identities was made known to ILWU members until after they were fired. [The discharged workers had no right] to counsel, to produce witnesses, to know the charges and to formal trial prior to judgment or sentencing. . . . Bridges' witchhunt methods and double standards make the bureaucratic procedures used to expel his union from the CIO . . . bland by comparison. (Weir 1967)

Bridges refused to concede anything to the dissidents, of whom Stan Weir was the most visible and outspoken. Seventeen years in various courts ultimately led to ILWU victory. Meanwhile, the ILWU carried on its "business as usual," while many of the fired B men never recovered, their resulting despair leaving many broken lives and homes in its wake. (Weir, interview with author, 1997)

Spurred on by the Mechanization and Modernization Agreement, worklife on the waterfront was changing rapidly in the early 1960s. The M&M contract was renewed in 1965, the job security clause being dropped since the Vietnam War was keeping everyone on overtime anyway. A new clause was added, however, known as "9.43." It allowed shippers to hire longshoremen directly to be their "steady men" running their expensive and "complex" new cranes.

The longshoremen were divided on the owners' demand for "steady men" to run their cranes. The older workers accepted at face value the owners' assertion that running these big container cranes was a highly skilled activity requiring special training and skills. The younger workers soon figured out that it was "no big deal." In fact, the new longshoring was considerably less skilled than the dangerous and varying work of loading and unloading ships in the pre-container era.

The ILWU severely weakened itself when it acquiesced to dividing the workers between those directly employed by the shippers as "steady men" and those regular longshoremen who continued to get work assignments through the union-controlled hiring hall. The almost sacred institution of the hiring hall, won at such great effort in the 1930s, withered as a consequence of this adaptation to "progress." The longshoremen's self-managed work-allocation system based on the hiring hall was outflanked by automation, which drastically reduced the number of workers needed. The shippers pushed their new edge further by insisting on choosing an elite group to be steadily employed, leaving union stalwarts with sporadic and insecure work assigned by the hiring hall. The economic advantages of becoming a 9.43 man (guaranteed full-time hours and higher pay) were irresistible to many, and divisions soon grew within the union.

After eleven years of automation, longshoremen struck in 1971. Rank-and-file activists were mobilized against allowing "steady men" to work the big cranes (versus those dispatched daily from the union hall), while Bridges and the union leadership focused the demands on who would be allowed to "stuff" containers and a wage increase. President Nixon's use of the Taft-Hartley Act failed to produce a settlement (96% voted to strike at the beginning, and 92% voted

Longshoring evolved over many decades into a fluid, cooperative, mutually dependent labor process.

to continue the strike after the Taft-Hartley injunction), but the strike's resumption after the mandated 60-day cooling off period failed to halt the use of new waterfront technology and its consequent division of labor. The strike lasted 135 days, but the union won only modest wage increases and little else. Left for arbitration was the contentious question of the 9.43 men, and the arbitrator's decision didn't alter the clause or the rights of management to divide the workforce.

There hasn't been another big strike on the West Coast since 1971. Former Local 10 secretary-treasurer Herb Mills thinks the 1971 strike was undercut from within by Bridges and the International leadership at the time. (Mills 1996) He says the damage done by 9.43 and the failure of the '71 strike has divided and weakened the workers a great deal. In fact, during the 1996 coast-wide contract negotiations, the rank-and-file of the two largest locals (Local 10 in San Francisco and Local 13 in San Pedro/Long Beach) rejected a contract proposal because it called for mild restrictions on steady men's ability to collect tens of thousands of dollars in "side deals" with the shippers. The same contract was passed on the second try after a full-court-press campaign by the union's top leaders. In any case, the labor relations deal that prevails on the Pacific Coast has allowed container tonnage to quadruple since 1980, while the number of work hours has remained constant for a workforce that has been reduced over 20 percent.

Pier 80. San Francisco built modern facilities like this one, but couldn't compete with Oakland's better transportation connections.

(Pacific Maritime Association 1995) Today's longshoreman is a well-paid worker who can easily afford an upper-middle-class lifestyle, but there are only about 9,000 longshoremen on the entire West Coast. The hiring hall is no longer the unifying institution it once was, and even if you could interest longshoremen in the social/political reasons for maintaining it, cell phones and modern telecommunications have made a central dispatch hiring hall obsolete. The special culture that longshoremen created at such sacrifice and with such imaginative brilliance has been broken. The power that once so intimidated San Francisco's rulers and planners has been bought off and made manageable by the apparatus of unionized collective bargaining, modernization and, as we shall see, co-optation.

The Home Front

Redesigning work to disconnect workers from their power was only part of the picture. After World War II, San Francisco's leaders faced an urban landscape full of both physical and social obstacles. Whole neighborhoods had to go—community stability had become an obstacle to rapid economic growth. The story behind several decades of "urban redevelopment" in San Francisco reveals a second front in our local class war. "Progress" was as readily invoked to justify evicting thousands while bulldozing whole neighborhoods as it had been to dismantle decades of workers' power on the job.

It is not accidental that the San Francisco neighborhoods most skilled in organizing, with the most active memory of how improvements were actually achieved, were the same neighborhoods that experienced the wrecking ball of redevelopment. Redevelopment targeted neighborhoods where relatively coherent subcultures within the working class flourished. (I speak of the predominantly African American Western Addition, the Italian produce district, and the South of Market single-room-occupancy hotels that housed thousands of retired workers who had participated in the great upsurge of the 1930s.)

The wrecking ball first cleared the old Italian Produce Market to make way for the Golden Gateway apartments and the eastward thrust of the financial district to the bay in the early 1960s. This project also led to the demolition of the old Alaska Fishermen's Union building between Commercial, Clay, the Embarcadero, and Drumm. With its demise the waterfront workers lost a vital social center that had served them for decades (the ground floor had housed the longshoremen's hiring hall, and several other maritime unions had offices there). Then the Geary Boulevard corridor, known in Redevelopment-ese as Western Addition A-1, cleared a two-block corridor westward from Cathedral Hill through the heavily populated Fillmore District. By mid-1967 the Western Addition A-2 plan had been made public and was well underway, removing over a thousand old Victorians in the Fillmore District and displacing over 10,000 African Americans in the process. Further redevelopment plans targeted the South of Market, Chinatown, and Mission Districts.

By the late 1960s, citizens groups were mobilizing in every neighborhood against redevelopment. The 1968–1969 Student/Faculty Strike at San Francisco State galvanized a whole generation of young activists, many of whom threw themselves into the blossoming neighborhood redevelopment and housing struggles around the I-Hotel, Chinatown, the Mission, South of Market, and the Western Addition. In the Western Addition, community opposition came together in the Western Addition Community Organization (WACO), while in the South of Market TOOR (Tenants and Owners in Opposition to Redevelopment) arose. (Hartman 1984) Thousands supported the ten-year struggle to save the I-Hotel, the last remnant of a once lively stretch known as Manilatown.

Justin Herman, head of the Redevelopment Agency, took a swing with "old reliable," the progress club, when he angrily denounced WACO as a "passing flurry of proletarianism," which was trying to "turn back the clock." (Mollenkopf 1983) But the mobilized, politicized community organizations, in some cases fused with the Black and Brown Power movements of the 1960s, could not be stopped by bureaucratic scorn alone. The "redevelopers" had to gain legitimacy to proceed with their plans. They used trusted labor leaders to create the appearance of a balanced, objective consensus for progress and redevelopment.

Co-optation

Largely supporting the pro-growth consensus of the early 1960s, union leaders were seen by ruling elites as reasonable men. Joe Alioto (head of the Redevelopment Agency himself in the mid-1950s) consolidated the integration of the big unions in town when he won the mayoral election in 1967 by building an old-style political coalition of big business and big labor with overt patronage. After winning the election with strong union support (major campaign supporters were Laborers Local 261, which was 65 percent black and 25 percent Latino, and ILWU Local 10, which was 70 percent black), Mayor Alioto appointed Harry Bridges to the Port Commission. He appointed Stanley Jensen of the Machinists Union and Joe Mosely, an African American dispatcher in the ILWU, to the Redevelopment Agency, Hector Rueda of the Elevator Construction Workers Union to the Planning Commission, and Bill Chester, another black ILWU official, was made president of BART.

Former ILWU clerk Wilbur Hamilton, an African American pastor with strong roots in San Francisco, was appointed to the Redevelopment Agency in 1968 and soon got the job of project manager for the Western Addition A-2 project, the Agency's largest project. Hamilton gave a black, pro-labor face to the essentially white racist "slum clearance" plan devised in the boardrooms of downtown San Francisco.

The unions already had a symbolically important role in the Democratic Party and the pro-development consensus. Jack Shelley had headed the San Francisco Labor Council in the 1950s before he went to Congress, and had become mayor in 1963. During his tenure he led the fight for the Panhandle–Golden Gate Park Freeway. His administration attempted to straddle the widening gap between the old blue-collar city and its ascendant incarnation as a corporate headquarters.

As social movements evolved through the upheavals of the 1960s and against the background of the permanent (cold) war, organized labor became an aggressive agent of the capitalist order. Unions supported anything that seemed to "create jobs," leading the charge for San Francisco's absurd and finally truncated freeway plan, as well as uncritically supporting Manhattanization and "redevelopment" of the residential neighborhoods in which workers lived.

In the South of Market, this pitted the once-vibrant and class-conscious unions against many of their own retirees during the fight over the Yerba Buena Center. Peter Mendelsohn, of TOOR, describes how the unions went after people fighting the Yerba Buena Center:

> They lined up all the unions against us. They went and got all the leaders. George Woolf sent a letter to Harry Bridges, asking Bridges to hear our side. We told him, "you've heard Redevelopment's side, now we'd like you to come down and hear our side." . . . It was guys like George Woolf and me who went out and raised money when they accused him of being a communist and tried to deport him. We were two of the main guys to defend him. . . .
>
> Harry Bridges' answer to our letter was "I heard Redevelopment's side, and Redevelopment's side is good enough for me. I don't want to hear your side." If the unions supported us, this could never have happened. But the unions are bought off. (*Redevelopment* 1974)

In fact, the ILWU got a choice redevelopment property on Franklin Street atop Cathedral Hill, where the Harry Bridges Memorial Building now stands, home to the union, its library, and its pension fund. Individual longshoremen got homes in co-op apartments built by the Redevelopment Agency in the Western Addition, and the Port Commission made available a South Beach lot for the ILWU's Clerks Local 34. This is not to insinuate that any corruption was necessarily involved. Rather, this kind of deal-making is the quintessence of modern capitalism's ability to propel itself, absorbing and redirecting oppositional movements.

Port of San Francisco. Once-bustling piers lie dormant in the shadow of San Francisco's
new economy, the corporate headquarters of the Manhattanized financial district.

Such co-optation contributed a great deal to the decline of trade unionism
as a political and economic force. At best, it represents an ironic complicity in
breaking transmission belts of working class culture and memory; at worst, it is a
classic case of selling out the class for narrow material benefits. Union leaders who
accept appointments to facilitate the corporate agenda offer us a disheartening
example of ignorance, naïveté, corruption, or all three.

Capitalist modernization and social control cannot be blithely attributed to
compliant union leaders, manipulative corporate planners, or complacent and
forgetful workers. Our epoch is one in which historical amnesia is the rule, not the
exception. Compelling visions of a different way of life (not organized to serve the
market) are invisible or absent. When workers show more solidarity and become
better organized, capital either mechanizes and restructures, or moves (or both).
Future workplace revolts will have to plan for this. The stunted, warped life we
live as "economic factors" rather than as full human beings has been utterly nor-
malized and removed from history or social choice. We chase the buck and pay
our bills because . . . well, what else is there?

Trumpeting San Francisco's special novelty glosses over the essential same-
ness of life in San Francisco and elsewhere. The world's most powerful capitalists
cut their teeth and sharpened their strategies and techniques in San Francisco.
Our daily life is the living proof that they have succeeded. These days "sudden
revolt" sounds like a perfume or a rock band, not an implicit possibility within our
collective revulsion at what passes for life.

Nevertheless, San Francisco continues to produce the seeds of revolt. The

The Progress Club   85

famous liberalism and tolerance for dissent helps make room for new initiatives that would be more difficult to embark on elsewhere. The half-century process of disrupting and disorganizing working-class communities at work and at home cannot prevent the inevitable re-emergence of real opposition. A new opposition, especially one that grasps the powerful levers available at work, remains to be defined. Among the fragments of our daily lives we must discover a language that reinforces our shared experiences and discoveries rather than emphasizing their identity-based differences. An inspired revolt based on a certainty that life can be much better than this is buried beneath the surface of our atomized existence. Can a new vision of progress help bring it up? Or will the progress club continue to bludgeon our aspirations for liberation? During the coming period the next chapters in San Francisco's epic class struggle will be written, hopefully in a radically new way.

References

Brecher, Jeremy. 1972. *Strike!* Boston: South End Press.

California, State of, 1940. *Handbook of California Labor Statistics*, Table 37: "Workers Involved and Man-Days Idle in Strikes, by Industry Group, California, 1927–1939" and Table 36: "Workers Involved and Man-Days Idle in Strikes, California, Los Angeles City and San Francisco Bay Area, 1927–1940"

California, State of, 1955, *Handbook of California Labor Statistics 1953–1954*, Table 54: "Number of Work Stoppages, Workers Involved, and Man-Days Idle, Major California Cities, 1941-1951"

Cobble, Dorothy. 1991. *Dishing It Out: Waitresses and Their Unions in the Twentieth Century.* Urbana & Chicago: University of Illinois Press.

Hartman, Chester. 1984. *The Transformation of San Francisco.* Totowa, NJ: Rowman & Allanheld.

International Longshoremen's and Warehousemen's Union, Information Dept. 1963. *The ILWU Story.* San Francisco.

Kazin, Michael. 1987. *Barons of Labor: The San Francisco Building Trades and Union Power in the Progressive Era.* Urbana & Chicago: University of Illinois Press.

Larrowe, Charles P. 1972. *Harry Bridges: The Rise and Fall of Radical Labor in the United States.* New York: Lawrence Hill.

Lens, Sidney. 1974. *The Labor War* New York: Anchor/Doubleday.

Mills, Herb. 1976. *The San Francisco Waterfront: The Social Consequences of Industrial Modernization, Part One: "The Good Old Days."* Beverly Hills & London: Sage Publications.

———. 1977. *The San Francisco Waterfront: The Social Consequences of Industrial Modernization, Part Two: "The Modern Longshore Operations."* Beverly Hills & London: Sage Publications.

Mollenkopf, John H. 1983. *The Contested City*, New Jersey: Princeton University Press.

Nelson, Bruce. 1990. *Workers on the Waterfront: Seamen, Longshoremen, and Unionism in the 1930s*. Urbana & Chicago: University of Illinois Press.

Pacific Maritime Association. 1995. *Annual Report*. San Francisco.

Quin, Mike. 1948. *The Big Strike*. Olema, CA: Olema Books

Redevelopment: A Marxist Analysis. 1974. San Francisco: Resolution Film Center.

Schwartz, Harvey. 1995a. "The March Inland" (ILWU Oral History Project Pt. IX), *The Dispatcher*, July 20.

———. 1995b. "Rank and File Unionism in Action" (ILWU Oral History Project Pt. XII), *The Dispatcher*, November 20.

Selvin, David. 1967. *Sky Full of Storm*. Berkeley, CA: University of California Press.

———. 1996. *A Terrible Anger*. Detroit, MI: Wayne State University Press.

Weir, Stan. 1996. "Unions with Leaders Who Stay on the Job." In *"We Are All Leaders": The Alternative Unionism of the Early 1930s*. Edited by Staughton Lynd. Urbana & Chicago: University of Illinois Press.

———. 1967. "USA—The Labor Revolt." *International Socialist Journal*. April & June 1967.

Yellen, Samuel. 1936. *American Labor Struggles*. Reprint: New York: Monad Press, 1974.

Zerzan, John. 1977. "Unionization in America." In *Creation and Its Enemies: The Revolt Against Work*. Rochester, NY: Mutualist Book.

The Silver Legacy
San Francisco and the Comstock Lode

by Jon Christensen

Landscapes can be deceptive. Sometimes a landscape seems to be less a setting for the life of its inhabitants than a curtain behind which their struggles, achievements and accidents take place.
— John Berger

THE CASUAL SAN FRANCISCO GAMBLER might be excused for taking the Silver Legacy at face value. The portal of the hotel and casino in Reno, an easy four-hour drive from the Bay Area on Interstate 80, is inscribed "Established 1895." The facade of the casino is familiar from the sets of TV Westerns. Imagine the TV Western "Bonanza" with a Victorian mining boom-town theme instead of cowboys. A row of stylized storefronts in a Victorian boomtown runs for a block along Virginia Street, Reno's gambling row.

The Silver Legacy was actually built in 1995. Theme casinos have taken over Las Vegas, but the Silver Legacy is the first of its kind in Reno. The conceit of the Silver Legacy is that a miner named Sam Fairchild built the casino right on top of a great silver mine. Inside the casino a huge stylized mining headframe—a pyramidal scaffold of beams—rises under a great dome upon which the heavens are painted. The colors of the sky shift from day to night and around again every two hours. As the sky darkens, the sounds of whippoorwill and crickets give way to thunder and rain, while the clink, clink, clink of coins in the silver pans of slot machines provides a constant reminder of what this fantasy world is based upon.

If a legacy is what has come down to us from the past and history is what we think about it, I had come to the Silver Legacy knowing that the history of the silver legacy, whatever it may be, was not likely to be found here. But I thought that maybe through the bald-faced lie of a casino I could begin to measure the distance between the history of this place and its relationship to San Francisco and the legacy that has come down to us. For a silver legacy does truly link northern

Nevada—Reno, Carson City, Virginia City, and Lake Tahoe—to San Francisco. People, capital, transportation, construction, labor, and recreation have flowed back and forth for almost 150 years. San Francisco shaped northern Nevada, both as a result of extracting its capital of silver and gold, and as a result of the periphery then shaping itself to exploit the center's capital through gambling and tourism after the extractive economy of mining went bust.

During a road trip from Reno to San Francisco, I set out to explore the evidence of this legacy on the land I love and to find the historical remnants of our connections. In Virginia City, thirty miles south of the Silver Legacy in Reno, the real Comstock silver mines are said to have made San Francisco into the City in the 1860s and 1870s. "The Comstock," wrote Grant H. Smith,

> lifted California out of a disheartening depression. It rejuvenated San Francisco, which in 1860 was but a ragged little town of fifty-two thousand people. In 1861 more substantial brick buildings were erected there than in all of the preceding years, nor did that growth ever cease. The opportunity for investments in the early years was limited, and nearly all of the profits from the Comstock were invested in San Francisco real estate and the erection of fine buildings.

For some, the City was a kind of shrine to the spirit of the hinterlands. "In beautifying San Francisco, sterile Washoe had come into her own," wrote George D. Lyman, in *Ralston's Ring: California Plunders the Comstock Lode.* But lest this begin to sound suspiciously like the usual lament of a colony that has gone through the expected progression from extraction to dependency, let me acknowledge at the start that this periphery has always been good at luring resources from San Francisco. Mining and gambling have always played to each other's hands in the relationship between northern Nevada and San Francisco.

While the Gold Rush expressed itself largely as freelance unaccountable anarchy that changed much of the world economy but built little within this region, the silver boom was all about organizing the regional economy. In this, the Silver Legacy stands as a fitting monument to the concentration of capital in a speculative economy that has straddled the Sierra Nevada for more than a century.

Inside the Silver Legacy casino I picked up a brochure that purported to reveal the "secrets of the Silver Baron's rig." I sat by a slot machine on a balcony overlooking the headframe that looms over the activity on the casino floor. "In the 1850s, a young prospector named Sam Fairchild journeyed west in search of a dream," the brochure said. "He found silver, the largest strike ever. But earth does not give up her treasures freely. Silver mining was a difficult and dangerous profession. So Sam enlisted a team of top engineers to design a revolutionary machine to simplify the mining process. The rig you see before you is an exact replica of that machine. Twelve stories high, it stands directly over the site of Sam's original claim."

The brochure goes on to explain how the over-stylized machinery of the mine works:

> Inside the mining shed, workers load all the raw material into large ore carts. When the ore carts reach the crusher, twenty 300 pound blades crush the massive rock. Then the conveyor belt brings the powdered ore up to the smelter burning continuously at temperatures of up to 1,000 degrees. The liquid silver is poured into silver bars and cooled at the top of the rig. The bars are then sent down the conveyor belt to the coin pavilion and minted into special "Sam" gaming coins. The coins are then dropped from a large funnel into the carousel windows, where they await the lucky winners.

It's such a great story it begs to be true. Gambling was indeed built on top of mining in Nevada, as this legacy was built on history. This spectacle at the casino hides history in plain view by creating a reassuringly familiar environment for gamblers to fritter away their money in hopes of a payoff. Slot machines ring the bottom of the Silver Baron's rig. Down in the pit, there is a tumult of people of all walks of life, nationalities, and colors pulling on the slot machines. They're dressed casually: gray-haired old ladies in polyester, bikers in leather, skiers in lycra, slackers in flannel, gang-bangers in baggy pants. Most of the gamblers in Reno are from northern California, and a great many are from San Francisco. There is a quiet frenzy as they pull the one-armed bandits and watch the wheels of fortune spin.

Of course, the customers are feeding the casino and not the other way around, but this is how it has always been in mining and gambling. Except for the casual style of dress that predominates today, even among high rollers who drop $100 tokens into slot machines while wearing sweats and sneakers, the scene on the casino floor reminds me of descriptions of the San Francisco Stock Exchange in the 1860s when the City was enthralled with the Comstock silver bonanza.

"The ladies were hurrying to the 11 o'clock session of the San Francisco Stock Exchange Board to gamble on Comstock stocks," wrote Lyman in 1937:

> Beautiful ladies with well-turned ankles; tightly laced ladies in rustling black silk; mysterious women in flowing black veils; perfumed women with sparkling eyes, flashing teeth and diamond-studded ears. The prodigious wealth of the Lode and the excitement attending the selling of these mining stocks had weaned them from homes, schoolrooms and the city's bright lights. Their silks and satins, diamonds and furs all recorded recently lucky encounters with the market. In all their fine black plumage they flitted about the Exchange, picking up "tips" on stocks and ready at a moment's notice to pounce upon some favorite with all the resources at their command. For Comstocks had been booming.

Some of the beautiful young employees of the casino are paid to stand around in such finery to help customers find their way to the oyster bar or the brewery or the craps pit. But in the casino the only hint of the real history of the silver legacy is a display in the hotel lobby of a Tiffany silver set on loan from the University of Nevada, Reno's Mackay School of Mines. John Mackay, one of the real Silver Kings, sent one of the first batches of silver from the big bonanza on the Comstock Lode east to Tiffany's to have a silver serving set made for his wife. (Lewis 1947) Aside from this relatively modest display, the true legacy of the bonanza is hidden from the view of tourists, who are enticed to participate in this fantasy and recycle their money endlessly while capital relentlessly accumulates to the house, as usual.

About thirty miles south of Reno and across a desert mountain range studded with stunted pinyon trees and dusted with snow, lies Virginia City. For a few years in the early 1860s, when the Comstock Lode was in its heady early bonanza days, Virginia City seemed like the center and San Francisco more of a waystation on the periphery. There was a lively exchange between Virginia City and San Francisco when the Comstock was booming and the whole country seemed to be booming with it. Speculators would come up from San Francisco to "see the elephant." The wagons would also bring oysters and champagne and traveling theater groups to the mountain.

"Everything in Virginia City from timber to banking, except the Washoe zephyr and the arsenic water, had been hauled over the ridge from California; and when a man made a strike on the Comstock his first thought was a palace on one of San Francisco's hills," wrote Franklin Walker:

> Features of San Francisco life in the fall of 1863 were Washoe silver stocks, Washoe widows, and Washoe journalists. Nearly everyone was speculating in "feet" on the Comstock lode, nearly as many were keeping Washoe widows from being too lonesome for their men across the mountain, and all who read newspapers had heard of the Virginia City *Territorial Enterprise*'s new humorist Mark Twain.

Virginia City is now a tourist trap that clings tenaciously to the skeleton of the Comstock. The bleached bones of the mining works and rock dumps lie scattered around. The buildings are leaning toward oblivion. Here it seems like the true history of the silver legacy might be comprehensible if one could push through the distracting gauze of T-shirts and candy shops, the old drunks, and the tinny clinking of slot machines. But just barely.

The story of the Comstock is a story of a boomtown that went bust in the late 1870s and ever since then has been looking for a way to promote its history.

At first it lived off its own myth. Stock manipulations and hype kept the mines going on paper even if they never produced much more from the ground. By the late 1870s the Comstock never again held San Francisco in its thrall. The Comstock didn't find a good draw until the postwar tourism boom and "Bonanza," which featured a studio lot version of Virginia City. This was Virginia City as a cow town, which it never was, but it became a way for the town to link itself with a popular image once again.

Virginia City still underestimates the value of real history. It has the real thing but does its best to cover it up. And if a good fantasy will do better at attracting tourist dollars, well then, by all means. The Ponderosa bar offers an "authentic mine tour." I went in for a drink and a look around. The bartender said the mine wasn't open during the winter. Just as well. Later I learned the tunnel in the Ponderosa was dug in the 1970s as a tourist draw. I still wanted to see a real mine, so I went down the hill to the Chollar mine, also closed for the off season, and prevailed upon the owner to open up the mine. Chris Keichler took me 600 feet back into the original heavily timbered six-foot-square tunnel to where miners had once hoisted silver ore from a beehive of tunnels below. Keichler has meticulously preserved and restored this small part of the mine. It is a good place to see the real structure of the mines and to get a view of the technological transformation of the Comstock that was made possible by the infusion of capital from San Francisco. My guide was familiar with all of this history. He not only provided a place where history could be seen, he also gave opinionated recommendations of several books to fill out my understanding. (His favorite authors are Grant Smith, Dan De Quille, Frank Crampton, Eliot Lord, and John Taylor Waldorf.)

Keichler was more comfortable with the actual workings of the mine than with speculating about the speculation that made the mines, Virginia City, and San Francisco. No one knows for sure how much of San Francisco's capital was sunk into speculative stock scams on the Comstock, but it may have been almost as much as the Comstock contributed to the building of San Francisco.

"Not less than four-fifths of the assessments collected by the mines throughout their history was contributed by stockholders in California and elsewhere," wrote Grant Smith:

> To the people on the Comstock, where money was expended, an "assessment mine" was almost as helpful as one that paid dividends; but they were the victims as well as the beneficiaries of the widespread mania, for they became inveterate stock gamblers. Nearly everybody gambled in mining stocks in those days—and knew that they were gambling. The aim of all was to "beat the game." The men who won, whether dealers or players, were admired and envied. It was a mark of distinction to be called a "big manipulator."

Across the street from the Ponderosa bar, in the *Territorial Enterprise* building, there is a hodgepodge of artifacts and T-shirts, none of which conveys much of the true history of the newspaper. Virginia City claims Mark Twain because that's where Samuel Clemens first called himself by his pseudonym. He spent a couple years there working for the *Territorial Enterprise*, which at the time had the largest circulation of any newspaper in the West. But Twain moved quickly—he went on to national prominence in San Francisco and parts beyond. "There was a popular saying that Washoe people hoped to go to San Francisco rather than heaven when they died," wrote Franklin Walker.

What Twain took from Virginia City was a jaded outlook that would serve him well in America. He never looked back to Washoe, which is what the desert country of western Nevada was known as in those days, so christened by immigrants who took the name from the Indian tribe that spent the summers around Lake Tahoe and wintered in the valleys east of there, where the wagon trains rested before crossing the mountains to California. (DeVoto 1932)

I too felt like going "down below" to San Francisco, as we all must from time to time, to seek a larger view. But first I would stop at Lake Tahoe, which Twain once described as "surely the fairest picture the whole earth affords." (Twain 1917)

Lake Tahoe lies at the crossroads between the Comstock and San Francisco. Thanks to a geologic miracle and a political accident, Lake Tahoe is the pivot point between California and Nevada. The mountains peak near 10,000 feet, rimming the emerald bowl of what was once some of the clearest water in North America. "The brightest gem in the mountain coronet of those twin queens, the Golden and the Silver States," as an over-the-top travel writer described it in the 1860s, Lake Tahoe has always been a wayfarer's refuge and a center of industry between San Francisco and northern Nevada. (Landauer 1996) In the 1860s, the main trail across the Sierra Nevada went by the south shore of Lake Tahoe, where today giant casinos crowd the state line on the Nevada side, and rows of motels, minimalls and second homes stretch around the lake on the California side.

When you travel Highway 50 to Lake Tahoe today, it appears in its large expanse as such a natural respite from artifice that one is hard pressed to see that the scene has been steadily shaped and reshaped as a center for recreation, an escape from civilized San Francisco on the one side and the boomtowns of Nevada on the other. The tourism industry of Lake Tahoe has been constructed in one of the most beautiful natural settings in the world, but there is trouble lurking in the history of this paradise—trouble rooted in its links to San Francisco and the Comstock.

Spooner Ridge (c. 1876). "The Comstock lode . . . the tomb of the forests of the Sierras"

The forests around Tahoe were clear cut in the 1860s and 1870s for the silver mines. "The Comstock lode may truthfully be said to be the tomb of the forests of the Sierras," wrote Dan De Quille, a contemporary of Twain's:

> Not less than eighty million feet of timber and lumber are annually consumed on the Comstock lode. In a single mine—the Consolidated Virginia—timber is being buried at the rate of six million feet per annum, and in all other mines in like proportion. At the same time about 250,000 cords of wood are consumed. The pine forest of the Sierra Nevada Mountains are drawn upon for everything in the shape of wood or lumber and have been thus drawn upon for many years. For a distance of fifty or sixty miles all the hills of the eastern slope of the Sierras have been to a great extent denuded of trees of every kind—those suitable only for wood as well as those fit for the manufacture of lumber of use in the mines. Already the lumbermen are not only extending their operations to a greater distance north and south along the great mountain range, but are also beginning to reach over to the western slope—over to the California side of the range.

Lake Tahoe has been an illusion straining to maintain itself for more than a century. In the early days the natural setting seemed grand enough to hide any flaws. Industry existed side by side with luxurious resorts for high rollers from the Comstock and San Francisco. The timber industry was part of the landscape of early tourism: as steamers plied the lake with rafts of logs headed for the eastern shore and Virginia City, they also carried sightseers on excursions. The San Francisco Water Company built a dam at the outlet of Lake Tahoe, hoping to find a way to bring more water to the City. It raised the lake level ten feet, but the water never made it west.

Though the denuded forests prevented Lake Tahoe from becoming a national-al park, and though the second-growth forest is crowded, dead, and dying—a tin-derbox waiting to explode—the ravages of tourism have been worse for the lake. (*Tahoe Tribune*, February 1996) First came the strip motels of the postwar tourism boom, when the automobile and vacationing middle-class families began to domi-nate the Western landscape. Then came the casino boom of the 1960s, which has-n't stopped yet. Tourism dominates the lake today.

A huge redevelopment project is demolishing a mile-long stretch of tacky 1950s motels and replacing them with a large-scale "rustic" development that parodies the myth of the West and Lake Tahoe. This is an era of consolidation in the tourism and gambling industries, similar to the consolidation during the last gasp of mining on the Comstock. The myth of the West is subject to further revi-sion for this era's concentrated capital investments.

The industry wants to make Lake Tahoe attractive to the same kinds of peo-ple it exploited in the early days when only the rich could afford to camp out on a long sojourn from the city or the silver mines. But the area is overcrowded and overloaded with sediment from building second homes and roads, and now envi-

Lake Tahoe (c. 1912)

ronmental restoration is necessary to appeal to the rustic sentiments of professionals on vacation.

So the casino tycoons have struck a deal to make peace with environmentalists. Some redevelopment money will go to restore wetlands that will catch sediment. The wetlands will open up more natural-*looking* space along the shore of the lake. Still, it will take hundreds of years to turn around the water quality of the lake and to restore the forests and wetlands. Central to the makeover is the tourism industry's discouragement of lower-class tourism, which is bad for Lake Tahoe's image and doesn't bring in much revenue.

The efforts to redevelop in an upscale way mask the fact that Lake Tahoe, while it is the wealthiest region of the Sierra Nevada (and one of the wealthiest in California and Nevada), has the greatest gap between rich and poor. On a drive around the lake, one sees gated communities containing the mansions of the scions of San Francisco and of Nevada casino moguls, while dilapidated apartments are the homes of Mexican families who live and sleep in shifts when they're not working in the casinos. Tahoe still hides what makes it possible.

I went on to San Francisco to search out the silver legacy at the center, knowing that there is little left. San Francisco has also been adept at turning itself inside out for speculation and redevelopment. "By 1864, the Comstock comet was blazing full blast across the Western horizon," wrote Lyman:

> Unmindful of her maritime past, San Francisco had become a mining city and had plunged wholeheartedly into a gambling mania, the like of which had never before been known on the coast. With millions of dollars in bullion in sight on Sun Mountain, Californians had thoughts for nothing but the stock market. As millions of dollars of San Francisco money were invested in Washoe hoisting machinery and reduction works, corporate organizations had been formed in San Francisco to which the mining claims were sold or exchanged for shares of stocks.

"The Comstock mines early became a synonym for stock devilment, for which the brokers and manipulators in San Francisco have been held solely responsible," wrote Smith. "True, theirs is the chief responsibility, but the gambling public must bear its share of the blame. The system early developed from a speculative investment in mining stocks into a gamble—then into a lottery."

"In flush times the leaders of stock operations were known by their purple and fine linen, their splendid equipages, and their lavish expenditures, generally in San Francisco, but sometimes in a trail of coruscating glory across the continent," wrote historian Charles Shinn.

"There were three active stock exchanges in San Francisco during the flush '70s, each with a large membership," wrote Smith:

Able and daring men gravitated to them by instinct. They were the liveliest places on the Coast and the focus of public attention. When "Jot" Travis, a well-known westerner, was being shown about the waterfront of San Francisco in the late '70s and one fine yacht after another was pointed out as belonging to a wealthy stockbroker, he finally inquired, with an air of childlike innocence, "W-where are the c-customers' yachts?"

Certificates of stock became tickets, and the holders won or lost on the turn of the wheel, wrote historian Eliot Lord. "A few prominent capitalists purchase the control of mines for the sake of dividends, and the profits of milling ore, but the great body of holders bought their shares to sell at an advanced price."

"A well-managed 'stock deal' was as acceptable to most holders as an actual development of ore," Smith concluded, in what is probably the most accurate accounting of the true history of the silver legacy:

> Control was often bought and utilized for the purposes of "rigging the market" and for the salaries, luxurious offices in San Francisco, and other perquisites that opportunity afforded. It should be said, however, that if San Franciscans milked the Comstock, they also fed it.

Calculating a final balance sheet for the Comstock, Smith estimated that from 1859–1882, the mines produced $320 million in silver and gold. Dividends totaling around $125 million were paid out to stockholders and around $74 million was invested in the form of assessments on stockholders for developing the mines. Smith estimated that private profits were not less than $20 million.

Yet today little remains. The mansions of the Silver Kings, the mining offices, the stock exchanges, and the newspapers that chronicled those days are either gone or remain as mere shells of their former selves, like the the Bank of California. Redevelopment is transforming San Francisco from the inside out while some of the historical shells are preserved. Some fading signs on the sides of buildings give a romantic air to the City that was, while the remnants of an old economy are transformed to serve the new.

It's hard to find stable reference points in a landscape that is constantly being remade. The center and the periphery are two parts of a self-reflecting fantasy. We want a comfortable history in which to sell the past. In northern Nevada, we fret about "Californication," in a titillating way. *The Reno News & Review*, the local weekly alternative paper, recently worried, "Are Californians Ruining Reno?" The paper is owned by a chain based in California. We don't have to leave Reno to feel connected to San Francisco. Going back home to Reno from the City, coming out of the mountains into town, I see a series of billboards advertising the restaurants in Harrah's casino: "It's like Fisherman's Wharf. It's like Chinatown. It's like Little Italy."

The shared history of San Francisco and Northern Nevada has become a legacy of speculation. Extractive industries have evolved to mine the imagination. In the process, they bury historical understanding in layers of fantasy, like the Silver Legacy. What begins in the glory of grand speculation ends in the endless grind of recycled images. Everywhere the real ties are obscured and mystified by a promotional and speculative economy that creates a legacy out of our history and throws it in our faces as if to say, "All that matters is what sells."

References

Berger, John. 1967. *A Fortunate Man: The Story of a Country Doctor*. New York: Pantheon Books.

Crampton, Frank A. 1956. *Deep Enough: A Working Stiff in the Western Mines*. Denver: Sage. Norman: University of Oklahoma Press.

De Quille, Dan (William Wright). 1876. *The Big Bonanza: An Authentic Account of the Discovery, History, and Working of the World-Renowned Comstock Lode of Nevada*. Hartford, Conn.: Nevada Publications. Reprint: New York: Alfred A. Knopf, 1947.

De Voto, Bernard. 1932. *Mark Twain's America*. Moscow, Idaho: University of Idaho Press.

Landauer, Lyndall Baker. 1996. *The Mountain Sea: A History of Lake Tahoe*. Honolulu, Hawaii: Flying Cloud Press.

Lewis, Oscar. 1947. *Silver Kings*. New York: Alfred A. Knopf.

Lord, Elliot. 1883. *Comstock Mining and Miners*. Reprint: Berkeley, CA: Howell-North, 1959.

Lyman, George D. 1937. *Ralston's Ring: California Plunders the Comstock Lode*. New York: Charles Scribner's Sons.

Shinn, Charles Howard. 1896. *Story of the Mine*. Reprint: Reno: University of Nevada Press, 1979.

Smith, Grant. 1943. *History of the Comstock Lode*. Reno, Nev.: Nevada Bureau of Mines, University of Nevada.

Twain, Mark. 1972. *Roughing It*. Berkeley, California: University of California Press.

Waldorf, John Taylor. 1970. *A Kid on the Comstock*. Palo Alto, California: American West Publishing.

Walker, Franklin. 1938. *The Washoe Giant in San Francisco*. San Francisco: George Fields.

Pecuniary Emulation
The Role of Tycoons in Imperial City-Building

by Gray Brechin

I DISCOVERED SAN FRANCISCO HISTORY in the Palace Hotel. For a kid up from the suburbs on the weekend, the Palace stood for the ultimate in worldly glamour, of metropolitan luxury, and of mythic individuals filtered through the writings of Lucius Beebe and Oscar Lewis.

Legitimated crime did not figure in that gauze of romance until years later when I had the chance to visit another deluxe hotel restaurant, in Scottsdale. The builder of that hotel and Arizona's most admired tycoon once sat in the very chair I occupied while making his legendary deals. A federal court had recently con-victed Charles H. Keating Jr. of seventy-three counts of racketeering, conspiracy, and fraud, and a state court was beginning its own investigation of alleged felonies. My mind drifted away then from peach-colored napery, *faux*-Fragonards, and all the other trappings of megasuccess in the Reagan era, all the way back to San Francisco in the Grant Era, to another banker, and to that other hotel on Market Street where I heard my calling as an historian.

San Franciscans have long prided themselves on inhabiting the Paris of the Pacific. William Chapman Ralston holds a cherished place as empire-builder in that fantasy. Just for starters, Ralston was founder of what was once the greatest financial institution of the West, the Bank of California. No less than four biogra-phies deal with Ralston's life and impact; one dubbed him *The Man Who Built San Francisco*. (Dana 1936) He has been called the West's Lorenzo de Medici. "He blazed the path for San Francisco's onward march to achievement and renown," claims a bronze plaque near the place where he drowned in the bay. By doing so, Ralston was saved the historical judgment and prison term that later befell Arizona's most notorious visionary. As Ralston's partner reportedly said on view-ing his corpse, "It's the best thing he could have done." (Ostrander 1966)

Ralston and Keating were born ninety-seven years and a hundred and fifty miles apart, in Ohio. San Francisco and Phoenix were boomtowns when the financiers respectively landed in them, the kind of go-go money machines that attract born speculators like honey does flies. Ralston had been involved in shady deals in Nicaragua before moving to San Francisco. (Lavender 1975) Lawyer Keating had been involved in shady deals in Cincinnati. Keating beat an SEC fraud rap by signing a consent decree swearing never to do it again; he was never a man to be slowed by promises. (McCombs 1990)

Throw bloody meat into a pool of sharks and you'll get something like the business climate of San Francisco during its formative years. Gold from the Mother Lode and silver from the Comstock Lode established an early pattern of high-risk gambling and damn-the-downstreamers exploitation that many historians believe has characterized Western behavior right to the present.

The first few years of placer mining did provide unusual opportunities for modest fortunes. But as the rich surface deposits ran out, hard-rock and hydraulic mining quickly took the place of freelance miners, and these required stock markets as well as the kind of venture capital that only financiers with international connections could raise. Nonetheless, the popular belief in anybody's gold became primary bait for those wishing to strike it rich on the market as others had struck it rich in the streams of the Sierra.

Capital concentration requires cities whose comforts and luxury beat the rigors of mining camps. Mining paper on the San Francisco exchanges excited frenzies resembling religious rapture. Only five of the hundreds of mines incorporated on the Comstock Lode ultimately proved profitable, but they were sufficient to lure thousands of suckers onto the San Francisco Mining Exchange where insiders had a second chance to strike it rich by swindling them of their savings. Gold Rush banker William Tecumseh Sherman sourly observed in 1856 that the very nature of the country begets speculation, extravagance, failures, and rascality. (Lavender 1975)

Many others, often approvingly, agreed with Sherman's judgment. In December 1883, the *Overland Monthly* editorialized that "The real peculiarity of our present Pacific civilization is that it is, perhaps, the most completely realized embodiment of the purely commercial civilization on the face of the earth." California was showing the way for less developed regions, particularly in its less exacting moral sense. Visitors concurred. The recently occupied tomb of William Ralston prompted tourist Joshua Speed of Kentucky to observe in 1876 that nearly all Californians were supermaterialists:

> They measure everything by the gold standard, men as well as mules. You never
> hear of Mr. Smith as a good man, or Mr. Brown as an honest man, or Mr. Jones

as a Christian. But Mr. S. has twenty thousand million and so on. The more he has, the better he is and it matters not how he got it, so he has it. (Speed 1876)

Economist Thorstein Veblen later dubbed this easy quantification of virtue "pecuniary emulation."

From the moment he arrived in San Francisco in 1854, Ralston was a leading player in the high-stakes game of Western exploitation. In a land whose abundant resources had scarcely been scraped and whose real estate values climbed with each new immigrant, the future belonged to the ruthless and to the lawyers who wrote the rules of the game for them. They were frequently the same.

Ralston dabbled in a number of schemes before finding his lode. Some things, like helping to finance the takeover of Nicaragua by soldier of fortune William Walker, just did not pay off. (Lavender 1975) It was to the Comstock Lode south of present-day Reno that Billy Ralston hitched his star soon after its discovery in 1859. Five years later he was treasurer or director of most of the bonanza mines. (Wilson 1969) In that year, Congress admitted Nevada into the Union as San Francisco's most lucrative colony, a state commonly known as the nation's great rotten borough.

Also in 1864, Ralston established the Bank of California. To his former partners' displeasure, Ralston took most of their best clients with him when he left to found the rival bank. Rumors abounded that Billy had been paid $50,000 to do so by the twenty-five or so bank directors with whom he surrounded himself. (Lavender 1975) With these men, Ralston entered ever-shifting partnerships and betrayals. They became known as Ralston's Ring, or, simply, the Bank Crowd, and they constituted the West's wealthiest capitalists during the Civil War period.

For the titular head of the bank, Ralston enlisted Sacramento's Darius Ogden Mills, the most respected financier on the coast, though Ralston actually ran the bank as its cashier. As his agent on the Comstock, Ralston installed a stock jobber named William Sharon.

To call Sharon a piranha would be to insult the character of the fish. Sharon adroitly devoured mines, mills, business associates, transportation, forests, and Virginia City's water works. He expertly manipulated the stock market with the advantage of insider information gleaned from the mineheads. He directed the profits back to his partners in the Bank Crowd.

Ralston converted his Comstock capital into coastal transport, insurance, telegraph lines, currency speculation, woolen and silk mills, canal companies, hydraulic mines, political and judicial bribery, Alaskan furs, gas works, refineries, and hazardous real estate schemes. It seemed that there was scarcely an enterprise in which Billy Ralston did not have an interest. Collis P. Huntington, boss of the

Central Pacific Railroad, wrote to his partner Mark Hopkins: "I think time will show that Ralston has got a larger institution than he is able to run." Ralston returned Huntington's trust by referring to him in coded telegrams as "Hungry." (Lavender 1975) Both were astute judges of character.

As long as Ralston rode the wave of riches, he was the city's paragon of virtue, a role model for pecuniary emulation. His lavish entertainments, his carriages, his ducal estate at Belmont, and his many charities earned him, like Keating later, a deserved place in the developmental history of his adopted city. He was unquestionably a visionary; his discussions with Frederick Law Olmsted, for example, led to the cultivation of Golden Gate Park. If it took insider trading, backstabbing, and wholesale political corruption to accomplish his ends, those were the rules of the game and everyone else who could afford to play was doing the same. Fortunately for Ralston, William Sharon cared little for popular opinion and served as the genial banker's lightning rod.

A confidential letter from Ralston to his partner suggests their modus operandi. Ralston advised Sharon to go easy on a wealthy associate who owned valuable stock that they wanted: "Give him sugar and molasses at present, but when our time comes give him vinegar of the sharpest kind. He is our friend and I think he will assist us." (Ostrander 1966)

Ralston's banking partner in New York wrote him in 1870 that "Everybody talks about you, your princely hospitality, and large-scale of expenditures. . . . All who go to California want to see you and want letters of introduction." (Lavender 1975) Those words could have been written about an equally spectacular banker more than a century later.

Arizona real estate tycoon Tom Arnold said of Charlie Keating's ever-ramifying companies of the 1980s:

> [They] just became bigger and bigger and bigger, until the projects were so large, there was just this sense of Big Business, with airplanes, helicopters, the Phoenician Resort built at hundreds of thousands of dollars per room, the Estrella development at 20,000 acres, just massive things. And everyone, I think, admired him, but wondered how he could do such things. (Lavin 1990)

So, increasingly, did pesky federal regulators trying to get some idea of what was happening inside Keating's $6.5 billion American Continental Corporation and its labyrinth of subsidiaries, Lincoln Savings and Loan chief among them.

ACC was the Phoenix-based holding company that, in 1984, swallowed Lincoln S&L with the digestive aid of $51 million in junk bonds provided by the leading authority in the field, Michael Milken of Drexel Burnham Lambert.

(McCombs 1990) The would-be free market heyday of the Grant Era provided the ideal at which the Reagan deregulators aimed, with a spectacular exception provided by Franklin Roosevelt's New Deal. Federally insured deposits enabled tycoons like Keating to treat S&Ls like Visa cards drawn on the U.S. Treasury, with the IRS acting as their collection agency. In five years, Keating's Crowd turned Lincoln's billion dollars in assets into a $2.6 billion liability for the U.S. taxpayer; this is known in the trade as a "zombie" because of its unnaturally prolonged life.

How did Keating and company accomplish such a prodigy? In short, they turned stodgy Lincoln into a pioneer in aggressive lending and creative accounting, according to the *Chicago Tribune*—a perfect cash cow, in the words of William Black of the Federal Home Loan Bank of San Francisco. (Lavin 1990)

Under Keating's creative management, Lincoln's federally insured deposits veered sharply out of home loans and into junk bonds, foreign currency speculation, legal and political fees, luxury hotels, and what is known in Arizona real estate circles as raw land—those full-color plates of saguaro-clad desert in *Arizona Highways* magazine that developers dream of scraping and covering with shopping malls, golf greens, and marinas. (Beard & Morrell 1990)

Keating in fact operated ACC like one of Billy Ralston's high-pressure hydraulic mines. Ralston's operations sent floods of mercury-tainted sludge downstream after extracting the gold, leaving behind a permanent wasteland for others to worry about. In what he called a tax-sharing plan, Keating upstreamed $94 million in federally insured funds from Lincoln to ACC, leaving depositors and regulators to pick through the gravel and bones that remained. (Lavin 1990)

To wreak such havoc required the kind of political contributions that in Ralston's time went by a shorter and much ruder name. Keating knew the price of men better than that of mules. He bragged that he had hired fifty accountants away from his auditors with munificent raises. He hired Alan Greenspan, longtime chairman of the Federal Reserve Board, to plead Lincoln's case as a financially strong institution in 1985, when it wasn't. He tried to hire Edwin Gray, the troublesome chairman of the Federal Home Loan Bank Board. (Lavin 1990) Politicians from Phoenix city council members to U.S. Senators shared in his generosity, as did Mother Teresa. The gratitude of those politicians was expressed in more worldly ways than the crucifix which the blessed Mother gave Keating for his campaign against pornography. (Irving 1989)

In the final five years of their spectacular careers, Ralston's and Keating's destinies converged and paralleled like iron rails. For both men, hotels and real estate

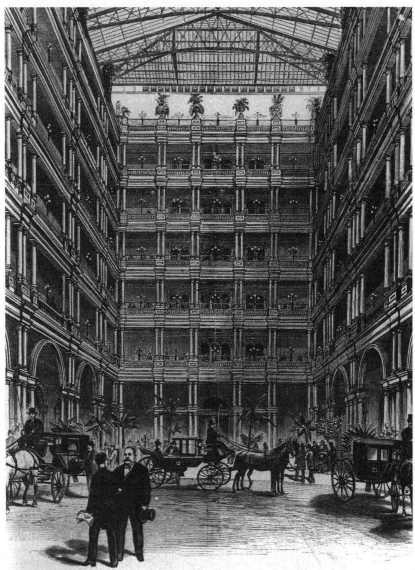

Palm Court of Ralston's Palace Hotel (*Frank Leslie's Illustrated Newspaper*, June 29, 1878). The spectacular drive-in courtyard of the West's most opulent hotel. The Palm Court was built largely to boost the value of Ralston's real estate holdings; the main entrance was placed on narrow New Montgomery Street rather than on the city's principal thoroughfare, Market Street.

became the obsessions that (they hoped) would extricate them from the tangled webs they'd woven, as well as insuring their reputations as city-builders.

During the silver boom of the 1870s, San Francisco's Montgomery Street became known as the Wall Street of the West. Just as Manhattan's Wall Street dead-ends at Broadway, so did Montgomery stop cold at Market. Ralston had plans to extend Montgomery's high-value real estate to potentially valuable land that he owned south of Market. Such an extension would require cutting through city blocks and leveling a hill on which his fellow magnates had built their mansions. No matter how powerful Ralston was, equally determined plutocrats who were not in on the deal blocked his New Montgomery Street two blocks south of Market, and that presented problems.

As Ralston's other investments turned rancid, the banker needed the lots he owned along New Montgomery to appreciate as planned. To attract investors to his land, he first built a million-dollar hotel called the Grand on the east corner of Market and New Montgomery. When that failed to work, he began the Palace on the western block.

Phoenician Hotel. Keating's opulent megaresort on Camelback Mountain was largely paid for by Keating's depositors and U.S. taxpayers.

Ralston's Palace was to be the opulent capstone of his career and ego. When completed in 1875, it was quite literally the grandest hotel in the world. Its luxurious appointments, high-tech gadgetry, Parisian restaurants, and tiered central light well placed it in a league with the finest hotels of Vienna, Paris, and New York. One historian noted that the state of California was run from the Palace bar, though he might have added several other Western states, territories, and Hawaii as well. Cost overruns ultimately drove the price of the Palace to nearly three times the original estimate. For San Franciscans, the hotel proved that their city had become world class in only twenty-five years. The Palace was also approximately four times too large for Ralston's city. It would not fill to capacity for decades. (Lewis & Hall 1940)

The building neared completion as Ralston's empire fell about him. He'd never been hampered by a firm boundary between his bank's finances and his own. He began selling properties and borrowing money on nearly everything that he owned and much that he didn't. Among the latter was San Francisco's private water company, on which he had an option and which he counted on selling back to the city at enormous profit. Other experiments in creative accounting included secretly over-issuing Bank of California stock. He borrowed $300,000 on Southern Pacific bonds that he'd removed from the bank vaults. (Lavender 1975)

Pyramid schemes based on the fantasy of perpetual growth are notoriously flimsy and grow more so as the economy slows down. On August 26, 1875, as rumors swept San Francisco, a run began on the Bank of California. At 2:35 p.m., its vaults empty, the bank closed its doors and thousands faced ruin. The details of their failures have never been told.

The Phoenician Hotel was an equally personal obsession with Charlie Keating. It was, like Ralston's, designed to skyrocket the price of adjacent land, but there was more to it than that. Keating loved that hotel. He and his wife haunted the building site, like Ralston had the Palace's. Their innumerable design changes hiked the final cost to an estimated $300 million. To this day, the Phoenician staff cannot tell for sure who the architects were, and say that it was mostly Charlie Keating. Again echoing his predecessor, Keating told a reporter, "I had the most successful resort, probably, ever built in the history of the United States." (McCombs 1990) Also one of the emptiest.

In the final months of his glory, Keating & Friends went on a bender similar to Ralston's, but bigger. His most famous stunt was to peddle a quarter billion dollars in ACC-uninsured junk bonds at Lincoln branches, those famous high-yield certificates that wiped out 23,000 chiefly elderly investors. (Lavin 1990)

House Banking Committee chair Henry Gonzalez later told those plaintiffs that they'd put their savings in inventive hands:

> We find Mr. Keating a player on the international scene, a dabbler in the foreign currency markets, an operator of a security subsidiary in General Noriega's Panama, a member of the board of a Saudi-European bank, [and] a good customer of Crédit Suisse, a banking corporation that played a big role in the Lincoln-Kuwait partnership in the $300 million Phoenician extravaganza in Phoenix. (Irving 1989)

On April 13, 1989, ACC declared bankruptcy and the following day the feds belatedly seized Lincoln. At midnight on November 16, 1989, federal regulators and armed FBI agents captured the Phoenician Hotel in a midnight raid. (McCombs 1990) When Keating came to work the next morning, the locks had been changed. He would soon be wearing a few of his own.

At the end, the bankers' fates diverged, for no federal regulators plagued Ralston. His corporate board summoned him to appear the day after his bank closed. It seemed that he owed the institution nearly five million dollars, approximately its entire capitalization. All directors professed shock and claimed to have no inkling of their partners' felonious activities, though subsequent lawsuits blew holes in their avowed naïveté. Years later, when lawyers cornered Darius Mills with a subpoena at the Palace Hotel, he suddenly grew deathly ill, retired to his bed, and lost all memory of everything pertaining to the management of the bank during his presidency.

On August 27, 1875, however, Mills's mind was in fine shape. He and his partners forced Ralston's resignation. They also made him sign over all of his assets to William Sharon who, they trusted, would attempt to straighten out the mess. Ralston left the bank for his daily swim. He was a strong swimmer, but on the day of his downfall he was under considerable stress. An hour after plunging into the bay, his body was retrieved by observers who watched him flounder and sink.

William Sharon had recently been elected to the U.S. Senate from Nevada, thanks to the generosity of his "sack bearers" in the Silver State. It was in the Senator's best interests to rehabilitate Ralston's reputation, for California law held him and his partners financially liable for the failed bank's debts. He did so with the same skill with which he played poker and the stock market.

Fifty thousand mourners marched in Ralston's funeral cortege. Orators thundered his virtues. The *Alta California* mourned that "His was the vast vision of the Builders and his like shall never pass this way again." Ralston biographer David Lavender claims that Sharon deliberately prolonged the city's emotional jag to make the work of the bank's reorganization committee easier. Sharon chaired that committee. (Lavender 1975)

The reclamation of both Ralston's reputation and institution worked like a charm. On October 2, 1875, the new Bank of California opened its doors. Jubilant crowds surged from the bank to the nearly complete Palace where Senator Sharon delivered a touching eulogy to his late friend. In addition to the Palace, Sharon now owned the Grand Hotel, New Montgomery Street, Ralston's country estate and town house, the city's water works, and so many other lucrative properties that he, rather than Ralston's widow, could claim to be California's second wealthiest citizen. He just trailed Darius Mills who soon left the state to cultivate a major dynasty in New York City. Sharon founded his own in California with his vastly enhanced fortune.

San Franciscans argue to this day whether Ralston's death was accidental. Historian Hubert Howe Bancroft, Ralston's

WILLIAM
CHAPMAN
RALSTON
1826 – 1875

HE·BLAZED·THE
PATH·FOR·SAN
FRANCISCO'S
ONWARD·MARCH·
TO·ACHIEVEMENT
AND·RENOWN

Ralston monument on Marina Green. Ralston's untimely death in the bay saved him from harsh historical judg-

contemporary, had no such doubts; in his copy of a city history, Bancroft scrawled in the margin that Ralston, though a daring, dashing pet of the people, was a bad man and committed suicide rather than face his friends, "after his frauds should become public [sic]." (Hittell 1878)

Although a habitual swimmer himself, Keating stayed around to serve time in a state prison while his attorneys fought to free him. His crash forced the Senate to investigate five of its own colleagues for their connections to Keating, including Senate Whip Allan Cranston of California, who soon resigned. California Governor Pete Wilson and President George Bush were momentarily brushed by the Arizona banker's dark wing. Had it not been for the cornucopia of other scandals during the Reagan years, the Keating chapter of the S&L disaster would easily rank with other national stenches such as Teapot Dome, Julian Pete, and the crash of Chicago's Sam Insull. Lincoln's $2.6 billion price tag represent-

"Keating: A Man Possessed" (*The Phoenix Gazette*, June 27, 1993). A man who was once a role model for pecuniary emulation.

ed the biggest of all thrift failures. (McCombs 1990)

The Resolution Trust Company sold the remainder of the Phoenician Hotel to the Kuwait Investment Company at a hefty discount. The Japanese had long before acquired the Palace with the Sheraton chain and the Bank of California in San Francisco.

Keating's appearance in manacles and jail togs during his first trial momentarily sated some of the tribal lust for revenge. In 1996, after serving considerably less than half of a nearly thirteen-year sentence, a federal judge sprang Keating from prison on a technicality. In the midst of a hysterical bull market in the late 1990s, the unwelcome lessons of the S&L crashes of the 1980s joined such ancient history as the Depression and the Grant Era and were happily forgotten. Keating's release, like so much else, was eclipsed by the saga of O. J. Simpson.

In the last analysis, Charlie Keating and Billy Ralston were far from the titans of free enterprise that their admirers claimed. Both danced a long and awkward tango with the government that they loved to hate.

Historian Bernard DeVoto once succinctly defined the Western attitude to the federal government as "Get out and give us more money." (DeVoto 1955) Despite his loud patriotism, Charles Keating had scant regard for the U.S. government when it got in his way. After one of his victories over the regulators hounding him, Keating leaped upon a desk with a foaming magnum of champagne and ripped open his shirt to reveal a T-shirt inscribed "Death to the Feds." (Irving 1989) It's a sentiment shared by many of his Sunbelt colleagues, along with Arizona's private militias.

The buccaneers of Ralston's era shared that sentiment as they built their fortunes on federal largesse. In personal letters to his attorney, Southern Pacific president

Collis Huntington referred to the judges and senators whom the railroad was forced to buy as damned hogs and worthless dogs. Congress, he felt, was the worst set of men that have ever been collected together since man was created. (Lewis 1938)

Such strong words were strange ingratitude for services rendered, for Huntington, Ralston & Friends had used their famous profit mill, the Contract & Finance Company (Wilson 1969), to skim off extra millions of public dollars and millions of public acres that were meant to finance the building of the transcontinental railroad. When Congress and creditors got nosy, the books got burnt.

A similar amnesia prevails in Arizona today, extending far beyond the federally insured deposits that built fortunes on the credit of the U.S. Treasury. The lakes, fountains, and Kilarney-green lawns essential for Keating's luxury developments were largely provided by the feds, along with the cheap energy that makes life in the desert bearable. Phoenix itself, with its astonishing boomtown sprawl, would have been impossible without the Bureau of Reclamation, created in 1902 by Representative Francis G. Newlands of Nevada. Newlands was Senator Sharon's son-in-law, and soon after the passage of the Newlands Act, moved on to the Senate himself.

"Oh! Fortuna, Thy Gold Doth Blind!" (*The Wasp*, May 10, 1879)—public-private partnerships in the Grant Era. Most great fortunes are based on gaining access to the public treasury. This is as true now—in the era of publicly subsidized sports stadiums and shopping malls—as in the era of railroad land grants, timber frauds, and municipal land swindles shown here.

Snaking over the mountains from the Colorado River, the Granite Reef Aqueduct of the $3 billion Central Arizona Project may, as water historian Marc Reisner has written, come as close to socialism as anything this country has ever done. (Reisner 1986) But for the moment it keeps the desert cities growing without end.

San Francisco in the 1990s has grown to its limits, and so must grow by tearing down and building anew. It does so in a giddy atmosphere of public-private partnerships that now extends all the way from the local level to Clintonian Washington, and relies, as it always has, on popular amnesia of how often the public gets snookered in such deals. "Free" enterprise is anything but, being virtually inconceivable without access to the public treasury and the paid cooperation of officials who hold the keys.

Urban redevelopment, for example, successfully transferred the land of the many to the hands of the few at major public expense, accomplishing in the South of Market area those very miracles of land appreciation that Billy Ralston unsuccessfully attempted a full century before. (Hartman 1984) As skyscrapers and tourist facilities moved south, wiping out cheap housing near the train station, Southern Pacific's land division planned a second downtown on the railroad's marshaling yards with the enthusiastic cooperation of state and city officials. They called it Mission Bay, for the inlet and marsh now filled with the city's trash and toxic wastes. A map produced after the 1906 earthquake suggested that Mission Bay would liquefy in a major seismic event, but that was of little concern to those who envisioned enhanced real estate values and new skyscrapers on the old dump. Then Assembly Speaker, now Mayor, Willie Brown's law firm represented the land division of Hungry Huntington's old railroad.

The scions of well-aged money keep a low profile today, marrying one another or those of metropolitan dynasties elsewhere. They constitute a cousinage almost unknown to those outside their circle. Five and six generations beyond, the fortunes made from the poisoned rivers and the fallen redwoods, from bribery or from the pockets of suckers picked on the stock exchange continue to propel numerous heirs through the *Chronicle*'s society pages. That destruction and those scandals have become local color, if remembered at all. The heirs regard the brassy nouveaux riches of Silicon Valley and Las Vegas with the contempt of the well-bred, and invest their capital in growth in those parts.

We must forget the mistakes of the past in order to repeat them again. The Keatings and Ralstons recur like avatars in every generation because we want them to. We need those men to give us hope. They are what the myth of the self-made man is all about. That the myth is often as much of a fraud as they were is fundamental to its eternal return.

References

Beard, Betty and Lisa Morrell. 1990. "Kuwait Turmoil Puts Deal for Valley Hotels on Hold." *Arizona Republic* (September 6).

Burck, Charles. 1973. "It's Promoters vs Taxpayers in the Superstadium Game." *Fortune* (March).

Dana, Julian. 1936. *The Man Who Built San Francisco: A Study of Ralston's Journey with Banners.* New York: Macmillan.

DeVoto, Bernard. 1955. *The Easy Chair.* Boston: Houghton Mifflin.

Furlong, Tom. 1989. "Arizona Hotel Exemplifies Lincoln S&Ls' Extravagance." *Los Angeles Times* (December 28).

Hartman, Chester. 1984. *The Transformation of San Francisco.* Totowa, NJ: Rowman & Allanheld.

Hittell, John S. 1878. *A History of the City of San Francisco.* San Francisco: A. L. Bancroft.

Irving, Carl. 1989. "Keating to Tell His Side of Story," *San Francisco Examiner* (November 19).

Lavender, David. 1975. *Nothing Seemed Impossible: William C. Ralston and Early San Francisco.* Palo Alto: American West Publishing.

Lavin, Cheryl. 1990. "Keating's Tarnished Image." *Chicago Tribune* (January 22).

Lewis, Oscar, and Carroll D. Hall. 1940. *Bonanza Inn: America's First Luxury Hotel.* New York: Alfred A. Knopf.

Lewis, Oscar. 1947. *Silver Kings: The Lives and Times of Mackay, Fair, Flood, and O'Brien.* New York: Alfred A. Knopf.

Lewis, Oscar. 1938. *The Big Four: The Story of Huntington, Stanford, Hopkins, and Crocker.* New York: Alfred A. Knopf.

McCombs, Phil. 1990. "Keating, Failed King of Thrifts: Lincoln S&Ls' Deposed Chief, Blasting Back at the Regulators." *Washington Post* (March 5).

Ostrander, Gilman M. 1966. *Nevada, The Great Rotten Borough, 1859–1964.* New York: Alfred A. Knopf.

Pizzo, Stephen, Mary Fricker, and Paul Muolo. 1989. *Inside Job: The Looting of America's Savings and Loans.* New York: McGraw-Hill.

Reisner, Marc. 1986. *Cadillac Desert: The American West and Its Disappearing Water.* New York: Viking.

Speed, Joshua. 1884. *Reminiscences of Abraham Lincoln and Notes of a Visit to California,* Louisville: J. P. Martin.

Wilson, Neil C. 1969. *400 California Street: A Century Plus Five.* San Francisco: The Bank of California.

Suicide in the City

by Ann Garrison

On July 18, 1955, the *New Republic* published "How to Be Happy #1053," a review of Dr. Arnold A. Hutschneker's *Love and Hate in Human Nature,* by San Francisco poet, musician, and filmmaker Weldon Kees. After scorning it as another how-to-do-it book, another guide to peace of mind and self-understanding, Kees lacerated Dr. Hutschneker for a pat approximation of Freud, an equation of Freudianism and science, and illiterate effusions on the science of psychology that could now save us from self-ignorance and lead us to the age-long dream of peace.

"Socrates, Proust, and Coleridge . . . had more self-knowledge and knew more at first hand of love and hate than the Doctor will ever know . . . and they never believed that self-knowledge could, in the long run, save them or us," wrote Kees. With bitter irony, he marveled at the publication of such a book "in our present atmosphere of distrust, violence, and irrationality, with so many human beings murdering themselves, either literally or symbolically." I can only guess that anti-Communist hysteria and the specter of nuclear annihilation partially occasioned his disgust.

On the day that "How to Be Happy #1053" was published, Kees's automobile was found abandoned on the approach to the Golden Gate Bridge. He had spoken to friends of suicide or of leaving to start a new life, perhaps in Mexico. His death was not officially recorded because his body was never found, but the poetry of his life and his possible suicide added to the mystique already woven around the bridge and its lethal appeal.

San Francisco celebrated the bridge's opening in 1937, and less than three months later, H. B. Wobber, a 49-year-old bargeman, strolled across it chatting with a tourist and then, halfway back, climbed up and jumped over the railing, without explanation and much to the tourist's alarm. Since then, more than 1,000 people have jumped to their deaths, and many who jumped unseen, perhaps at night or in fog (possibly including Weldon Kees), have washed out to sea uncounted. A strong current runs oceanward beneath the bridge and sharks feed there and beyond.

Suicide is only one of many dramas acted out on the bridge; the city's landmark structure has long been a stage for street theater. Protesters stopped bridge traffic to protest the Gulf War, the politics of AIDS research, and recently, corporate plans to cut down the ancient redwoods of the Headwaters Forest. Local legend has it that draft dodgers climbed the bridge towers and threatened to jump in order to earn mentally unfit draft status during the Vietnam War. While bridge theater has ranged from the revolutionary to the farcical, suicide has been the tragic and most oft repeated performance.

Jim Jones, leader of the People's Temple, delivered one of the most momentous bridge soliloquies on Memorial Day 1977 when he and a group of his followers joined 400 antisuicide activists in the bridge toll plaza to commemorate bridge suicides and demand the erection of a preventive barrier atop the railing. Jones, by then feeling persecuted by defectors, the media, and the government, told the crowd that he had been in a suicidal mood himself that day, and that he had "personal empathy for what we are doing here today." The next year, on November 18, 1978, he and 913 followers committed mass suicide at their compound in Guyana, after killing all of their dogs, fish, and farm animals as well as their pet chimpanzee, Mr. Muggs. (Chidester 1988)

Long before the toll of Golden Gate Bridge suicides reached 1,000, the bridge had become the best-known suicide site in the Western world, and San Francisco had been accused of taking a perverse pride in its reputation. Tour bus drivers cited the death toll as they passed the bridge, the city's daily papers announced each leap, and other newspapers, magazines, and even television documentaries described "The Esthetics of Suicide" (*Newsweek*, January 9, 1961), "The Golden Leap" (*Time*, August 24, 1970), "The Bridge of Sighs" (*Newsweek*, August 13, 1973), and "The Golden Gate Bridge: Site of Beauty and Despair" (*AAS Newslink*, July 1987).

When 997 people had purposely concluded their lives on the bridge, authorities stopped releasing the number for fear that potential suicides would rush to make headlines with the thousandth leap. Nevertheless, the *San Francisco Examiner* announced number 1,000, having kept its own tally.

Though bridge suicides have accounted for only a minor percentage of all San Francisco suicides, the city at the same time became known as the country's suicide capital, year after year reporting a higher rate of self-murder than any other U.S. city. The *San Francisco Bay Guardian* (May 17, 1996) called its home "suicide city."

Golden Gate Bridge from Crissy Field

The significance of the statistics has been questioned by several researchers who found that our Medical Examiner's Office is far more diligent than most, performing autopsies at an extremely high rate and doing unusually extensive testing for drugs and other poisonous substances. Office statistician Donna Allison says that examiners do autopsies of all cases in which there is any question about the cause of death, and they test for every potentially lethal drug on the market, legal or illegal. Firearms are by far the most common method of committing suicide nationally, but poisoning is the most common method in San Francisco. In 1994–1995, our Medical Examiner's Office counted twenty-four suicides by firearms and thirty-seven by poisoning, while the nation counted 2,559 by firearms and 2,110 by poisoning. The suicidal may simply prefer poisoning to firearms here, but it also seems possible that San Francisco reports more suicides than the rest of the country because conscientious examiners detect more purposeful self-poisoning.

Our high suicide rate also seems less dramatic when one considers that it makes a great deal of sense demographically. Who is most likely to commit suicide? Elderly people and unmarried people, especially those widowed or divorced. Caucasians and Asians. Alcoholics and other substance abusers. Men, who attempt suicide half as often as women, but succeed three times more often. The upper and upper-middle classes. And the terminally ill. San Francisco has high concentrations of all these groups. The median age is well above the national average, and there are far more unmarried people here than in the outlying Bay regions or other more suburban locales. We are less Caucasian than most American cities, but more than 40 percent of our large minority population is Asian. Our alcoholism and substance abuse rates are high. We are also, on average, one of the richest and best educated urban populations in the United States. And many San Franciscans are terminally ill; as a gay Mecca, the city has been a center of the AIDS epidemic.

Whether or not it can be explained by demographics or by a conscientious coroner's office, San Francisco's leading suicide rate has added to its mystique and given rise to popular romantic theories about why there is so much suicidal despair in a prosperous urban center celebrated for its beauty, mild climate, and tolerant, freewheeling, often frivolous ways.

This is the end point of the country's westward movement, say some. There's no place left to go once you've chased your dream all the way to the Pacific, so if you're still depressed or anxious, or if you feel like you've failed, it may seem like the time and place to give up. Even author Joan Didion has rhapsodized about California as the end of the trail, the last chance. It's a poetic image, but the great western movement came to an end at the turn of the century and people have continued to chase their dreams every which way. Suicide rates are, indeed, highest in the West and lowest in the East, but the state with the highest rate is Nevada, not quite the end of the trail. Los Angeles's suicide rate is typically half that of San Francisco, although both cities face the big empty Pacific from the end of the trail.

Another romantic theory is that suicide rates are high in this and other vibrant, glamorous cities for the same reason that suicide rates peak in spring; loneliness and despair are harder to bear when the world all around you is budding and blooming, or when the people around you all seem to lead charmed lives. April is the cruelest month, San Francisco the cruelest city. In "Suicide Capital? A Study of the San Francisco Suicide Rate" (*Bulletin of Suicidology*, December 1967) Berkeley psychologist Richard Seiden pointed out that neither Tacoma nor Sacramento had much cosmopolitan sheen, but both had high suicide rates. He added that San Francisco and Sacramento shared the nation's highest reported rates of alcoholism, a well-known relative of suicide, with San Francisco placing first.

Since the 1980s, the growing homeless population has further damaged the despair-amidst-glamour-and-gaiety theory by giving the city's glamour and gaiety a cruel tinge. Our often theatrical street life still offers charming moments, but the homeless now beg throughout the central city, most often in front of restaurants, theaters, and other urban pleasure haunts. Their pleas for spare change interrupt cultured chat over cappuccino and cause the well-dressed to avert their eyes. The homeless are more visible here than in many American cities because San Francisco was built for nineteenth-century street life; we lack space for cars but still have pedestrian thoroughfares for the homeless to beg on, unlike the sprawling freeway-based cities where people rarely leave their cars between suburb, office, and mall.

Our suicide rate would jump even higher if we counted drug overdoses among the homeless, but their deaths lack clear intention; here as elsewhere, straightfor-

Reclaiming San Francisco

ward self-murder is most often a resort of the upper and upper-middle classes, who more keenly feel the weight of great expectations. Those who struggle just to get by tend to turn their anger and frustration outward.

A premise of the end-of-the-trail and despair-amidst-glamour-and-gaiety theories is that San Francisco suicides are often newcomers who arrive with big dreams and suffer big disappointments. Even Boyd Stephens, the city's Chief Medical Examiner, told the *Bay Guardian* (May 17, 1996) that San Francisco was the city at the end of the rainbow, a place where many people fail to find all they'd hoped for.

Richard Seiden dented the newcomers theory when he reported (in the previously cited 1967 paper) that suiciding residents actually tended to have been here longer than the general population; of that year's 187 suicides, 54 had been here for between four months and nine years, but 133 had been here for ten years or more. By contrast, the average American remains in the same place for only five years. And although people may bring more yearnings and less stoicism here than to Pittsburgh or Detroit, the really big dreamers head for L.A. or New York, so wouldn't dreams die even harder there?

The suicide rate has declined very slightly since mid-1991, when someone assigned the task of retrieving the bodies of Golden Gate Bridge jumpers to the Marin County Coast Guard Station. Now, to be counted in San Francisco, one has to jump far enough on the city side to land on the ground. As a result, the city has counted only nine Golden Gate Bridge suicides in the past four years, compared to fifty-six in the four preceding years.

While our suicide rate may not lead the nation's for poetic or romantic reasons, we may indeed lead the nation in our support of suicide as a personal choice that authority should not contravene. As the AIDS epidemic advanced, the city's gay community organized not only to help the afflicted live but also to help them die. In 1993, Hemlock Society co-founder Derek Humphries spoke here, saying that AIDS had permanently transformed the right-to-die movement:

> For the first five years we were an elderly organization; it was just me and a bunch of old women. And then, in 1985, when AIDS became quite a public matter, we went from the sea of grey-haired ladies to a lot of young people. And then a lot of nurses and doctors who treated AIDS patients started getting involved because it changed for them when they saw young people dying. (*Bay Area Reporter*, May 20, 1993)

Though AIDS has probably increased the actual rate of suicide in San Francisco, it has not significantly increased the reported rate. The Medical Examiner's Office does not perform an autopsy if a doctor is willing to certify that the deceased has died of an illness. In February 1997, the *New England Journal of*

Medicine reported that 53 percent of prominent San Francisco AIDS doctors privately admitted assisting AIDS patients in suicide.

Long before AIDS, many San Franciscans defended the right to suicide by opposing an antisuicide barrier on the Golden Gate Bridge, where one can easily climb the chest-high railing and take a 240-foot, four-second, 80-mile-an-hour flight to near certain death. The Bridge Authority commissioned the first design for a barrier in 1953, but even though fifteen more designs have since been commissioned and the estimated price has gone from $200,000 to $3 million, they have never proceeded with construction. Instead, officials bought a closed-circuit television for the toll office, so that workers can scan the bridge and dispatch highway patrol officers when anyone behaves suspiciously.

Each time suicide prevention activists press for an antisuicide barrier, arguments rage in the daily newspaper columns and letters to the editors. It would mar the beauty of the bridge, say the opponents. The force of high winds blowing against a rigid barrier could damage the bridge's superstructure. It would cost too much and people who really want to kill themselves will eventually do it one way or another. And why shouldn't they be able to jump off the bridge if that's what they want to do? Two-thirds of letters to bridge directors have opposed a barrier, and many have defended personal freedom to commit suicide.

Those San Franciscans who insist on the right to design one's own death echo an argument with roots in ancient Greece and Rome, where suicide was on the whole a respected choice. Socrates committed rational suicide; Plato taught that suicide was justifiable in cases of extreme sorrow, unavoidable misfortune, or intolerable disgrace; Epicurus urged men to weigh carefully whether they would prefer death to come to them or would go themselves unto death; and the Stoics held that "he who does not wish to live is at liberty to die."

The Catholic Church condemned suicide as the greatest of sins during the Middle Ages, and bodies of suicides were dragged through town squares, hanged, and, in England, buried at crossroads with a stake through the heart. John Donne, David Hume, Montesquieu, and other Enlightenment writers resumed the defense of suicide as a personal choice during the seventeenth and eighteenth centuries.

Though the Catholic Church still lists suicide as a mortal sin, the task of suicide prevention passed from the moral to the medical professions during the eighteenth and nineteenth centuries. Like homosexuality, self-murder was condoned in the ancient world, condemned during the Middle Ages, and then pathologized with the rise of medical science and psychiatry. Accordingly, mental health professionals make most of the arguments for a suicide barrier on the Golden Gate Bridge. Despite their compassion, commitment, and often lifesaving assistance to those who seek it, their arguments for a barrier, which would prevent personal choice, disturb me as much as Dr. Hutschneker's happiness prescriptions disturbed Weldon Kees.

Now, in March 1997, the Golden Gate Bridge Authority is again considering a suicide barrier. They say that the latest design, a fence of high-tension wires extending six feet above the existing railing, eliminates aesthetic and engineering safety concerns. The narrow wire would be unobtrusive, fenceposts would be placed one hundred feet apart to keep views open, and the barrier's flexibility would keep it from endangering the bridge structure during high winds. Those who object to the $3 million cost and those who defend the right to die may be the new design's only opponents.

Forty-four years have passed since the Golden Gate Bridge Authority set the first barrier design aside. Although the Authority has never embraced the personal liberty argument, repeated decisions against erecting a suicide barrier have been consistent with San Francisco's longstanding preoccupation with personal freedom. Gay Mecca, heart of the hippie revolution, bastion of political radicalism, home to left, right, center, and cyber libertarians, this is a city where morning and evening traffic reporters routinely warn of demonstrators who are slowing cars to assert their rights or the rights of others. Less often, they warn of traffic jams on the bridge caused by suicides or attempts. What are we known for more than our tolerance and determination to pursue our own paths, except, perhaps, for our beautiful but lethal Golden Gate Bridge?

Acknowledgments

Thanks to Charlotte Ross, Richard Seiden, Lonny Shavelson, Myra Morrant, Donna Allison, and the staff of the San Francisco Public Library.

References

Chidester, David. 1988. *Salvation and Suicide: An Interpretation of Jim Jones, the Peoples Temple, and Jonestown*. Bloomington: Indiana University Press.

Remarks on the Poetic Transformation of San Francisco

by James Brook

IN HISTORICAL CITIES, built on the sediment of countless generations, you could use the richness of the past to criticize the misery of the present. In a city such as Paris or London you could, until recently, question the streets and buildings and the faces in the crowd about fundamental things and expect a response. A poetic relationship to the city was possible in part because the past—with all its contradictions and conflicts—was embedded in the place. Memory, however deeply buried, informed the contemporary experience of the city: the stuff of the city was packed with explosive charges composed of hope, desire, and frustration. When ignited, objects gave off a flash of recognition and poetry. In these old cities Surrealism—a late but the most radical manifestation of Romanticism—could function as a blasting cap. A golden age could suddenly be recaptured in a moment's confrontation with an object found in a flea market or glimpsed in a shop window. Poetry could be found in a passing stranger's gaze, a forgotten statue, or an uncanny sequence of events. You could "read" traces of subjectivity in the stones and in the air.

Young cities like San Francisco and most American cities have not just a different history but a different kind of history. They have no "romantic *ruins*" (Breton 1969), no abandoned castles, few neighborhoods left unimproved (even in poverty and neglect slums once allowed life to go on without surveillance by power). Little in the built environment of American cities predates the nineteenth century—urban archeologists can't uncover deeply buried secrets. As the United States expanded westward, cities were laid out and constructed as needed—without a period of "organic" growth from, say, Greek or Roman beginnings and without a prehistory related to the land and ancient patterns of use and settlement. (On this continent, only Indian villages like those still in existence in Hopi Land had the long run-ups to history resembling European towns.)

American cities seem to come out of nowhere—to be the instantaneous products of intersecting sums of money and goods bound for market. These are cities of relentless development and disruption and, in their growth and change, more given to destroying and rebuilding themselves than expanding by accretion and reuse. American cities are always new—they are not the kind of place where poetic energy could easily gain a foothold. In America the *noir* vision—the gothic of capitalism—developed and flourished. In lieu of the call-and-response of desire and the play of *correspondances* between psyche and object, there were the fearsome projections of paranoia, the madness of the white man as he took possession of the "empty" continent. The equivalent of the Surrealist "unwonted" (*l'insolite*) in America would be the Americans themselves—lost in the landscape they conquered—and not the dressmaker's dummy or the beautiful woman a European poet might have glimpsed on a street corner. Here the poetic spirit is in constant conflict with the *noir* sensibility of a Jim Thompson, a James M. Cain, or San Francisco's own Dashiell Hammett.

San Francisco, with its radical instabilities—rapid changes of fortune in a constantly shifting population renting quarters on very shaky ground—is fertile ground for the *noir*, as it is exemplified in *The Maltese Falcon*, the paranoid realist portrait of the city. The difficulty lies in finding or creating conditions "stirring human sensibilities" (Breton 1969) in a less cynical and gloomy direction.

Nicolas Calas, a Greek Surrealist in exile who settled in New York City during World War II, noted in *Confound the Wise* (1942), that "Without *encounters*, there would be no *surprise*, and without *surprise*, poetry cannot be brought into the world." Calas was familiar with several old European cities—Paris, Athens, and Lisbon, among them—formed by the countless lives of their inhabitants, builders, destroyers, and invaders. With a clairvoyant eye he discerned the subtle determinants of poetry-in-the-world in the twists and turns of garden paths, elevator cages, shop windows, billboards, the grandeurs and mistakes of architecture, the songs of the people (back when they had songs and sang them), streets of ill repute. . . . Even a line of verse would do, in a pinch. The individual and collective poetry of the city was available to any "reader" who happened by.

Calas devotes the final chapter, "The Evil Eye," to his response to New York, a city unlike any other that he had known. New York was even the antithesis of the city as Calas understood it. Endless ledger-like rows and columns of blank windows perforated the skins of featureless skyscrapers, machines for living and working in. Unlike the transformative windows of the Baroque or of a Manet painting, these repetitively punched holes displayed neither the exterior to the inhabitants nor the inhabitants to passersby. Privacy was paramount—in order to hide the empty and impersonal from public scrutiny. Forty years before the advent of the Walkman, Calas observed that "people now carry little windows of noise. 'Why do you go about with a portable radio?' I once asked an intelligent and well educated young girl. 'So as not to hear myself singing when I walk alone.'"

Calas discovers a simulacrum of nature in his first American city: "When describing New York it is easier to call it fantastic than beautiful. . . . New York is a landscape and we admire it as we do the Alps, from a distance." People climb up and work in "mountains," and "they sleep and make love in rooms that are like the caves of the primitives." The city of the machine develops toward the panorama—in its negation of the European city, Calas holds out the hope that this romanticism of the artificial landscape prepares the ground for something new: "How beautiful mountains can be when great fires brighten the precipices and extinguish the stars." The way to New York's poetry led through an intensification of all that contradicted the inherited idea of the city. The project of transformation by the poet—whose job title, in this extended sense, might read "engineer," "filmmaker," "graffiti writer," or "arsonist"—could have no recourse to a nostalgia for the products of another civilization. "I claim that the vision of the poet should be diabolical, that he must have an evil eye if light is to be thrown on images and new forms are to come into existence." It was André Breton who noted (1969) that "The marvelous is not the same in every period." The problem is discovering just what is peculiar to the era we live in.

The newly built environment is refigured as a pre-urban landscape. Calas poses the question of the kind of lives possible in such a setting. He recognizes that the American city was not commensurate with, was not a distortion or failed imitation of, the far older European city. This is important when we look at the fate of cities: if in the last twenty-five years European cities have been rapidly destroyed by what is called Americanization, a process that has been described by both right and left as "degeneration," a similar critique cannot easily be applied to American cities, which have not accumulated centuries of experience, custom, and sentiment. In the critique of the lamentable state of American cities, there can be no appeal to nostalgia for lost traditions and ways of life; our appeal can be only to the future. This should not necessarily excite optimism.

San Francisco makes New York, Boston, and other Eastern cities look ancient. San Francisco is barely 150 years old, but even this figure belies the youth of the city. Burnt to the ground half a dozen times before the 1906 earthquake and fire flattened downtown, San Francisco is a twentieth-century city. Mineral wealth financed the overnight building of San Francisco; there was no city before the discovery of gold in the Sierras. From the beginning, the city has been "under construction" without let-up: natural catastrophe merely cleared the field and accelerated development.

Early on, hills were leveled and the bay shore filled in; lots still under water were surveyed and put up for sale. Vast sand dunes were planted and built on. Ugly speculative and makeshift architecture spread like the tailings of a silver mine. Rough and wonderful adventures were available to all comers—there was cash and all the hazards of freedom from law or custom. Capital, sweat, and cat-astrophe built, destroyed, and rebuilt the city. Today the catastrophe of capital—a disaster that, in a dark moment, could make one long for another great temblor if social revolution fails to set things right—is once again transforming the city's face and character.

Sometimes pretending to the title of Paris of the Pacific, other times claim-ing to be the Wall Street of the West, San Francisco is trapped in self-delusion, believing in its own boosterism. As high-rises succeed high-rises in the financial district, and as the financial district extends to the South of Market, China Basin, and Mission Bay, with downtown interests controlling the development of the Army base of the Presidio (a national park-for-profit), the Navy base of Treasure Island, and the old shipyard at Hunters Point, San Francisco is witnessing one of the biggest land grabs of its short life.

Perhaps it's the very newness of the city that encourages San Franciscans to imagine an "Old San Francisco" cobbled together from true stories, half-truths, and outright lies about the Spanish past, the Barbary Coast, sudden reversals of fortune, the life of the prospector, Victoriana, and so forth. When a newly restored print of Alfred Hitchcock's Vertigo (1957) showed at the Castro Theater last year, the audience paid reverential attention to the travelogue of the "Old San Francisco" enclosed within the San Francisco of the 1950s that constitutes the first half of the film; few seemed to know or care that most of the buildings used to evoke the mythical past were erected in the early twentieth century.

In his 1982 film, Sunless, Chris Marker reflects on the complicated relation-ships between memory, time, historical event, and geography as well as the difficul-ties involved in speaking of these things or depicting them. The narrator of Sunless quotes from a traveler's letter: "He wrote me that only one film was capable of por-traying impossible memory, insane memory: Vertigo." As the voice-over narrates the traveler's "pilgrimage to all the film's locations," the narration is accompanied by shots from *Vertigo*, which alternate with contemporary footage of the same locations from the same points of view. Marker rewrites Hitchcock even as he follows in his footsteps—or as his camera follows Hitchcock's. The murder mystery is radically rewritten to reveal a story of desire attempting to triumph over time. The geography of the city is reduced to an absolute moment of yearning and loss, of memory filling all of space: "Vertigo of space and reality stands for the vertigo of time," with the swirl in Madeleine's hair symbolizing "the spiral of time." The myth of the city in *Vertigo* is made true through being made more mythic. Scotty, "as time's fool of love, finding it impossible to live with a memory without falsifying it," invents "a double for Madeleine in another dimension of time, a zone that would belong only to him, and from which he could decipher the indecipherable story that had begun at the Golden Gate, when he had pulled Madeleine out San Francisco Bay, when he had saved her from death before casting her back to death. Or was it the other way around?" But the truth of the myth also obliterates the reality of the city: neither *Vertigo* nor its rewriting in *Sunless* relates to San Francisco except as a series of fetish images connected to a private ritual.

A little later in *Sunless* the narrator outlines the plot and themes of a science-fiction film that will never be produced. In it, a being from the year 4001—an era when the human brain will have evolved to its full capacities and total recall will be the norm—goes back to our period to rescue us, like a "Che Guevara" of chronology, because we suffer from "infirmities of time," and we struggle to remember and to commemorate by means of a piece of music or a portrait of a beloved face. The future overfull of memory and the past impoverished of it. The narration of this unmade film (like an unmade bed at the far end of another, earlier film, *La Jetée*) accompanies another travelogue of San Francisco, this one of the contemporary city. The rapid series of shots is empty, without atmosphere: Montgomery Street downtown, the "banker's heart" sculpture in front of the Bank of America building, a used-car lot with the Civic Center in the background, a view of North Beach and the Golden Gate Bridge from the top of Coit Tower. The images are empty of imagination and desire: without its memories, the city is a dead place, and this has "something to do with unhappiness and memory."

Cities have had their poets whose images have changed our experience of these places. But San Francisco, home and haven to many poets, has not been fortunate in poets who delve into its urban life. If Calas is right that "culture has always developed where gold lies" and that "Poets today, as of old, run away from goldless lands," then only a peculiar dialectic can explain why the poets of San Francisco turn their backs on the city. San Francisco has never really had a poet of its streets. There's no Walt Whitman of its epic founding, no Charles Baudelaire of its continual transformation, no Vladimir Mayakovsky of its bay-spanning bridges, no André Breton of its secret desires, no Frank O'Hara of its conversation and broken hearts, no Thomas De Quincey of its labyrinths and penury, not even a Raymond Chandler of the dark precincts of its soul.

The city has been hospitable to poets—their presence has even contributed an aura of popular and rebellious culture to the image of San Francisco. Turn-of-the-century poets like George Sterling rhapsodized "the cool grey city of love" (as he viewed it from Carmel). But they did not write well or memorably. Better poets, who were technically and culturally equipped for the task, came later, but most of these had other subjects. Their writing was often anti-urban, avoiding the city as subject. They wrote of mental states and personal relationships, the beauties of nature (or, at least, the attractions of the parks system), and the formal properties of writing itself. In any case, if there was poetry in the city, the poets rarely found it, at least at the level of recognizable description.

No lack of knowledge or failure of technique explains why Kenneth Rexroth, for example, did not write his best poetry about a city with whose cultural and political life he was so passionately involved. (It was largely through Rexroth's efforts that San Francisco became a destination for poets after World War II.) But in his poetry Rexroth was more at home camping out with a woman in the Sierras than, say, imitating a *flâneur* in the Paris of the Pacific. Is this because he had already seen the Paris of the Atlantic? And New York and Chicago? Speaking in general terms, Rexroth observed that "A lot of western migration was in the first place to get away from the destructiveness of the big metropoles and then to find new spiritual roots." (Rexroth 1971) (It's a pity that Allen Ginsberg didn't call San Francisco home—more urban in consciousness than most local poets, *he* could have been its poet "under the shadow of the mad locomotive riverbank sunset Frisco tincan evening sitdown vision." ("Sunflower Sutra" in Ginsberg 1984))

On the other hand, while San Francisco poets tend to look away from the city or admire it from afar—as a landscape or panorama—some have evoked the paranoid genius loci. Jack Spicer's parodic verse apparatuses and Philip Lamantia's gothic Surrealist lyrics read like emanations from the civic soul in distress. Spicer despairingly defaces the torn-up map of the center of town: "When they number their blocks they mean business." ("For Nemmie" in Spicer 1975) Lamantia names the paranoid landscape as he addresses the ghosts of the murdered Indians and insurrectionaries and the extinct flora and fauna that haunt the vertical and horizontal planes of concrete and glass. With Poe-like hypersensitivity, Lamantia notates the shudder of vice: "On the pillars of nicotine/the word *pleasure* is erased by a dog's tongue." ("Hermetic Bird" in Lamantia 1997) (The gothic Surrealist tendency can also be seen in Bruce Conner's work with its air of violence, rot, and decay, some of it "inspired by the slow annihilation of the Victorian houses in Western Addition black community." (Solnit 1990) The same tendency emerges much later in the circle around V. Vale and his *Search & Destroy* and *Re/Search* magazines. Beginning in the 1950s, Surrealism—as method and as ideology lending support to a diffuse mysticism—was central to San Francisco artists and poets like Jess, Robert Duncan, Wally Hedrick, Bob Kaufman, and others.)

Whereas Lamantia marks the no-man's-land between the *noir* and the poetic impulses, the extreme literary representation of the paranoid landscape of San Francisco is Dashiell Hammett's *The Maltese Falcon*. Here the separation between the *noir* and the poetic is absolute: all desire is alienated and projected in this tale of a homophobic and misogynist detective who gets mixed up with a gang of homosexuals and a double-crossing woman. Avid of every deadly sin, the thieves and the private eye roam over the downtown grid as if it were a chessboard. San Francisco is an empty space where they can play their game, a game that mimics the unbridled capitalism that ran roughshod over the city of the late 1920s. Names and addresses are just labels—the look and feel of the city are never described, the city is drained of all affect. *The Maltese Falcon* provides the reader with precise directions—you know where a character turned left and how far he walked before hailing a cab, but you never see the city streets, the exteriors of buildings, or the faces in the crowd. The city is dead, invisible, unmagnetic. In fact, to give some feeling for the site of the action, one edition of *The Maltese Falcon* was illustrated with period photographs of downtown. (Hammett 1984) While these succeed in filling in the blanks in description, they add a falsely nostalgic patina to an era that was as hard and ruthless as they come.

In its depiction of the manic activity of the prideful, envious, wrathful, slothful, avaricious, gluttonous, and lustful, *The Maltese Falcon* is like a photographic negative of the classic Surrealist narratives of desire in the city, André Breton's *Nadja* and Louis Aragon's *Paris Peasant*. *Paris Peasant* was published in 1926, *Nadja* in 1928, which makes them roughly coeval with *The Maltese Falcon*. But what a world of difference between Hammett's San Francisco and the Surrealists' Paris! Reading Breton and Aragon, we leave behind the petty inferno of the criminal world, to be swept into a poet's laboratory where the routine cynicism of economic man is subjected to destructive testing.

In *Nadja* and *Paris Peasant* layers of urban paranoia are peeled back to reveal the kernel of desire within mad projections and sudden, overwhelming fears: "Beauty will be CONVULSIVE or it will not be at all." (Breton 1960) The mute hostility of blank walls and anonymous crowds gives way to a kind of psychic magnetism: "Reality is the apparent absence of contradiction. The marvellous is the eruption of contradiction within the real." (Aragon 1994) Objects and places speak to the wanderers who have deciphered their languages: "I am not talking about your poems." (Aragon) But such objects, places, wanderers, and languages were less possible in San Francisco than they were in Paris. The San Francisco of 1928 was a city too naked and raw for the Surrealism of the Paris of 1928. In any case, with only a limited notion of construction, Surrealism was more successful at "reading" the city than at "writing" it.

Poetry in San Francisco cannot be realized through the transposition of the Surrealist method to inhospitable terrain, however much we treasure the passions that Surrealism stirred up in its place and time: "In our mouths/Their mouths/There is/Hope." ("Surrealism" in Spicer 1975) San Francisco poets are faced with inventing a poetry of the city without recourse to the explosive "finds" (*trouvailles*) that were strewn about Paris or Lisbon once upon a time.

In the years since World War II the poetic impulse, verse aside, has made its presence felt in many different ways in San Francisco. Many elements combined to make San Francisco a congenial place for experimentation. There were the Italian anarchist milieu, the black Fillmore jazz scene, and the none-too-controlled waterfront. There was San Francisco's cultural and geographical distance from New York, which gave artists and writers less recognition but more freedom to do as they pleased. There was the GI Bill, which financed many an education on and off campus. (Solnit 1990) And there was cheap rent. The poetic tended to surface in new ways of living—like the early beat, Haight-Ashbury, and punk scenes in the periods before marketing and ideological fixation turned them into consumables.

The poetic impulse has also propelled the body impolitic to riot, spontaneous demonstration, and what you could call "public close reading of the text." Here are a few examples:

In May 1979 Dan White, the embittered right-wing and homophobic assassin of Mayor George Moscone and Supervisor Harvey Milk ("The Mayor of Castro Street"), was found guilty of manslaughter by reason of "diminished capacity" and sentenced to less than eight years in prison. This light sentence set off a long night of rioting with pitched battles between mostly gay rioters and the police. Over a dozen police cars were burned to illuminate the proceedings. More than a few participants attended the evening's revels at the Civic Center, whose Beaux Arts security architecture failed to deter rioters, and the Hall of Injustice just for the hell of it.

In January 1991, as the bombs began to fall on Iraq, thousands of people spontaneously gathered to run through the city streets to express their rage in "unofficial demonstrations" against the Gulf War. Without leaders, program, or organization to encumber and direct them into "constructive channels," these demonstrations were, for a few precious days and nights, the life of the city. You could breathe again after years of the Yuppie Rampant under Presidents Reagan and Bush. (Later on, the demonstrators were persuaded to join normal, orderly, boring, and ineffectual weekend marches along a deserted Market Street for the benefit of the media—which weren't interested in broadcasting images of opposition to the war.)

At rush hour on the last Friday of every month hundreds or thousands of bicyclists gather downtown to ride—"an organized coincidence" without leaders, organization, program, route, or political demands—through the automobile-choked city under the banner of Critical Mass. Critical Mass is a sort of critique on two wheels—ideal melding of critical thinking and useful technology!—of how San Francisco has been sacrificed to the circulation of the automobile. Although in constant danger of becoming just another civic event or sanctioned demonstration—like the Gay Pride Parade or Carnaval—Critical Mass's disruption of the daily grind and the homeward commute continues to open up space for the public imagination.

And then there is the writing on the wall: dominated by corporate messaging, the media landscape of San Francisco has long been challenged by the interventions of the Billboard Liberation Front, graffiti artists, and others who show what can be done with a little forethought, cheap materials, and adventurous friends. Not long ago, an unnamed group ruined (improved) a Calvin Klein ad with its trademark emaciated models, by changing the caption from "Just Be" to "Just Buy." And now on the sidewalks of Valencia Street—the current bohemia of young professionals— a spray-painted stencil depicts a woman with flowing hair, full skirt, and upraised whip demanding that we "Discipline the Rich!"

PHOTO CHRIS CARLSSON

Anonymous social critique underfoot on Valencia Street

San Francisco exists—that much is incontestable. And, evidently, there are San Franciscans. But it's not easy to describe or delimit city or citizen. The tourist trail shows one version of San Francisco: following the map to Yerba Buena Center, Powell and Market Streets, Union Square, Civic Center, cable cars, Chinatown, North Beach, Coit Tower, Fisherman's Wharf, Pier 39, Alcatraz Island, and Golden Gate Park, tourists see a Potemkin Village or theme park, a San-Francisco-in-quotation-marks. Strange to say, people who live in San Francisco are not immune to the utopian function of tourist destinations: they cherish the postcard view of the city—it's their dream of the place, how it should be, how it could have been, even if they wouldn't be caught dead wearing a souvenir T-shirt. In fact, workaday San Francisco intersects more and more with tourist San Francisco, with the office towers staffed by suburbanites.

The identity of San Francisco and San Franciscans is not easy to establish without resorting to mere statistical description. Every hour of the day and night there is an exchange of people coming into and leaving the city for all kinds of reasons. There are people who live and work in San Francisco, people who live there and work elsewhere, people who live there and don't work at all, people who work there and live elsewhere, and people who come to the city for cultural activities and the nightlife and to see their friends. Definitions were easier in the Greek city-state, with its rigid class structure, strict hierarchy of rights and duties, and geographical limits. . . .

Does San Francisco extend to Oakland, Berkeley, Marin, and Burlingame? Are the residents of these places San Franciscans? Are residents of San Francisco who work across the bay less a part of the city? What do these groups have in common? Why doesn't all this coming and going result in more fortuitous encounters? Is there a recognizable San Francisco type—as there is a Parisian type or a New Yorker type?

For the first hundred years the city was known for one kind of man: a white immigrant from the East Coast or Europe, unruly and individualistic, a petty bourgeois turned prospector eager to extract riches from the earth or his neighbor. The international thieves and resident detective of *The Maltese Falcon* are late examples of this type—businessmen without constraint of regulation or custom. If this type is disappearing under the waves of immigration from Asia and Central America, so much the better. But perhaps only the specifically European aspects of the type are receding while the interest in getting ahead persists in full force. The Silicon Valley millionaire is usually white and male, but his employees, who are well paid and who have the chance to strike it rich, come in all nationalities and colors (though there is still strong bias against African Americans in the technical jobs).

Calas warns: "Where there is certainty there can be no surprise, sensibility is not aroused, and poetic shock can not be reproduced." The surveyor's grid, the urban planner's charts, the architect's plans, and the banker's calculations influence the shape of the city and the range and quality of experience. In our lived environments we see the results of the application of the logic of capitalist development: we cease wondering at the strange combination of sociological diversity and geographical separation that limits our interactions with one another. The bourgeois ordering of space—from local fantasies of Haussmann's Paris to the current mania for security architecture and entertainment complexes—produces monotony along with its (fortunately) unsuccessful attempts to impose social order.

Fortuitous encounters are necessary to poetry: free association is its raw material, whether on the street or in the psyche. The poetic encounter undermines bourgeois order—and stimulates the creation of new kinds of order, subjectively determined and acknowledged as such.

All cities are more or less segregated—that's the history of class society. But San Francisco has to be in the vanguard of separation by ethnicity, class, income, profession, family type, sexuality, age, style of dress, and other markers; even when people rub shoulders, their differences almost ensure that interaction will be perfunctory and asocial. "Diversity" has been folded into the requirements of development, and fortuitous encounters grow ever more rare, with crime and commerce now being the most effective ways of bringing dissimilar people together. Responding to economic and social pressures, neighborhoods tend toward homogeneity, and few public accommodations serve a demographically mixed clientele. This ever more nuanced separation is not simply the by-product of anonymous market forces: our betters in the corporate boardrooms are not geniuses of strategy, but they do have their vision of the city and the will and means to impose it with a measure of success.

Before World War II, San Francisco was a white city. That began to change when the shipyards and other industries began to attract large numbers of African Americans, swelling the black population from the low thousands to the tens of thousands. As late as 1966, when the Civil Rights movement was already well advanced, the San Francisco Planning and Urban Renewal Association (SPUR), a downtown business front still very much in operation, was not embarrassed to combine worship of high-tech "clean" industry with fascist social "selection" in its *Prologue for Action*:

> If San Francisco decides to compete effectively with other cities for new "clean" industries and new corporate power, its population will move closer to standard White Anglo-Saxon Protestant characteristics. As automation increases, the need of unskilled labor will decrease. Economically and socially, the population will tend to range from lower middle-class to lower upper-class. . . .

> Selection of a population's composition might be undemocratic. Influence on it, however, is legal and desirable for the health of the city. A workable though changing balance of economic levels, social types, age levels, and other factors must be maintained. Influence on these factors should be exerted in many ways—for example, changing the quality of housing, schools, and job opportunities. (Quoted in Hartman 1984)

Clearly, SPUR is the spiritual if not the genetic heir of the white settlers of nineteenth-century San Francisco. In the past thirty years the planners got most of what they wanted. Manufacturing and port-related jobs are gone, and the old working-class culture has gone with it. Housing has largely been gentrified—even well-paid professionals have a difficult time finding an affordable home or apartment. While unskilled labor still exists, the nature of the unskilled work has changed—as have the complexions of the people laboring on construction sites, cleaning homes, taking care of the white children, sweeping up in offices, flipping burgers in fast-food restaurants, or sewing behind the doors of sweatshops. If the planners did not succeed in keeping people of color out of the city, it was because they could not control immigration legislation and the evolution of the global economy. But without two "middle-class" incomes, poorer families live in crowded apartments in dangerous and neglected areas of the city—or they move south to Daly City or across the bay to Oakland.

The second time I came to San Francisco was for a demonstration against the Vietnam War. Chased down Market Street by the riot police, I thrilled to the freedom of the city. The air was different from any other that I had ever breathed, and not because of tear-gas. That feeling of liberty eventually brought me to live in San Francisco. Thirty years later the police are a little better behaved, while the freedom of the city is much diminished. The contrarian streak in San Francisco still resists the corporate and bureaucratic agenda, the programmed slide toward uniformity of population and cityscape. But its victories have been limited: battles have been won, but the war is being lost. And yet. Given that the city is tending toward uniformity—accepting of the imposition of a kind of capitalist certainty— we need not succumb to the no-less-false certainty of despair. The impermanence of land, city, and people gives cause for hope. . . . Chance may switch sides and clear the way for the poetic transformation of San Francisco. Who knows? A stock market crash, an earthquake, a popular movement, or some other constellation of forces may lend a hand. Or, perversely, the town could become so dull that boredom itself will provoke a response. The self-destruction of the city may turn out to be the molting of a phoenix.

Acknowledgments

Thanks to Beth Grundvig, Stephen Vincent, Sandra Phillips, Susan Schwartzenberg, Heather Woodward, Nancy Peters, and Chris Carlsson for their criticism and encouragement; special thanks to Bruce Elwell for directing me to Nicolas Calas.

References

Aragon, Louis. 1994. *Paris Peasant*. Translated and with an introduction by Simon Watson Taylor. Boston: Exact Change.

Breton, André. 1960. *Nadja*. Translated by Richard Howard. New York: Grove Press.

Breton, André. 1969. "Manifesto of Surrealism (1924)." In *Manifestoes of Surrealism*. Translated from the French by Richard Seaver and Helen R. Lane. Ann Arbor, MI: University of Michigan Press.

Calas, Nicolas. 1942. *Confound the Wise*. New York: Arrow Editions.

Ginsberg, Allen. 1984. *Collected Poems 1947–1980*. New York: Harper & Row.

Hammett, Dashiell. 1984. *The Maltese Falcon*. San Francisco: North Point Press.

Hartman, Chester. 1984. *The Transformation of San Francisco*. Totowa, NJ: Rowman & Allanheld.

Lamantia, Philip. 1997. *Bed of Sphinxes: New and Selected Poems 1943–1993*. San Francisco: City Lights.

Rexroth, Kenneth. 1971. "Interviews." In *The San Francisco Poets*. Edited by David Meltzer. New York: Ballantine.

Solnit, Rebecca. 1990. *Secret Exhibition: Six California Artists of the Cold War Era*. San Francisco: City Lights.

Spicer, Jack. 1975. *The Collected Books of Jack Spicer*. Edited and with a commentary by Robin Blaser. Los Angeles: Black Sparrow Press.

You Are Here (You Think)
A San Francisco Bus Tour

**by Bernie Lubell, Dean MacCannell,
and Juliet Flower MacCannell**

You think therefore you are.
　　　　—after Descartes

You think where you are not.
　　　　—Jacques Lacan

ONLY A DECADE AGO, places that spent the most money on tourism development were the least popular destinations. People went to what seemed most "authentic." Now, the promoted, constructed tourist sites (Las Vegas and Disneyland, for example) predominate. People are no longer free to choose the "authentic alternative" as every region comes under the sway of corporately modeled tourism.

"You Are Here (You Think)" originated in a chance comment. Lydia Matthews, then Acting Program Director for Headlands Center for the Arts, convened Headlands artists to ask for new ideas for a series of lectures and workshops on the topic of cities. Instead of proposing another event discussing cities out in the bucolic surroundings of the Marin Headlands, we suggested taking people back to the city on a bus for an irreverent tour that would challenge and analyze tourism even as we visited sites normally not found on the tourist map. Our remark was made in the spirit of the free flow of jokes and ideas that marked a delightful evening. Imagine our surprise when Lydia called a few weeks later saying she had arranged for rental of a Gray Line bus and driver and asked us to pick a date for our "tour."

Tourism has unconsciously shaped our ways of experiencing cities, even when we are not officially on tour. We picture the city as it is on tourist maps and postcards. Could a tour allow tourists to realize San Francisco not as given by corporate tourism but for themselves? Our aim was to get inside the original human connections that inspired the touristic quest, to go beyond the paradox of constructed experience by engaging the consumer in the constructions consumed.

We started out with little more than a list of unconventional sights and an odd ordering. The fifty places on the bus were filled almost immediately by members of Headlands Center, residents of Marin County who had never seen much of San Francisco beyond the Civic Center. We had purposely avoided telling our friends to come so that we would have a real test of our tour. There was one "real" tourist from Israel who had read about the tour in the *Guardian*; he was told it was sold out, but came anyway. Fortunately, there was a cancellation. A few artists were timely enough to make reservations, and managed to get on board.

Before the tour, we asked our tourists to make a metaphor of the city. Afterwards, we asked for a second metaphor. We gave them blank notebooks as guidebooks; a blank postcard on which to create an attraction; a felt-tip pen and a sheet of suggestive words they could paste into their books and cards. We also gave them each a bottle of water. Except for the water, this experimental model for experiencing the city was not organized around bits assembled for easy consumption.

We wanted to reconnect the tourist quest to the fundamental human desire to see and know something else, resisting the conventional forms that have grown up around that desire, over-organizing and killing it.

Our bus circled the city, sliding by the most commercialized tourist sites— Fisherman's Wharf, Pier 39, and Ghirardelli Square—pointing out their touristic conversion from serious work sites to sites of commodified leisure. We traversed the nearly deserted Financial District (on a Sunday), noting the resemblance of this ultra-urban site to natural landscapes of canyons and gullies replete with migrating falcons. We then went to the first of several "empty spaces": "Psycho Alley," an ugly vacant lot off Market Street, whose grim blank walls had been alleviated by successive efforts of anonymous graffiti artists to beautify them. (The alley's dazzling graffiti have since been painted over.)

Noting the similarity between the commercialized tourist environments at Pier 39 and the new condominiums along the Embarcadero, we motored across the Lefty O'Doul Bridge into the vast emptiness of unused railroad right-of-way south of Mission Creek. A feeling of insecurity often attaches to these empty spaces. Perhaps that is the nonfinancial reason for the rush to urban in-fill; in this case, the Mission Bay project. Yet a certain void is a crucial counterpoint to urbanity: cities are, as Lacan once put it, purely products of human desire. We need to have unplanned, chance blanks or voids inserted in the webs or texts of cityscapes to experience desire anew. No rational grid can prevail forever over the fundamental chaos of human life; its limits should be encountered, not glossed over; its gaps should be filled with the unknown, the imagined. Only emptiness can fill a space with possibility.

The tourists before embarkation

Continuing farther into the *terra incognita* on the AAA tour map of San Francisco, we drove into Bayview–Hunters Point, past the Bayview Opera House, and stopped to visit Cathy Sneed's Prison Garden Project, run by former County Jail inmates. Both sites are community-based efforts to imagine ways of filling "empty spaces" as an alternative to the plans for the same spaces driven by corporate greed. Ironically, the Prison Garden Project is behind and adjacent to a Foodland supermarket.

No tour would be complete without a "shopping stop." We acknowledged the inseparability of tourism and commerce as we paused at Good Vibrations, a woman-run, family-style sex emporium. As a contrast to all forms of commerce we disembarked at Golden Gate Park and watched the bus drive off while we strolled across the polo fields. In this "thinking wild" exercise, we backed our tourists onto an unusual group of shallow pools with no signs to mark the site, and then marveled at the imaginative suggestions they made about where we were.

Our last stop was at the Palace of the Legion of Honor, where we discussed themes of authenticity, public art, and the relationship of life and death.

Addressing the "Tourists": Before You Get on the Bus

Before getting on the bus at Marin Headlands on the morning of July, 10, 1994, the three of us in the role of tour guides addressed a few remarks to our would-be metatourists.

Bernie Lubell: I guess I am fundamentally a city boy, so I naturally began thinking about this tour by thinking about cities in general. Cities are repositories of memories. They are a mixed nostalgia for the not-yet and never-was, a desire for the opportunity of youth. The streets fan out in a pattern of paths and opportunities for chance discoveries, returns and redundancies, strange encounters and accidents. You might turn a corner and confront yourself. Italo Calvino says that cities are full of "images of things which mean other things." They are the traded tales that constitute memory and desire.

Maybe I would be less romantic about them if I were not a city person. But still, I think cities were the beginning because cities are about our need for each other. Historians say that first we were agrarian and that farms created the wealth that built the cities. I say, "No way." First, we needed each other, and then we built the cities and said, "Hey, we've got to eat!" Of course, they may have looked like warrens of caves, but human needs must have been somewhat the same.

There is always a conflict between a city and the individual, and yet the city is where you can find yourself. Not all cities are equal in this regard. I came to San Francisco because it is especially open and tolerant and easy. Whatever I wanted to be I might be, here. It must be something like the feelings of the '49ers when they arrived looking for gold. And the speculation of the Gold Rush has become the cliché of self-actualization, a New Age Rush, if you will.

The conflict of all those individuals and the need for order often make great cities miserable places. Cities are where the real fundamental forces of the universe are: chaos, irony, and paradox. Which is just another way of saying that great cities are where great people are.

Juliet Flower MacCannell: Through boom and bust San Francisco has kept speculating—and dreaming. Raised instantly, it has been repeatedly razed—and raised again. Whenever disaster strikes the City, there is immediate, unanimous agreement to rebuild it. Why is there so much libidinal investment in this town?

Sartre said that for the European, "city" means the "past"—Rome the eternal—but, in America, it stands for "what is yet to come." The "to come" appears often in our shaky town: it needs love in order to exist at all. After the 1906 quake, H. G. Wells said, "Nowhere is there any doubt but that San Francisco will rise again, bigger, better and after the very briefest of intervals."

A new formation of the human subject is possible here in San Francisco. Sartre called it an Asian city. Ferlinghetti said San Francisco doesn't look like America when you come upon it—it looks like "Tunis seen from the sea." But, no mere Mediterranean look-alike, San Francisco is really, he continues, the place where "the West comes to an end." That is more than an interesting phrase. Although the Ohlone Indians were here first, the "official" history of San Francisco usually begins with the Western advent—the conquistadores and the Spanish missions, even though Mission Dolores was feckless and the soldiers posted here inept.

San Francisco was not much of an outpost for the Church or the military. What's more, nobody could adequately farm its sand dunes. So the three main self-concepts of what it meant to be a male citizen of the Western world—Soldier, Priest, Farmer—never took real root here. San Francisco had other origins, the heart and liberal mind perhaps, than the spirit of conquest and conversion inherent in these three.

The City, at least, began with a love story, with William Richardson, a skilled English whaling man, seeing what was then a backwater outpost of Mexico—a hilly, treeless, sandy place—and falling for its beauty like the proverbial "ton of adobes" even before he fell for the Mexican commandant's daughter. Marrying her, he became a citizen of Mexico, Don Guillermo Antonio Richardson, and built the first civilian house on what is now Grant Avenue in his Yerba Buena (San Francisco). Only then did San Francisco really have its start as a dwelling place, something more than a colonial outpost.

In those sands, was it Robinson Crusoe's desert isle that Richardson saw?

The pursuit of happiness, more than the pursuit of power and prestige, had staked its claims here, bracketed by the Romantic era, the time of democratic revolutions and colonial revolts (Mexico's independence redistributed Church lands in California). There was a new openness to possibilities, new forces in government, new forms of life.

I think there is another source for the libidinal charge around San Francisco. Perhaps the sudden fulfillment of one of Western man's oldest dreams—gold—

Shooting spree

altered a basic coordinate of human desire. Wealth was created in a way that mirrored the earliest origins of human society—the direct exploitation of the earth (or the Mother)—without having to go through the usual layers of human exploitation that characterize life in civil society. Opportunism was always here, of course. Sam Brannan, who sold equipment to miners, and Levi Strauss were among the biggest winners in the '49er "free-for-all."

Still, for a moment, everyone seemed to be distracted from trying to extract wealth directly from their fellow humans. With the Big Four—Hopkins, Huntington, Stanford, and Crocker—the railroad barons who imported Chinese labor, this form of abuse arrived soon enough. But for a brief time, it was not the dominant tone.

The dizzying ecstasy of that successful contact with the origin may have liberated the imagination to begin dreaming less of a new frontier than of its possible end, of starting off on a new footing—psychologically, if nothing else. I agree with Ferlinghetti: San Francisco is, in every sense, where "the West comes to an end."

Of course, maybe we just love San Francisco because it disappears before our eyes at least once a day under the fog, and reappears—alluring, light and mysterious.

Dean MacCannell: My assignment is to talk about the "nature of the touristic act" and then to explain some things we are going to do, hopefully disruptive of the usual tourist experience. I want to generate some involvement with the characteristics of tourist involvement. We have tried to invert the usual structure of the tour, but we cannot completely escape its determinisms. We are about to make you tourists in your own city. Tourists and locals stand to one another in a relation of mutual visibility and isolation—they can't really make contact through this thick pane of sound-proof glass. You may feel slightly paranoid and divided internally when the tourists look up at you trapped in the bus. "Hey, I'm not really a tourist, I live here."

What happens on the tour is the production of a common narrative of the city; the manufacture of collective experience. We will discover that this experience is not of San Francisco. This is where our theme of emptiness begins to emerge as necessary to any understanding of the city that is based on the tour.

We are not going to see San Francisco. Instead, we are going to see a string of sights and attractions: the Bridge, the Wharf, the Vista Point, the Park, the Museum, etc. These are all merely parts of San Francisco, an unstated San Francisco, which can only exist in the empty spaces or gaps between them. Of course, these spaces are not truly empty. They are filled with things that are not officially designated as worthy of the tourists' attention.

Ask yourself, "What kinds of things are tourist attractions?" Napoleon's hat is a tourist attraction, and so are the Grand Canyon, the Hope Diamond, and the ovens at Dachau. Roy Rogers' stuffed horse, Trigger, is a tourist attraction. There is nothing generic about tourist attractions. Anything can be one. But the one thing they all have in common is they are all marked as such. Tourist attractions have labels on them, they have brass plaques on them, they have entries in guidebooks. They have spiels coming out of the mouths of tour guides (like us) on tour buses.

So between your consciousness (as tourist) and the attraction, there is this mediating thing, the marker. A marker stands between you and the attraction just as the attraction stands between you and San Francisco. There is no San Francisco out there except for the tour-narratives that string attractions together. As tourists, our relationship to the thing we come to see is doubly mediated.

The markers that constitute the tourist experience take two very different forms. One is site specific—it cannot be said about any other place. The other is a generic comment one could make about almost anything: "The Golden Gate Bridge needs to be maintained and therefore gets repainted every four years." (This was actually said to us on the Gray Line Tour we took in preparation for this tour.) That could be said about any bridge. It is a kind of marker designed to separate you from the Golden Gate Bridge as a specific object.

The point to generic markers is to send the tourist back home self-satisfied and content. It is reassuring that you already possess everything you needed to know about San Francisco: the bridges there need to be painted, there are traffic jams at rush hour, etc. The tourist is encouraged to retreat into his or her own ego and hometown, proud of their self-sufficiency without any real need for "San Francisco."

Site-specific markers, on the other hand, might disrupt you, put you beside yourself, and engage you in some kind of relationship to the place. This alternative way of marking emphasizes the specificity of place and origins, confronts possible alternative ways it could have evolved, and does not avoid irony.

On this tour, we are going to be re-marking San Francisco. But we don't want to be alone in this act. So that's why we have passed out some materials.

You have nouns, verbs, and adverbs on a sheet in your packet. These words are purposefully designed not to be like generic tourist language. Tourist words are: "It's the original," "It's typical," "It's authentic, "It was the first," "It was the longest. . . ." Tourist language returns you to the self-sufficiency of your ego: all egos want to be original, autonomous, and authentic. We are encouraging you to build some markers around these nontouristic nouns, verbs, and adverbs. Go ahead and paste them into your book and write some stuff around them about the things you see.

Be critical of the things that we do and say on this tour. Mark our oversights and missed opportunities or something that isn't there yet or something that used to be there. Think of yourselves as responsible for the creation of a new brass plaque—or the destruction of an old one.

Last Stop: The Palace of the Legion of Honor

Bernie: If this were a normal tour, you'd be taken to an open art museum. But this closed one has a swirl of controversies that summarize much of the tour. Here is a real work site that converts the entire museum into a back region. The construction work, which has closed the Palace of the Legion of Honor for seismic upgrading and remodeling, has exposed the underbelly of the Palace.

The Palace of the Legion of Honor was a gift of Alma de Brettville Spreckels in 1922. Conceived as a three-quarter-size replica of the Palais de la Légion d'Honneur in Paris, it serves as a memorial to the California soldiers killed in World War I. The building is surrounded by wind-swept trees and a golf course on the bluffs overlooking the outermost corner of the Golden Gate. There are views of the Golden Gate Bridge, the Marin Headlands, and the northern part of the city. Below the sheer cliffs are nude beaches, ruined roads, forts—paths created by people in their search for golf and empty space.

When excavation began in the courtyard (beneath Rodin's *Thinker*) some archaeological remains were anticipated, but the extent of the finds was both a surprise and a problem. It seems that the palatial memorial to the dead had been built

Excavations at the Palace of the Legion of Honor

directly atop the graves of paupers from the Gold Rush era. Bodies of gold diggers from all over the world were interred here. These earliest settlers had been buried in the San Francisco Cemetery and were moved to Lincoln Park (the site of the Palace) in the 1870s to make room for the burgeoning city. In 1909 the graves were supposed to have been moved again to Colma to make way for a golf course, but most of the graves were never moved—the markers had simply been kicked over and covered with dirt. When the Palace was built in 1922, its foundation was poured directly on top of the redwood coffins of the city's pioneers. Nude bathers routinely find headstones and markers in the gullies that lead down to China Beach. Every time there is any construction human skeletons appear.

During the retrofit about 800 bodies were recovered, and thousands more remain, some as backfill against the walls of the new museum café. The opportunity for discoveries about life in early San Francisco was immense, and there was even the possibility of identifying some remains. But the rainy season was approaching and further archaeological removal of bodies was consuming time. After months of supporting the archaeology, the coroner suddenly cut it off. Bodies were rushed off to Colma without detailed study, and field notes and photos from the dig were confiscated by the museum. (San Francisco, in its headlong rush to fill all available space with the pursuits of the living, has regularly removed its dead to Colma, a short distance south on the Peninsula. Colma has always had a larger population of dead than living.) To date, only a cursory analysis of the immense store of knowledge has been budgeted for. Fortunately, Richard Barnes, who photographed the excavation, maintained the rights to his work, which he has assembled in a traveling exhibition, "Still Rooms and Excavations." (Barnes interview in *Photo Metro*, Vol. 15:144, 1997)

The museum took the project out of the hands of the archaeologist, even disallowing a private fundraiser suggested by the archaeological team to support a thorough analysis of the findings. Why was this research stopped and the affair covered up? One answer lies in the legal minefield of obligations that the identification of any bodies might lead to.

But, more basically, history holds a different meaning for everyone involved, from the coroner to the museum trustees to the golfers and the archaeologist. And the past was holding up the future—but whose past? Although San Francisco is proud of its mythical past, actual remains keep getting in the way of present pleasures and future needs.

Influential and wealthy families setting out to build memorials to themselves faced wildly escalating costs brought on by the dead. If these had been the bodies of the wealthy with important descendants, would they have been treated differently?

We like to think we revere the past, but this has always been a city of speculation, eyes set firmly on the future. This new rush to ship off the bodies mirrors the original disinterment and successive cover-ups of 1909—when the bodies weren't moved—and the construction of the museum on top of their coffins in 1922.

There is even more death around this peaceful hillside. Across the road, tastefully hidden below a corner of the parking circle in the sweep of a 270-degree turn with vistas of the ocean to distract your vision, is a poignant Holocaust memorial by George Segal. "Oh yes," people say, "I was there but I couldn't find the memorial."

The timing for our trip to the Palace could not have been better (or worse?): it happened that the City Art Commission proposed to install a Richard Serra sculpture of massive steel plates at the focus of the plaza directly across from the museum. Serra's heavy steel plates have accidentally killed workers who did not follow directions during installation. But the most interesting questions arising from Serra's proposal are about the nature of this site as an attraction and what constitutes authentic experience. As soon as his sculpture was commissioned, the public protested that such a work would block or spoil the view. Serra's work was compared to a giant lunch bag. Others likened it to a permanent tour bus. . . . It was "art versus nature" as the attraction.

Kenneth Baker, the *San Francisco Chronicle* art critic, argued that, although the sculpture would conflict with our unconscious romantic views, it would force us to be really here and now and to wake up to a true experience of place and time, which the view was supposed to provide in the first place, an experience that people "vainly try to seize with a camera." The conflict was, however, soon resolved. Mindful of a similar controversy in New York City, Serra angrily withdrew his proposal, but the issues of authenticity remain.

[We planned the following "spontaneous" argument to mark the place of controversy just before we reboarded the bus:

—This huge steel thing is going to block my view.

—It's really not that big—just stand on the view side.

—It's not its physical size, it's the kind of thing it is. It's not natural.

—That's the whole point: it's supposed to disrupt your view. You come here looking for a postcard. Something had better disrupt your view.

—Does it have to be ugly to be authentic?

—Is the only really authentic experience of place a nostalgic one for you?

—It would take away from the site as an attraction.

—Bull! Serra's steel plates will become just another attraction.

—You mean the sculpture could become a marker for the view?

—Or even for the controversy.

—So, the Serra sculpture is the perfect marker for the site?

—No, anything sufficiently large would do.

It is possible that the only authentic experience is a transformational one, formed in the crucible of controversy.]

One Year Later

In 1995 we met at Headlands Center for the Arts to discuss that first tour of the City.

Bernie: This tour was an outgrowth of personal relationships to the city as site and as metaphor—but also to this city we have chosen to live in. It was an opportunity to share San Francisco's tolerance of ambiguity, its speculative nature, to sample some surprise and discovery, development and emptiness—to tour San Francisco as a landscape for the imagination.

This city lives on its conflicts. Despite homogenizing forces seeking economic predictability, San Francisco remains fervently ephemeral. It is still a city where individuality and diversity are a premium, where you can find yourself. Aside from the Grateful Dead, I came to San Francisco because there is a fog of opportunities here. And the city has a history of collective imagination. It is the birthplace of the beats, the Mecca for the Summer of Love and many religious cults, and the home of interdisciplinary art.

We come wired with two competing drives: a desire to return to the communal bliss of the Garden of Eden and wanting to get to El Dorado and strike it rich (either materially or spiritually). This city attracts both the community and the individual—and its landscape is the embodiment of our conflicting desires. Because of the physical and social topography of San Francisco, every corner or hill allows for discovery and chance encounters. Suddenly we are drawn outside ourselves by something strange yet familiar. Cities remove us from our natural habitat—yet the experience of landscape and people in the city is a kind of abstraction of our ancestors' primeval experience. On the tour we crossed a field and walked without a path through the woods to come upon the backside of a series of eerie, shallow artificial pools (later revealed to be fly-casting ponds). We hoped to slow people down and bring them to consider mystery and surprise, as though they were hunters: the tunnel as though it were a cave, the exposure of the savannah-like polo fields, the enclosure and loss of direction in the woods and the discovery of possibility in the clearing. As we lose open space and are accosted by blank walls in a city groaning with population our reactions reveal an identity we must make time and emptiness for. A tour can remind us of who we are and what the forces are that shape our environment.

But my biggest surprise was the contribution of the tourists on the bus. We gathered stories from them about public art in the financial district, the club scene South of Market, how "Divisadero" meant the edge of civilization, and their quirky reactions to things we hadn't even noticed.

The isolating drone of the bus engines poses a real challenge to create an interactive tour. Nevertheless, our future tours could incorporate: interviewing other tourists at Fisherman's Wharf, or getting hopelessly lost, having a picnic on Mount Tamalpais with a view of the city as fog, observing street life during rush hour or in the Tenderloin, creating designs to make Market Street into a city park, discussing our sex lives with an expert at Good Vibrations, or planning new messages for the "Jumbotron" at Union Square—exercises to discover and remark the empty spaces. If anything can make the old sites new, it is the possibility of reconnecting them to individual experience—personal and social discoveries through real interactions with places as they are now—as we are now. The tourists would become the tour.

Dean: After the tour Bernie, Juliet, and I went for a walk in the Headlands. Bernie and I began complaining that there were no relatively undiscovered neat things around—no big boulders with garnets in them, no really good blackberry patches that hadn't been picked clean, stuff like that. Not even when we started rambling off the path. Bernie said that it was because in our lifetime we witnessed the filling up of the earth with people to the point that every square inch had been picked over and played out.

I was not ready to concede so much to a mechanical model driven by population density. I was holding on to some grandiose hope that our New Tourism could budge the grid of human experience slightly off its current numbingly predictable coordinates. Can't we try to undo the framework of designations that direct attention exclusively to Fisherman's Wharf, Pier 39, Grant Avenue, and so forth? Can't we discover and describe grounds for new desires in the abundant stuff that is overlooked by sightseers who follow conventional guides? Or, perhaps, if Juliet is correct in her belief that conventional attractions are only there to hide and suppress the unconscious, we might find new grounds for excitement beneath and behind the conventional. Wasn't that the real reason we went under the Palace of the Legion of Honor, and for our excitement when we discovered that human remains were found where they should not have been?

What exactly is it that the minor, personally meaningful site lacks, that the major, official, public attractions, no matter how worn out they may be, can take for granted as a source of enduring power?

We cannot answer this question by appeal to the popularity of public attractions. Except for the pretentious simulacra of attractions manufactured by capital (Pier 39, for example), everything that eventually became an attraction certainly did not start out as one. There was a time when the Mission Dolores was just a mission, when Fisherman's Wharf was just a fisherman's wharf, when Chinatown was just a neighborhood settled by Chinese. All these places were, no doubt, deeply personally meaningful to some people before they became famous attractions. What transformed these places into the centerpieces of the enormous tourist industry of the City of San Francisco?

The key I have been looking for is that the place became something other than a spatial coordinate, something other than a spot of protected intimacy for like-minded persons. It became, in addition, the locus of a human relationship, an urgent desire to share—an intimate connection between one stranger and another through the local object. It is the "You have got to see this, or taste this, or feel this" that is the originary moment. This moment has become depersonalized and automated in conventional attractions—the reason they are at once both powerful and dead—like everything that is wrong with "tradition." But as key, this arrangement of actors and sentiments can be displaced into new things as cause, source, potential. What is required is a simultaneous caring and concern for the other person (host and guest) and for the object that is shared but never possessed.

So, for me, the tour itself becomes the missing key: the buttonholing, imperious, insistent sharing of the overlooked; working but not overworking the transformation between what is personally meaningful and what is eventually powerfully cool. Not to everyone. That is what makes it a new kind of tourism. Open to everyone but closed to all but the few who are tolerant of the sometimes weird moralities that are implied.

Juliet: When we began the tour I wanted the tourists who came not to be allowed simply to "go home again" when it was over. I asked Dean and Bernie if we might end the tour by having the tourists get "lost." I also wanted to show them many empty spaces, and to call their attention to the fog, so they would not be able to "see" in any usual sense of the term. Why these desires? I wanted San Francisco to be, for them, a conspicuously imaginary object.

Normally, a tour's aim is to bring you home again. The route taken is a pursuit, disguised, of being back home. This was confirmed by our experience of the commercial tour we took in preparation for ours: each bit of information imparted by the guide was designed to send visitors straight back to Ohio or Tokyo, delighted that they did not have to deal with San Francisco's earthquakes, high costs, gloomy weather, and homosexuals.

This touristic strategy is ultimately a ruse of patriarchy (and capital), which sends us out of the primary family in pursuit of the world and goods, only, in the end, to return home, to mother. You're supposed to get somewhere, but your final goal is really a return. Desire is forced into a circle. My question was, could a different itinerary break into the spaces forbidden by that circle, and shape our tour as and by a "desire for something else"? Could we find how or where San Francisco was driving toward "something else," remaking and re-marking "pleasure"?

We needed to create a certain tension to break the circle of Freud's pleasure principle: repetition that lowers tension to zero. Besides, the deep politics of circular pleasure are doubtful: Aristotle says pleasure is the leisure to contemplate—freedom from work. Pleasure depended, therefore, on someone else's unpleasure—in Aristotle's case, slave labor. Is this appropriate for a true democracy? The pleasure principle is death-driven, serving and satisfying an abusive power (the *jouissance* of the Other). Phallic modes of enjoyment have had their say, their day, and their play. Can't there be an other *jouissance*?

Since tourists are notably supposed to enjoy a passivity that represents leisure to them, how could we incite them to experience San Francisco's unique tensions and conflicts as pleasurable? To encounter a new object of desire, we would need a different mode of enjoyment in touring.

We directed our tourists toward unmarked, but not pristine, spaces to punctuate networks of meaning with clearings—spots without familiar coordinates. Coming unexpectedly upon a pool divided by several rows of concrete, with slanted sides that ran into the shallow water, our tourists were taken with wonder: they asked "What is it?" and "Is it a swimming pool for people in wheelchairs?" The site was the fly-casting pool; but for our tourists, it was a site for the play of musement.

Our City can be a collaborative work of art, not designed for permanence but for constant reconstruction. This labor implicates everyone and therefore differs from "development" imposed from without. Razed periodically through natural and other means, its daily disappearance in the fog perpetually reshapes it. It has welcomed a community of strangers who have not been pressed out of some melting pot into uniform molds; its habitués need not be blood brothers. And it has perspicuously recognized a feminine factor: one hundred streets are named for women, none of them particularly famous or infamous.

Acknowledgments

We would like to thank Miley Holman, archaeologist in charge of the excavations at the Palace of the Legion of Honor, for taking the time to relate the saga of the experience to us.

Location: San Francisco

by Marina McDougall
and Hope Mitnick

The cinema demands a limited view of things—especially in a location, so the viewpoint must be chosen with the greatest possible concern.

. . . .

The tourist seeks the definitive view, the economic identifying viewpoint with the maximum amount of sensory gratification.
                    —Peter Greenaway, Film Director

Establishing Shot

Throughout the world San Francisco projects a stream of post-card views, a series of identifiable markers that have come to symbolize "San Francisco." It is the work of the media, tourist bureaus, and city planning agencies to shape, reshape, and sometimes undo this collective mental picture of the city. Hundreds of films shot in San Francisco over the last century draw upon a standard repertoire of local imagery. Transforming the city into a set, film production designers have used it as a back lot for the staging of Hollywood fantasies, comedies, dramas, and thrillers. Though San Francisco figures in films like *Barbary Coast, Dark Passage, Lady from Shanghai, Vertigo, The Conversation, Bullitt, What's Up Doc?* and *The Joy Luck Club* in very different ways, the city typically serves as scenographic background to a film's storytelling. Most often this one-dimensional backdrop expresses almost nothing of the place.

The city is also a set in the way that it architecturally packages itself for another pervasive form of entertainment: tourism. Disneyland-style thematization runs rampant in a city that attracts 16 million tourists and business travelers annually. Whole neighborhoods have been destroyed, recreated, and redecorated as tourist destinations by urban planners who use the same strategies as film production designers to transform the city into a collection of picturesque façades.

In seeking an authentic experience of the city, both natives and tourists attempt to penetrate the fakery of the set. What happens to this quest when the façade is indistinguishable from the real thing?

The Props

The Planning Commission and the Redevelopment Agency view the revitalization of San Francisco's neighborhoods as revenue-generating, location-based entertainment. Theme-park thinking has contributed to the touristic success not only of Chinatown, but also of Japantown, North Beach, Pier 39, and Yerba Buena Gardens. Urban design elements including street furniture and landscaping visually identify these thematic zones. New props appear regularly: dark-green Parisian self-cleaning toilets, bilingual "Heart of the Mission" banners, palm trees lining Market

Street and Herb Caen Way, and vintage streetcars imported from other municipalities.

The decorative architectural detail or *chinoiserie* of San Francisco's Chinatown was predominantly planned and designed by non–Asian Americans in cooperation with Chinatown merchants to increase tourism. After the 1906 earthquake destroyed the original Chinese settlement, designers combined Edwardian architecture with the curved eaves, balconies, and lattice work that duplicate stylistic elements of buildings in Beijing. In 1925, street lanterns were installed for San Francisco's Diamond Jubilee celebration, and telephone booths with Chinese characters reading "electric voice house" were installed by Pacific Telephone in the 1960s.

In a notice put out by the Redevelopment Agency seeking design services for streetscape and urban design enhancements along Fillmore Street, the agency described its vision for the future of the neighborhood as "establishing Lower Fillmore Street as a destination dining and entertainment district organized around the theme of the 'Old Fillmore Jazz Preservation District.'" Considering the role of the Redevelopment Agency in leveling the neighborhood in the 1960s and attempting to remove the African American community from the lower Fillmore, these attempts at "revitalization" seem especially ironic.

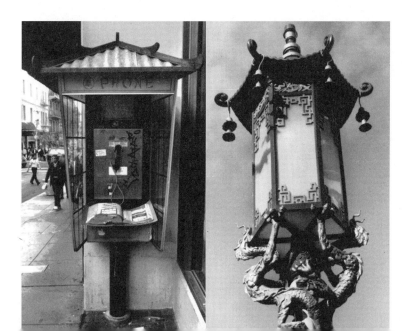

Framing

Designers of visual media gravitate toward the iconic, the symbol-ic, the reductive marker that stands for something larger. When real things are elevated to a mythic realm of signification, some-thing of their history and founding purpose drops away. In the sou-venir shop it is difficult to see the Golden Gate Bridge, Fisherman's Wharf, and Alcatraz as more than mere representations of San Francisco.

No other city in America can offer such breathtaking vistas, such friendly and diverse people, such a colorful cultural history or such familiar locales. . . . In a city that boasts historic cable cars, an exotic Chinatown, lively Fisherman's Wharf, colorful North Beach, eerie Alcatraz, the majestic Golden Gate Bridge and so much more, there is plenty to offer any film project. San Francisco has it all—and it all looks great on film!

—Mayor Willie Brown in *San Francisco Film Production Guide*

A row of file cabinets in the San Francisco Film Commission Office is filled with Polaroids of San Francisco sites. This image bank of cafés, parks, Victorians, churches, and alleys provides a look that saves footwork for the production designer.

According to the Film Commission Office, the city earns over $50 million in film-related revenue annually.

Location Scouting

The San Francisco movie map lays the world's most beautiful movie set at your feet. See the city in a whole new way and become part of your movie memories.

—San Francisco Movie Map

More and more frequently the "behind-the-scenes" of the set blurs into everyday neighborhood activities.

The Mission Dolores cemetery is the setting for the scene in Alfred Hitchcock's *Vertigo* where Madeleine visits the grave of "Carlotta Valdes." According to legend, the wooden grave marker used in filming the movie remained in the cemetery long after the shooting was over. Like Kim Novak's character Madeleine and James Stewart's Scotty, people continue to haunt the cemetery, possessed by a memory—but in this case, the memory of a film. Another layer of vertiginous irony is added, considering that Madeleine only pretends to be haunted by Carlotta in order to fool Scotty and the audience, which is duped along with him.

During the recent shooting of the television show "Nash Bridges," a catering truck was on the set on Grant Avenue in Chinatown. When it came time to serve the crew dinner, elderly residents of the neighborhood lined up behind the gaffers, makeup artists, and supporting actors. The caterers dished out the food and local residents sat down and ate along with the crew.

Off Screen

How does the off-the-beaten-track get on the beaten track? Whole parts of San Francisco remain unframed by Hollywood, thematically uninterpreted by city agencies, and unidentified with the city's cultivated image. Seldom is Mission Street captured on a glossy postcard, or the Sunset chosen as a film location, or the city's dilapidated piers—now slated for retail uses—described in a tourist guidebook. Where tour buses unload daily, places evolve into strange versions of themselves—interpreted, rehearsed, and economically motivated by the needs of one-time visitors.

There are benefits to visual underrepresentation: theme-free zones leave more room for the imagination.

Acknowledgments

Andy Bellows, Robin Eichman, Polly Platt, Phil Keppeler

References

Greenaway, Peter. *The Stairs*. London: Merrell Hobberman, 1994.

MacCannell, Dean. *The Tourist: A New Theory of the Leisure Class*. New York: Schocken, 1989.

Monk, Dave. *The San Francisco Movie Map*. San Francisco: The Reel Map Co., 1996.

San Francisco Film Production Guide. San Francisco: San Francisco Film & Video Arts Commission, Office of the Mayor, 1997.

"S.F. Chases Movie Bucks," *San Francisco Chronicle*, January 1, 1995.

Sorkin, Michael. *Variations on a Theme Park: The New American City and the End of Public Space*. New York: Hill & Wang/Noonday Press, 1992.

Wong, H. K., ed. *San Francisco Chinatown in Picture and Story*. San Francisco: Chinese Chamber of Commerce, 1961.

Yip, Christopher Lee. *San Francisco's Chinatown: An Architectural and Urban History*. San Francisco: University Microfilms Dissertation Information Service, 1985.

Another View of Chinatown
Yun Gee and the
Chinese Revolutionary Artists' Club

by Anthony W. Lee

WE KNOW VERY LITTLE ABOUT the activities of what was surely a remarkable artists' collective in San Francisco's Chinatown, the ambitiously named Chinese Revolutionary Artists' Club. The facts are scant. The Club was formed some time in 1926 and was devoted to "doing [modernist oil] painting that is essentially Chinese," as the San Francisco painter Otis Oldfield tried to explain. The Club's studio was located in a small, cramped room at 150 Wetmore Place, on the western fringe of present-day Chinatown. Its initial membership was comprised entirely of young Chinese immigrant men, most of whom had taken to oils only a few years before, and as far as can be discerned, they took each other, Chinatown's streets, its daily inhabitants, and several selected studio props—mostly objects from Chinatown's stores—as their primary subjects.

Perhaps the Club's most important public event took place in late 1930 or early 1931, when it hosted a much-anticipated reception for the Mexican muralist Diego Rivera. From what we can reconstruct, the reception was intended to be quite inclusive, since it was attended only in small part by the Club's members and in much larger part by Rivera's traveling entourage and doting guests. Judging by surviving accounts, the event must have bordered on the comic. The cramped quarters overflowed with unrecognized people; the food and drink ran out very quickly; and the young men had a difficult time maintaining decorum. Not only was the large Rivera physically uncomfortable on their tiny, square, lacquered stools ("he overflowed on all sides," as a guest happily recorded, which "must have cut him in two"), but he was unable to communicate with his hosts, since none of them spoke Spanish, French, or Russian, his familiar tongues. (Oldfield 1982) To compensate, Rivera is said to have lectured in excited, demonstrative gestures, and he spoke sometimes in Spanish, sometimes in French, hoping that a familiar word or two would find a comprehending ear. He apparently listened patiently to the members' incomprehensible questions. And he concluded by pronouncing in lengthy and convoluted prose, as was his occasional wont, on the artistic and political implications of a mural practice, though none of the young men was likely to undertake anything so artistically ambitious.

It is unclear how Rivera's grand visit affected the Club's members, if at all, but it is a fact that, soon after, they admitted their first and only female member. For its efforts at a new inclusiveness, the Club received a brief write-up in the *San Francisco Examiner*, which praised the "boys" for their "bravery." But the bravery in this case only partially referred to a question of gender parity. The *Examiner* writer was probably also referring to a new manifesto issued by the painters themselves, in which they proclaimed a new determination to establish a "Chinese academy of art, where [we] can spread [our] theories of art to all Chinese students." (Gee n.d.) But the publicity and new resolve to reach out to Chinatown's other students—an ambition perhaps initiated by the socially minded Rivera—apparently came to naught. The Club disbanded sometime in mid-decade, during the city's darkest Depression years. In the late 1930s, some of its former members and fellow travelers continued to have an individual but mostly modest impact on Chinatown's obscure artistic scene; and this consisted chiefly in encouraging a next generation of Asian American painters. By the beginning of the 1940s the Club was largely forgotten; very little of the painters' works survives. As far as we know, the young men themselves held rare, irregular exhibits during the Club's decade or so of existence, and only one among their small number, Yun Gee, ever went on to show his work with any kind of critical acclaim elsewhere. What happened to Mrs. Chan, the only female member, remains a mystery.

This scant history, fragmentary and anecdotal as it is, would seem to argue for the Club's less than prolific (not to say occasionally comic) quality, and provide a rather self-evident set of reasons for its historical obscurity. Simply put, the Club does not seem to

Figure 1. Yun Gee, *The Flute Player* (c. 1928), oil on canvas

have left much of a mark on a larger artistic scene, either in works left behind or in the influence it had on other, more notable painters. Indeed, in the years since its quiet dissolution, it has remained important only as a footnote to readings of the more famous Gee. (Brodsky 1979) And though he hardly merits more than a passing reference in histories of early San Francisco art, Gee (fig. 1) can at least be identified against the backdrop of recognizable exhibitions and works. His more conventional career took him from the Club to San Francisco's mainstream galleries, and then to Paris's famous salons. He had his modest beginnings in a local, hardly noteworthy painting group, or so the history goes.

Yet we do a youthful Gee and the Club's other members an injustice if they are cast aside as just another of those Saturday afternoon painting groups; and we certainly normalize their ambitions if we read them only against the city's regular mill of professional exhibitions and criticism. They did, after all, comprise a nec-essarily segregated Chinese painting collective and held some sort of vision about the possibilities within that marginalized space—visions that may not have accorded with the institutional requirements of the city's nascent dealer-critic sys-tem, visions that were surely rare and fraught with contradiction during a moment of explicit antagonism between insulated Chinese immigrants and their white counterparts, and between the collective nature of an ethnic cultural identifica-tion and the demands of an increasingly consumer-driven art marketplace. But with so little evidence, how can we recover what this collective and its art were working toward? How can we strip away the layers of overpainting at 150 Wetmore Place, to revisit an early Asian American cultural project? How are we to regard the hybrid cultural ambitions of early immigrant painters? And finally— the main subject of this essay—how might we understand their relationship with and desires for the regular subject matter of the paintings themselves—the streets, people, and commodities of the new, spectacular, touristic Chinatown?

Let me say from the outset that I will not be answering these questions with anything resembling conclusiveness, given the elusive nature of the subject. But I think the speculations are worth the effort, especially if we are ever to rethink the antinomies of Chinatown's imagery.

A Glittering Ghetto

The German-born photographer, Arnold Genthe, once made a living with his photographs of Old Chinatown. In the late nineteenth century, as a young man, Genthe regularly descended Nob Hill, sauntered up and down the length of Dupont Street (present-day Grant Avenue), and photographed Old Chinatown's busy inhabitants. He was continually struck by the alien quality of the place and its people, and despite (or perhaps because of) the pervasive abjection, the crowded quarter became for him a space of authentic cultural contact. He was not, of course, alone in believing this; and his pictures, which tried to give photographic detail to the street-level hubbub of the neighborhood, fed the appetites of a like-minded patron class. (Lee 1995) By the turn of the century, the energetic Genthe had accumulated some 200 glass negatives and lantern slides; after Old Chinatown's destruction in 1906, his pictures became perhaps the most complete record of its past life. Selective and deracinated as they were, the pictures were soon assembled, narrativized, and released as a certain kind of documentary effort. They went through three well-received editions and continue today as a historical tableau (an invidious one, to some). They helped to shape the image of Old Chinatown and, just as importantly, provided a basis with which to gauge the development of the new.

The experience of the old quarter lingered with the photographer, and when he visited the rebuilt Chinatown in the 1910s and 1920s, Genthe was not fooled by its new, tourist-friendly glitter. He searched for the remnants of Old Chinatown, details that would confirm the logic of his recently anthologized photographs. He observed:

> On brilliantly illuminated streets, smoothly asphalted, filled with crowds in American clothes, stand imposing bazaars of an architecture that never was, blazing in myriads of electric lights. Costly silk embroideries in gaudy colors, porcelains of florid design, bronzes with hand-made patina, and a host of gay Chinese and Japanese wares which the wise Oriental manufactures for us barbarians, tempt the tourist to enter, while inside cash-registers and department-store manners, replacing abacus and old-time courtesy, indicate up-to-date methods. In one store the Chinese owner even wears a proud tuxedo. Yet even to-day, in these ware-houses of quite modern Oriental art, as well as in the modest store of the small dealer next door, may the patient searcher discover a precious bit of lacquer, a charming piece of brocade.

Genthe is quite specific about the new Chinatown's faults: its fabricated architecture, utterly clean pavement, carefully offered commodities, consumer-driven etiquette. We sometimes think that it is only through our careful hindsight that Chinatown's early artificiality can be named; but as Genthe's testimony will evidence, some contemporaries easily recognized the fabrication and complained that the object-desires of modernity were too transparently organized. They may differ from us in that some of them held the belief that a truly authentic quarter lay beneath the rubble, palimpsestic in the alleys and corners. In Genthe's case, the past was observable in lacquered bits and brocaded pieces—ironically, in the fragments of an earlier consumer culture.

Genthe was not alone in his suspicions of the new Chinatown and its masquerade. Sociologists pointed to the unchanged poverty of its inhabitants; reformists raised fears of illegal drug smuggling; moralists denounced the unseen sex trade; journalists wrote often of the entrenched Tong associations and gang warfare. As late as 1925, a year before the founding of the Chinese Revolutionary Artists' Club, San Francisco police regularly raided the new shops and storage basements in search of opium and imported prostitutes. (Dillon 1962) As much as Chinatown was dominated by glitter ("new pagoda streetlamps!" a journalist wrote excitedly), many contemporaries argued for its garish make-believe. A new, gaudy tourist world was being constructed, true, but the marks of its manufacture were left showing.

This refusal to be deceived is what a celebrated photograph (fig. 2) tries to tell. In a public event that took place sometime around 1919, San Francisco police burned confiscated opium in the middle of rebuilt Chinatown. The event was apparently worth photographing several times and, as this picture informs us,

Figure 2. Burning confiscated opium in Chinatown (c. 1919)

was well attended. To our eyes, the public burning may represent many things— the formal display of civic authority, the ritualized expunging of sin, the vigilant surveillance of Chinatown's streets, the symbolic punishment of vice in the public sphere. Indeed, the photograph tries to capture something of the medieval, penal quality of the event. It insists upon the orderliness, attentiveness, and dapper appearance of the crowd, as if it were assembled for an important public execution. What was being burned was not the body of a particular sinner but the recalcitrant body of underground Chinatown itself. All the more important that a large ring of men was commanded to be in attendance, the better to stand witness to the argument.

The burning and the photographs gave ceremonial form to the claim that the new tourist quarter, like the old, was still ridden with vice, despite the appealing pagoda lamps and colorful streaming banners. They insisted that the new, material objects were to be regarded with skepticism, and that a fundamentally and originary Chinese culture lay hidden in difficult relation with them. We might readily suggest that this early argument still obtains today, when Chinatown is continually regarded as a double simulation. On the one hand, it is held to be a fabulous fabrication for the benefit of its visitors' desires; the busloads of tourists only seem to confirm its continued hold on the imagination. On the other, it is often viewed (by San Franciscans, who know better) as a careful ethnic dissimulation, which, through the insistence on things to buy, strategically displaces concerns over the quarter's social, economic, and sometimes moral abjection. The argument itself is predicated on the belief that an "authentic" culture resides somewhere outside of the street-level glitter, since its hollow shell holds only uncertain attachment to the real and unsurveilled lives of its citizenry. Genthe's comical picture of a Chinese merchant in tuxedo, donned for the unsuspecting customer, is a condensed image of this larger, still-pervasive anxiety. Another collective life must lay beneath the natty coattails and tie.

In contrast to this general reading, I will suggest that Glitter Chinatown was built on the fantasy of a hidden life and, in fact, represented and continues to represent that life by staging its perpetual absence. The fantasy of a hidden Chinatown harbors both the fears and desires of the non-Chinese visitor and, most importantly, polices the continuum of the touristic experience. Edward Said might very well view this as yet another example of an Orientalist discourse, since it provides an "accepted grid for filtering through the Orient into Western consciousness." In this case, the "Orient" was increasingly subject to the historical momentum of West Coast capital, and its main features were best glimpsed, as Genthe observed, in a culture of mass-produced objects "that never was." A whole subculture of abjection was construed in order to naturalize the increasing commodification of an ethnic neighborhood and culture—and its attendant anxiety. Glitter Chinatown could never be allowed to exist legitimately, a hollow shell without a hidden culture. It could not readily become a mere simulation, an object of the tourist's fancy. The Chinese themselves must be held responsible for capital's ruthless colonization.

This illicit fantasy might seem to constitute a hopeful picture of Chinatown's history, at least from the point of view of Chinese painters, since it offers the possibility that an alternative imagery—one more or less based on the quarter's hidden lives—had always existed as an absent (and necessarily absent) impelling force. It is sufficiently grim, however, in that the alternative imagery is nothing but a touristic fabrication, too. Chinatown's underground was only representable as a nexus of desire and loathing.

We must prepare ourselves for the possibility that some Chinese, like Gee and his cohorts, held quite similar views—that Glitter Chinatown was a tenuous putting-into-place of another, replacing image and that it did in fact produce a fantasy of the "real" lives of its citizenry. The singular difference may have been the worry that both halves of that equation—the tourist world and the representation of an unsanctioned subculture—were all that the new Chinatown seemed to amount to in imagery. "I was an oriental from Chinatown," Gee later wrote, "and I suppose the interpretation of such a person was that he was only a Launderer or a Restaurateur." (Brodsky 1979) What else could there be?

An Old World and a New

In contrast to the thrills offered to the sauntering Genthe, the experience of Chinatown was markedly different for Yun Gee. He probably did not view the crowded streets and smelly alleys as signs of cultural authenticity; he was less likely to consider his freedom to stroll with the same *flâneur* sensibility. To judge by existing accounts, he, like his contemporaries, understood the boundaries of Chinatown's streets, which were permeable in only one direction. The most obvious complication for him was the overwhelming suspicion about the legitimacy of his very presence, which made the very act of strolling in public potentially an uncomfortable one. He was, simply put, regularly suspected of being a criminal.

This general suspicion was the result of two separate developments—one, a series of laws culminating in the 1924 Immigration Act, which excluded all Chinese (except government officials, merchants, teachers, and students) from entry into the country; and the other, a series of countermeasures by the Chinese themselves, intended to circumvent the laws (the fraudulent claims of "paper sons," the rapid increase in "students"—the second of which may now provide us with more understanding of what the Club meant when it issued its desire to reach out to more "students"). To a frustrated police force known as the Chinatown Squad, the circumventions were often more successful than otherwise, since Chinatown's streets seemed to be augmented far too frequently by new arrivals (Yun Gee and his fellow Club members included)—this, despite the fact that the quarter's population had dwindled in the early 1920s to a very modest 61,000. Police anxieties led to harsher crackdowns, to which the photograph of the public burning may be said to belong.

This measured, sometimes uncomfortable experience on the streets needs to be weighed against the ongoing links between Chinatown and China, for once again judging by the evidence, the Club's members, like many Chinese men, preferred to stay within the harshly circumscribed eight-block district than to return to the East. For them, Chinatown still represented the possibility of renewal, even within a surveilled environment. Between 1906 and 1917, for example, Chinatown regularly served as a founding point for larger nationalist and reformist political agendas on the mainland. In San Francisco, in 1910, the revolutionary Sun Yat-sen established the radical T'ung Meng Hui, the forerunner to the Chinese Nationalist Party. There, too, he founded the *Young China Daily*, which along with three other Chinatown newspapers served as an exiled journalistic organ advocating the overthrow of the Manchus. A politicized population in half-exile—that is what I think Chinatown often meant to Yun Gee.

The consistent undercurrent of political activity is an important subtext to the redevelopment of Chinatown and the Revolutionary Artists' Club's relationship to it. In an odd confluence, a political sensibility was nurtured and given fantasy within the increasingly consumer-friendly tourist quarter. We must remember that the 1911 October Revolution, which effectively ended three hundred years of Manchu rule in China, was almost completely financed by overseas Chinese; that is, many of those same tourist shops and tuxedoed merchants helped to fund the overthrow. With Glitter Chinatown, we are faced with the possibility that a founding opposition in radical behavior, between an embrace of politics and the tourist industry, was at one time not held to be so reducible. Young, radicalized Chinese painters attempted to include, rather than repress or discard, the products and desires of the American commodity fetish. The attempts to make use of the commodity were not quite the same as those of the Club's famous near-contemporary, Walter Benjamin, who took the eminently reproducible object as an interventionist force within the "parasitical dependence on ritual," the cult of "aura" in art; in one reading of that argument, a revolutionary political significance was based precisely on mass reproduction's contamination of high culture and its fetishization. Nor were the attempts quite the same as what Dick Hebdige today calls "style as a signifying practice," where marginal subcultures appropriate the products of mass culture for subversive, defiant, and ultimately self-constructing ends. In the case of the Revolutionary Artists' Club, the spectacle of Chinatown, with its precious porcelains, silk brocades, asphalt streets, and electric lamps, was an ideological space still in the making. The self-conscious fabrication of a consumerized ethnic subculture was a way of elaborating a nationalist political stance. Painting, categorizing, fixing, and displaying the industrialized kitsch products of the Chinese was the means by which to articulate a nationalist identity from a distance. "Dr. Sun had told us that our main job in America was to raise funds," a young revolutionary once observed. (Nee & Nee 1972) To fight, he became a dry goods clerk, peddling Chinese and American goods to the quarter's new visitors. In the early development of touristic Chinatown, the collected objects and colorful environment inspired a collective wish-image for a nation-state.

The disparity between means and ends—between the modest teapots and a larger nationalist dream—must not prevent us from seeing either the seriousness or productive fantasy of the project. For the dream of a nation-state could transform all manner of goods into metaphors of health, well-being, fecundity, and rebirth. The delicacy of edge-to-edge and volume-to-volume in the still lifes in Yun Gee's self-portrait (fig. 1) posits a pictorial relationship whose logic is not only compositionally but metaphorically driven. The teapot pours apples from its spout, as if bringing forth sweet, ripe fruit. The apple closest to its tip resembles it in shape and color; those dropping below have become more differentiated and are now ready for the taking. The womb-like teapot provides sustenance to its beholder and those who know how to take from it. The paint brushes and fan in the upper left jut out from a porcelain vase, like flowers in a pot. They echo each other in a series of triadic segments, whose symmetry posits a relationship between the tools of painting and the objects of luxuriant pleasure. The whole assembly is raised on a pedestal of green and, through the cast shadows of the fan, is given a weight and monumentality far in excess of its modest contents. And it is the painter himself who sits amidst the objects of Chinatown's stores, playing a song to their significance and allowing them to endow him with a painterly identity as he transforms them into a nationalist poetics. The tilt and angle of his fingers are matched only by the wisp and bend of the teapot necks, each describing the other in much more than simply compositional rhythm.

Something of the sort is claimed by Gee himself. In one of the few surviving written fragments from this early period of his career, Gee addresses the potential relationship between the possibilities of Western-style painting and the developing aims of the Nationalist revolution on the mainland:

> The aim of this school is not to cultivate merely an art of compromise, nor a safe, middle-of-the-road art, but to create an art that is vital and alive that will contribute to the development of Chinese painting technique [and subjects]. This is no easy task. But, since the republic is young and art is long, time will be an ally in the successful development of the new style. (Brodsky 1979)

"This is no easy task," he portends, but the attempt is revealing in itself. The development of painting (modernist oil painting "that is essentially Chinese") and a republican identity were at one time hinged together. The art itself was a strangely hybridized, modernized variety, but it was meant to articulate a vocabulary and visualize the signs—the commodities-as-signs—of a republican culture.

I wish to alert us to a current impasse in our reading of this fragment, for Gee tried to understand Western oil painting of Orientalized kitsch as devoid of any inherent contradiction. It did not cause him to pause over the inherent race relations and conflicts that such a slippage might sometimes suggest, nor over the ways in which such works contributed or would continue to contribute to an Orientalism in paint. In fact, modernist painting and its general subjects—uncannily Cezanne-like at times—were held to be compatible with the Club's political

Figure 3. Yun Gee, *San Francisco Chinatown* (1927), oil on paper board

sensibility. This difficult transformative act will certainly put into relief the cumbersome name for the group itself, the Chinese Revolutionary Artists' Club. For as much as "revolutionary" may characterize a set of medium-based experiments, it is also quite clearly meant to reference a political sensitivity and affiliation. Furthermore, it is meant to describe the shift—the slide—from one to the other, from a medium-based style to a larger nationalist identity. It really comes as no surprise that the card-carrying Rivera wanted to meet the young men, lacquered stools and all, to expound on his ideas for a politically responsible public art, which for him was founded partially on rediscovered fresco techniques. He, too, had a stake in reconfiguring a Europeanized painterly manner for nationalist ends.

The general linkage between the objects of the tourist's world and a political sensibility ought to cause us to reconsider a historical commonplace about the early development of Chinatown. At one time, both private fantasies and collective goals were articulated through the commodity. And if we have lost one half of that equation today, it is because we have also lost the nationalist specter haunting the imaginations of the Chinese. That is not the only reason for our amnesia, of course, for we can also stress the instability of this general linkage to begin with, one which Yun Gee articulated himself. In terms of material goods, the offer of kitsch objects made the elaboration of a radicalized identity subject to the whims of the marketplace. "Make tourists WANT to come," a Chinese newspaper editor once commanded, but implicit in the call was a recognition of the variable lures that were needed, the various goods that had to come and go. But it was not simply the rotating goods on offer that made it difficult or even necessary to stabilize an iconography; it was also the new and compelling lure of the goods themselves that Yun Gee could not quite overcome. "I bought a coat," he once wrote in great excitement, and proudly displayed it in his painting (fig. 1).

The Revolution in Art

A comparison of some paintings by Gee may well offer an example of how the potentially disjunctive accommodation of the object-desires of Chinatown and a nationalist agenda might have appeared. When he painted Chinatown's streets in a small picture called *San Francisco Chinatown* (fig. 3), Gee found it best not to include any inhabitants, as if the quarter was most amenable to picturing when comprised entirely of its new pagoda streetlamps (with bright rays emphatically jutting in all directions) and tall building façades. Chinatown seemed most coherent and consistent as a brilliant spectacle, devoid of social relations and daily activity. Its identity was best understood as a carefully constructed place. Part of the modernist, pseudo-cubist aesthetic lent itself to such an attitude, for it insisted on fitting

Figure 4. Yun Gee, *San Francisco Street Scene with Construction Workers* (1926), oil on paper board

together component parts into an overall set of surface relations. Brushes and strokes fell into jigsaw patterns, and the particular task for the painter was to provide a level of visual interest in the play of colored facets and edges.

At Chinatown's outskirts, however, Gee's attitudes changed. One scene, *San Francisco Street Scene with Construction Workers* (fig. 4), is a familiar one to San Francisco Chinese, then and now, since it is the Stockton Street tunnel that separates Downtown from Chinatown proper. We see the cavernous mouth of the tunnel at the bottom center, just beyond the crest of the hill that is the intersection of Stockton and Sacramento Streets. It is a significant location insofar as we are positioned at the southwestern edge of Chinatown, the boundary of the policed quarter beyond which, through the tunnel, an entirely non-Chinese San Francisco begins. Gee places us on the inside of the gilded ghetto, looking out, mindful of the quarter's boundaries, watching the city take shape over the tunnel on California Street and observing its activity from a necessary distance. The workers themselves are held on an impossibly precipitous slope, as if they were tacked onto the picture's surface and absorbed into its fiction, as if they constituted a tableau beyond the quarter itself. A street sign to the far right, barely legible as "Cali[fornia]," is the name for the street above, not the intersection below, and thus holds particular, metonymical value. It is a link to the burgeoning space beyond Chinatown's closed borders, towards the precipitous space at the upper half. A stroller (a *flâneur*), convulsive in his step, makes his way past the sign, southward to the tunnel and an imaginary freedom—or at least one denied to the bulk of young San Francisco Chinese. He sports a pipe and probably is a stand-in for the painter himself, who regularly pictured himself with pipe in mouth (fig. 5). But it is a stroll that the young Gee was only allowed to make infrequently, and the pathos of the image is in the carefully measured step of the surrogate, who crosses a boundary that the painter himself could rarely cross. The whole scenario of *flânerie* must take place in the fantasy of the painting.

Figure 5. Yun Gee at his easel in San Francisco (c. 1927)

Compared to the general pictorial strategies in *San Francisco Chinatown, Construction Workers* is decidedly different. It does not imagine the visual delight of the streets to be similar to the careful construction of the painting. It is, instead, awkward, with the facets and edges unable to smooth over the disjunctions of place, and unable to handle the strolling figure in anything but facile, abbreviated terms. I will place a particular stress on the differences between these two paintings and the near breakdown of the latter, for it points to the instability of the nationalist vision based partially on a fabricated, contained tourist culture. *San Francisco Chinatown* is a view inward and, to the painter, was best understood as a self-sufficient image with a disembodied aspect. Its composition aims for a certain internal consistency, with a careful symmetry of vertical and horizontal elements and a rhythm of overhead triangles, as if that kind of consistency came from the place itself. Chinatown's streets and storefronts, it seems, were a carefully arranged image that readily gave themselves over to painting. At the quarter's edge, however, the spectacular self-sufficiency broke down. *Construction Workers* is a view outward and, with that as a subject, seemed to suggest the pull of the tunnel, the distant vista, and the hint of a complex urban space beyond Chinatown's edge. But the painting does not seem to manage that combination comfortably and is interrupted by the convulsive desires of Gee himself. At Chinatown's borders, he was most aware of his physical presence to the city outside—most aware of his difference in racist San Francisco—and this required that he encode that knowledge into the painting's logic.

In Gee's extant paintings, then, we might be able to glimpse something of the uncomfortable or at least unstable vision of a radical Asian American artistic sensibility. On the one hand, the new Chinatown inspires fascination and self-sufficiency; on the other, self-consciousness and loss. At one end of town, the streets insist on Chinatown's own fullness and offer the possibility of delight; at the other, they require a sense of the quarter's isolation and distance. At Chinatown's heart, the brilliant corners and elegant lamps do not require any singular bodily awareness on the part of the stroller but promise a collective fantasy of plenitude;

Figure 6. Yun Gee, *Chinese Man in Hat* (1928), oil on paper board

at the edge, the fantasy disappears, and a simple comparison with the space beyond quickly demands an imaginative surrogate.

The closest Gee came to placing the two attitudes together in one painting occurred in a small oil on paper board, *Chinese Man in Hat* (fig. 6). The painting is probably a portrait of a Club member, since the painters' subjects tended to be so insular. Running halfway down either side of the central figure is Chinese verse On the left side, it reads:

I am thinking, thinking of me, I am thinking of me;

I am worried, I am happy, I am at once worried and happy;

I have nothing, I have something, I have at once nothing and something;

I am dreaming of myself, I am dreaming of myself.

This set of contradictory states and the desire to see himself at a hallucinatory distance are taken up in the verses on the right. They read:

Who creates, creates whom, who creates whom;

Who is alive, who is dead, who is both dead and alive;

Who knows, who is enlightened, who knows and is enlightened;

Who changes whom, who changes whom.

"I am thinking of me," he writes on the left, and as if in response on the right, he asks, "Who creates whom." The acts of thinking and painting are hinged together, but the process itself is riven with a deep anxiety. It causes the painter to imagine himself as two relatively distinct selves—the "I" on the left, directed and possessive, who has and does not have, who thinks and dreams of himself; and the "Who" on the right, an exteriorized and disembodied self, who changes and creates but is dead and enlightened in the knowledge. The central figure points to himself, as if to lay claim to the dissonant set of characterizations and their contradiction. The pathos of the image is in the belief that the painted subject will accommodate the competing selves within

PHOTO COURTESY ANTHONY W. LEE

Figure 7. Yun Gee (c. 1929)

his body, somehow managing the potential for fragmentation. Unlike the paintings of Chinatown's streets, where the contradictions of its culture could be separated by the inward or outward gaze, the paintings of the Club's members themselves had to locate and attempt to accommodate the dissonance in a single figure. Their bodies were made over into the ritualized spaces over which the antinomies of the Club's artistic ambitions had to be displayed.

The argument of the paintings did not simply reside at the level of painted fiction, for it spilled over into Yun Gee's growing sense of himself on Chinatown's streets. As the street paintings might suggest, Gee apparently relished the experience of the sidewalks and storefronts and was sensitive to his relation with them. He frequently moved up and down the steep hills, trying to find a particularly sketchable subject. Like the *flâneurs* before him, he walked with attentiveness and alertness, typically scouring for a useful street scene to transform into the stuff of art. What is especially significant on these strolls is that he apparently dressed for the part too. As photographs tell us (fig. 7), he regularly donned the various outfits of the urbane stroller—fedora, broad lapels, flowing tie, and walking cane—as if to masquerade as a privileged non-Chinese and to pass along the length of Grant Avenue as Genthe had once done along Dupont Street. One account suggests the absurd, overproduced manner of his make-believe. Out on a stroll with the painter Otis Oldfield, Gee

had fitted himself out to be a Chinese carbon copy; he'd gotten the beret; he

Another View of Chinatown   177

had a suit made that was as close as it could be, identical to the one that Otis wore most of the time; he'd gotten a cane and a pipe. . . . The beret stuck up on top of that wiry Chinese hair; it wouldn't fit down on his head at all. The one that he had bought had not had that little thread that comes out of the top, so he got a piece of yarn and sewed it on. He had to have everything exact. (Oldfield 1937)

It is an odd, comical picture, this. We can only imagine Gee twirling his cane, jauntily stepping past the tourist shops and beneath the colorful canopies, disguised as the francophile Oldfield, down to the added yarn. There is obvious pleasure in the masquerade, brought about by wrapping his body within the object-desires of modernity. But, as in the accounts of Chinatown itself, the costume is ill-fitting and subject to suspicion. It is worn in vulgar explicitness, almost as a parody or even a self-parody.

Gee as self-conscious *flâneur* suggests the deep awareness of Club members about the unstable nature of their project and hints at an underlying tension between the means and ends of a nationalist program. It is as if the West—its fashions, products, etiquette, fetishes—cannot be sufficiently encompassed and must be taken with both an awareness of its lack of fit and its undeniable pleasures. This was not simply the result of commodities having an unconscious—one that overwhelms any attempt to use them. Rather, it was the result of specific

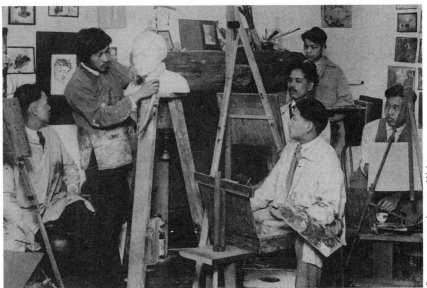

Figure 8. Yun Gee and the Chinese Revolutionary Artists' Club (c. 1927)

social and political conditions of the Chinese in America—conditions that continued to remind the painters of the policed nature of their touristic living environment. The utopian vision of radicalized Asian American artists always confronted the material bases of immigrant life. Despite the presence of an occasional celebrity like Rivera, life at 150 Wetmore Place was probably no different from that on the streets.

A Budding Modernist

We have already rehearsed most of what is known about the early career of Gee, the Club's most celebrated member. One other photograph (fig. 8) of Gee and other Club members tells us a bit more, but not much. He is found amid his fellow painters, modeling an impeccably clean white bust of a man. While the Club was collective in nature, the photograph tries to tell us that Gee was sometimes its center. The rest of the painters are ostensibly at work on their canvases, but he in fact remains their focus of attention. But it is an awkward kind of attention, which betrays a now-familiar underlying problematic. The seated painters have taken to Westernized dress, their starched collars and neck ties donned even in the splattered environs of the Club's cramped studio. The standing Gee keeps to his distinctly Chinese smock, allowing the paint to coat but not strip away an outwardly ethnic identification. If the Club was indeed "Chinese" and "revolutionary," Gee was going to try to insist on what the combination of those terms at one time tried to mean, or at least how it ought to be photographed. A revolutionary Chinese artists' club had to hold the contact of two generalized cultures, the New East and the New West, in some kind of awkward, explicit, visible tension.

Remove Gee and his friends, and 150 Wetmore Place takes on a decidedly different appearance. For the "Chinese" quality of the Club quickly fades and, with the single exception of a landscape painting in the back, does not seem to remain or reside in the artworks themselves. The sketches and drawings attached to the walls are vaguely cubist in style and certainly Parisian in origin. Indeed, the still lifes of tumblers and saucers seem more suited to a studio at the Bateau-Lavoir than one in Chinatown—this, remember, in 1926, when photographs of Parisian studios amply displayed a similar ambiance. "Revolutionary," the art on the walls seems to tell us, belongs more properly to certain stylistic affinities with the École de Paris. Only that white bust of a man, whose features on closer inspection can be construed as Asian, may give away the studio's regular inhabitants. Even the bust's presence is not without ambiguity, for it may well stand as a convenient model for a painter of Orientalist exotica ("orientalia," as Gee once said in disdain). (Brodsky 1979) Given the strange conventionality of the interior, we cannot even tell if the unfinished paintings in the background belong to the Club's seated members, since each of their canvases is turned away from us and remains strategically hidden behind the monochrome of wood support panels. Gee himself is preoccupied by the one decidedly nonmodern object.

The artistic activity in the photograph—Gee's intimate rapport with the Asian bust and the rapt attention of his colleagues—contribute to the tension in the entire public image of the Chinese Revolutionary Artists' Club, between the explicitly Modernist ambitions in the paintings and the developing ethnic identification of its members. Two cultures have met, the photograph tells us, but it is unclear how (under what set of terms) the meeting was productive.

Figure 9. Yun Gee, *Man with Pipe* (c. 1927), oil on paper board

This general tension and ambiguity, its pathos and historicity, are what we must hold onto if we are ever to revisit the conflicted, anxious vision of an early Asian American artistic practice. The Club's painting of Chinatown's streets and commodities was an attempt to imagine a utopian model of nationalist artistic production to accompany a process that had barely begun in China itself. It developed within an increasingly industrialized subculture in the West which, in this early moment, still permitted the ethnic commodity to contain various, competing collective meanings in relation to private fantasies. That ambitious project has been all but erased, though in the previous pages I have tried to hint at its conflict and complexity. Though this vision is now small and discrete, there is still something at stake, especially if we are to recover both the repressed portions of

Chinatown's imagery and a largely "present absence" in the celebratory, touristic images that followed.

From the perspective of conventional San Francisco art histories, the Club's achievements were altogether unambiguous and, modest as they were, have been construed (in footnotes) as relatively productive, since the Club produced Gee. The young immigrant, so it is argued, took the formation of the Club as an opportunity to hone his skills as a developing modernist painter. Why else would he have made a huge bonfire just months before the Club's founding, in order to destroy all of his previous work (the bonfire, now, may remind us of another event of ritualized burning)? Yes, he had been trained in traditional Chinese watercolor painting as a student in Canton, but it is clear that soon after his arrival in the city, he quickly took to oil painting with great enthusiasm. By 1924, he could be found enrolled at the California School of Fine Arts, working closely with the Paris-trained Oldfield; and the two took painting trips together for the single purpose, as one early chronicler would have it, to "train the oriental mind in occidental ways of art." (Hailey 1937) Under Oldfield's watchful eye, Gee's repertoire of subjects expanded, and the young painter even took his teacher as a sitter (fig. 9). Soon, all of Gee's early, conventionally "Oriental" watercolors were discarded—if not before 1926, then certainly in the celebrated bonfire. Later that same year, he joined the so-called Modern Gallery, which included his mentor Oldfield and virtually all of the city's experimental modernists; and as a gesture to his stylistic turn and exceeding precociousness, the gallery board gave the immigrant painter its first solo exhibition in November 1926. The selection of paintings told of his recent conversion: brightly colored Chinatown landscapes, conventional still lifes, urban genre scenes, small portraits. There were seventy-two canvases in all, and most sold. Many of the remaining works were re-hung on the occasion of Oldfield's wedding, a ceremony orchestrated by the young devotee and mimic, Gee. Apparently, the wedding and festive environment were a success. When asked if he minded that the paintings had slipped sideways from all the thumping and dancing, Gee is said to have responded, in good modernist argot, "Oh, no, it just gives them movement!" (Oldfield 1982) A year later, in 1927, not only Chinatown's but San Francisco's art scene could seem too provincial for a painter who had taken to oil paint a mere three years before, and Gee left San Francisco for Paris. In December, he held a solo exhibition at the Galerie Carmine; by April of the following year, he held another at the Galerie des Artistes et Artisans. In 1929 he exhibited in that most hallowed of modernist venues, the Salon des Indépendants, and later that year, he had yet another solo show, this time at the venerable Galerie Bernheim-Jeune.

The awkward tension evident in the Club's photograph of Gee and his friends in San Francisco must seem to be a charming moment of early innocence. Two cultures had met, a certain modernist cultural history says, and one would completely absorb the other. So it did.

References

Benjamin, Walter. 1969. "The Work of Art in the Age of Mechanical Reproduction." In *Illuminations*. Translated by Harry Zohn. New York: Shocken.

Brodsky, Joyce. 1979. *The Paintings of Yun Gee*. Storrs, CT: University of Connecticut.

Dillon, Richard. 1962. *The Hatchet Men*. Sausalito, CA: Comstock.

Gee, Yun. n.d. "Oriental Group is Developing New Technique." Unpublished scrapbooks, vol. 1 (Aug. 1930–Jan. 1936).

Genthe, Arnold. 1913. *Old Chinatown: A Book of Pictures* by Arnold Genthe. New York: Mitchell Kennerly.

Hailey, Gene. 1937. "Otis Oldfield." *WPA California Art Research* 19.

Hebdige, Dick. 1979. *Subculture: The Meaning of Style*. London: Methuen.

Lee, Anthony W. 1995. "Chinatown and the Flâneur in Old San Francisco." *JASAT* 26.

———. 1996. "Picturing San Francisco's Chinatown: The Photo Albums of Arnold Genthe." Visual Resources 12 (2).

Nee, Victor, and Brett de Bary Nee. 1972. *Longtime Californ': A Documentary Study of an American Chinatown*. New York: Pantheon.

Oldfield, Helen. 1982. "Otis Oldfield and the San Francisco Art Community, 1920s to 1960s." *Interviews on Art and Sculpture in the San Francisco Bay Area*. Berkeley: Regional Oral History Office.

Said, Edward. 1978. *Orientalism*. New York: Pantheon.

Takaki, Ronald. 1989. *Strangers From a Different Shore*. New York: Penguin.

Black Consciousness in the Art of Sargent Johnson

by Tommy L. Lott

HISTORIANS TELL US THAT San Francisco was unlike many Eastern cities that had heavily populated black ghettos in the 1920s and 1930s, as a result of Southern migrations at the turn of the century. Two major studies of San Francisco's black community, Douglas Daniels's *Pioneer Urbanites* and Albert Broussard's *Black San Francisco*, employ demographic comparisons with Eastern cities prior to World War II to account for the absence of a black ghetto in San Francisco. The invisibility of the black community in San Francisco seems to have come full circle. With a noticeably shrinking black population, political gains wrought by the Civil Rights struggle, including the legislative career of Mayor Willie Brown, have not affected the rate of black migration from the city. One important political implication of the current demographic shift is increased marginalization of the black community, a consequence that is incongruous with San Francisco's image of itself as socially progressive.

The history of African American political struggle in San Francisco is inextricably linked with demographic change. Harlem Renaissance historian Nathan Huggins, speaking as a native of San Francisco, credits black San Franciscans before World War II with a political complacency that accommodated social inequality. (Daniels 1990) Both this complacency, as well as the myth of racial tolerance that has long been associated with San Francisco, can be viewed as a function of demographics. Prior to World War II, the much larger Chinese and other Asian groups suffered the brunt of racial violence in San Francisco. (Broussard 1993) By comparison with the Asian experience, black San Franciscans appear to have been tolerated, because they were not the focus of race riots and lynchings. Many of the early black migrants interviewed by Daniels seemed grateful that they were spared the experience of African Americans in other parts of the country. They escaped the fate of their more populous Asian brethren because, with a population of less than 5,000 until 1940, African Americans posed no political threat.

Huggins also noted that in the absence of "conspicuous numbers," black San Franciscans were more apt to submerge racial identity and to minimize difference. For African Americans living in San Francisco during the twenties and thirties, acceptance by the mainstream was contingent on racial invisibility. The political leverage to begin demanding fair treatment and respect would not come until the black migration of the 1940s. Since resistance to discrimination required a strong assertion of racial identity, black San Franciscan's were faced with Du Bois's classic dilemma of double consciousness. But given their small numbers, the question of whether to assert racial identity or to seek absorption into the mainstream was not a genuine choice. Prior to 1940 they could do neither. To expose the city's image of racial tolerance as a false one, historians often cite employment and income data that clearly indicate discrimination against African Americans in San Francisco prior to World War II. I want to take a closer look at the manner in which this myth supports a system of racial discrimination.

Sargent Johnson, an accomplished Bay Area multimedia artist, negotiated the Du Boisian dilemma with great success. Born in Boston on October 7, 1887, Johnson moved to San Francisco in 1915 after spending his young adult years living in Pennsylvania and Chicago. He was a versatile and innovative artist, who in addition to sculpting, painting, and etching used enameled porcelain steel panels to create large murals. With African Americans virtually locked out of every skilled profession, how was it possible for a black artist aligned with the Harlem Renaissance to excel in San Francisco's elite artist community in the 1920s and 1930s? Although Johnson's art, especially in his later period, was not exclusively devoted to racial images, he gained early recognition through his prize-winning submissions in the Harmon Foundation exhibitions of the work of Negro artists, as well as in other local and national competition. He managed to assert a strong black identity in his art without losing the racial invisibility required for mainstream acceptance. This apparent contradiction reveals an important insight regarding the ideological function of San Francisco's myth of racial tolerance; namely, that by relying on political complacency it masks social inequality.

There were many personal as well as philosophical influences on Johnson's art and aesthetic view. Commentators often note the multicultural aspects of his art, but they have little to say regarding the possible influence of his mixed-race family background or his multicultural experience in San Francisco. Alain Locke's classic anthology, *The New Negro*, is often cited as a major philosophical influence on

Johnson's view of African American art, yet many of the details of Locke's view that are crucial to fully understanding the place of African art and Southern black folk culture in Johnson's practice are ignored. (Locke 1925) In addition to Johnson's African-inspired work, which focused on a rather tenuous conception of a "pure American Negro," Locke's teachings regarding African American art also accommodated the mixed-race image of African Americans that Johnson sometimes constructed (perhaps inadvertently) on the model of a Third World hybrid. Johnson's multicultural orientation was in keeping with Locke's general view of the relation between African American art and mainstream American art, as well as with some of his more specific claims regarding the role of the African American artist in America's "cultural democracy." Indeed, the influence of Asian and Mexican art, quite prominent in Johnson's large-scale public art, never detracted from his desire to produce the African-inspired images he reserved mostly for galleries, collectors, and museum exhibitions.

In many respects Johnson's career provides a paradigm of Locke's "New Negro" artist, whose work would display elements that were racial, national, and universal. Locke outlined a twofold cultural strategy: a vibrant race tradition in art would contribute to American art and, in turn, this achievement would help bring about social equality. One of the writers Locke had mentored, Langston Hughes, deemed the Harlem Renaissance movement a failure because it was motivated by a fantasy that the race problem could be solved through art. (Hughes 1940) Hughes rightly questioned whether the contributions by an elite

PHOTO TOMMY L. LOTT

Sargent Johnson, *Untitled* (n.d.). This log sculpture is in the median of Webster Street at Bush Street.

group of black intellectuals to American culture would bring about social change for the masses of African Americans. Johnson's art had very little impact on segregationist policies, yet the eventual incorporation of his "Negro" art into mainstream American art fulfilled the aesthetic mission that Locke had set for African American artists in 1925.

A Colorful Art for a Colorful Race

More than any of the other Renaissance artists, including Locke's protégé Aaron Douglass, Johnson epitomized Locke's teachings regarding aesthetics and black consciousness in art. Locke was well known for his denunciation of propagandistic art. Johnson shared Locke's aversion to the social realism of other so-called New Deal black artists such as Jacob Lawrence, Elizabeth Catlett, and Charles White. Unlike these latter artists, the black consciousness displayed in his work was not meant to disturb status quo racial inequality. He is reported to have remarked that working people "are sure they don't look as awkward, as earthy, and as unbeautiful as that." (Arvey 1939) This apolitical aesthetic stance, one of the problematic aspects of Locke's philosophy of art, served Johnson well. His highly acclaimed "Negro" art peacefully co-existed with widespread racial discrimination against black San Franciscans in the 1920s and 1930s. When we consider the fact that, despite the influence on his art by Diego Rivera and the Mexican muralists, Johnson chose not to engage in social commentary for ostensibly aesthetic reasons, we must wonder whether his success as a black artist in San Francisco was predicated on his taking a strong position against propaganda in art.

The only surviving statement of Johnson's aesthetic view seems to be his often quoted remarks in a *San Francisco Chronicle* interview he gave in 1935. In what appears to be a series of highly edited quotations, Johnson distinguished between the "culturally mixed Negro of the cities" and the "more primitive slave type," and insisted that Negro art is devoted to a study of the latter as representative of the "pure American Negro." He agreed with Locke regarding the need for a group-conscious art and with Locke's view that the African American artist should turn to the American South to study his cultural roots, rather than to Europe to imitate the European masters. Some of his remarks clearly indicate that he remained committed to expressing a strong sense of racial pride in his art long after the official demise of the Renaissance. In a declaration that has been compared with Langston Hughes's famous manifesto, "The Negro Artist and the Racial Mountain," Johnson asserted, "I am concerned with aiming to show the natural beauty and dignity in that characteristic lip, that characteristic hair, bearing and manner. And I wish to show that beauty not so much to the white man as to the Negro himself." When we associate these remarks with the voice of a visibly mixed-race black man living in San Francisco in the mid-thirties, other readings are suggested. Why would a person of mixed-race ancestry insist that, of all things, the "pure" African American be represented? Perhaps Johnson's preference for the "pure" Negro of the South can be understood as a criticism of black San Franciscans and their aesthetic values, for his claim to want to reveal a black aesthetic to the African American himself ends with the added comment, "And this is not so easily accomplished." He may have realized that his task would be especially difficult to accomplish in San Francisco. With very few Southern black migrants in the Bay Area in the mid-thirties, it was quite likely that his use of images of black Southerners to represent the race would fail to be appreciated by San Francisco's more status-conscious black urbanites.

It is worth noting that Johnson speaks of black Southerners as "primitive," based on his perception that they were not "culturally mixed." His use of "primitive slave type" comes quite close to Locke's notion of "racial types." Johnson further specifies an African identity for this type with the stipulation "as it existed in this country during the period of slave importation." His appeal to this image of Southern black people to construct what he considered to be more authentic visual representations of the race follows many of Locke's stipulations regarding "genuine Negro portraiture" and "true Negro types." For example, Locke referred favorably to the painter Aaron Douglass' earlier "Negro type studies," but was critical of Ronald Moody for his inattentiveness to "racial types." (Locke 1939) In visual art, as in ethnological studies, a racial type is constructed from certain physical features that are selected and idealized as a model for representing a particular group of people. For Locke, the visual representations of ideal racial types were meant to counter not only the negative effects of racist stereotypes and caricature, but also "Nordicized" images created by African American artists. Locke invoked the need for "representative" African American art when he defended his choice of German artist Winold Reiss to illustrate the 1925 "Harlem" edition of *Survey Graphic*. (Locke 1925a) Just as Locke must have known that he would face heavy criticism from many who thought he should have commissioned an African American artist to portray African Americans from the usual Eurocentric perspective, Johnson must have known in 1935 that his rejection of the "mixed Negro of the cities," in favor of representing the African "primitive" type, would confront similar expectations from San Francisco's black urbanites.

Following Locke, Johnson advocated the study of Southern black folk culture and African art as sources of inspiration for African American art. But since Johnson never visited Africa and only traveled once to New Orleans, his own representations of the "pure Negro" were largely idealized physical features he copied from African Americans he encountered in the Bay Area. (Arvey 1939) This observation is not meant to diminish the critical praise he received for his use of African sources, as demonstrated by his numerous awards. With regard to Johnson's copper masks, for example, commentators have noted that, rather than merely imitate African art, as so many other artists had done, he employed a thorough knowledge of the structural aspects of African art and applied that knowledge to create representations of African Americans. (Porter 1943; Arvey 1939) The concern Locke often expressed regarding the superficial use of African art by both European and African American artists did not apply in the case of Johnson.

Even as a mentor who pulled strings behind the scene to arrange exhibitions of both African and African American art, Locke often criticized the work of the Renaissance artists. He was primarily concerned with the development of Negro art and often stated his criticisms generally. Hence, it is not always clear whether he had Johnson's work in mind. His scant remarks specifically on Johnson's work were always favorable, but some of his criticisms of the Africanist school of African American art, if applied to Johnson's art, would constitute a misunderstanding. This suggests that, at best, Locke's attitude toward Johnson's work was indifferent. There is a bit of irony in Locke's oversight of Johnson's work, for, more than anyone else, Johnson demonstrated the veracity of the aesthetic principles Locke advocated.

The most telling criticisms of Johnson's art were leveled by other African American artists. In some cases the criticism of his art impugns Locke's aesthetic theory as well. James A. Porter, a student of Johnson's aunt, May Howard Johnson, and a co-exhibitor with Johnson in some of the Harmon Foundation exhibitions, praised Johnson's modeling technique but preferred to view him as a "ceramic artist," rather than as a sculptor creating works of fine art in various materials. (Porter 1940) Needless to say, this charge presupposed a questionable theory of art to which neither Locke nor Johnson subscribed. Porter rejected Locke's call for a race tradition in African American art. He argued that this would foster the segregation of African American artists from other American artists. Putting aside the question of whether Locke's strategy for bringing about the incorporation of African American art into mainstream art was sound, there remains a question of whether the work of artists who are inspired by African art to study ancient craft and decorative styles should be considered fine art. Although Locke did not want to grant primacy to museum art as a standard of aesthetic achievement, his mild praise for Johnson's art suggests that he expected African American artists to produce work that surpassed both the African and

European masters. He invoked one of the guiding principles of African decorative art, "beauty in use," to contest the idea that only museum art has aesthetic value or counts as fine art. Locke even quoted art critic Roger Frye's comments regarding the technical superiority of African sculpture to support his own belief that sculpture would be the forte of African American art. (Locke 1946)

Locke praised Richmond Barthe's famous sculpture of a mother holding her lynched son as a work of fine art, and took special note that it contained non-propagandistic racial content. We can only speculate as to whether he would have said as much for Johnson's masterpiece, *Forever Free*, a wood sculpture covered with lacquered cloth. This piece, along with one of his lesser known works, *Negro Woman*, were based on the mother-child theme in one of Johnson's earlier drawings, titled *Defiant*, and in numerous abstract works from his later period. Both *Negro Woman* and *Forever Free* display Johnson's preference for the ancient technique of applying color to sculpture. According to Johnson these forms allowed him to express a racial dimension in his art. "I am concerned with color not solely as a technical problem, but also as a means of heightening the racial character of my work. The Negroes are a colorful race. They call for an art as colorful as it can be made."

It was precisely this art deco feature of Johnson's work, along with complete disregard of his endeavor to develop techniques better suited to capture racial aspects, that provided the basis for Porter's low esteem. Locke instead seemed more dissatisfied that none of the African American sculptors, including Johnson, had advanced beyond either the European or African masters. Perhaps Johnson's attempt to transform ancient practices went largely unnoticed by Locke because he viewed decorative arts as a less advanced cultural development. For him, decorative arts would constitute the "raw materials" for fine art. He argued that, in its mature stage, African American art will display universal aesthetic principles derived from many different cultures. Unfortunately, Locke failed to realize the extent to which Johnson's study of ancient techniques of applying color to sculpture, his use of images of Third World people, as well as his commitment to representing the beauty and dignity of the Southern black peasant, followed through on this proposal. (Johnson 1935)

Art Big Enough to Belong to Everybody

Although Johnson's interest in African art and the visual representation of African Americans was shaped largely by his association with the Harlem Renaissance artists and the influence of Alain Locke, his distant location on the West Coast was an important factor in his development as an African American artist. Commentators fail to consider the social significance of Johnson's mixed-race background in this context. With Johnson's African American identity in mind they often conclude that he was "isolated." If this claim is taken to mean either that he was not a part of the art scene (centered on the East Coast), or that he was not connected with the black community, it is very misleading. Johnson participated in all ten of the Harmon Foundation exhibitions of Negro art as well as in an equal number of local and national exhibitions. In newspaper articles from the 1930s and 1940s, either his identity as an African American artist was taken for granted because of the racial content of his art or ignored as irrelevant. To use Dick Hebdige's phrase, Johnson seems to have been "hiding in the light." Knute Stiles points this out in his review of the Oakland Museum's retrospective of Johnson's work. Stiles claimed to have "known Johnson for several years before he mentioned that he was a Negro; I hadn't noticed. I was to learn that he had publicized his blackness during the political thirties and always acknowledged his dedication to raising his black brothers out of poverty and misery." (Stiles 1971) Unlike some of his family members who preferred not to identify themselves or live as African Americans, Johnson chose not to pass, although he apparently was not opposed to capitalizing on his status as ethnically indistinct. There were several reasons Johnson's career in San Francisco during the 1930s and 1940s was not hampered by his racial background, but a paramount factor was that he was not perceived, in many circumstances, to be a black person.

Another important factor in Johnson's successful career was his close association with two well-known Bay Area sculptors, Beniamino Bufano and Ralph Stackpole. Johnson came to San Francisco specifically to pursue his career as an artist. He studied drawing and painting at the avant-garde A. W. Best School of Art. Even though his interest in sculpting can be traced to his earlier experience of observing his aunt, May Howard Jackson, as she modeled clay, he was thirty-two years old when he began studying at the California School of Fine Arts. There he worked for two years with Stackpole and for several years with Bufano. Even as a student, he won awards for his sculptures of Elizabeth Gee (a Chinese neighbor's child) and of Pearl (his daughter), and by the mid-thirties he was at par with his teachers, co-exhibiting and serving on juries with them. Some of Johnson's sculptures were included in Stackpole's Court of Pacifica at the Golden Gate International Exposition in 1938. In 1940 he was selected by officials at the Works Progress Administration Federal Art Project (WPA) to replace Bufano, who had been fired from a project at George Washington High. The fact that this much-publicized scandal was never viewed in racial terms by the press, or by anyone directly involved, is a sure sign that Johnson had fully arrived in San Francisco's art community. In addition to training him to work in various media, Johnson's teachers, as WPA artists, also communicated a multicultural orientation that would have a lasting influence on his art.

Johnson's selection to replace Bufano was not the only indication of recognition by his peers. He was elected in 1932 to the San Francisco Art Association, and two years later he was appointed a member of the council. In 1936 he was hired by the WPA as a senior sculptor, advancing almost immediately to the position of unit supervisor. Working from his shop at 15th Street and Shotwell, Johnson began producing large-scale public art. His first public art project was a 22-foot-long organ screen for the California School for the Blind in Berkeley. This screen was carved in redwood with a center panel that featured African American singers whose faces resembled some of his earlier masks. Johnson is known to have produced at least four other works for the WPA, including a two-part work comprised of a 30-foot-long, 14-foot-high greenish-gray slate façade titled *Sea Forms*, which was placed over the main entrance to the Maritime Museum on Polk Street, and a 125-foot-long, 14-foot-high glazed tile of green-and-white abstract patterns resembling sea forms that covered the stairwells to the promenade deck. His group of animals of cast terrazzo (camel, burro, grasshopper, duck, hippopotamus, and elephant), colored coral, green, and gray, were placed in the child care center playground of the Sunnydale Housing Project. Ten years later he was commissioned by the architect

Sargent Johnson, *Sea Forms* (1939)
at the Maritime Museum

PHOTO CHRIS CARLSSON

Albert Williams to create an abstract pattern incorporating pots and pans with fired enamel on iron 14 feet wide and 28 feet long. This façade was designed to be placed over the entrance of the Dohrmans building, located on Geary Street in Union Square. What is important to notice in connection with Johnson's work for the WPA is that his large-scale public art projects required him to collaborate with other Bay Area artists in both the public and private sector while, in some cases, supervising their work.

Johnson is sometimes depicted in art history books working on the massive 185-foot-long, 12-foot-high relief frieze of cast stone he installed on the retaining wall across the back of the football field at Washington High School, at 32nd Avenue and Anza. (Dover 1960) When he was selected by the WPA to replace Bufano, his design had to be submitted for approval to the San Francisco Art Commission, which initially rejected it. Some of the committee members went on record declaring support for the retention of Bufano, whose design they had already approved. Johnson eventually won approval by creating a clay model 12 feet high and 3 feet long. It is worth noting that while the art commission was split on the merits of Johnson's plans for the Washington High frieze, this same group voted unanimously to accept Diego Rivera's mural for the yet-to-be-built San Francisco City College Library. This is extremely important to consider in connection with the political aspects of Johnson's dispute with Bufano.

Bufano and Johnson jointly contributed to other public art projects for the WPA prior to Bufano's dismissal. Bufano had created two stylized animals carved in brown and black granite, *Seal* and *Frog,* for the promenade deck of the Maritime Museum, which were not installed until 1942. A 1938 photo of Bufano working in his studio with four of his assistants, including Johnson, accompanies an essay Bufano wrote for Francis O'Connor's anthology of essays by WPA artists. (O'Connor 1973) Less than two years after this photo was taken, Johnson would literally betray his former teacher and collaborator. Several commentators have erroneously reported the circumstances surrounding Bufano's dismissal. For example, we are told by Romare Bearden and Harry Henderson that "Johnson's design won him the commission for this athletic frieze. . . . The award outraged Beniamino Bufano . . . who felt his own design should have won, and ended their friendship." The only truth in this assertion is the fact that their friendship ended. It is not at all true that Bufano became bitter because he lost a competition to his former student. Rather, what really happened was that the Art Commission had already commissioned Bufano to do the frieze, but WPA officials objected to the political content in Bufano's design and assigned Johnson to take over the project. According to Richard McKinzie, Bufano was fired when WPA officials learned that he had used the Marxist labor leader Harry Bridges as a model for the frieze. (McKinzie 1972) The *San Francisco Chronicle* reported that "When [Joseph] Allen changed the locks on Bufano's workroom, to impress on him that he was fired, the clay that Bufano was molding into the heroic figures of the frieze became Johnson's to work with." Keeping in mind that the workroom from which Bufano was barred had been a training ground for Johnson's development as a sculptor, the official story repeatedly told by politically naive commentators evades many of the important issues raised by Johnson's betrayal of Bufano. (Montgomery 1971; Bearden & Henderson 1993)

Although Johnson clearly benefited from his collaborations with Bufano and Stackpole on public art projects, he was highly critical of some of his more politically minded colleagues—in particular, the Coit Tower muralists. His ability to relate to the art establishment, especially collectors, was to a large extent due to his well-known political neutrality. His opposition to political messages in art places him closer to Locke than to Bufano on questions of ideology and aesthetics. In his essay on public art, Bufano presents a philosophy of contemporary art that is thoroughly political. (O'Connor 1973) Bufano maintained that art must become democratic by being "big enough to belong to everybody, too big for anyone to put in his pocket and call his own." Rather than produce art to fit over some patron's fireplace, he invoked a notion of public art that is created for the benefit of the masses. He maintained that the function of art is to create a universal culture "that will guide the future course of world destiny to a better way of living." When Bufano spoke of guiding the future course of world destiny, he assigned a political role to artists in combating the rise of fascism and modern warfare.

Unlike Johnson, who is reported to have shrewdly studied the tastes of patrons by working in an art gallery in order to meet them, Bufano maintained an antipatron stance. He quoted the "whining complaint and recrimination" in a letter he received from an ex-patron to illustrate the need for artists to be less dependent on patrons to survive. The patron was incensed at Bufano for proposing a monumental St. Francis made of stainless steel and copper overlooking the bay, insisting instead that Bufano's best work was represented by his little statues of children, rabbits, deer, and puppies. Bufano then asked, "How can such a man understand the Sun Yat-sen or the Statue of Peace?" "How can a cultural pattern be developed for America if art and the artists are subjugated to the whims and idiosyncrasies of a few overfed decadent merchant princes, carryovers from the days of feudalism?" (O'Connor 1973) Rather than capitulate to the economic pressure of survival, Bufano advocated the radical practice of offering his service to any community that could simply pay him day wages and supply the materials.

He wanted to produce art for the masses with materials and designs that would "reflect public service and functional objectives." He maintained that public art allows artists to give something to the world and enables their voices to be heard beyond the provincialism of their immediate locales.

According to Johnson's own testimony, the desire to produce public art that would be available for future generations motivated him to paint murals in large buildings. (Arvey 1939) As in the case of his abstract design for the Dohrmans building, he sought white patronage to paint religious murals in several black churches in Oakland. Because Johnson's reliance on patrons contrasts sharply with Bufano's teachings, Locke's view of the WPA seems more relevant to understanding Johnson's relationship with his patrons. Bufano believed that the WPA would lay the foundation for a renaissance of art in America, whereas Locke viewed it as a means of sustaining the earlier generation of Harlem Renaissance artists. Given Locke's influence on Johnson's identity as a black artist, Johnson

Sargent Johnson, frieze at Washington High School football field (1942)

was placed in the predicament of having to negotiate the black quest for self-esteem that he shared with the Harlem Renaissance artists and his own recognition of the cogency of Bufano's antipatron stance. Under the rubric of "cultural democracy" Locke aimed primarily to include the African American image in mainstream American art, but he expected African American artists to earn the recognition and esteem of rich patrons. Bufano's notion of "democratic art" was a rejection of Locke's elitism. The renaissance Bufano spoke of would move art into the public domain, whereas Locke conceived the Harlem Renaissance as a means of changing the image of black people in art and socially elevating black artists.

Certain aspects of Bufano's view of art seem to dovetail with Locke's view. For example, Bufano criticized American artists, claiming that they have "borrowed some decadent European form and have pursued it in true merchant fashion." He advocated a more "universal" art that included ancient and non-Western practices. I have already noted traces of this doctrine in some of Johnson's remarks. His view, however, involves a more complex blending of the teachings of his mentors. The technical aspects of his art—e.g., applying color to sculpture—were heavily influenced by Bufano, but his turn to Africa as a source of inspiration was a consequence of Locke's influence. Bearden was critical of African American artists such as Johnson because he believed they had not progressed beyond the influence of their teachers. Bearden's criticism exposes Johnson to one of his own criticisms of other African American artists; Johnson was in no position to criticize them for going to Europe only to imitate the masters, when he seems to have imitated some of his white teachers—specifically Stackpole and Bufano.

Bearden's criticism seems misguided in the case of Johnson, even if he was right to note traces of Bufano's influence on Johnson's style. The fact that Johnson's technique was indebted to Bufano is not sufficient reason to dismiss his art as imitative. Even though Johnson's sculpting technique was acquired from Bufano, the content of his art was considerably different. Bufano's penchant for creating statues of "great men" contrasts sharply with Johnson's preference for African American "primitive types" and ordinary people of all races. With regard to the politics of representing Southern black folk culture, Johnson's practice seems to have been influenced by both Locke and Bufano. Both advocated a return to folk sources, only Locke had mainly ideological concerns in mind, whereas Bufano was more concerned with technical issues pertaining to the use of what he called "pure forms" in modern art. Johnson followed Bufano's teachings regarding the use of both ancient and modern materials as a matter of technique, but he also wanted to meet Locke's demand for African American art with a racial content. He accomplished both by using the technique he acquired from Bufano to emphasize universal themes in his

WPA projects, while reserving the expression of black consciousness for his pieces geared to collectors.

Johnson's art reflects many Asian-Pacific elements that can be found in the work of other Bay Area artists, including his teacher Ralph Stackpole. Lizzetta LeFalle-Collins maintains that Johnson's statues of the Incas, which were created for Stackpole's installation at the International Exposition on Treasure Island, represent his attempt to depict the "pure Indian." (Lefalle-Collins 1996) What might be considered by critics as imitative in Johnson's style enabled him, in fact, to collaborate on public art projects with other Bay Area artists. LeFalle-Collins notes, for instance, a striking similarity between the divers and swimmers in Johnson's athletic frieze at Washington High and the swimmers shown standing and diving in Rivera's mural at City College of San Francisco. But to suppose that he was only interested in pre-Columbian or contemporary Mexican art as a marketing-networking strategy would be misleading. It makes more sense to suppose that he actually found a style, in the work of Stackpole and Bufano, most suitable to expressing a multiracial perspective. Indeed, his own Indian background provided a motive for his interest in the art of the Zapotec. His interest in Third World cultures was not limited to African and pre-Columbian Indian art. In addition to his travels to Mexico to learn technique from the Zapotec Indians, he also went to Japan to visit Shinto shrines and study Japanese art.

What is the relevance of Johnson's success as both a Harlem Renaissance artist and a WPA artist for understanding the myth of racial tolerance? This question involves several issues pertaining to the relationship between elitism in art and the politics of representation.

When Locke advocated the appropriation of black folk culture by artists, he had a European model of nationalistic art in mind. Harlem would be a Mecca for the black renaissance in art just as Dublin and Prague were centers where European artists gathered to mine their national folk cultures. But what about the excavation of folk culture by intellectuals, black or white? Johnson's art is not to be confused with the folk expression of the Africans or the Indians, whose technique and imagery he appropriated. But if Johnson was black and Indian, why should we construe his use of folk techniques as an "appropriation"? Both Locke and Bufano expected modern art to rely on folk cultures as a source of inspiration for contemporary ideas. When Johnson began working in the black Oaxacan clay used by the Zapotec Indians, he was not interested in making pottery or sculptures that were a part of their traditions. Nor were any of the African masks in his series meant to be part of African religious tradition. Rather, he aimed to incorporate ancient principles of aesthetics regarding sculptural forms into a transformative practice by combining Western with non-Western elements. This hybrid form is not to be confused with any of the folk forms from which it is derived. We can best understand Johnson's appeal to folk sources as appropriation in the sense that African art forms were used by European artists such as Georges Braque, Pablo Picasso, and Amedeo Modigliani.

There is a certain amount of ambivalence that can be associated with Johnson's appropriation of folk art, as well as his representations of Southern black folk. He was quite aware of the political thrust of his images of African Americans in an era of legal segregation and racial oppression. For this reason he subscribed to Locke's philosophy and attempted to create a new black aesthetic in contemporary American art. His peer acceptance by other Bay Area artists boded well for the social objective Locke had set for the renaissance artists. Johnson was a perfect instance of Locke's notion of "cultural democracy," whereby American artists of all races are at liberty to draw on native folk sources for raw materials and inspiration. The problem with this notion, as we have seen in connection with Bufano's philosophy, is that the inclusion of African American images in mainstream art is quite compatible with the denial of social equality to African Americans. Brazilian culture provides a case for comparison. The inclusion of the African and Indian cultures of Brazil into the national culture has not resulted in any significant social change for blacks and Indians in Brazil. This criticism seems to apply to the lack of impact Johnson and the Harlem Renaissance artists had on the institutionalized practice of racial discrimination in the United States.

San Francisco's myth of racial tolerance is much like Brazil's myth of "racial democracy." (Nascimento 1977) If we situate Johnson's art in the context of what Bay Area artists were doing, it clearly reflects a cultural pluralism that did not exist in other parts of the United States. It is in this sense that the myth is sustained by Johnson's success. But if we consider the fact that Johnson consciously avoided raising political issues in his work, we come closer to understanding why the idea of racial tolerance in San Francisco is only a myth. Johnson's role in the silencing of Bufano is unforgivable, for Bufano was a very strong voice for social change in America. He produced art that advocated resistance to oppression. "I sculptured 'Peace' in the form of a projectile, to express the idea that if peace is to be preserved today it must be enforced peace—enforced by the democracies against Fascist barbarism. Modern warfare, which involves the bombing of women and children, has no counterpart in a peace interpreted by the conventional motif of olive branches and doves." (O'Connor 1973) The ambivalence of those of us who take ourselves to be progressive sometimes feel toward Johnson's art derives from his refusal to use his art to advocate social change. When we consider

Johnson's relationship with the black community, the question arises as to whether he trained any black artist to paint murals in black churches or whether as a WPA unit supervisor he included any black artists on any of his projects. Virtually nothing has been written about his relations with other Third World artists in the Bay Area. When we celebrate Sargent Johnson as one of San Francisco's great artists we must not fail to consider his success in relation to the social environment from which he emerged—including the community of black artists with whom he associated in San Francisco.

Acknowledgments

I gratefully acknowledge assistance from Beth Bresnan and Lizzetta Lefalle-Collins.

References

Arvey, Verna. 1939. "Sargent Johnson." *Opportunity* 17 (July) 213–14.

Bearden, Romare, and Harry Henderson. 1993. *A History of African-American Artists: From 1792 to the Present.* New York: Pantheon.

Broussard, Albert. 1993. *Black San Francisco.* Lawrence: University Press of Kansas.

Daniels, Douglas. 1980/90. *Pioneer Urbanites.* Berkeley: University of California Press.

Dover, Cedric. 1960. *American Negro Art.* New York: Graphic Society.

Locke, Alain, ed. 1925/68. *The New Negro: An Interpretation.* Boston: Atheneum.

———, ed. 1925a. "The Art of the Ancestors," *Survey Graphic* VI, 6 (March) 673.

———. 1936/91. *Negro Art: Past and Present.* Salem, NH: Ayer.

———. 1939. "Advance on the Art Front," *Opportunity* XVII, 5 (May) 132–36.

Hughes, Langston. 1940, *The Big Sea.* New York: Farrar, Straus & Giroux.

Johnson, Sargent C. 1935. Interview, *San Francisco Chronicle* (October 6) D3.

LeFalle-Collins, Lizzetta, and Shifra M. Goldman. 1996. *In the Spirit of Resistance: African-American Modernists and the Mexican Muralist School.* New York: The American Federation of Arts.

McKinzie, Richard D. 1973. *The New Deal for Artists.* Princeton, NJ: Princeton University Press.

O'Connor, Francis V. 1973. *Art for the Millions.* New York: Graphic Society.

Porter, James A. 1943/92. *Modern Negro Art.* Washington, D.C.: Howard University Press.

The Beat Generation and San Francisco's Culture of Dissent

by Nancy J. Peters

MORE THAN TWO THOUSAND PEOPLE from diverse communities and generations gathered in April 1997 at a memorial service for Allen Ginsberg at San Francisco's Temple Emanu-El. The presence of so many celebrants from the liberatory movements that followed in the wake of the Beat Generation demonstrated the strength and range of the city's abiding culture of dissent. San Francisco has always been a breeding ground for bohemian countercultures; its cosmopolitan population, its tolerance of eccentricity, and its provincialism and distance from the centers of national culture and political power have long made it an ideal place for nonconformist writers, artists, and utopian dreamers. An outsider literary lineage originated with the Gold Rush satirists, continuing on through such mavericks as Frank Norris, John Muir, Ambrose Bierce, Jack London, and the San Francisco Renaissance writers of the 1940s. The beat phenomenon that took shape in San Francisco in the mid-fifties not only dislodged American poetry from the academic literary establishment, it invigorated a democratic popular culture that was to proliferate in many directions: the antiwar and ecology movements, the fight against censorship, the pursuit of gay, lesbian, minority, and women's rights. Drawing on Whitman's ecstatic populism, the prophetic radicalism of William Blake, and the performance heritage of oral literatures, the beats created a style of poetic intervention that inspired following generations to challenge oppressive political and cultural authority.

The idea of bohemia caught the imaginations of writers in early San Francisco with Henri Murger's *Scènes de la Vie de Bohème* (1844), which depicted life in the Latin Quarter of Paris, where artists had been renouncing their bourgeois origins since the revolution of 1830 to live for love and a more egalitarian society. It was thought that Bohemia was the country of origin of Gypsies, who were regarded as an ideal nomadic community that flourished outside the constraints of established society. Mürger's book enjoyed immediate popularity, and by the 1860s word of it had reached San Francisco writers. In those days San Francisco was a rapacious society that offered boundless opportunities for the savage exploitation of man and nature. There was certainly no literary canon, and literary expression took the form of exaggeration, hoaxes, and the kind of boisterous humor that reached its high point in Mark Twain's mining novel *Roughing It*. Many writers were manual laborers, shopkeepers, housewives, and transients; and the realistic narratives of pioneers and miners who survived the hazards of emigration and settlement were often so harrowing that they surpassed the wildest fiction. The city's earliest literature, then, was both democratic and anarchic; at the same time, the lawlessness of the city seemed to elicit from some of its poets a nostalgia for classical literary forms and an imagined lost civility of remote times and places, so that a vaguely Apollonian standard of order and proportion coexisted anachronistically with violent and macabre stories and homespun accounts of daily life. Literary carpetbaggers from the East Coast occasionally tried their hand at taming the literary frontier, but most left town in defeat, proclaiming the city illiterate, chauvinistic, and pretentious. Although class society in San Francisco bore little resemblance to that of Paris, the city's writers were not blind to the obvious attractions of *la vie de bohème*, and they reveled the nights away in Montgomery Street bars and restaurants. The popular press was full of references to bohemians. Before he struck it rich with his sentimental gold-field fables, Bret Harte used the pseudonym "The Bohemian" and even wrote a column of whimsical vignettes in *The Golden Era* called "The Bohemian Feuilleton." Although women intellectuals and writers such as poet and actress Ada Isaacs Mencken and journalist Ada Clare, who had been friends of Walt Whitman, found San Francisco appallingly provincial, they welcomed the sexual and social freedom the frontier town's literary scene offered.

Another, later, bohemian community developed in the 1880s and 1890s around the intersections of Pacific, Washington, Jackson, and Montgomery Streets, where food was cheap and low-rent artists' studios were abundant. When the Montgomery Block building (at Montgomery and Columbus)—which in the 1850s had been the center of business, banking, and mining speculation—emptied out as the commercial center moved south, artists and writers moved in. Over the years, more than 2,000 of them are reputed to have had spaces there, making the loss of this historic building in 1959 a black episode in the city's cultural history. (The Transamerica Corporation Pyramid now occupies the site.) Some of the notable writers and artists who lived in the "Monkey Block" were Ambrose Bierce, Joaquin Miller, George Sterling, Jack London, Sadakichi

Hartman, Frank Norris, Yone Noguchi, Margaret Anderson, and Kenneth Rexroth. Frida Kahlo and Diego Rivera lived there while Rivera was painting the allegory of California's riches on the ceiling of the California Stock Exchange (now a tony private luncheon club).

When the Montgomery Block studio space was taken over by business offices following the earthquake and fire of 1906, the writing community dispersed. The city's unofficial poet laureate, George Sterling, moved to Carmel, where between 1906 and 1912 he and a small group of writers and artists attempted to create an alternative community that would use art as the basis for an ideal society. Hardworking writers, idealistic social reformers, muckrakers, and various classes of bohemian artists made up the population of the colony. Sterling and his friend Jack London, both ardent socialists, brought a political orientation to the group; Jimmy Hopper and Fred Bechdolt collaborated on a novel, 9009, that exposed prison conditions; and Upton Sinclair, who had come West after Hellicon Hall, his utopian colony in New York, had ceased to be viable, worked on plays and new social reform plans. One of the most gifted members of the group was Mary Austin, who was a feminist and early champion of Native American languages and cultures. Other residents and visitors to the community were writers Ambrose Bierce and Sinclair Lewis, photographer Arnold Genthe, poet Nora May French, painters Xavier Martínez and Ernest Peixotto, and muckrakers Lincoln Steffens and Ray Stannard Baker.

"There are two elements, at least, that are essential to Bohemianism," Sterling once wrote in a letter to Jack London. "The first is devotion or addiction to one of the Seven Arts; the other is poverty. . . . I like to think of my Bohemians as young, as radical as their outlook on art and life, as unconventional. . . ." (Walker 1966) About as far as you can go from poverty, art, and radicalism is San Francisco's Bohemian Club, of which both Sterling and Jack London, ironically, were once members. Organized in 1872 as a drinking club for male journalists, the Bohemian Club's membership soon solicited wealthy businessmen to support its theatricals and other activities. Since World War II, this "official" bohemia has been composed of the city's political and financial elite, along with some establishment writers and commercial artists. Members meet in town (to hear readings of poetry by the likes of Henry Wadsworth Longfellow and Edwin Markham) and also at the Bohemian Grove, a notoriously exclusive retreat on the Russian River that hosts an annual summer exercise in ruling-class cohesiveness, where CEOs and directors of the Fortune 500 companies camp out in secrecy with presidents and congressmen, cabinet members, and Pentagon brass. (Domhoff 1974)

After the Carmel experiment foundered, Sterling returned to San Francisco, depressed and feeling isolated. His hopes for a literary community were dashed and his ornamented verse failed to find favor in the East. He committed suicide in the Montgomery Block in 1927. That same year the poet Kenneth Rexroth arrived in San Francisco in quite a different mood, delighted to find a literary scene so under-developed and noncommercial—an inviting *tabula rasa*. Neither the modernism of Eliot and Pound nor the latest critical fashions had reached the city, which despite its pretensions was in the late 1920s a real cultural backwater. Rexroth, with his wide-ranging intellect, prodigious memory, and ferocious temper, believed himself just the man to transmute the city's literature and culture along radical new lines. Rexroth had come out of the anarchist tradition of socialism and during the Depression worked as a labor organizer and for various WPA projects; he was active with the Randolph Bourne Council, the John Reed Clubs, and the Waterfront Workers Association. An admirer of Kropotkin's *Ethics* and *Mutual Aid*, he was a fiery advocate of a communalist society that would be created through civil disobe-dience. Rexroth opposed European cultural chauvinism, and introduced transla-tions of Asian poetry to American readers. Confronting the Eastern literary estab-lishment, which was by the 1940s immersed in formality, ironic distance, and a value-free aesthetic, he insisted that poetry should have moral significance and bear personal witness against the "permanent war state." Rexroth's "Thou Shalt Not Kill," a polemic against consumer culture, was a precursor to Ginsberg's "Howl"—but was much more vitriolic.

After World War II, the United States began to solidify its enlarged role as an imperialist power and to incorporate useful features of fascism: militarization, nationalist ideology, state support of large corporations ("What's good for General Motors is good for America"), and the creation of enemies for purposes of social control. The mass media celebrated common sense, social adjustment, conformi-ty, churchgoing, and togetherness. The good life was defined by a house in sub-urbia, a new car, and synthetic products; the economics of planned obsolescence fanned the flames of market growth. Blacks who had served in the armed forces were mustered out to segregated neighborhoods, and women who had worked in war industries went to the new suburbs to be housewives, childbearers, and the principal victims of restored sexual puritanism.

However, returning GIs brought home with them a new interest in foreign cultures, and San Francisco, with an eye on potential markets abroad, stepped up its commercial contacts with Asia. In fact, the city then was receptive to many outside cultural influences and offered a receptive environment for radicals, anar-chists, communists, populists, Wobblies, abstract expressionist painters, assem-blage artists, and experimental theater troupes. Jazz and bebop began revolutionizing music and pulling in enthusiastic crossover audiences. And behind the rhetoric of consumerism and togetherness a current of dissent ran just below the surface. Philip Lamantia recalled the city in the late 1940s:

> San Francisco was terribly straight-laced and provincial, but at the same time there were these islands of freedom—in North Beach at bars like the Iron Pot and the Black Cat, where intellectuals met to talk. There was a whole underground culture that went unnoticed by the city at large. An amazing music scene was going on, black music. *Ebony* magazine ran a story about how San Francisco was the best city in the country for blacks. Down in Little Harlem around Third Street and Howard you could hear all-night rhythm and blues. The Fillmore was the center of the bebop revolution, with frequent appearances by Charlie Parker and Dizzy Gillespie, and San Francisco was unique for the open and friendly relations between blacks and whites who had gone underground, much more so than in New York. Blacks accepted the white hipster poets, and the musicians generously let a few talented young white musicians jam with them.

Writers who were conscientious objectors during World War II and interned at the Waldport, Oregon, CO camp came down on furlough to meet with Bay Area writers. Among them were Adrian Wilson, an innovative fine press printer, and the poet William Everson, whose Untide Press published Kenneth Patchen's poetry of social protest. Between 1946 and 1952, Rexroth held Friday evening soirées at his home at 250 Scott Street to discuss poetry and ideas. Regular participants included William Everson, Robert Duncan, Philip Lamantia, Muriel Rukeyser, Morris Graves, Gary Snyder, James Broughton, Lawrence Ferlinghetti, Michael McClure, and Thomas and Ariel Parkinson. (Hamalian 1991)

Additionally, the anarchist Libertarian Circle met on Wednesdays on Steiner Street, where a community of free spirits drank plenty of red wine and set about refounding the radical movement. They met for big parties at Fugazi Hall on Green Street in North Beach, and the writers and artists of the Rexroth group were joined by old Italian anarchists, longshoremen, doctors, cabbies, professors; sometimes as many as two hundred people attended these gatherings, which featured political debate, dancing, picnics, and hiking trips. Out of this Libertarian Circle came Lewis Hill, who conceived the idea of a listener-sponsored, cooperative radio station as a means to reach greater numbers of people. He and Richard Moore aspired to make available a life of the mind for working people who couldn't afford a university education. Thus was born KPFA/Pacifica, which aired experts on public affairs and philosophy, literature and film, classical music and jazz, expanding the social influence of the region's progressive intellectuals.

Literature began to be a communal experience, with poetry readings and

Lawrence Ferlinghetti in front of City Lights Books (1959)

discussions drawing substantial audiences. Regular readings were organized at San Francisco State College by Robert Duncan and Madeleine Gleason, and in 1954 Ruth Witt-Diamant formalized them with the foundation of the San Francisco Poetry Center there. English professor Josephine Miles coordinated similar events in Berkeley, and the California School of Fine Arts (now the San Francisco Art Institute) was a center for literary performances as well. Spirited literary journals sprang up on both sides of the Bay: *Goad*, *Inferno*, and *Golden Goose*. George Leite published *Circle* magazine (1944–1948), influenced by surrealism, which attempted a new synthesis of antiauthoritarian politics, pacifism, and internationalism in letters. *The Ark* urged spontaneous revolt in order to transform social relations. This constellation of political engagement and literary expression became known as the San Francisco Renaissance, and it marked the beginnings of a shift of cultural gravity from East to West.

In 1947 *Harper's* published an article by Berkeley writer Mildred Edie Brady, "The New Cult of Sex and Anarchy," which unwittingly drew national attention to the Bay Area's special appeal. She took a dim view of the region's art and intellectual life, describing two camps of bohemians. The first, she said, were devotees of Henry Miller who were attracted by the sex in his books and by his pacifist manifesto, "Murder the Murderers"; they were embroiled in "mysticism, egoism, sexualism, surrealism, and anarchism." The second group could be found in association with Kenneth Rexroth: these read Peter Kropotkin and Wilhelm Reich. Both groups, she reported, glorified the irrational and did nothing but count their orgasms. Two young New York writers, Lawrence Ferlinghetti and Allen Ginsberg, would remember this summons to possibilities far more appealing than Empson's *Seven Types of Ambiguity* and the agenda of the New Criticism.

The principal writers of the Beat Generation—Allen Ginsberg, William Burroughs, and Jack Kerouac—had met in New York City in the early 1940s, when Ginsberg and Kerouac were students at Columbia University. They were experimenting with new writing based on uncensored self-expression and altered states of consciousness induced by trance or drugs. Joined by Neal Cassady, Gregory Corso, and Herbert Huncke, they hung around Times Square, fascinated by marginal subcultures, and picked up the style and language of addicts, con men, carnies, hustlers, and small-timers. (Schumaker 1992) In the world of the dispossessed urban dweller they saw an escape from postwar mass society. These Easterners were disaffected, urban, *noir*, while the poets of what would later be considered the Bay Area branch of the Beat Generation—Gary Snyder, Philip Lamantia, David Meltzer, Joanne Kyger, Bob Kaufman, Michael McClure, Lawrence Ferlinghetti, and Philip Whalen—were more politically and ecologically oriented. And while the vitality of

African American culture influenced writers on both coasts, the Western poets were more open to Asian and Native American traditions.

The poet hipsters converged in San Francisco in the mid-fifties, when, for a brief few years, an energetic literary community produced readings, small publications, and multimedia events in collaboration with assemblage artists Jay de Feo, Wally Berman, Joan Brown, Wally Hedrick, and Bruce Conner. (Solnit 1990) Lawrence Ferlinghetti had come from Paris to San Francisco in 1950, where he met Peter D. Martin, son of the anarchist Carlo Tresca, and together they founded the City Lights Bookstore in 1953 as a literary meeting place. Two years later Ferlinghetti issued his first book of poems, *Pictures of the Gone World*, launching City Lights Publications. Jack Kerouac and Neal Cassady sped back and forth between New York and San Francisco, measuring the disappearing landscape of freedom, an experience portrayed in Kerouac's novels. With the publication of *On the Road* in 1957 the *Village Voice* noted that "Jack Kerouac, the Greenwich Village writer (with Allen Ginsberg and Gregory Corso), had to go to San Francisco to become a San Francisco writer and become famous." Ginsberg arrived in 1954 and wrote "Howl" that same year and the next, while living at 1010 Montgomery Street in North Beach. Ferlinghetti had rejected Ginsberg's earlier poems, but when he heard Ginsberg read "Howl" at the Six Gallery in 1955, he knew it was the defining poem of the era. This long incantatory work describes the destruction of the human spirit by America's military-industrial machine and calls for redemption through the reconciliation of mind and body, affirming human wholeness and holiness.

Howl and Other Poems, which City Lights had had printed in England, came to public notice after the second edition was seized by U.S. customs in March 1957 on charges of obscenity. On April 3 the American Civil Liberties Union (to which Ferlinghetti had submitted a copy of the manuscript before it went to the printer) informed Chester MacPhee, Collector of Customs, that it would contest the legality of the seizure. City Lights announced that a new edition of *Howl* was being printed in the United States, thereby removing it from customs jurisdiction. A photo-offset edition was placed on sale at City Lights Bookstore and distributed nationally. On May 19, the *San Francisco Chronicle* printed a defense of the book by Ferlinghetti, who stated, "It is not the poet but what he observes which is revealed as obscene. The great obscene wastes of *Howl* are the sad wastes of the mechanized world, lost among atom bombs and insane nationalisms." Customs released the books, but then the local police took over, arresting Ferlinghetti and the bookstore manager, Shigyoshi Murao, on charges of selling obscene material.

A long court trial lasted throughout summer, during which City Lights and

Photo Charles Daly

Grant Avenue, North Beach (1959)

Howl were supported by poets, editors, and critics. J. W. Erlich, an attorney of national renown who had defended Billie Holiday and other artists, agreed to take the case, along with Albert Bendich and Lawrence Speiser of the ACLU. (Erlich 1960) When it was learned that Municipal Judge Clayton Horn, a devout Christian who taught Bible classes, had been appointed to hear the case, Ferlinghetti's lawyers foresaw trouble. It was unusual for the Municipal Court to hear constitutional cases, and Horn took his responsibility seriously, especially in the wake of his previous case. Several young girls visiting the city from Los Angeles had been caught shoplifting, and Judge Horn had sentenced them to read passages from the Bible and to see Cecil B. DeMille's *The Ten Commandments*, which was filmed partly in San Francisco and had just been released. The sentence provoked a great public outcry: Judge Horn had violated the principle of separation of Church and State. So Horn asked for a recess so he might read other obscene books that had been banned throughout history, and then proved himself a conscientious man, determining that *Howl* was not obscene because it was "not without socially redeeming importance." He then went on to set forth certain rules for the guidance of authorities in the

PHOTO COURTESY CITY LIGHTS BOOKS

The *Howl* trial. Lawrence Ferlinghetti and Shigeyoshi Murao, front-row bench (1957).

future, establishing the legal precedent that enabled publication in the next decade of Lawrence's *Lady Chatterley's Lover,* Miller's *Tropic of Cancer*, and other prohibited literary works.

Like Mürger's book about Paris bohemians, the novels of Jack Kerouac chronicled the half-imagined, half-real lives of the artists. His *On the Road* and Ginsberg's "Howl" seemed to awaken the collective American id, arousing desire and fear, rage and envy. To the astonishment of the poets, who were going about their work writing poetry and editing small literary journals, the Luce empire unleashed its full arsenal at a perceived challenge to the Puritan ethic. The beat poet was excoriated as juvenile delinquent, drug addict, and sexual outlaw. In one piece, *Life* magazine asserted that "bums, hostile little females and part-time bohemians are foisted into polite society by a few neurotic and drugged poets. . . . [They are] talkers, loafers, passive little con men, lonely eccentrics, mom-haters, cop-haters, exhibitionists with abused smiles and second mortgages on a bongo drum—writers who cannot write, painters who cannot paint, dancers with unfortunate malfunction of the fetlocks." Paul O'Neil wrote a piece in *Life* called "What Is It That Beats Want?" paraphrasing Freud's famous question about women, noting that the beats, too, were illogical, emotional, and irrational. Things went so far that at the 1960 Republican Convention FBI Director J. Edgar Hoover warned that America's three greatest enemies were Communists, Eggheads, and Beatniks.

A cry of outrage came from yet another quarter: establishment intellectuals disliked beat populism and the lack of respect for tradition, the latter a complaint that continues in academia today in new guise in the debates over multicultural- ism, curriculum, and the canon. Writers Herb Gold, James Dickey, and John Updike attacked the beats; and Diana Trilling labeled them "unholy barbarians." The poet and critic John Hollander saw in "Howl" the "ravings of a lunatic fiend," and John Ciardi wrote in the *Saturday Review*: "The fact is that the Beat Generation is not only juvenile but certainly related to juvenile delinquency through a common ancestry whose name is Disgust . . . little more than unwashed eccentricity." Norman Podhoretz was hysterical: "We are witnessing a revolt of all the forces hostile to civilization itself—a movement of brute stupidity and know- nothingism that is trying to take over the country. . . . The only art the new Bohemians have any use for is jazz, mainly of the cool variety. Their predilection for bop language is a way of demonstrating solidarity with the primitive vitality and spontaneity they find in jazz and of expressing contempt for coherent, ratio- nal discourse. . . ." This diatribe calls up the usual racist stereotypes in its com- parison of beats to African Americans, to whose marginalized culture the writers were much indebted, as they openly claimed. Conservatives nearly a half century later are still sputtering about those who make careers of "execrating American values," as George Will observed in an April 1997 syndicated obituary of Allen Ginsberg. In September, *New Criterion* editor Roger Kimball said in the *Wall Street Journal* that "Allen Ginsberg, William Burroughs, and the rest of the Beats really do mark an important moment in American culture, not as one of its achievements, but as a grievous example of its degeneration."

Even the anarchist Paul Goodman, who was sympathetic to the beats and applauded their "dropping out of the system of sales and production," regretted that "They have no moral code, no positive political or social program, are mere- ly the symptom of the failure of industrial society to provide a challenge to the young." (Goodman 1959) He went on to regret the beats' cynicism, neglect of ethical goals, and ignorance of civilized values. Radicals of the old left (many of them now of the new right) opposed the beats' apolitical stance and their anar- chist views. "[They] are only reflections of the class they reject," wrote Irving Howe in the *New Criterion*, and he attacked them for having no political program. Indeed, the beats had no programmatic politics and rejected institutional forms of protest, declining party memberships and sect affiliations altogether.

Countercultures offer an irresistible narrative opportunity, with a colorful cast of characters and the seductive themes of transgression, exile, and utopia. The beat story, set in San Francisco, New York, and the long American highway in between, is part fiction, part autobiography—a narrative in the counterpoint voices of author and media. With a nice blend of condescension and malice, *Chronicle* columnist Herb Caen coined the word "beatnik" after the 1957 launch of the Russian satellite sputnik, conferring on the writers just a hint of anti-Americanism. A city reporter dressed in all-black, donned beret and false beard and went to the pads of North Beach to report on the exotic sexual practices of the misfits. (Watson 1995) All this coincided with the inordinate attention sociologists were then giving to alienated youths stuck at the "aggressive stage," and doomed to be social pariahs. The juvenile delinquent was being represented in an exciting way in such films as *The Wild One* (1953) and *Rebel Without a Cause* (1959). A film company offered Kerouac and Cassady a huge sum of money (which they refused) to pose as armed and vicious killers to promote a beatnik genre film: Albert Zugsmith's *The Beat Generation* featured a sociopathic rapist pursuing suburban housewives. Exploitation novels had such titles as *Lust Pad, Bang a Beatnik*, and *Sintime Beatniks*. The popular sitcom *The Lives and Loves of Dobie Gillis* introduced the unthreatening beatnik for family consumption in the goateed Maynard G. Krebs, a figure reprised in the 1980s in *Happy Days* as "the Fonz." For the kids there was even a muppet called Ferlinghetti Donizetti ("I don't wash. I don't have to!"). Press coverage finally brought young people to North Beach from all over the country; they dressed as hipsters and tried to be beats; they were followed by tourists who came to see beatniks; and finally, commodities were created to sell to both beatniks and tourists. This commercial appropriation would be replicated a decade later in the Haight-Ashbury, with the hippies.

By the time the Coppolas began working on their definitive film of *On the Road* in the early nineties, the beat writers had become subjects of doctoral dissertations and as iconic as the city that claimed them for itself. A *San Francisco Examiner* story, "Icons" (Nov. 1996), noted "the cultural detritus" being exhibited at museums: art works featuring Elvis, Marilyn, Lucy, and "Beat Culture and the New America: 1950–1965," which had shown the year before at the Whitney in New York. "Whether it's Dennis Hopper's photos of alienated youths, Michael McClure, Bob Dylan and Allen Ginsberg gathering in hip colloquy or a slouching Jack Kerouac, the Beat attitude is integral to the Bay Area's identity." Billboards of Allen Ginsberg and Jack Kerouac in Gap khaki have loomed over the downtown freeway, while William Burroughs was pictured in *Vanity Fair* in Nikes. Major corporations regularly solicit the City Lights Bookstore for location shots against which to display

Photo Larry Keenan, Jr.

Michael McClure, Bob Dylan, and Allen Ginsberg at City Lights (1965)

their products. In efforts to turn the neighborhood into a theme park, the North Beach Chamber of Commerce modified its logo to "Little Italy and the Home of the Beat Generation." A recent float in the Italian Heritage Parade (formerly the Columbus Day Parade until Native American protesters motivated a name change) revives the stereotypical image of the "beatnik" with beret and bongos. In fact, a steady exodus of Italians from North Beach to the Marina, the Mission, and the Excelsior has been going on since the 1906 earthquake, making "Little Italy" a misnomer today. And although a bohemian community established itself in North Beach, with coffee houses, galleries, and the City Lights Bookstore as pivot points, the brief period of close collaboration of beat writers and artists was over by 1956, when Ginsberg, Burroughs, Kerouac, and others left San Francisco, just as North Beach was moving center stage in the public mind.

The beats succeeded surprisingly well, however, in sidestepping mainstream appropriation. For one thing, they were not a school; formal stylistic agenda was something they avoided. For another, they were more a historical moment than a cohesive literary movement in which Ferlinghetti's Chaplinesque populism could coexist with William Burroughs's paranoid dystopia or Philip Lamantia's urban surrealism with Gary Snyder's bedrock common sense. Moreover, most of the Western writers never identified themselves as "beats" at all. We see over the years that a succession of independent press publications and loosely organized readings and other events brought together writers who were distinctly individual in aesthetic sensibility, subject matter, and personal interests. The beats marked a point of transition between the old bohemian utopias and the postmodern era of decentralization and "difference." The writers had the advantages of both mobility and a unifying narrative. Ginsberg's resolute vision of a community of poet comrades and his energetic media skills perpetuated the larger story of a "generation" with a common agenda, which helped to focus attention on the writers and to give them a public forum. However, the wide compass and heterogeneity of the beats was fundamental to their far-reaching appeal: Diane di Prima's feminism, Phil Whalen's zen whimsy, Bob Kaufman's dada black humor, Jack Kerouac's apolitical romances. City Lights, too, played a role in widening the definition of "beat." Ferlinghetti, who never considered himself a beat writer, saw the group as part of a larger, international, dissident ferment. His idea was to encourage cross-currents and cross-fertilizations among writers and thinkers from different cultures and communities both in the books sold at the store and in its publication program. In this sense the beats are just one phase of the outsider literary line, and "the beat goes on" in City Lights' books and journals that presented such younger writers as Anne Waldman, Guillermo Gómez-Peña, Sam Shepard, Sara Chin, Andrei Codrescu, Karen Finley, Ellen Ullman, James Brook, Rodrigo Rey Rosa, Charles Bukowski, David Henderson, Gary Indiana, Ward Churchill, Michael Parenti, Alberto Blanco, Rebecca Brown, Janice Eidus, Gil Cuadros, Jeremy Reed, Nathaniel Mackey, La Loca, Rikki Ducornet, and Peter Lamborn Wilson.

With no set allegiances to political parties or agendas, the beats were important as exemplars of creative resistance. As Allen Ginsberg often claimed, candor—the expression of authentic personal experience—was foremost, and beat work helped to bring private life into public discourse. The beat challenge to power was in the practice of a kind of mobile guerrilla poetics. Because the beat period is usually dated 1945 to 1960 (or 1965), the writers' mature years are seldom taken into account, the years in which they were most active in national and community issues, especially Ferlinghetti, Snyder, Ginsberg, and di Prima, who had moved permanently to San Francisco in the early 1970s. Snyder was a leading force in the back-to-the land ecology movement. Di Prima taught in schools and prisons and founded a school of healing arts. San Francisco's poets gave benefit readings, marched and demonstrated and sometimes went to jail. Some were active in support of the United Farm Workers and other union struggles; others were at the forefront of protests of the Vietnam War and, later, U.S. military and CIA interventions in Latin America. Allen Ginsberg was a Pied Piper of poetic interventions: levitating the Pentagon in 1967 and chanting with the Yippies at the 1968 Democratic Convention, and then testifying with humor and common sense at the ensuing Chicago Conspiracy Trial. He spent many years documenting evidence of CIA drug dealing. On one stay in San Francisco in the mid-seventies, he so pestered CIA chief Richard Helms on the telephone that Helms made a bet with him. He promised to investigate Ginsberg's charges and vowed that if Ginsberg proved to be right about the agency's heroin trafficking he would meditate every day for the rest of his life. Within a couple of days, the City Lights publishing office received a call from Helms: "Please tell Mr. Ginsberg that I began my first meditation session this morning." Another prolonged investigation that Ginsberg undertook with PEN American Center uncovered reams of documents proving extensive FBI sabotage and destruction of the independent press that had been a vigorous force in the 1960s and 1970s. (Rips 1981)

The "rucksack revolution" Kerouac had prophesied in *The Dharma Bums* arrived in the Bay Area in the early 1960s. Once again, a new music—this time rock—drew a new generation of rebellious youths to San Francisco. The hopes of this massive counterculture to enlighten national consciousness through a psychedelic-erotic politics eventually proved futile. Although breakthroughs were made in sexual liberation and the arts, particularly multimedia and performance work, the community self-destructed under the weight of Dionysian excess, political naïveté, and the impossibility of creating a utopia that would serve macrocosmic needs. As in other bohemias, a society of dropouts is never as free as it seems and cannot exist outside the organized catastrophe of oppression. This later became clearer as the numbers of the hippie counterculture grew. (Smith 1995)

A post-hippie underground sensibility emerged in the early seventies in the social-critique proto-performance work of such artists as Sam Shepard, Karen Finley, and in projects by filmmakers and photographers at the San Francisco Art Institute. At the Mabuhay Gardens later in the decade punk musicians began mocking the star system of stadium rock and repossessing their own creativity. V. Vale perceived in the punks a healthy defiance of commercial youth culture and, with seed money from Ginsberg and Ferlinghetti, began documenting (and catalyzing) this impetus in his tabloid *Search and Destroy* and in the publications of Re/Search, which covered—in addition to the punk scene—reggae, situationism, surrealism, marginalized artists, and the particular legacies of Burroughs, Lamantia, and J. G. Ballard.

By the mid-seventies, oppositional communities began to be based on gender and ethnicity. "Difference" was the focus, and difference no longer referred to white male bohemians dropping out of mainstream society, but instead to perceived "genetic" difference. (Davidson 1989) Aware of multiple histories, writers grouped themselves as gays or lesbians, Latinos, blacks—with subdivisions within those groups. Ethnic writers and artists gathered in the neighborhoods to explore issues of identity and to foster small-group cohesiveness. Such groups as the Kearny Street Workshop and the Mission *Raza* Writers in San Francisco and the Before Columbus Foundation in Berkeley discovered and published fresh ethnic voices who had different stories to tell and had never had the opportunity to be heard. Interlingual poetry flourished, as did new performance work. These developments were instrumental in alerting New York publishers to a substantial new audience they had scarcely touched. In the eighties, a new formalism began to obscure the popular voice. In the ferment of deconstruction and postmodern theory, elitist language and theory in the universities began to dominate as they had in the 1950s. Globalized ideologies make pluralism and diversity useful in eluding appropriation, but the doctrine of fragmentation and decentralization makes problematic recognizing and acting on common interests. It is instructive to note that when the Berlin Wall fell, East German *Stasi* (secret police) documents revealed that the government had paid agents to infiltrate the literary underground in order to put an end to beat-inspired writing by subsidizing "pomo" theory and the new formalism, which was believed could divert attention from social issues.

The renewed popularity of the beats in the nineties goes beyond nostalgia for a period that now seems innocent in its freedom of the road and for its pleasures of unrestrained sex and drugs. The 1950s and 1990s have much in common, both periods characterized by paradigmatic technological and economic change, government capitulation to corporate power, the rise of religious fundamentalism, and a media-imposed anti-intellectual culture. Public resources for education, libraries, and the arts have been savagely curtailed, bringing to crisis a long period of cultural vigor in the Bay Area. An oppositional culture today faces formidable challenges now that the global economy has transformed work and the dynamics of urban life. In San Francisco, as elsewhere, upscale development, real estate speculation, and consequent high rents make the marginalized life of the independent writer and artist almost impossible. Additionally, the commodification of transgression and the instant appropriation, re-formation, and marketing of dissent have eliminated older channels of social contention. While the much-heralded democracy of electronic communication makes it easier to disseminate radical ideas, they are more easily drowned out in the glut of information pouring through the Babel of the Internet. Corporatization of bookselling and publishing also contribute to the dumbing-down effect. Fortunately, many people in San Francisco and the Bay Area have resisted the lure of Starbucks-Best-Seller culture, continuing to support independents. Talented writers and artists still manage to survive in the Mission and South of Market, producing experimental theater, performance works, digital arts, chapbooks, and zines; and so there remain in the city vital pockets of dissident culture that continue to confront the question of how to create art that uses anger and desire to motivate adventure, self-realization, and community. The future viability of this culture depends on what directions the city takes now.

References

Davidson, Michael. 1989. *The San Francisco Renaissance: Poetics and Community at Mid-Century.* New York: Cambridge University Press.

Domhoff, G. William. 1974. *The Bohemian Grove and Other Retreats; a Study in Ruling-Class Cohesiveness.* San Francisco: Harper & Row.

Erlich, J. W. 1960. *Howl of the Censor.* San Carlos, CA: Nourse Publishing Co.

Ferlinghetti, Lawrence, and Nancy J. Peters. 1980. *Literary San Francisco.* San Francisco: Harper & Row.

Ginsberg, Allen. 1956. *Howl and Other Poems.* San Francisco: City Lights.

Goodman, Paul. 1959. *Growing Up Absurd.* New York: Random House.

Halperin, Jon. ed. 1991. *Gary Snyder: Dimensions of a Life.* San Francisco: Sierra Club Books.

Hamalian, Linda. 1991. *A Life of Kenneth Rexroth.* New York: W. W. Norton.

Rexroth, Kenneth. 1957. "Disengagement and the Art of the Beat Generation." *Evergreen Review* 1, 2.

Rips, Geoffrey. 1981. *Unamerican Activities: The Campaign Against the Underground Press.* San Francisco: City Lights.

Schumaker, Michael. 1992. *Dharma Lion: A Critical Biography of Allen Ginsberg.* New York: St. Martin's Press.

Smith, Richard Candida. 1995. *Utopia and Dissent: Art, Poetry and Politics in California.* Berkeley: University of California Press.

Solnit, Rebecca. 1990. *Secret Exhibition: Six California Artists of the Cold War Era.* San Francisco: City Lights.

Walker, Franklin. 1939. *San Francisco's Literary Frontier.* New York: Alfred A. Knopf.

Walker, Franklin. 1966. *The Seacoast of Bohemia; an Account of Early Carmel.* San Francisco: Book Club of California.

Watson, Steven. 1995. *The Birth of the Beat Generation; Visionaries, Rebels, and Hipsters, 1944–1960.* New York: Pantheon.

Riffs on Mission District *Raza* Writers

by Juan Felipe Herrera

FROM MY MOTHER'S tiny dark windows, I looked out one night to the Lochman furniture store signs on Mission and 17th and saw a fat red neon bellboy fixture pinned over Shapiro's Furniture—a giant clock over the Mission mainline that signified two things: one, the myth of a unitary machine or system that could point me to a universal equilibrium of meaningfulness; two, this barrio was about to explode and time was ticking itself into another category. In the decades that followed, I would become part of many missions, covert and subterranean, local and international, elusive, foolhardy and miraculous, whose task it was to dismantle that time-keeping unit of day-to-day comfort culture and at a deeper level: the pain of multiple exiles, my mother's life as poet washerwoman, my father as a campesino with dream fragments of a ranchito in the impossible future, and my own emergence. Almost out of fate I would join bands of literary marauders, many born and many made in the Mission District, street comrades and word-spitters, opal-eyed and sequined-dressed investigators unpacking passion, language detonators for a new city and society.

1968: The Tropics of Pocho-Che

Ysidro Ramon Macías, a fair-skinned and brainy Chicano from Fresno, founded the Pocho-Che Collective in 1968 and recruited Mission writers such as Roberto Vargas, René Yañes, and Alejandro "Gato" Murguía. Pocho-Che ignited the *visión tropical.* The collective felt there had to be a forum for the social issues confronting the Mission and its people. They wanted to fuse two disparate realms of political and cultural turmoil and potential collective power: Latin America and the Chicano territories of the United States and Mexico. With this in mind, they chose the name Pocho-Che: "pocho," a pejorative term used to signify the "half-breed" Chicano/a caught in the fracture of identity, neither American nor Mexican, a mere pocho, a stuttering kind. Being pocho was to reacquire, to transform. "Che" was Latin America itself, its possibility for political change; the revolutionary figure of Che Guevara, a key thinker and actor in the Cuban revolution, hovered over the palm trees of San Francisco.

Alejandro Murguía recalled its beginnings:

> It had to do with living in San Francisco, the Central American and Mexican barrios; the contact among us all. It was a year and a half after Che's death, which sparked a lot of reading, interest, and investigation into Latin American guerrilla and political movements. . . . The call for the *zafra* [sugarcane harvest] came from Fidel (Castro). Latin American movements were very strong in the late sixties. It forced you to find out who Carlos Marighela was, or who Camilo Torres was; Pocho-Che came out of this mixture. It was a sense of community. We said, 'Here is our barrio [Mission District], here is our *gente*—but we are also part of *la Raza*, you can't deny it.'

On July 26, 1969, commemorating the tenth anniversary of the Cuban revolution, the young poets came out with the first mimeographed issue of *Pocho-Che*, featuring a cover of Fidel Castro and the Cuban military hero, Camilo Cienfuegos. The project had been a nocturnal secret, printed at night in the Mission's Neighborhood Arts Program where Roberto Vargas worked as a program administrator. In this issue, an essay by Macías, "The Evolution of the Mind," seemed to herald the political charter for new *Raza* writers of the Southwest. It underlined the Third World as the literary audience for the new artists in the Mission, a very different focus than that taking place in other parts of California. Macías stressed the progression of historical consciousness from the initial plane of "Mexican-American" to "Third World" and then "Humanist" awareness. Although the number of copies was meager—only 500—and although they sparsely filled the bottom shelves of some of the sundry stores and magazine shops of the Mission—they reached a highly mobile, articulate set of young activists and artists across the States.

The second issue of *Pocho-Che*, an offset production with cardboard covers, was published in the spring of 1970. This time, Macías persuaded a friend to print the magazine on a press at the Berkeley Alternative School, housed in a Presbyterian church at Sacramento and Grove. Alexandra Murguía assisted in the editing, making sure that it would be finished in time for the second Denver Chicano Youth Liberation Conference. Murguía had already gone to the first Denver Youth Liberation Conference in 1969. This time, he and Ysidro, Roberto Vargas, and a friend called "Teen Angel" packed up in a VW van, riding through the snow, carrying a fresh set of *Pocho-Che*. At the conference they learned what others were doing across the nation.

By 1973, the Pocho-Che group had produced two additional issues, journeyed to Cuba to work in the Third Venceremos Brigade, assisting in the sugar cane crop, meeting young Angolans and Vietnamese, intensifying their internationalist perspective, their *visión tropical*. By this time they had also initiated the Pocho-Che Editions project, publishing small double-backed poetry chapbooks. These early Mission poets, along with Latina and Latino writers and activists such as Nina Serrano, Alejandro Stuart, Fernando Alegría, and Rupert García, provided some of the necessary rethinking for the *experimento tropical*—the search for a Latino discourse that was intent on reconnecting strong international histories and social movements throughout the Americas into the Mission *conciencia* (consciousness). This "greenness" had been in motion for a while. The exodus of Latin Americans and Southeast Asians from their homelands, which were in economic and political turmoil, had released sociopolitical and nostalgic claims for a New Greenness. Early poets, artists, and writers in the Mission moved and wrote to the mix and flow of exile and displacement, romantic memoir, and a new-found politicized love.

They enlarged the group in 1973, as the Third World Communications Collective, with such new members as Janice Mirikitani, Ntozake Shange, Jessica Tarahata Hagedorn, Serafín Syquia, Geraldine Kudaka, George Leong, and Victor Hernández Cruz—all major figures in the Mission's literary world. They quickly produced two landmark anthologies: *Time to Greeze: Incantations from the Third World* and *Third World Women*. Ironically, the TWC lasted only six months. Hectic schedules, lack of economic support, and the death of one of their members, Serafín Syquia, toppled the collective. Later in the year, on October 4, "Gato" Murguía and Roberto Vargas met with Fernando Alegría and others to plan an emergency support reading event for Chile. This took place downtown at the Glide Memorial Church, featuring Pocho-Che poets and others such as Diane di Prima, Kathleen Fraser, and Lawrence Ferlinghetti. Formless and at the edge of breakdown, the group continued its mission of internationalist poetics and consciousness. Yet all these projects seem to be preliminary heats for the mega-event about to erupt in the late spring of 1974: El Festival Sexto Sol. The Pocho-Che called for all artists and poets to conjure the Sixth Sun, to make the tropicalized word and world live.

1974: El Sexto Sol Shines for You

With the Sexto Sol Conference, the poet rebels launched the refiguration of La Misión as a Green Center with the palm tree as the image of the new vision, the new Latino aesthetic. Alejandro Murguía and Roberto Vargas had met with Stanford University supporters—Fernando Alegría, Jean Franco, and various student organizations headed by MECHA-and had agreed to hold the Sexto Sol event at three sites between March 30 and April 1: Stanford, San Francisco State College, El Club Tropical, and the Palace of Fine Arts in San Francisco, overlooking the Golden Gate Bridge.

As plans for Festival del Sexto Sol finally materialized, Vargas feverishly poured out in his diary:

> The Festival del Sexto Sol is a reality—Meztizo Prophets gathering en la bahía to define liberación in all dialects (Pocho-Spanish). Che saw this when he was Sandino, when he was Martí. This afternoon was work and wet weather, then home again. The telephones are ringing everywhere about the festival. Symbols pour out of our earhorns' shapes of Neo-Indios xeroxed copies of the Popul Vuh and Che Urban Guerrilla warfare. Another phone call among bags of oranges and chicken. . . .

Sexto Sol was a collective occasion of cultural crossovers and political affirmations. Jazz riffs, dance, and salsa music: two *folklorico* ballet groups, and four political *teatros*—Teatro de los Mascarones, Los Topos from Mexico City, Teatro Cena, and Teatro de la Gente from the Bay Area. Among the critics were Carlos Monsiváis, also from Mexico City, and Jean Franco, Fernando Alegría, and Arturo Madrid. Some of the Bay Area writers included Avotja, David Henderson, Carol Lee Sánchez, Dorinda Moreno, Natalia Rivas, Alejandro Murguía, Roberto Vargas, Victor Hernández Cruz, Alurista, and me. Among the poets at the edge of the movement who followed the Sexto Sol call was Nina Serrano, whose poem "Sexto Sol / Sixth Sun," published in 1980 in her first book, *Heart Songs*, the last surge of the Pocho-Che Editions publication project, invoked the new Mexican age to come. Enriquetta Vásquez from New Mexico and Ricardo Sánchez from Texas stood up for the heartlands of the Southwest. Also present were Miguel Algarín and Miguel Piñero from New York. Various music groups such as Kafala and Spice—sixty in all—inspired the moment. We were armed with a thick set of voices, tropical categories for our word.

The Red and the Green Nations

New collaborations emerged with poets from the broken edge of the borderland, San Diego, Tijuana, where the Náhuatl nations were being recast through the new hot language of a primordial Aztec Amerinda: the Red Nation.

In Southern California, the poetics of the Red Nation had been in the making for a while. Alurista, Jorge González, and others had been instrumental in reinterpreting the notion of the Aztec sunstone as a cultural and historical wheel of social change, prophecy, and as a literary epicenter that could still be applied symbolically to our current social conditions. Maestro Andres Segura, an Aztec healer from Mexico City, made annual forays to the area with his *danza azteca* ensemble Xinachtli; San Diego song writer Enrique Ramirez had just written his popular song "El Quinto Sol," which was later adopted by many groups throughout the Southwest. Alurista's first book, *Floricanto*, published in 1971, had broken ground with its Náhuatl Aztec voice and referents. I stood between the green and red projects, between the Mission district's call for a new tropics in the metropolis—a refigured internationalist discourse and consciousness—and the Southern poesy of Chicano Aztequismo, of Quetzalcoatl and muralized tzompantli skull racks for sacrificed literary practices, old Western regimes of voice, text, and Eurocentric word.

Ysidro Macías met Segura when he was at the University of Irvine. Segura, a Náhuatl ritual officer, was a magnetic figure who would provide the Mission poets with a refreshing language of origins and of transformation because he just happened to walk into the Mission as the Green Tropical internationalist vision was taking hold. Segura's explanation of indigenous concepts, symbols, and observances fit the radical utopian visions of the Pocho-Che. Although his ideas were enclosed in a nationalist frame, he was, ironically, well received by the globally oriented Pocho poets. Perhaps it was because the post-sixties open-ended experimental moment was crystallizing here, in the nexus of urban santería, Mexican-Chicano nationalism, and a unique Bay Area international *tropicalismo*.

Segura toured, holding *danza indígena* workshops, with young Chicana and Latino writers and artists who were already exploring pre-Columbian notions of culture. In fact, his dialogues on Mexican prophecy provided the Sexto Sol icon and theme, that of a new solar age. El Pocho-Che maneuvered Red Nation poetics into political art forms that had been successfully shaped by Chicano *teatros* and writers throughout the South-North axis, along the borderlines of Arizona, New Mexico, Texas, and, most significantly, Southern California.

In the south writers were attracted to the Red poetic voice. Growing up, San Diego's Chicano-Indio poets were my posse—Toltecas en Aztlán—along with the Centros music groups such as Trio Moreno, Servidores del Arbol de la Vida, and Rondalla Amerinda, who were more in tune with corridos and boleros spun to the Mexican tales of Aztlán, a neo-indigenous nation grounded on the heartbeat and ruins of the entire Amerindian continent. Few of us talked or wrote about the Third World, which was a foreign concept to us in the south. We were so close to Mexico, to the native American Diegueño reservations in San Diego county, and also to the conservative right-wing and military tilt of a region economically supported by naval industry. We were more familiar with the cultural traffic that poured in from Mexico and the adjacent agribusiness center of the Imperial Valley where many of our friends and families labored. We did not see Che Guevara as our emblem or Latin America as our center; rather, the Aztec poet-prince of the Valley of Texcoco, Nezahualcoyotl, and Amerindia—the indigenous continent. We did not focus on Fidel Castro's speeches and manifestos. Here, we examined Angel Garibay's and Miguel León Portilla's translations of ancient Náhuatl texts. In San Diego, the literary universe was cloaked in Mexican Indian history, symbol, and meaning; we were quasi-Aztec word-lovers eager to rebuild working-class barrio temples, pyramids, and stone monuments to a Indio Paradise lost and renewed.

A few months after Sexto Sol, Isabel Alegría from the Berkeley Comunicación Aztlán Collective introduced me to David Henderson, who had just come out with his first book of poems, *The Mayor of Harlem*. She interviewed us about poetry, the writer's link to the world, our manuscripts-in-progress. The show aired on KPFA a few weeks after our meeting. Later, David gave me a fresh copy of *Umbra*, a Third World anthology he had recently edited and founded in New York, where he had been part of the Black Arts Movement there, with its connections to the Mission writing scene. Other travelers on the East/Village-West/Mission trail were writers like Ishmael Reed, Jessica Tarahata Hagedorn, Victor Hernández-Cruz, and Amiri Baraka. The Mission Latino writers worked on an East-West literary net as the south worked on a Norte-Sur interconnection. In the *Umbra* issue of 1974 I read about Felipe Luciano's jaunt to China and remembered that I had met him at Sexto Sol. I noted, too, the quick political pace of Mission writers such as Roberto Vargas, who was chanting a Latino bilingual voice about Latin American political reality, about Sandino, Ernesto Cardenal, and "Tachito" Somoza. The *visión tropical* of the Mission was as clearly demarcated as the indigenous Red vision of the Southlands. The blur and intersections between these two poetics and corresponding literary missions were ever present.

1975–1977: *Tin Tan* and El Centro

After the Sexto Sol it was time to build: either the Green or the Red would have to take charge or perhaps we would come up with a "third form": a tropicalized cultural arts center in the Mission District would establish *lo tropical*, a headquarters for the Pocho-Che writers, from which they could coordinate their internationalist investigations and missions for revolutionary change. This was the next step.

From 1975 to 1977, the members of the old Pocho-Che published *Tin Tan*, a magazine with a series of incisive articles, reviews, and literary features of Latin American political reality. Co-edited by Murguía and Daniel del Solar, regular

Verano 1977
Issue No. 5
$1.50

LITERATURA
SALVADOREÑA

PEDRO JUAN PIETRI

FRANCISCO X CAMPLIS

RAY BARRETTO

RALPH MARADIAGA

JOSÉ LUIS CUEVAS

STUDENT SPEECH

contributors included Victor Hernández-Cruz, Nina Serrano, Gilberto Osorio, and Roberto Vargas. The magazine merged out of the various Latin American issues affecting the Mission community and the various official roles played by key Pocho-Che members. *Tin Tan* would no longer mimic Pachuko working-class idioms and fashion styles on the silver screen—now he would dress as a Mission poet *congero* would dress, in white cottons and mango-watermelon-colored shirts, talking about apartheid, and about oppression in the Americas.

By late 1974, Roberto Vargas had become Associate Director of the San Francisco Art Commission, which at this point was interested in establishing new projects in the ethnic communities. Since Murguía had editorial and graphic arts skills, he was a natural candidate for the new magazine publications instructor position offered by the Commission—a perfect niche for the production of the new *Tin Tan*. In addition to this, the locale for the *Tin Tan* workshop on 22nd Street and Bartlett—*La Gaceta Sandinista*—was a decisive working environment and turning point for the Pocho-Che group, one that would nurture its internationalist networks and aspirations.

Beginning in 1972, the writers aimed to establish a Latino arts center in the Mission, and they broadcast the idea through the pages of *Tin Tan*. The Board of Supervisors at that time was funding a major arts complex in the city—the Davies Performing Arts Center—and felt that every ethnic neighborhood should have a separate neighborhood mini-arts center. By 1976 ideas for the Centro Cultural de la Misión were being debated by competing Mission cultural arts leaders. After heated discussion, a new Mission Arts Alliance was formed. Led by Gato Murguía, it began to formulate the actual Centro proposal. The coalition met at St. Peter's church on Alabama Street for its first meeting.

Murguía remembers:

The first meeting was held at St. Peter's, where representatives from the Art Commission came down and many community artists attended and spoke up about what we wanted—the big dream to build a pyramid and have ceremonies at the altar. The first scheme was to buy the armory at 14th and Mission Street and turn that into a cultural center, but it was too big. Some people liked the armory because it had firing ranges on one floor. There were several groups that submitted proposals for a cultural arts center. One group was led by a reactionary woman on the Art Commission, Elvira Martínez, who, along with the group from the Palmetto Museum, was pushing for an old mortuary building. Other people wanted little sites like the Precita Park Center. We said we wanted a place for theater, a place for a gallery. . . . We gave them a manifesto.

The City gave way to the well-organized Alliance and purchased the "Shaft," an old four-story furniture store between 24th and 25th on Mission

Street. In the summer of 1977 the fifth issue of *Tin Tan* celebrated the opening of the Centro Cultural de la Misíon, attended by over two thousand Mission residents and inaugurated by Nicaraguan poet Ernesto Cardenal, who baptized children at the site. *Tin Tan* as well as other Mission publications—*El Tecolote, El Pulgarcito,* and *La Gaceta Sandinista*—were housed on the third floor. Alejandro Murguía was the director of the center—the "third form" seemed to be in place.

The Mission could now shout louder south of Market Street—a region seen as dangerous, noisy, and devoid of literary power and writing culture by the commercial presses of the Bay Area and by the mainstream. La Misíon was dressed in full regalia now. The shifting literary currents that once had fostered the Beat Movement in North Beach in the fifties and the Haight-Ashbury literary explosion of the sixties were pulsating south of the slot in the late seventies. The Pocho-Che group immediately began to work on a new series of poetry books by Nina Serrano, Roberto Vargas, and Raul Salinas. They were meeting regularly at Cesár's Latin Palace on Mission and Army (formerly Cesár's Latin Club in North Beach) and at El Señorial, also in the vicinity. Yet another shout was being heard in the Mission—the increasing military conflicts in Central America, which

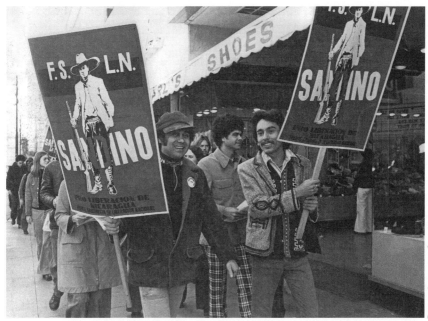

Roberto Vargas and Alejandro Murguía on Mission Street (1976)

would soon engage many of the Pocho-Che group and other Mission activists and artists in the new Centro. The literary missions of writers would soon be taken to task, would be pushed to the "fourth form," and to revolution.

1978: Nicaragua

The following year, in 1978, a bulletin arrived from the Sandinista networks in Central America calling for immediate action and support for the Nicaraguan revolution. People started to leave the Centro to participate actively in the Sandinista guerrilla offensive. Gato Murguía and Roberto Vargas were invited by the World Peace Council to attend a conference on "Racism and Racial Discrimination" in Basal, Switzerland, and a few months later Murguía boarded a plane to Panama to attend a solidarity meeting with Nicaraguan representatives. After this he went to Costa Rica and met with Daniel Ortega and Victor Tirade López, two principal leaders of the Sandinista Liberation Front (FSLN), and was named the official Bay Area FSLN representative. Vargas and others had already left the Centro and were on their way to Managua. Murguía was left with managing Centro affairs and heading the Nicaraguan Solidarity Committee; later, he too headed to Central America, leaving the cultural center in the hands of an artist relatively new to the Mission.

Home from the Nicaraguan offensive, when the Pocho-Che cadre reunited in 1979, they found that the Centro had been transformed and had a new director. To their surprise, they also found that their political activities had been denounced in one of the major local art tabloids—*City Arts*. Murguía recalls:

> It was the biggest mistake—how the separation was made. The Centro was turned over to someone who had no political experience and who, in fact, wound up being a staunch reactionary who denounced us to the State Department. He wrote in *City Arts* that the Nicaraguan movement had divided the Mission and that he was able to unify it by expelling politics from the Mission Cultural Center.

The tropical vision had met its odd end at the highest peak of its development—the actual participation of Latino Mission poets in Nicaraguan revolutionary practice. By the end of the seventies the Pocho-Che affiliates went back to their apartments in the Mission, wondering what had gone wrong. Everything they had labored for in the last decade seemed to have slipped away. The Mission Cultural Center was hostile territory, their makeshift books and tabloids were out of print, the green *tropicalismo* had faded. In 1980 Pocho-Che finally disbanded, and within a short time Roberto Vargas moved to Washington, D.C., as Nicaragua's cultural attaché, and Murguía went underground in the Mission and co-founded a new group, the Roque Dalton Cultural Brigade, with Magaly Fernández, Wilfredo Castaño, Jack Hirschman, Jorge Herrera, Barbara Paschke, David Volpendesta, Tony Ryan, María Rosa Galdamez, Francisco X. Alarcón, Victor Martínez, Tina Alvarez, and me. The Pocho-Che poets had accomplished much during that decade. What would rise from the ashes of the Green and Red Nations?

Late November 1996: From a Letter to Victor Martínez

You point your finger at me and say that if one Chicano or Latina makes it, then we all make it. You keep on telling me that Chicanos are authentic Americans, that this is the first lesson. This takes me back to Pocho-Che days when we hoisted up Che Guevara and Lolita Lebrón as our American figures. America, we chanted through rain, meetings, snow, demonstrations, more meetings, scuffs, and sleet. We are the real thing, you tell me, been breaking new ground for decades, inventing ourselves a new set of categories, fresh art forms, an authentic discourse, we been hashing it out, without much to go on, except this fiery fuel inside, we put up cultural centers on pennies, Teatro Chicano, Teatro Latino, lesbian ensembles, Latino gay performance, we did it with khakis and wino shoes, you name it, we've broken through the wall, against all odds, from *frijoles* to *murales*, from stealing sacks of chiles to re-appropriating our language and sexualities. Now that's American, *carnal*, you tell me, with your raspy voice. American originals. Maybe this is the key—invention. Is it possible? Original? What are we renewing? From what to what? How long-suffering is the transition?

The concept is provocative Vic, archaic, the whole thing about rising from the ashes, dressed in *campesino* shorts, working off a *molcajete*, the good ol' Indio Chicano stone mortar and pestle, mixing diverse elements, mashing them into pulp and juice, into a new blood force. Resurrections without a body, or is the body the words, the dead poesy? Resurrections? Have we been locked into a religious frame, a vicious and regressive underlying morality without knowing it, the grammar of the Second Coming? And yet things and moments seem pliable, transformative, we move out into the open mix of coffee houses, homeless tenements, beaten-down chartreuse *movimiento* rooms, past the old Victoria Restaurant, Gómez-Peña's loft on César Chavez Street with velvet O. J. Simpson paintings on the walls, New Age gargoyle trilingual low-riders, swamp art spaces, Kulingtan workshops and Pinay poetics, verse-riffs and *performero* do-wop, *mercados* featuring papaya and jitomate sales, gentrified Victorians cutting through the old Irish, Mexicano, and Latino neighborhoods; things appear new, our poesy missions appear refurbished, then the fog from the Pacific rolls in again, homicide stats pile up on the curb, more death, then light, rain, more rain.

Have you seen the young ones, the generations of *Raza* poets and writers spit out "Aztlán," talk about new stone idols, ring up workshop poetics, quote Archibald Macleish, Marianne Moore, Berryman, then "Chicano power" and "Quetzalcoatl" one more time? And the gallon of hand-me down nationalist sewage? The New gnaws at me. Or is it ground zero? Is it the fact that we never did fall, truly alone and shivering, into the furnace of an authentic experience and explosion of community across assigned boundaries and voices, into the colossal and marvelous thing called change, called reality, this Thing-just-like-this? Wipe my face, squint, make sure I say what I mean.

American originals, I repeat, then I think of time. Maybe time more than historical content or appropriation was the key to our missions. Maybe we wanted to simply acknowledge and conjure a crazy realignment with peoples and places cast out into a fabricated arena of temporal loss and jinxed distances, maybe we are at heart time-killers, we want an exploded time, of things, ideas and knowledge that we can feel at our side, inside of us, a complex chronos-fission, as though refracted in our mother's tiny living rooms, our ringed hands, in thunderous accelerations, potholes, street signs, *ranchero* hats, Frida Rigoberta fists, tawdry publications and voices in Maya, rendings, *rendijas*, all sewn together, really, at random. We are rebel marauder Tiempo Pilots pillaging the day-to-day linear progression of Western time, of linear history that desires nothing more than to leave us all behind, accompanied only by its own guilt-processing time-keeping unit strapped to our "Modern" psyche. And maybe, if we are here, unshackled, in this aura of the awakened present and its chambers of gnashing trade systems, global and virulent, in every *maquila* shoe, aesthete café cup and madras shirt, we can now ask ourselves, well, what is foreign and distant? What belongs to a past that must not be ours, a slavery net that we left eons ago? How can our writing unlock time, snap us all into a plenum of actual realities? The year ends and a new one starts with these questions and riffs; the old Lochman Furniture store clock on Mission Street ticks again, then falls apart. . . .

Battles, missions, experiments, just as the feelings of chaos, frenzy, and passion continue and intersect, everything rocks on ice. Chiapas coughs up more Indian cadavers, they slide up through Peru, Oaxaca, and Guerrero—America speaks louder than our tiny books. So many Americas, that's the point: between 16th and César Chavez Streets, in the southern quadrant where Salvadoreños peek out a makeshift newspaper cape on Hampshire Street cement, *viejítas* climb innumerable stairs into abandonment, down by the new police squad adobe on Valencia Street, orange siren lights smear across storefront tins and a cat with a Forty-Niner cap invites you to lean on a crucified figure, sand-brown Vietnamese *empanadas* and an uptown Mercedes mix colors, more gold neck-chain sales and steamed rice along the main line, punctuate this with cheap plastic black luggage and fried chicken, listen to the *vato* preach on the corner about the coming of Quetzalcoatl Two, this time the Mutton God will be dressed as a Shriner with an Uzi between his teeth firing away at McDonald's employees.

I want writing to contain all this because we contain all this—is this closer to what you mean by saying we are Americanos? Is this your mission? You know Victor, I am going to say it: no more movements, nothing about lines or metaphors or even about quality and craft. Perhaps the notion of being American is off center—there is no center, I guess that's the thing. AIDS is not a line or a metaphor or an iambic construct, or a national artifact, a session on meter. You can't lean it on quasi-nationalisms, or Aztec sloganeering. You can't prop it up as a *mariachi* Rimbaud gone Latino wearing a vest of alienation and a paisley button that reads "Peasant Power!" It is not enough to go about ranting "qualified" ethnic know-how, "minority" bombast, harpooning dead islands, manifestos, and poets—that boat ride is over, baby. Any flirtations with "language" aestheticism sprinkled with a taste of retro-bohemia will not pull us through. Language seeks linear time and history, it wants to appear monumental, greater than us. In a sense, language wants to ignore the facts; now I am sounding Tibetan, I feel like I am talking about the wheel of illusions. These are facts, for now: the mottled flesh-sheet of viral invasion, global and phantasmagoric, these facts break through our mouse-hole, our underground, our missions, our sacred bundle of wired words. At this very second AIDS gnaws away at our pretensions, at our internal cellular texts; this event alone, by itself, without further elucidation, unites us, moves us, informs us, gives us death and spirit. Blood writing: the last manifesto and true axis of this millennium. The ante has never been so high for us. To write "ethnic folk drama" is not sufficient, to join the Hispanic Movimiento Advertising Machine whose main function is to pat its own rhetoric on the back and spawn a new generation of "melting pot" ventriloquists is out of the question, to huddle around a literary agent who tells us to keep it current, PC, and racy, to install a refurbished femme Virgen de Guadalupe over the ruins, once again, is not sufficient, to stay in the "color" game, the hetero-sex gang and never unite with sisters and brothers will annihilate us, we got to match wits with the RNA Gila Monster inside of us, we got to keep close to all of our lives as they suffer, as they bleed all around us, the mission is on, Vic. . . .

> Rwanda in our living rooms,
> this full empty street with anti-graffiti artists,
> this City cutting through the plutonium, the last tropic, the one
> with history tearing through its palm-shaped heart.

Acknowledgments

I want to thank Margarita Luna Robles for her critical comments on this paper, the late Tede Matthews and also the late José Antonio Burciaga, beautiful friends, for granting interviews in 1992; also Alejandro Murguía for 1984 interviews and invaluable information on the evolution of the Pocho-Che Collective and *Tin Tan*, and finally thanks to Ray Gonzales for encouraging this essay, which appeared in a preliminary draft as "Mission Street Manifesto," in the *Guadalupe Review*, 1992.

Street Subversion
The Political Geography of Murals and Graffiti

by Timothy W. Drescher

YOU CAN'T LIVE LONG IN SAN FRANCISCO without becoming aware of its neighborhood murals, especially in the Mission District. Nearly a thousand murals were painted in communities all over the Bay Area between the early 1970s and the present, and by 1978 over 700 of them enlivened the walls of San Francisco, and Berkeley and Oakland in the East Bay. Although urban renewal in various guises, gentrification, "routine" maintenance, and natural deterioration have taken their toll, the number of murals in the area continues to increase.

The City is also particularly rich in murals of the New Deal/WPA period, painted from 1934 (Coit Tower, the model for the WPA murals program) to 1947 (Rincon Center, the last New Deal mural project). Also, the famous Mexican artists Diego Rivera and Frida Kahlo spent many months working in the City during the Depression and were later an inspiration to the community muralists of the 1970s and after. Painted in the 1930s social-realism style, these paintings and the political and aesthetic traditions behind them inspired several leading muralists in San Francisco's early mural movement.

The community murals movement, which began in the mid-1960s, was shaped by shifts in funding sources, forms of project administration, and types of political engagement. The initial phase lasted until about 1974; then, when murals began to be funded through CETA (the federal Comprehensive Employment and Training Act of 1974), many artists worked in teaching jobs and their murals often served as important training projects. With the end of CETA in 1981 and the ascension of Republicans to power (along with a significant economic recession), murals were put on hold, although a handful of influential works was produced, including the important Balmy Alley project off 24th Street, in the Mission District. Until the 1990s, San Francisco muralists shared basic modernist principles—they sought centralized, integrated, focused themes, and usually worked in teams. Then a new nationwide phase began to show the beginnings of postmodern influences. These are seen in style and method of organizing some larger mural projects, and are often also connected to the spray-can art proliferating throughout United States cities. "Street Subversion" compares some of the "pomo" characteristics of the new phase mural works, especially spray-can works, with those of the previous modernist, social-realist generation. It focuses on two mural clusters in the Mission District, which differ in significant ways that throw light not only on the motives and methods of their creators but on their divergent political and cultural orientations.

I. From Prehistoric Caves to the Contemporary City

Murals have existed for tens of thousands of years, since prehistoric cave paintings. In historic times, tomb paintings celebrated the lives of royalty and the upper classes. In Europe, patrons from the Church and the nobility supported the creation of magnificent frescos and secular murals beginning in the late fifteenth century, but murals were still an elite expression until the 1920s, when they began to be commissioned for public buildings in Mexico. The Mexican artists of this period are obvious influences on San Francisco's early community muralists. The three leading Mexican muralists were Diego Rivera, David Alfaro Siquieros, and José Clemente Orozco, a trio that became know as "Los Tres Grandes."

Among these, Rivera is particularly significant for San Francisco because he painted four murals here. Rivera is important for other reasons, too. His anthropological studies informed his depictions of ancient Mesoamerican cultures, which included the great murals of Teotihuacan and Bonampak. Perhaps most importantly, his Communist political activism inspired many local muralists to commit their own skills to struggles for social justice in the 1960s: civil rights, women's liberation, the anti–Vietnam War movement, and celebration of local poor, ethnic, and working-class communities.

At the same time Rivera was painting in the United States, the New Deal mural programs were beginning at Coit Tower. Some of Rivera's assistants were significant New Deal artists who later became involved in San Francisco's community mural movement: Emmy Lou Packard, Lucienne Bloch, and Stephen Dimitroff. The main lesson of the New Deal murals was stylistic: social realism. They had a story to tell, and a message to communicate: realism was selected as the appropriate vehicle.

The period from 1960 to roughly 1974 saw grassroots political activism at unprecedented levels throughout the United States. Beginning in mid-decade, artists and community activists began painting on neighborhood walls murals that addressed issues and explored perspectives that were rarely presented in the mass media. In focusing on these issues, the community murals movement added "community" to the historical mural tradition. Earlier murals in Europe were painted at the behest of aristocrats or for the general population; this was public art, not community art. An example of the shift from the New Deal mural paradigm to that of the community mural movement may be seen in two groups of San Francisco murals, those painted inside Coit Tower and the others on the open walls along the streets of the Mission District.

The public art images of the New Deal murals, with very few exceptions, tended to narrate a single master history rather than grapple with the complexities of multiple histories. Maxine Albro's 1934 Coit Tower fresco shows workers in the orchards and flower farms of California busily and happily harvesting the state's rich agricultural bounty. They work thanks to the National Recovery Act, and they are are grateful to have jobs. And they are all white. That the state's labor force had never been monolithic in race or attitude went unmentioned. Fifty years later, Juana Alicia painted *Las Lechugueras/The Women Lettuce Workers* at 24th and York Streets, in the Mission District, and was impelled to articulate a different reality appropriate to the time and to her mural's audience. The style is still basically realistic, and the mural is beautifully painted. She shows women lettuce workers following behind a harvester driven at a pace controlled by the bosses (or is it the Immigration Service, the hated *migra*?), who look on from the background. The women, including a prominent figure visibly pregnant, are being sprayed with pesticides as they work. The impact of the more recent mural indicates a major shift from the perspective recorded in the New Deal piece. Not least in the differences between the two murals is the fact that this one was painted on the street, giving the viewer access not only to the finished image, but in some cases to the process of its painting and the opportunity for discussion with the muralist while she painted.

Early community muralists saw their work as part of a larger political effort to alter the organization of society to meet the needs of all its members, not just the wealthy. This goal manifested itself in several ways. One was the style of expression (social realist, coherent, consistent). Another concerned the organizational processes of the projects. The murals' emphasis on social realism in the 1960s was largely a legacy of the thirties and leftist influences, where clear communication was important because "educating the masses" was the primary function of tendentious art, including murals. Another area dealt with the subject matter, which ranged from critique and opposition to the celebration of marginalized groups. In the sixties the mere assertion of a nondominant culture, the expression of marginal voices, functioned as a challenge to the dominant myth of a coherent, centralized, white U.S. culture. Even if the images themselves were not openly oppositional, the mere fact that black artists might paint large public statements celebrating black culture was viewed as a provocation by conservatives. There were, nationally, relatively few images suggesting that it was time to take up arms and seize state power, but in the atmosphere of the times, it seemed as if there were many more such murals because those that existed became widely known.

Always what was most subversive in community murals was their process. The physical reality of people getting together to make their own decisions for their own reasons about what would appear on their own community walls was a genuinely democratic experience. Group consensus was the goal. After all, these muralists were beginning to build a coherent community, and their models derived from political groups that began by hammering out "principles of unity" to which all participants could agree. Consistency of style was consistent with such goals and appropriate to the modernist sensibilities that sought coherence, focus, unification—all suggested under the rubric "centralization."

The Balmy Alley mural project represents in many ways the organization and painting style of some of the most important community murals painted during the first two decades of the movement. Then, within only a few years, a new style of mural established itself in the city, this time in the North Mission area near the intersection of Mission and 16th Streets. The two projects can serve as representatives of the shift in sensibilities from modern to postmodern.

II. 1984: The Inner Mission District, Balmy Alley, and Political Modernism

The Mission District is ethnically mixed, but the Inner Mission (roughly the area from Potrero on the east to Dolores Street on the west, and Chavez [formerly Army] Street on the south to 20th or 21st Street on the north) is dominated by Latino culture. From the late nineteenth century through the early 1950s, the dominant group was Irish, but now the population of the Mission District is largely a mixture of Central Americans, Mexicans, and South Americans. The main streets are Mission and 24th Streets, which feature Mexican bakeries, small stores, taquerías, and restaurants offering cuisine from many Latin American countries. The area has a history of political activism, many service agencies, and a local newspaper, *El Tecolote*. Neighborhood murals show a wide range of Latino cultural references. For example, a mural painted in 1974 by the Mujeres Muralistas, *Latinoamerica*, includes imagistic references to four or five different Latin

Balmy Alley

American cultures within a single, unified design.

Balmy Alley (formally Balmy Street) is a block-long alley between 24th and 25th Streets. It had been the site of significant murals since 1972, when two women who came to be called the Mujeres Muralistas painted their first team mural. A few murals were added sporadically along the alley until 1984, when Ray Patlan brought some three dozen mural activists together and proposed a joint project in which each garage door or fence segment along the alley would have a mural painted on it. They would be linked by dual theme: the celebration of indigenous Central American cultures and/or protest against U.S. intervention in Central America. The organizational rubric for Balmy was *Placa*, which in Spanish refers to the tag, or mark made by taggers. It is an assertion of self and group.

The residents and owners whose property backed onto Balmy were mostly Latino, and while some were initially skeptical about giving permission for murals to be painted on their garages or fences, nearly all embraced the project once it began and they could see the results. In the summer of 1985 twenty-seven murals were painted, and a dedication celebration was held in September of that year. The project was funded (at $2,500) by a single grant from the Zellerbach Foundation, and a generous provision of paints was donated by the local distributor of Politec Mural Paints, formulated especially for outdoor mural work. Balmy became a highly influential project, leading to the La Lucha Continua Art Park in New York City the following year.

A key to Balmy's impact was that the murals were painted in a single location, which gave them a more powerful presence than any single piece could have commanded by itself. There had been earlier clusters, such as Estrada Courts in Los Angeles, and the minipark a few blocks down 24th Street in San Francisco. Clusters of murals had also been painted at the Palacio de Bellas Artes in Mexico City, not to mention the Vatican: they were honored by virtue of their location in august surroundings, whereas Balmy Alley itself was elevated by the murals painted there. So the idea was not original, but in the politically conservative atmosphere of the mid-1980s, the theme, the more than two dozen murals in a single space, and the excellence of the painting made Balmy a special project.

Most of the Placa muralists had been painting murals for over a decade or shared the basic outlook of those who had. Community murals could be designed with a group of members drawn from the mural's projected audience, its community, but they could also be designed by individuals or by groups of artists who were aware of the interests of that audience. In Balmy Alley, the latter was the case. Community-based murals were part of the political activism of the sixties, and they drew on a history of labor organizing from the thirties, as well as on work done by New Deal artists in the United States and by the Tres Grandes of Mexico. Representative titles of the Balmy Alley murals include *Youth of the World, Let's Create a Better World/Juventud del mundo vamos a creer un mundo mejor, United in the Struggle/Unidos en la lucha, After the Triumph/Después del triunfo, We Hear You Guatemala/Oímos Guatemala.*

Mural projects based in political modernism sought a unified, coherent expression (sometimes complex) of a didactic lesson, often in the form of symbols from the cultural/mythological/historical traditions of marginalized people. Mural makers sought to achieve in the process of creation what the murals' messages called for—the unity of diverse people, liberation from racial, gender, and, occasionally, class oppression. For example, in the *ILWU mural-sculpture* located at Mission and Steuart Streets, at the Embarcadero (a two-year undertaking that coincided with Balmy Alley and two-thirds of whose ten members also took part in the Balmy project), a decision was made to adopt a single painting style so that the finished work would not appear to have been painted by ten separate hands. The only focus was the history and principles of the ILWU. Men and women of different races, with different politics and painting styles, found consensus stylistically and thematically in order to produce the mural sculpture. Balmy's characteristic as a cluster, directly expressing an agreed-on theme in mostly social-realist style identifies it also as a modernist production.

PHOTO DIMITRI LOUKAKOS

Clarion Alley

III. 1994: The North Mission, Clarion Alley, and Postmodernism

The North Mission is demographically different from the 24th Street corridor. The North Mission is less vital economically, and while it borders on the predominantly gay and lesbian Castro District to the west, it also borders on the once industrial but now gentrifying South of Market area. Its residents come from a wide variety of cultures, and although there are taquerías in the area, there is no sense of a dominant Latino (or any other) culture. For nearly two decades, the North Mission was the location of the American Indian Center. In the 1990s, it is a center of young, hip-hop culture, and the BART stop at 16th and Mission is infamously the most dangerous in the system. The North Mission's "answer" to Balmy Alley is Clarion Alley, running a block away from the BART stop, just south of 17th Street, from Mission to Valencia.

The rubric for Clarion is CAMP—Clarion Alley Mural Project. Clarion has no thematic focus comparable to Balmy's, and the originating group was part of a new generation of community-based public artists. None had participated in Balmy, although they knew of the project. What is more, none had a background in mural painting, bringing an entirely new sensibility to the creation of a mural cluster. The project, or rather the tone of the project and the style of most of the

Graffiti by Twist (Barry McGee). These panels were spray-painted on temporary wooden walls erected around the rehabilitation of the San Francisco Unified School District administration building in the early 1990s.

pieces in it, may be labeled "postmodern" insofar as they exhibit the pluralism and self-consciousness that are characteristic of the new style. The specific context of Clarion was different from Balmy's. Clarion Alley's residents and owners were ethnically more diverse than Balmy's. It was the site of serious drug dealing and use, and was frequently used as an outdoor toilet by drug addicts and the homeless. Clarion opens onto Valencia Street directly across from a new district police station, yet this had no apparent impact on the alley's illicit drug users. One of the thoughts of the mural organizers was that if the alley became the site of artworks that brought visitors, its "inhabitants" would be inclined to go elsewhere to defecate and shoot up. After three years of the project, there was some indication that this was happening, but it was still wise to be careful when visiting.

A selection of Clarion's murals must suffice to indicate its character. Starting at Valencia Street, one sees a sign that announces the project in several of the languages spoken in the vicinity; it includes a telephone number to call. The sign has remained in place for years without defacement, showing that the project continues, and is respected by local taggers. There are mural images of animals that lived in the area before the City was settled, a tag of horses by Reminisce, and an abstract piece by Chuy Campusano, an early San Francisco social-realist muralist whose style shifted to abstract/geometrical in the 1980s. Campusano's piece is black against a white background, with a UFW flag and caricatures of former Mayor Dianne Feinstein, Governor Pete Wilson, and the Pope. A small, vertical, four-by-eight-foot mural called *Faux Mission Man* mocked in cartoon style visitors from the suburbs who came into the area on weekends because of its "cool" and slightly disreputable ambiance. There were initially two poems in Clarion, selected by the poetry editor of the steering committee. There is a collage, two doorways with full-length portraits of performing artists, and a particularly striking monochrome realist painting of an escalator. Two old-style murals were painted by Precita Eyes Muralists and by Fresco, a team of Ray Patlan and Eduardo Pineda, both of whom had worked in Balmy and on the *ILWU mural-sculpture*. These latter murals are distinguished by their naturalistic painting styles and use of a full palette. At the Mission Street end, Kenneth Huerta painted a three-story portrait called *Mojo Man*. His work is immediately identifiable by his sketching initially in collage, a technique that enables him to create images very quickly and transfer them to a larger mural surface without gridding or projection. Huerta's design process also refers to that of photomontage artist John Heartfield.

The overall effect of Clarion is complex and is a departure from previous murals. With no guiding theme or shared palette or stylistic consistency, there is no claim to a unified perspective or even of agreement on what issues are important. In fact, Clarion is notable for its lack of issue-oriented murals. They are expressive gestures of individuals—they could even be called existential—and only three murals focus on explicitly political issues.

Funding for Clarion came from private donations, small foundation grants, local businesses, and the City. The mural group is adamant, however, that it would rather reject a grant than sacrifice any autonomy. Politically, CAMP incorporates much of what gave the community mural movement its initial strength: the participants are ethnically and sexually mixed, the content is spontaneous and relevant to the visions and concerns of the people who live with the images on a daily basis, and it is supported financially by those same people. Whereas earlier murals fought against racism Clarion provides a forum for individual sensibility and expression of a racially diverse group of artists, the "next generation" of muralists.

In the mid-nineties, CAMP's position was that of allowing the "masses" (by which is meant local inhabitants) to express themselves. This educates everyone to neighborhood diversity and fosters a mutually respectful intercommunicative community. This is different from an "everybody do your own thing" attitude. A framework is provided: location, social context, specifics of the urban environment, and a collective spirit that is neither collaborative nor competitive.

The organizers of CAMP, some of whom live in an apartment in the alley (which itself has a long history of housing artists, including an important second-phase muralist, Michael Mosher), have been involved in two other projects in the nineties: the Bloody Thursday *ILWU mural-project* and the Redstone Building project. Each in its way signifies the new generation's shift from earlier viewpoints. Their projects manifest the influence of the spray-can writers in San Francisco. One of CAMP's goals is inclusiveness (open to anyone who shares their views); and their work evolves over long periods of time, which is possible because they are not constrained by funding cycles that define a limited time period in which "officially" funded projects must be completed. They work as a collective of different styles, almost none realistic, their differences representing authentic complexities and indeterminacies of the world they live in. Their process is open, and is less hierarchically or bureaucratically controlled. Perhaps most important of all, they make no attempt to agree on a single message to be presented to an imagined audience. Barry McGee said (in an October 1996 interview), "I never wanted my graffiti to be absolute—'this is the way it is.' I wanted to bring a smile—empty shirts with ties for example. I want a dialogue, so the most effective work is humorous because it engages the viewer, as does leaving the meaning a little bit unclear."

Artists in the new group share some interesting ideas about their work, their influences, and spray-can venues. For example, several younger artists mention the influence of comic books. Local artists Barry McGee and Rigo, for example, incorporate a sophisticated application of comic-book principles to the artists' own ends, challenging the distinction between high and low art. The conceptual level of their work is very high. For McGee, a plain drawing style makes his work accessible and it allows him to develop irony simply by placement of a figure geographically, relative to such urban features as billboards, large buildings, abandoned industrial sites, and so on. When placed where they can be seen by freeway commuters, for instance, his world-weary characters elicit wry smiles.

Rigo demonstrated his commitment to making his art easily understood in his Balmy Alley piece, painted in 1995. Its simple, familiar style appeals to the youths who view it, and this makes the multicultural, antigang message of the mural more effective. Elsewhere, because of its association with comic books, the flat style led Rigo to use text as image. *Extinct*, for example, reminds us of a road sign warning of danger, with its diagonal yellow and black stripes. The question is, what is extinct? To answer that, we look at its location, next to a Shell gas station, and make the connection with Shell's deplorable environmental record. The mural is painted on a single-room-occupancy hotel, and thus points to the virtual (if not actual) extinction of poor people in the city. The road-sign style is also used in *One Tree* and *Innercity Home*. The latter ironically refers to Interstate 80, from which the mural can be readily seen. *One Tree*, at the base of an entrance ramp to southbound Highway 101, is perhaps his most humorous work, pointing as it does to a single tree incongruously standing in a vacant lot between a corrugated building wall and the freeway ramp.

McGee's comic-book style developed somewhat differently. He favors a monochrome that grows out of the two-color throw-ups (large, balloon lettering outlines with a single color filling in the letters) of spray-can graffiti tags. This style, in its simplicity, allows for spontaneity, which enables him to work quickly in "non-permissional" circumstances. As it turns out, he values spontaneity in any case, feeling that the sense of immediacy contributes to the meaning of his figures. The drips falling from the bottom of his figures announce both his spontaneity and his subtle challenge to graffiti writers, among whom "no drips" is an unstated rule.

Traditionally, community murals used text primarily as commentary or to explain the "point" of the accompanying image. A recent example is Johanna Poethig's *To Cause to Remember*, which shows the Statue of Liberty lying on its side and quotes "Give me your tired, your restless. . . ." The juxtaposition of these welcoming words with the plight of the unemployed, the homeless, and immigrants

Extinct by Rigo, 5th and Folsom Streets

makes the point. For Rigo and for spray-can artists effecting wild-style lettering, the text is the point, although Rigo often depends on locational context to establish the full "statement" of his works. Seyed Alavi's 1992 *Words by Roads* project in Oakland heads in the same direction. Each of the four murals consists of large letters painted on freeway underpasses: for example, "eRACISM" and "INFORM(N)ATION."

McGee's spontaneity, even in "permissional" projects, can be compared with the Ramona Parra Brigade in Chile during the Pinochet regime, which developed a quick style of painting because of the very real dangers of being beaten and tortured by military thugs. Even if there is not the same threat of violent reprisal that there was in Chile (although reports of police beatings are common enough among writers), it is still preferable not to be caught.

Perhaps the clearest departure from traditional murals by these new artists is the rejection of realism. Indeed, the planning process is often a key element in the subversive character of traditional mural work because democratic experience runs so counter to our normal experience. But the spontaneous spray-can artists vie for public space simply by doing it, by taking it, and then leaving it up to "the authorities" to challenge their appropriation. This contestation is more dynamic because it is an ongoing challenge and response played out publicly on the walls of public space, even if often on private property. Some graffiti art thus becomes, as McGee puts it, a type of performance art, whereas traditional murals are more conventional, static espressions.

For McGee, graffiti may be a kind of "striking back" at injustice by any powerful institution, creating an "instant dialogue" that is carried out in action. Traditional murals may oppose institutional positions, but real dialogue is rare unless provided by the mural itself; an example of such is a 1995 Chicago work by Olivia Gude, *Where We Come From, Where We're Going*, which incorporates substantial portions of text into the mural, statements made by passersby to the site, who comprise the figures represented in the mural.

Oddly, for a style that communicates a ready *joie de vivre*, McGee's figures are clearly world-weary in contrast with the generally high-energy and humorless figures of traditional murals, which require much planning and intend to convey serious messages. In fact, one is hard pressed to think of examples of humor in San Francisco murals, with the notable exceptions of some of the early and comix-inspired works of Michael Rios, Gilberto Guzmán, and Spain (and the single R. Crumb mural, painted for the Mission Rebels building).

Traditional muralists were sometimes concerned with both geographical and architectural environments as well as audience. Appropriate locations usually meant highly visible ones. The images sometimes took into consideration the observer's visual field, and sometimes incorporated the architectural characteristics of the building on which the mural was painted so that the entire mass of the building was appropriated as part of the painted image. But spray-can artists have a different conception of political geography; that is, a different set of criteria determine the appropriateness of a site. They favor tunnels and rooftops, partly because the Department of Public Works does not buff pieces in those locations. As antigraffiti programs have expanded, writers have found it discouraging to have their efforts scrubbed or painted out almost immediately. Taggers and muralists inspired by spray-can writing do not have these problems because of the relative quickness of putting their tags up. McGee favors rusting surfaces, and old, abandoned areas that are marginalized anyway, so less likely to be a focus of maintenance. Not only will writings put up in these locations last longer, the deteriorated surfaces and locations contribute to the impact of his tired, bemused figures.

IV. Billboard Corrections

One area in which writers and muralists converge is in billboard corrections. These must be distinguished from mere alterations and vandalism. A billboard correction seeks to modify the advertisement as quickly and subtly as possible in such a way that the message of the ads is turned around and "shoots itself." A subgroup of spray-can artists mounts such a challenge, and some traditional muralists (if rumor is accurate) have also occasionally indulged in billboard corrections.

An advertisement correction confronts not only the ad's content but also the claim of public space by advertisers. Regardless of what one thinks of tags and other spray can writing, it is difficult to defend the appropriation of public space by billboards as a socially beneficial activity. In some cases, the effect is relatively benign, but liquor and tobacco ads are obviously harmful and these have been the targets of most billboard corrections. Besides, apt corrections elicit humor, all too rare in public art of any sort, by cleverness of execution and by subverting the obnoxious message of an advertisement. A Bank of America billboard in Berkeley, for example, was corrected from "Banking on America" to "Feeding on America"—short, sweet, exactly to the correctors' point. In a 1995 billboard design to announce a Galería de la Raza show, Kenneth Huerta and Diana Cristales painted "Mal burro," a parody of Marlboro cigarette advertisements in which Huerta replaced the magnificent horse of the Marlboro Man with a "bad donkey." The catalyzing influence on Huerta was Enrique Chagoya, a distinguished printmaker who was for a time in residence at the Galería de la Raza. Chagoya is well known for his satirical images, such as his Goya meets Mickey Mouse. Huerta applied this ironic use of icons to advertisements, with telling results.

A "replacement" by the Billboard Liberation Front, shortly after the Exxon Valdez oil spill. The original billboard advertised a radio station: "Hits Happen!"

But changes are afoot even in billboard corrections, initiated largely by the spray-can community. Writers have found a new venue in the bus shelter advertising kiosks found throughout the city. The trick is to get a key so that they can open the locked kiosk. Some have replaced the artwork with their own work. Some have corrected ads: for example, they exchanged a soft-porn Bebe ad with their hard-porn version.

In another example, a Miller Genuine Draft beer ad featured an image of bottle caps, each inscribed "MGD." The writers removed the ad, changed the "D's" to "V's," which then read "MGV," the writers' own tag. As is usual in such instances, they then locked in the new, corrected ad to protect it from "graffiti vandals" and waited to see what would happen. The advertising company, apparently not noticing the change, simply rotated the corrected ad to other bus shelter kiosks in their normal fashion, inadvertently moving MGV's tag throughout the city.

Traditional mural locations in San Francisco are usually announced by the Mayor's Office of Community Development or offered by private property owners. Designs are then composed which may or may not take specifics of the location into account, but invariably take specifics of the social location into account. Spray-can writers are less bound by official approval for their sites, and billboard corrections in fact take advantage of the carefully chosen advertising locations in order to maximize their works' exposure in exactly the same way the advertising companies have selected their sites. Of course, the writers are still bound by the pre-selected locations of bus stop advertisements, but they continue to turn them to their own purposes of subversion.

Acknowledgments

I am indebted to Aaron Noble, one of the CAMP organizers, for the generous sharing of his time and knowledge of the Bloody Thursday *ILWU mural-sculpture* and the Redstone Building projects.

This essay makes no attempt to be exhaustive or even inclusive of community muralists practicing in San Francisco. It focuses on a group of younger muralists and spray-can writers whose work departs from the tradition and shows signs of being significant for future community public art. Muralists such as Miranda Bergman, Juana Alicia, Susan Greene, Johanna Poethig, Susan Cervantes, Josh Sarantitis, and others cannot be forgotten, nor should it be suggested that they are not doing important work. It's just that the subjects of this essay are going a different direction—or the same direction differently.

References

Drescher, Timothy W. 1994. *San Francisco Murals: Community Creates Its Muse, 1914–1994.* St. Paul: Pogo Press.

A "replacement" by the Billboard Liberation Front (1977)

The Miracle Mile
South of Market and Gay Male Leather
1962–1997

by Gayle S. Rubin

THIS IS A STORY of several separate realities and their convergence: a complicated San Francisco neighborhood, a distinctive segment of the gay male population, the harsh imperial dreams of urban redevelopment, and a ravaging epidemic. It is a tale of sex, gender, real estate, morality, money, and medicine.

The Site

> More than any other neighborhood in the city, South of Market is the part that contains the whole: the one matrix that subsumes unto itself every successive layer of urban identity in the history of the city. Here indeed is the anchor district of San Francisco: the site of all of its early institutional life—churches, orphanages, schools, unions, hotels, and public institutions. Here is the residential district of its most diverse population. . . . South of Market was an urban district containing the full formula of the city. (Starr 1995–6, 370)

Market Street is one of the primary corridors of San Francisco. It cuts a sharp diagonal across the city from the Ferry Building to the base of Twin Peaks. The trolley rails along Market Street have long marked a physical and psychological boundary (the Slot) between the area north of Market, where the local centers of political and commercial power are situated, and the predominantly poor and working-class area "South of the Slot."

The South of Market was first settled during the Gold Rush: "A tent city sheltering perhaps a thousand would-be gold miners, it was called Happy Valley for its sunshine, shelter from prevailing winds, scrub oaks, spring water, and carefree inhabitants." (Bloomfield 1995–6, 372) Much of the present neighborhood was then a marshy swamp or entirely under water. Like most of San Francisco's shoreline, the South of Market was largely manufactured through the liberal

Rubble of the Tool Box at 4th and Harrison Streets (1971); inset: Chuck Arnett Photos Michael Kel
(left) and Bill Tellman (right) at Satyrs Badger Flat Run (1966)

application of landfill. Most of the city's early industries were located here, including iron foundries, boiler works, machine shops, manufacturers of bullets and shot, breweries, and warehouses. The wharves South of Market were a focus for shipping and shipbuilding. The residential population worked in these industries or in other nearby commercial enterprises. (Bloomfield 1995–6, Averbach 1973)

Leveled by the 1906 earthquake and fire, the South of Market was quickly rebuilt, and became "part of San Francisco's commercial downtown. The South of Market did not, however, match North of Market in uses. Here there were no major department stores, fashionable boutiques, banks, or except for the Palace, leading hotels. The owners did not anticipate such high-rent tenants and they built accordingly." (Bloomfield 1995–6, 387) While the postquake South of Market sheltered many working-class families, it was also an area with a high concentration of single working men and seasonal laborers. This had been the case since the Gold Rush days, when miners and field hands wintered in San Francisco, and seamen and transient workers stayed when they were between jobs or looking for work. (Averbach 1973)

This pattern intensified after the 1906 earthquake and fire. Most of the labor force that rebuilt San Francisco lived in the South of Market and much of the housing constructed there after the quake consisted of residential hotels. The city's shipping industry continued to dominate the eastern portion close to the waterfront. Seamen and dockworkers lived nearby, and service businesses in the neighborhood catered to them. The headquarters of maritime unions were in the South of Market, and the area seethed with labor activism. (Issel & Cherney 1986, Bérubé forthcoming)

World War II brought new working populations. Averbach notes that

South of Market emerged in 1950 with almost nine times the black population it had held before the war. . . . This recently arrived group was part of the great wartime migration of workers who followed numbers of Chicanos who had begun to move into South of Market in the early 1930s. . . . During the 1950s, the southwestern half of South of Market served as a reception area for a Filipino population of seasonal migratory workers. (Averbach 1973, 215)

While the ethnic composition of the transient poor changed, the general character of the neighborhood remained relatively stable until the 1950s. Then came the era of slum clearance and urban renewal.

Redevelopment

This land is too valuable to permit poor people to park on it.
—Justin Herman, Executive Director, San Francisco Redevelopment
Agency, 1970 (Hartman 1974, 19)

The South of Market area for many years has been recognized as an area of blight producing a depressing, unhealthful, and unsafe living environment, retarding industrial development, and acting as a drain on the city treasury. This study of 86 blocks is concerned with the problems of blight and with ways and means of improving the area through the use of the redevelopment process. . . . The South of Market Area ranks among the most severely blighted sections of the city, along with Chinatown and the Western Addition. . . . [T]he conditions of blight are such as to be highly conducive to social disintegration, juvenile delinquency, and crime. . . . The present wasteful use of potentially valuable land must be stopped if the South of Market area is to become a well functioning part of the city's environment. (Redevelopment Agency of the City and County of San Francisco 1952, 1–2)

Dreams of urban renewal drove a great deal of postwar urban planning and politics. Redevelopment promised cleaner, more livable, and more prosperous cities; in practice, it often eliminated low-cost housing occupied by poor and working people and replaced light industry, warehousing, and wholesaling with high-rent offices, fancy hotels, and expensive restaurants. Urban renewal also provided opportunities for large and politically well-connected developers to amass huge fortunes, often subsidized by public funds.

Some of San Francisco's biggest redevelopment projects have been in the Western Addition, the Embarcadero just north of Market, and in the South of Market. The Western Addition, then one of the city's largest concentrations of African American residents, was targeted for redevelopment in 1954. In 1959, the old wholesale produce district and waterfront area north of Market were designated as the Golden Gateway/Embarcadero–Lower Market Redevelopment Project Area. As early as 1953 large sections of the South of Market were approved for redevelopment by the San Francisco Board of Supervisors. At that time, the South of Market still contained light industry. It housed the bus terminals and the cheap hotels for transients, seamen, and other single working men. While the main streets were lined with low-rent commercial businesses, a working-class residential population occupied the smaller side streets and alleys. Many of the charities serving the urban poor were located in the South of Market, which had a substantial concentration of homeless, drug-addicted, or alcoholic street people. The district, with its lower rents and physical proximity, was ideal for housing the service businesses for the large downtown firms. These factors made it a juicy redevelopment plum. (Hartman 1974, 1984; Hoover 1979)

In 1952 the Redevelopment Agency of the City and County in San Francisco released its first comprehensive proposal, which called for displacing the residential population in favor of more industry. Then, in 1954, today's Yerba Buena and Moscone Convention Center were foreshadowed when local developer Ben Swig unveiled a "San Francisco Prosperity Plan." Swig's plan included a convention center, a sports stadium, and several high-rise office buildings. Much of that ambitious agenda has been accomplished, and the sports stadium now also looms as inevitable.

"One obvious prerequisite to South-of-Market development was the removal of the 4,000 residents and more than 700 small businesses. . . . In 1966, following final official approval of the plans by the Board of Supervisors, land acquisition and relocation began in earnest." (Hoover 1979, ix) Then in 1969, local residents and owners formed Tenants and Owners in Opposition to Redevelopment (TOOR) and filed the first of the many lawsuits that delayed redevelopment and reshaped its ultimate manifestations.

During the period of political and legal wrangling, the old neighborhood was significantly dismantled. Housing was demolished and entire streets disappeared. But the construction of new office towers and public buildings awaited the outcome of litigation, so the new neighborhood remained largely unrealized. In the interregnum, different kinds of residents and enterprises flowed into the disrupted niche. There were plenty of vacant buildings, both residential and commercial. Rents and land values were cheap, until speculation and resurgent redevelopment activity began to drive them higher. Street life at night was sparse. The streets emptied out when businesses closed and the daily work force departed. Parking at night was plentiful. The South of Market became a kind of urban frontier. The area began to attract artists looking for affordable studio space, musicians in search of practice venues, squatters who occupied the abandoned factories, and gay men. The relative lack of other nocturnal activity provided a kind of privacy, and urban nightlife that was stigmatized or considered disreputable could flourish in relative obscurity among the warehouses and deserted streets.

The Population

There had certainly been men engaging in homosexual activities in the old South of Market. A common pattern in which male homosexuals had relationships with masculine "trade" (straight-identified men who performed only insertive sex acts) has been well documented in other waterfront and working-class enclaves in late nineteenth- and early twentieth-century U.S. cities. (Chauncey 1985, 1994)

Moreover, research by Allan Bérubé shows the extent to which gay life in New York and San Francisco overlapped and intermixed with the world of sailors and merchant seamen. San Francisco's Embarcadero was known as a gay male cruising area at least as far back as the 1920s. At that time it was considered a "tough" area, so "only the boldest" went there. Bérubé's research shows that there were also many homosexual seamen who were well integrated into the working-class culture that once dominated the neighborhood. (Bérubé 1993, forthcoming)

> Along the waterfronts in port cities were complex sexual cultures that incorporated . . . erotic arrangements between men, often with the threat of danger and violence. On the Embarcadero in San Francisco, for example, before the 1960s, were hundreds of cheap hotels, taverns, lunch rooms, cafeterias, union halls, and the YMCA where maritime and waterfront workers and servicemen hung out and interacted with others outside their worlds. By the 1950s, what might have been described as the early gay bars and nightlife in San Francisco might more appropriately be called the homosexual aspects of waterfront culture. These often attracted gay men from other parts of the city. (Bérubé 1993, 10–11)

Bérubé notes that a 1954 police crackdown on San Francisco's "sex deviates" targeted the area at the base of Market Street where it meets the Embarcadero. Police action against gay haunts in the 1950s was typically expressed in political and moral terms, such as the crusades against communism

Fistfucking "time line"—poster for Fist Fuckers of America (FFA) night at the Folsom Street Barracks, by Bill Tellman (c. 1972)

or the need to protect women and children from the putative dangers of sexual psychopaths. (Freedman 1987; D'Emilio 1989b) The timing and severity of such crackdowns were usually determined by election campaigns, morality drives, or sensational and highly publicized crimes. (D'Emilio 1983, 1989a) However, raids and arrests also had significant economic and geographic consequences for the distribution of sexual sites in U.S. cities. For example, police attention toward the bars at the foot of Market Street helped "clean up" the area, which soon became the Embarcadero Center, whose hotels, office towers, and massive retail complex now span eight city blocks and comprise San Francisco's largest single real estate development.

Paul Gabriel (Member of the Board of Directors and Oral History Project of the Gay and Lesbian Historical Society of Northern California) notes that the "Gayola" crackdowns in 1960 and 1961 focused on the lower Market and waterfront bars. (D'Emilio 1983) These raids drove most of the gay bars from the area. Both Gabriel and Willie Walker (Archivist of the Gay and Lesbian Historical Society of Northern California) observe that as gay sites were driven out of the lower Market and the waterfront, gay occupation in the Tenderloin and Polk areas increased. (Walker & Gabriel personal communications 1997; Garber & Walker 1997; Walker 1997) Similarly, the gay presence in the South of Market shifted westward. It was during the course of the 1960s that the Polk and the Folsom became densely and visibly gay. Police action and redevelopment have had substantial impacts on San Francisco's gay (and sexual) geographies.

During the 1960s, San Francisco's major gay areas acquired different dominant stylistic characteristics, although these overlapped and were not mutually exclusive. Before the emergence of the Castro in the 1970s, the Polk and Tenderloin were the major gay areas. Polk Street became a commercial center. Its variegated gay economy included gay bars and baths, shops that provided gay or sex-related items, and many gay-owned shops that dispensed less specialized goods and services ranging from groceries to antiques. The territories of male hustlers, drag queens, and transsexual sex workers spanned the lower Polk and the adjacent Tenderloin. The Folsom and the South of Market drew a different population, the "leather" crowd. The gay men who began to filter into the South of Market in the 1960s were predominantly a group called "leathermen."

Leather

The South of Market district of San Francisco has been synonymous with leather sexuality for so long—nearly 30 years—that the terms are almost interchangeable.
—Joseph Bean (1988, 4)

"Leather" is a term for a distinctive subgroup of male homosexuals who began to coalesce into coherent communities by the late 1940s. Leather communities appeared first in the major cities of the United States, but later developed in other urban centers and in most industrialized capitalist countries. The leather subculture is organized around sexual activities and erotic semiotics that distinguish it from the larger gay male population. (Mains 1984; Rubin 1994, 1997; Thompson 1991) "Leather" serves as a marker for a kind of community, a collection of sexual practices, and a set of values and attitudes. However, the leather "community" is not unitary or monolithic. In addition to the common cleavages of class, color, ethnicity, geography, and faction, the apparent homogeneity of "leather" camouflages several major subpopulations divided along lines of sexual semiotics and practice.

If gay male leather can be said to have a core meaning, it would have to be gay masculinity. In the late 1940s and early 1950s, homosexuals were presumed to be effeminate—fairies, pansies, and queens. Gay men who were masculine in their personal style, and especially those who wanted other masculine men as partners, began to carve out alternative gay social spaces. Many of these men rode motorcycles, and as one man later explained to me, "The motorcycle was the symbol of homosexual masculinity."

Biker gear was also coded as masculine. Leather jackets, jeans, boots, and Harley caps all became markers for butch gay men interested, sexually and socially, in other butch gay men. Bars catering to this leather crowd emerged by the mid-1950s. "Leather" bars were contrasted to "sweater" bars, a nickname for the establishments that catered to an ostensibly swishier set.

In the mid-1950s, gay bikers also established gay motorcycle clubs. The first such club was the Satyrs, founded in Los Angeles in November 1954. The Satyrs were followed by the Oedipus in Los Angeles, the New York Motorbike Club, and early San Francisco clubs such as the Warlocks and California Motor Club (CMC). These clubs would host country runs and city celebrations which served as social occasions for leathermen. In the early days of leather, these bike club events comprised much of the leather social calendar. The Satyrs had a popular annual Badger Flat Run. The Warlocks were known for their Witches Christmas, and the CMC was famous for a giant Carnival. The leather bars, the bike clubs, and private parties were the major institutions of the early leather community.

Like most important symbols, leather acquired many meanings. Leather came to mean more than gay masculinity. It also connoted brotherhood and group solidarity, on the one hand, and a kind of rebellious individualism on the other. Like other black-clad rebels of the 1950s, the gay leather crowd expressed its own disaffection with post–World War II America, although mainly with its antigay attitudes and staid sexual moralities. In addition, leather became the major symbolic and social location in the gay male world for various kinds of "kinky sex."

By "kinky sex" I mean primarily activities such as sadomasochism (SM), bondage and discipline, and fetishism. Among gay men, the social organization of sexual sadomasochism and fetishism is generally structured by the idioms of leather and the institutions of leather communities. Some leathermen consider leather to be fundamentally an expression and symbol of SM. Other members of leather communities have no interest in sadomasochism and may even resent any association with SM.

During the mid-to-late 1960s, another subgroup precipitated around a practice called "fistfucking," also known as "handballing" or simply "fisting." Fistfucking refers primarily to the insertion of the hand or arm into the rectum of a partner, although later, as women began to self-consciously embrace the practice, it also came to refer to the use of the entire hand to penetrate the vagina. Edgar Gregersen has noted that fisting "may be the only sexual practice invented in the twentieth century." (Gregersen 1982, 56–57) By the late 1960s, fisting had became so popular that its enthusiasts quickly comprised another major group among leathermen. "Fisters" have become perhaps the third significant subdivision of the leather population along with sadomasochists and men who eroticize masculinity or motorcycles.

Folsom Street: The Miracle Mile

This is the city's backyard. . . . An early morning walk will take a visitor past dozens of small businesses manufacturing necessities; metal benders, plastic molders, even casket makers can all be seen plying their trades. At five they set down their tools and return to the suburbs. . . . A few hours later, men in black leather . . . will step out on these same streets to fill the nearly 30 gay bars, restaurants and sex clubs in the immediate vicinity. Separate realities that seldom touch and, on the surface at least, have few qualms about each other.
—Mark Thompson (1982, 28)

Gay male leather communities have been markedly territorial in major U.S. cities. In San Francisco, leather has been most closely associated with the South of Market neighborhood since 1962. Earlier, in the 1950s, leathermen had mostly patronized the waterfront bars, such as Jack's on the Waterfront, the Sea Cow, and the Castaways. The first dedicated leather bar in San Francisco was the Why Not, which opened briefly in the Tenderloin in 1962. When the Tool Box opened later that year on the corner of Fourth Street and Harrison, it was the first leather bar located in the South of Market.

The Tool Box was a sensation. It was wildly popular and even attracted nationwide media notice. Herb Caen wrote about the Tool Box in his famous *San Francisco Chronicle* column:

As I noted a few days ago, some of the young fellers who hang out in the Tool Box at Fourth and Harrison wear and "S" or an "M" on their shirt pockets to indicate "Sadist" or "Masochist." Which prompted a relieved message from Harold Call. "I'm so glad you printed that," he said. "All this time I thought it meant 'Single,' or 'Married!'" (Caen 1964)

WHY NOT

Poster from the Why Not (1962)

The most celebrated element of the Tool Box was a huge mural painted by Chuck Arnett, a local artist who worked at the bar and whose paintings and posters were also featured at such later bars as the Red Star Saloon and the Ambush. The mural was a massive black-and-white painting that depicted a variety of tough-looking, masculine men. In 1964, when *Life* magazine did a story on homosexuality in America, a photograph of the Tool Box was spread across the two opening pages. (Welch & Eppridge 1964) In it we see the mural and some of the bar patrons, including Arnett and several others who would play significant roles in San Francisco's early leather history, as the managers, bartenders, bouncers, and above all, the artists and decorators of local leather establishments. Standing next to Arnett is Bill Tellman, another artist who has contributed a great deal to the local iconography. He designed the poster for the Slot, one of the earliest leather-oriented bathhouses. He also did graphic design for the Ambush, and a made a backlit stained-glass depiction of fist-fucking that eventually adorned the Catacombs.

Jack H. is also in the photo. In 1965 Jack and a partner opened the Detour at 888 McAllister Street when the popularity of the Tool Box began to subside. Later he was a co-owner of Febe's, one of the first leather bars to open on Folsom Street. Jack also later opened the Slot, and some stories even credit him with having invented fistfucking at a party in his basement in 1962.

Mike Caffee, another artist, is there, too. Caffee worked in and did graphic design for many leather businesses. In 1966, he designed the logo for Febe's and created a statue that came to symbolize the bar. He modified a small plaster reproduction of Michelangelo's David, making him into a classic 1960s gay biker:

> I broke off the raised left arm and lowered it so his thumb could go in his pants pocket, giving him cruiser body language. The biker uniform was constructed of layers of wet plaster.... The folds and details of the clothing were carved, undercutting deeply so that the jacket would hang away from his body, exposing his well-developed chest. The pants were button Levis, worn over the boots, and he sported a bulging crotch you couldn't miss.... Finally I carved a chain and bike run buttons on his [Harley] cap. (Caffee 1997)

This "leather David" became one of the best-known symbols of San Francisco leather. The image of the Febe's David appeared on pins, posters, calendars, and matchbooks. It was known and disseminated around the world. The statue itself was reproduced in several formats. Two-foot-tall plaster casts were made and sold by the hundreds. One of the plaster statues currently resides in a leather bar in Boston, having been transported across the country on the back of a motorcycle. Another "leather David" graces a leather bar in Melbourne, Australia. One is in a case on the wall of the Paradise Lounge, a rock-and-roll bar that opened on the site once occupied by Febe's.

PHOTO JOE WINTERS

Original Febe's statue, by Mike Caffee (1966)

Despite its enormous influence, the popularity of the Tool Box was short lived. By 1965, it had competition from the Detour and On the Levee, and by

1966, Febe's opened and became the leading leather bar. Although the Tool Box was open until 1971, it was never again the dominant leather bar. However, when the building that housed the Tool Box was torn down for redevelopment in 1971, old patrons came by to get bricks to keep as mementos. During demolition, the wall with the mural was left standing for some time, all alone in a sea of concrete rubble and twisted steel. In his memoir of Chuck Arnett and the Tool Box, Jack Fritscher recalls:

> [T]he Tool Box, long deserted, was torn down by the city for urban renewal. Somehow, though, the wreckers ball failed to knock down the stone wall with Arnett's mural of urban aboriginal men in leather made famous by *Life*. For two years, at the corner of Fourth and Harrison, drivers coming down the off ramp from the freeway were greeted by Arnett's somber dark shadows, those Lascaux cave drawings of Neanderthal, primal, kick-ass leathermen. (Fritscher 1991, 117–118)

The leather scene moved to what would become its Main Street in 1966, when Febe's and the Stud opened up at the western end of Folsom Street. Several other bars soon opened along a three-block strip of Folsom Street, establishing a core area that anchored a burgeoning leather economy with various commercial establishments, which continued to develop and expand in the 1970s to become one of the most extensive and densely occupied leather neighborhoods in the world. The area still functions as the local leather "capital." As a result, the South of Market acquired a number of nicknames, including the Folsom, the Miracle Mile, and the Valley of the Kings.

This last appellation was coined by local leather columnist Mr. Marcus. By the late 1970s, Mr. Marcus had given each of San Francisco's three major gay neighborhoods a nickname. The "Valley of the Kings" conveyed an image of powerful, cocky, independent, and sexy masculinity. It contrasted with Marcus' nickname for Polk Street, the "Valley of the Queens," in reference to the older and sometimes more effeminate population of gay men associated with the area. He dubbed the Castro the "Valley of the Dolls," an allusion to its hordes of young and beautiful men.

By the late 1970s, the Castro was unquestionably the center of local gay politics, but the Folsom had become the sexual center. The same features that made the area attractive to leather bars made it hospitable to other forms of gay sexual commerce. Many of the nonleather gay bathhouses and sex clubs also nestled among the warehouses. Just before the age of AIDS, the South of Market had become symbolically and institutionally associated in the gay male community with sex.

The Coming of AIDS and the Fall of the Folsom

Protestations from gay leaders notwithstanding, the AIDS epidemic hit Folsom St. afi-cionados sooner and much harder than it hit other gays, long ago sending the S and M subculture into a tailspin from which it has never recovered.
—"The Death of Leather" (1985)

The years between 1966 and 1982 were a period of triumphant expansion, but by the mid-1980s, both the neighborhood and community were devastated. The AIDS epidemic brought a tsunami of mortality to gay men in San Francisco, and the South of Market appeared to bear the brunt of its fury.

In the Castro, businesses closed as their owners died. Each week the obituaries announced more losses: singers, artists, therapists, doctors, bartenders, community activists, and politicians. An anguished pall hung over the Castro in the mid-1980s, but while the neighborhood suffered a period of stunned shock, the economic and social reversals did not decimate the neighborhood. Although it lost the joyous innocence it once had, the Castro recovered and remains culturally vital, politically active, populous, and prosperous. By contrast, many of the changes in gay South of Market have been dramatic and enduring. When leather bars or sex clubs closed in the mid-1980s, new ones did not replace them. Most were succeeded instead by restaurants, bars, and dance clubs with a predominantly heterosexual clientele.

By 1987, the institutional infrastructure of leather had undergone substantial attrition, and the South of Market had become a case study in urban succession. Instead of the hordes of gay men en route to the baths and leathermen on the prowl, the Folsom was suddenly filled with the mostly nongay and nonleather patrons of the new eateries and music halls. These changes likely account in part for a persistent belief, often expressed within both the gay community and the nongay press that the leather population has been hit harder by AIDS than other groups of gay men.

However, there are no demographic studies that prove or disprove such assertions, or any hard data demonstrating such differential AIDS mortality among gay sexual subpopulations. Mortality within the leather community has been severe, as has been the overall—and overwhelming—gay male mortality in San Francisco. But the belief in greater AIDS mortality for leathermen is unsupported and probably unwarranted. So why has the Castro prospered while the South of Market has undergone such profound deterioration as a gay neighborhood?

While I do not want to underestimate the devastation that has resulted from the sheer loss of life, the effects of AIDS on the leather community have been mediated through other factors. The displacement of gay leather South of Market resulted from geographic competition for the area that long preceded AIDS, and from public policy decisions about disease control, as much as it did from AIDS itself. Moreover, rather than destroying the leather community, AIDS has both reinforced some aspects of its social structure and produced changes in others.

While the level of neighborhood change in the South of Market led to presumptions of greater mortality among leathermen, prior prejudices about leather sexuality also contributed to the notion that men who hung out in the leather bars were more subject to the disease. Stereotypes that leather sexualities—particularly SM and fisting—were inherently dangerous, undesirable, or unhealthy have been easily assimilated into concerns over AIDS-related risks and hazards. Thus, leather sexualities have been prominent among the ideological scapegoats for AIDS fear, panic, and loathing.

Poster for Up Your Alley Street Fair, Ringold Alley (1985)

In the gay press of the mid-1980s, it was commonplace to blame "sleazy South of Market leathermen" for the disease:

> We have been a plague upon ourselves! In the late '50's and early '60's, when I first came out, backroom bars were non-existent, baths few and far between, the S&M scene a small, closed and very secret society. Fist-fucking was almost unheard of and "rimming" almost never done. . . . The leather scene was now being written up by gossip columnists in various big-city newspapers. Even Bloomingdales, in the mid-70's, did a major promotion featuring black leather clothing. In the late 50's almost no one had ever heard of terms such as "scat," "water sports," fist-fucking, tit clamps, etc. Now, not only does everyone know what these terms mean, but many have actually experienced them as well. . . . (Knapp 1983)

Clutching our carcinogens and holding butch poses, we treat each other's bodies like disposable bottles, stumbling drunk and wasted through smoke-filled
bars, giving and getting attitude, while a cancerous angel of death spreads his
black leather wings and prepares to fly over Folsom and Castro. (Evans 1982)

Leathersex and leathermen had become easy targets for AIDS blame. Leathermen
were already disdained, and their sexual practices were often feared or disparaged.
Moreover, since leathermen were often characterized as more "sexual" than other
gay men, it was easy to consider them more prone to exposure to a sexually transmitted disease. Even the South of Market neighborhood became a geographic
magnet for AIDS-related apprehensions.

Closing the Baths: A Classic Sex Panic

Before there were any openly gay or lesbian leaders, political clubs, books, films,
newspapers, businesses, neighborhoods, churches or legally recognized gay
rights, several generations of pioneers spontaneously created gay bathhouses
and lesbian and gay bars. . . . [G]ay baths and bars became the first stages of a
movement of civil rights for gay people in the United States. . . . Gay bathhouses
represent a major success in a century-long political struggle to overcome isolation and develop a sense of community and pride in their sexuality, to gain their
right to sexual privacy, to win their right to associate with each other in public,
and to create "safety zones" where gay men could be sexual and affectionate
with each other with a minimal threat of violence, blackmail, loss of employment, arrest, imprisonment, and humiliation. . . .

As a historian, it is clear to me that yet another government campaign to dismantle gay institutions, even in the well-motivated attempt to stop the spread
of AIDS, will only backfire. . . . Instead of wasting its time defending its bathhouses, its bars, and its very right to exist, the gay community must be allowed
to devote all its resources, including the bathhouses, toward promoting the
research, health programs and safe sex educational measures that will save lives.
(Bérubé 1984)

While bathhouse closure may appear tangential to the impact of AIDS on the
leather community, the links are strong. Bathhouse closure exemplifies the way in
which public policy decisions driven by misplaced passions often had unintended
and unanticipated consequences. As with other sexually transmitted diseases, early
attempts to explain and combat AIDS often assumed a profoundly moralistic cast
that had little connection to the exigencies of epidemiological intervention. Sex
prejudice, sex moralism, and sex panic often powered analysis and policy. (Brandt
1988; Bérubé 1988; Patton 1985; Triechler 1988)

Proponents of bathhouse closure, such as Randy Shilts, argued that their program was an obvious common sense measure to save lives. They portrayed the debate about closure as one pitting public health against civil liberties. Shilts in particular wrote as if public health professionals were in agreement on the desirability of closing the baths, and that only political considerations were preventing them from doing so. (Shilts 1987)

On the contrary, bathhouse closure, far from being an obvious public health measure impeded by political pressure, was a case of political pressure overwhelming public health considerations. Public health professionals were not unanimous about the necessity or desirability of closing the baths, which stayed open in most other cities. It is ironic that while there are still no legal gay bathhouses within the San Francisco city limits, establishments in nearby municipalities such as Berkeley and San Jose have continued to thrive.

It is arguable that what mattered in the long run was changing behavior, not its location. Closing the baths may have actually impeded the progress of safe-sex education. Even in situations where the ownership did not cooperate, safe sex was spreading, like the epidemic itself, from person to person, through sexual contact, as men would engage each other in discussions of what they were or were not about to do. Wholesale closure eliminated opportunities for sex education along with opportunities for sex. At the baths, the concentrated populations of those at high risk for AIDS provided opportunities for educators to disseminate condoms along with written guidelines for AIDS risk reduction. (Murray & Payne 1988; Bolton 1992)

The social costs of closing the baths were treated cavalierly. Those who pushed for closure appeared to assume that nothing important or good ever happened in the sex palaces. They failed to recognize the baths and sex clubs as important institutions that served many needs within a diverse gay male community. (Bérubé 1996) The major gay baths had deep pockets and expensive attorneys, and could afford a protracted legal fight. By contrast, many of the leather clubs were relatively small operations in which a dedicated owner had invested most of his capital and a great deal of personal commitment, and they could not afford prolonged litigation. Calls for closure quickly claimed most of the specialized leather, SM, and fisting sex clubs even before any city actions were taken, and as the agitation intensified, most of the men who ran the leather clubs elected to shut down and limit their losses. The wider social and economic fallout from closure was also substantial. While the owners of bathhouses were frequently vilified as greedy capitalists (and some undoubtedly were), the debates never grappled with the importance of the baths to gay male social life or the economic impact of closure on the gay economy.

New sexual spaces eventually began to reemerge by the end of the 1980s. Many were small, some were dirty, and most were ill-equipped and lacking in the accumulation of small improvements that had made the older clubs comfortable and sexy. Some of the clubs lacked even the most basic of the amenities taken for granted in the old facili-

Graffiti on 2nd St. between Bryant and Harrison (1986)

ties. The infrastructure of semipublic sex was degraded as a result.

This began to change only in 1992, with the opening of Eros and Blowbuddies, two clubs that permit only safe sex on the premises. They have been followed by others, and something of a sex club renaissance is now under way. The infrastructure of gay male commercial sex is being slowly rebuilt. Nonetheless, few of the current facilities can compare with the sex palaces of yesteryear. Nostalgia for those well-developed installations has contributed to recent calls in the local gay press for removing all of the regulations put in place by the closure campaigns. Instead, new regulations have been adopted. Removing the regulations might hasten the recovery of baths and sex clubs, but some changes are irreversible. One of these is the displacement of the gay and leather communities from the South of Market.

"South of Market Dies Screaming"

> Once the rough threatening preserve of welders, wholesalers, butcher supply houses, winos, struggling artists and gay men who dressed in black leather motorcycle outfits and metal studs, Soma has suddenly become fashionable. . . . Now the streets are lined with shiny BMWs and Mercedes. . . .
> —"Off-Beat Rough Toward Chic Very Fine" (1988)

> When Gay people take over a neighborhood, they call it gentrification. When straight people take over a neighborhood, they call it a renaissance.
> —Tom Ammiano (1988)

By forcing the leather-oriented sex clubs to close, the war against the baths eliminated an important social and economic sector of leather community life.

Because so much of the gay commercial sex establishment was in the South of Market, closure eviscerated a substantial segment of the nonleather gay economy there as well. The loss of the bathhouses and sex clubs, which drew gay customers and employed gay men in the neighborhood, weakened the gay presence in the area. Abrupt bathhouse closure and damage from urban renewal were significant factors in the startling collapse of gay South of Market in the mid-1980s.

The visible changes in the neighborhood occasioned dozens of articles in the local and even national press celebrating the area's sudden respectability and trendy "renaissance." Virtually all the commentary cited AIDS as the cause of the South of Market's shifting demographics. But these changes had been underway for some time. A major factor was the physical position of the South of Market neighborhood. While the Castro was far away from the centers of retail power, finance, and redevelopment, the proximity the leather neighborhood to downtown San Francisco, once a convenience, had become a threat to its survival.

Redevelopment had suddenly escalated in the late 1970s. As Chester Hartman observes, South of Market redevelopment "spanned the political lives of five mayors—George Christopher, John Shelley, Joseph Alioto, George Moscone, and Diane Feinstein." (Hartman 1984, 24) Moscone was elected in 1975. His administration was "more oriented to neighborhood concern and consequences of downtown growth," and his appointments to the Planning Commission reflected these priorities. (xvii)

Dianne Feinstein became Mayor when George Moscone was assassinated by Dan White in 1978. Feinstein's friendlier stance toward development was reflected in an unprecedented building boom and in a marked increase in the pace of "urban renewal" in the South of Market. Among Dan White's legacies is a measure of responsibility for the accelerated Manhattanization of San Francisco in the 1980s.

The convention center named after Moscone, who might have opposed its construction, was completed in 1981. That year, the San Francisco Planning and Urban Research Association (SPUR) released a report on South of Market development and held a conference to promote its findings. The flier for the conference showed Mayor Feinstein about to fire a starter's pistol for the developers preparing to sprint across Market Street in quest of the "South of Market Pot O' Gold." Sticking out from under the "Pot O' Gold" is the hand of someone crushed beneath, an apt image for the fate of the old neighborhood.

Leather bars in old Victorian houses were not suited to compete with new high-rise, high-rent buildings or even the mid-level eateries and other enterprises that would service them. Long before AIDS was a factor, conversion to straighter, more respectable, more expensive bars and restaurants was well underway in the

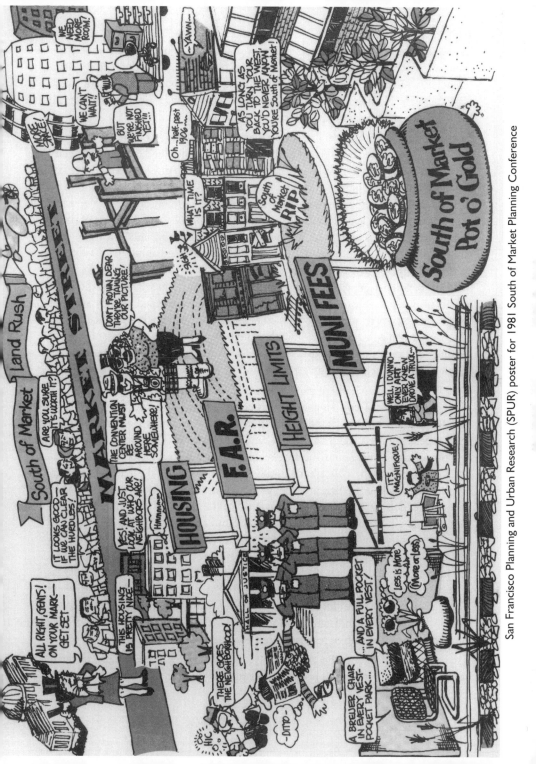

San Francisco Planning and Urban Research (SPUR) poster for 1981 South of Market Planning Conference

South of Market. Redevelopment is now rapidly invading and encircling the Folsom. At the northeast corner is the Moscone Center and the Yerba Buena complex, which includes two new museums and a performance center. More large civic projects and many private developments are planned. What remains of the leather bar area is within a few blocks of Yerba Buena.

At the southeast corner is a large and growing retail complex which now includes Toys 'R Us, the Bed and Bath Superstore, Trader Joe's, and an entire city block devoted to a huge Price-Costco warehouse store. An Office Max store has recently opened just behind the San Francisco Eagle, one of the remaining leather bars. The back of the Costco parking lot faces the Eagle on one corner and the Lone Star, another leather bar, on the other. Shoppers laden with carts of paper towels and a year's supply of Windex are not a promising mix with gay men dressed in leather. The potential for conflict and violence along these ruptured territorial membranes is immense. In October 1995, three men attacked and severely beat a patron leaving the Lone Star. He dragged himself over to the Eagle to obtain assistance, and his assailants were soon apprehended as they stood in line to get into a nearby music club, the DNA Lounge, which had once been a leather bar named Chaps. It is difficult to imagine how these businesses and populations can continue to coexist. The differences of scale between Costco and the leather bars in size, capital investment, and mayoral benediction are extreme. It is quite evident that if anything gives, it will not be Costco.

The corner of Folsom and 11th Streets is a vivid example of neighborhood change. At the height of leather occupation, this intersection was a major part of a circuit between the various bars, baths, and eating places. There were leather bars on two of the corners, and the intersection formed a corridor between the bars located further south or west, such as the Ambush, Arena, and the Eagle, and bars further east, such as the Brig and the Ramrod. Once the heart of the Miracle Mile, the intersection became a barrier to gay male leather traffic by the late 1980s, having become a major thoroughfare of nongay San Francisco nightlife. On weekend nights, hordes of predominantly heterosexual revelers throng the area. Their presence draws hungry panhandlers, as city policies have driven much of the homeless population out of the major tourist neighborhoods and into adjoining areas such as the South of Market. Street crime has increased as both affluent club patrons and the vulnerable poor are targeted by a variety of scammers, muggers, and thieves. The police cars that endlessly prowl along Folsom and 11th are evidence of how highly charged this strip of real estate has become.

To move among the remaining leather bars, a gay man must navigate through crowds that can be hostile and dangerous. In 1987, a young heterosexual tourist was assaulted and murdered near the corner of Folsom and 11th after he was apparently mistaken for a homosexual. It is deeply ironic that, contrary to stereotyped expectations, the displacement of those "threatening men in black motorcycle outfits" by a mostly heterosexual street population has made this neighborhood considerably less safe than it used to be.

The Resilience of Leather: Changes and Continuities in the Leather Community

Against all odds and expectations, the San Francisco gay male leather community has weathered AIDS, sex panics, and urban renewal. The structures of leather social life have undergone substantial change. But the community and its culture have adapted and survived. For example, AIDS has unquestionably contributed to substantial erosion among some leather institutions, particularly the gay motorcycle clubs. Many major clubs and the events they sponsored did not survive into the 1990s. The Warlocks, one of San Francisco's oldest motorcycle clubs, is among those that vanished, and important events, such as the CMC Carnival and the Satyrs Badger Flat run, have also been suspended.

However, while some of the older institutional forms are foundering, new ones are thriving. Virtually every public event in the gay male leather community raises money for AIDS, and much of leather socializing now occurs at AIDS fund-raisers.

Moreover, there is a palpable, visible recovery taking place. New clubs are being founded, new bars are opening, and leather businesses are once again flourishing. A few

Detail from poster for Folsom Street Fair (1997)

PHOTO JIM WINBOURN; POSTER DESIGN MICHAEL J. WILLIAMS GRAPHIC DESIGN of these are in the Castro, but most are still in the South of Market. The Folsom is still the central focal point for local leather and it remains a magnet for leather tourists.

The leather occupation of the South of Market is thinner and more dispersed than it once was. The leather bars and businesses are interspersed among the music halls, upscale restaurants, and big-box warehouse stores. The intermingling of gay or leather sites with straight or mainstream undertakings has meant a loss of the very privacy that once drew leathermen to the South of Market. The leather presence is also more episodic. Where there used to be leathermen constantly thronging the Folsom, such hordes now only appear for major leather holidays and festivities.

Two street fairs are important in maintaining the Folsom's leather ambience. In 1984, a group of community organizers and housing activists decided to start a street fair in the South of Market. The Folsom Street Fair was intended to make a political statement that the South of Market, far from being an empty slum in need of urban renewal, was already occupied. The fair, it was thought, would bring together and display all the disparate elements of a vital and viable neighborhood. Thus the fair has never been an exclusively gay or leather event. Nonetheless, the founders included leathermen, and given the strong presence of leather in the area, the fair has always had substantial leather participation.

Like most San Francisco street fairs, the Folsom Street Fair has entertainment, sales booths, and opportunities for political organizing, fundraising, and education. While most commercial booths feature generic street fair merchandise like polished rocks and mediocre pottery, the fair is also a showcase for services and crafts directed at leather consumers. These include piercers, makers of bondage furniture, whipmakers, and purveyors of other SM equipment. SM clubs do small-scale rummage sales to raise funds, and various community service organizations hand out literature and sign up members. The Folsom Street Fair has become an occasion for the leather community to come out in force and in full dress.

A second South of Market street fair was started in 1985 on Ringold Alley. It was called the Up Your Alley Fair, or Ringold Alley Fair. In 1987 the Up Your Alley Fair moved to Dore Alley between Harrison and Folsom. A single nonprofit organization now runs both the Folsom Street and Dore Alley fairs. These street fairs have become important social and economic events for the leather population.

Although AIDS has made the leather community smaller, it has also made it tighter and more socially integrated. Suffering and the sense of common struggle have drawn people together. Leather society is certainly more gender-integrated than it was even ten years go, and it is also more nationally confederated and politically cohesive.

In the long run, the South of Market is probably lost to the leather population, despite the stubborn vitality of a few remaining strongholds. San Francisco's entire eastern waterfront is about to be rebuilt, and what is left of the old docks, piers, factories, warehouses, and low-cost housing along the bay is about to be replaced by large and expensive edifices of concrete, glass, and steel.

A new baseball stadium planned for China Basin will anchor one end of this expansion, and there are plans to rebuild the bay front all the way to Pier 70. Several mammoth projects for Rincon Point, South Beach, China Basin, and Mission Bay are in the planning stages or awaiting approval. (Port of San Francisco 1997) This would take the rebuilding boom almost to Bayview–Hunters Point, one of the last strongholds of African American residents within the city limits. On the other side of Bayview–Hunters Point, a new half-billion-dollar football stadium and retail mall will anchor the southern limit of the city's eastern flank. New condominiums, malls, offices, and sports facilities will occupy much of what little is left of the city's last major strip of light industry, low-rent commerce, and low-cost housing. There are no leather bars or low-income residents in the blueprints for these developments. If the leather community must leave the South of Market, it may establish itself in some other urban niche. But finding any corner of the city left unmolested by large-scale construction is becoming an increasing challenge.

Nonetheless, the leather community has shown itself to command robust social reserves, surprising economic vigor, and flexible adaptability. Despite the repeated losses of key individuals to AIDS and the implacable march of urban renewal, the gay male leather community has continued as a viable and evolving social form. For now, leather continues to be a vital part of the mix in San Francisco's extraordinary South of Market.

Acknowledgments

Without the assistance and generosity of several individuals, this essay would not have been possible. I owe thanks to Liz Highleyman for emergency editing, to Allan Bérubé for permission to quote from his remarkable ongoing research in gay and labor history, to Paul Gabriel for sharing important insights from his unpublished work, to Willie Walker for his encyclopedic knowledge of San Francisco gay history, to Jay Marston for enduring encouragement and support, and to the editors of this volume for patience and persistence.

References

Averbach, Alvin. 1973. "San Francisco's South of Market District, 1858–1958: The Emergence of a Skid Row." *California Historical Quarterly* 52(3):196–223.

Bean, Joseph W. 1988. "Changing Times South of Market." *Advocate* (California supplement) (29 March) 4–7.

Bérubé, Allan. 1984. "The History of the Baths." *Coming Up!* (December).

———. 1988. "Caught in the Storm: AIDS and the Meaning of Natural Disaster." *Outlook* (Fall).

———. 1993. "'Dignity for All': The Role of Homosexuality in the Marine Cooks and Stewards Union (1930s–1950s)." Paper presented at Reworking American Labor History: Race, Gender, and Class conference. Madison.

———. 1996. "The History of the Bathhouses." In Dangerous Bedfellows, eds. *Policing Public Sex: Queer Politics and the Future of AIDS Activism.* Boston. South End Press.

———. Forthcoming. *Shipping Out.* New York: Houghton-Mifflin.

Bloomfield, Anne B. 1995–6. "A History of the California Historical Society's New Mission Street Neighborhood." *California History* (Winter).

Bolton, Ralph. 1992. "Aids and Promiscuity: Muddles in the Models of HIV Prevention." *Medical Anthropology* 14:145–223.

Brandt, Allan M. 1988. "AIDS: From Social History to Social Policy." In Elizabeth Fee and Daniel M. Fox, eds., *AIDS: The Burdens of History.* Berkeley: University of California Press.

Caen, Herb. 1964. Column. *San Francisco Chronicle* (July 3).

Caffee, Mike. 1997. "The Story of the Fe-Be's Statue, As Told by Its Sculptor, Mike Caffee." Unpublished manuscript.

Chauncey, George Jr. 1985. "Christian Brotherhood or Sexual Perversion? Homosexual Identities and the Construction of Sexual Boundaries in the World War One Era." *Journal of Social History* 19 (Winter):189–211.

———. 1994. Gay New York: *Gender, Urban Culture, and the Making of the Gay World, 1890–1940.* New York: Basic Books.

"The Death of Leather." 1985. *San Francisco Focus* (November).

D'Emilio, John. 1983. *Sexual Politics, Sexual Communities: The Making of a Homosexual Minority in the United States, 1940–1970.* Chicago: University of Chicago Press.

———. 1989a. "Gay Politics and Community in San Francisco Since World War II." In Duberman, Martin Bauml, Martha Vicinus, and George Chauncey, Jr., eds., *Hidden from History: Reclaiming the Gay and Lesbian Past.* New York: New American Library.

———. 1989b. "The Homosexual Menace: The Politics of Sexuality in Cold War America." In Kathy Peiss, Christina Simmons, and Robert Padgug, eds., *Passion and Power: Sexuality in History.* Philadelphia: Temple University.

Evans, Arthur (aka The Red Queen). 1982. "Milk Milked." Letter to the editor, *Bay Area Reporter* (24 November) 6.

Freedman, Estelle. 1987. "Uncontrolled Desires: The Response to the Sexual

Psychopath, 1920–1960." *Journal of American History* 74(1):83–106.

Fritscher, Jack. 1991. "Artist Chuck Arnett: His Life/Our Times." In Mark Thompson, ed., *Leatherfolk*. Boston: Alyson.

Garber, Eric, and Willie Walker. 1997. "Queer Bars and Other Establishments in San Francisco." Gay and Lesbian Historical Society of Northern California. Unpublished data.

Gregersen, Edgar. 1983. *Sexual Practices: The Story of Human Sexuality*. New York: Franklin Watts.

Hartman, Chester. 1974. *Yerba Buena: Land Grab and Community Resistance in San Francisco*. San Francisco: Glide Publications.

———. 1984. *The Transformation of San Francisco*. Totowa, NJ: Rowman & Allanheld.

Hoover, Catherine. 1979. "Introduction." In Ira Nowinski, *No Vacancy: Urban Renewal and the Elderly*. San Francisco: Carolyn Bean.

Issel, William, and Robert W. Cherney. 1986. *San Francisco 1965–1932: Politics, Power, and Urban Development*. Berkeley: University of California Press.

Knapp, Don. 1983. "A 20 Year Cycle." *Bay Area Reporter* (10 March) 13.

Mains, Geoff. 1984. *Urban Aboriginals: A Celebration of Leathersexuality*. San Francisco: Gay Sunshine Press.

Murray, Stephen O., and Kenneth W. Payne. 1988. "Medical Policy Without Scientific Evidence: The Promiscuity Paridigm and AIDS." *California Sociologist* 11(1/2):13–54.

"Off-Beat Rough Toward Chic Very Fine." 1988. *New York Times* (September 15).

Patton, Cindy. 1985. *Sex and Germs: The Politics of AIDS*. Boston: South End Press.

Port of San Francisco. 1997. *Waterfront Design & Access: An Element of the Waterfront Land Use Plan*. Draft (May 7).

Redevelopment Agency of the City and County of San Francisco. 1952. *The Feasibility of Redevelopment in the South of Market Area* (June 1).

Rubin, Gayle. 1994. "The Valley of the Kings: Leathermen in San Francisco, 1960–1990." Doctoral dissertation, Department of Anthropology, University of Michigan.

———. 1997. "Elegy for the Valley of the Kings: AIDS and the Leather Community in San Francisco, 1981–1996." In Martin Levine, Peter Nardi, and John Gagnon, eds., *In Changing Times: Gay Men and Lesbians Encounter HIV/AIDS*. Chicago: University of Chicago.

Shilts, Randy. 1987. *And the Band Played On: Politics, People, and the AIDS Epidemic*. New York: St. Martin's Press.

Starr, Kevin. 1995–6. "South of Market and Bunker Hill." *California History* (Winter).

Thompson, Mark. 1982. "Folsom Street." *Advocate* (8 July) 28–31, 57.

———. 1991. *Leatherfolk: Radical Sex, People, Politics, and Practice*. Boston: Alyson.

Triechler, Paula. 1988. "AIDS, Homophobia, and Biomedical Discourse: An Epidemic of Signification." In Douglas Crimp, *Cultural Analysis, Cultural Activism*.

Walker, Willie. 1997. "Gay Bars, Bathhouses and Restaurants in San Francisco 1930–1969." Gay and Lesbian Historical Society of Northern California. Unpublished data, charts, and graphs.

Welch, Paul, and Bill Eppridge (photographer). 1964. "Homosexuality in America." *Life* (26 June) 66–80.

From Manila Bay to Daly City
Filipinos in San Francisco

by James Sobredo

IN THE MIDDLE OF UNION SQUARE, one of the choice tourist spots in the city, stands a monument "Erected by the Citizens of San Francisco to commemorate the Victory of the American Navy under Commodore George Dewey at Manila Bay." This monument, dedicated to the prowess of the Navy in the 1898 Spanish-American War, is surrounded by such symbols of Western capitalism as Macy's, Tiffany, Saks, Hermes, the Westin Hotel, and the Grand Hyatt. Unbeknownst to many of the millions of tourists who pose by the monument for their souvenir photos—indeed, to most San Franciscans—is the fact that this great American naval victory also led to a bloody war waged against Filipinos fighting for their independence.

Just a few blocks away from Union Square, in the basement of 407 Sansome Street, the Filipino American poet Al Robles serves lunch at the Manilatown Senior Center. One of the Filipino regulars is Felipe Daguro, a retired stevedore who is 91 years old. When Daguro immigrated to America in 1918, he was a young boy who ended up working on the sugar plantations of Hawaii. He came to San Francisco in 1946 and worked for the Port of San Francisco. Daguro is one of many *manongs* (elder brothers) who come daily to the Manila Senior Center kitchen for the $1.25 lunch. Why do these *manongs* come to the Center? What is the Manilatown Senior Center doing in a place surrounded by prominent capitalist icons such as the Pacific Stock Exchange and the Transamerica building? Like Daguro, these *manongs* used to live only a few blocks away, at the International Hotel at Kearny and Jackson Streets. And, like Daguro, twenty years ago the *manongs* were forcibly evicted from their homes by San Francisco police and sheriff's deputies. Today, at the site of the former International Hotel, there remains a huge hole surrounded by barbed-wire and chain-link fence. Right next door sits the twenty-seven-story Holiday Inn, where tourists from all over the world register daily in the main lobby. Soon they, too, will visit Union Square for their souvenir photos. Some may even read the inscription at the base of the monument, but no one will make the connection between the Union Square monument, American imperialism, and the huge empty hole at Kearny and Jackson.

José Rizal's Quarantine and the Nightmare of Imperialism

The great nationalist hero of the Philippines, Dr. José Rizal, came to the Bay Area on April 28, 1888. Rizal was the leader of the nascent nationalist movement against Spanish colonialism in the Philippines. Unfortunately for Rizal, he arrived during one of the most anti-Asian periods in American history. Only six years earlier, Californians successfully convinced the U.S. Congress to pass the 1882 Chinese Exclusion Act, an immigration law that excluded Chinese laborers from entering the United States. Upon sailing through the Golden Gate, Rizal discovered that he was not allowed to set foot in San Francisco. Instead, he found himself quarantined at Angel Island. The following day he wrote a letter to his parents in the Philippines:

> Here [in San Francisco] we are in sight of America since yesterday without being able to disembark, placed in quarantine on account of the 642 Chinese that we have on board coming from Hong Kong where they say smallpox prevails. But the true reason is that, as America is against Chinese immigration, and now they are campaigning for the elections, the government, in order to get the vote of the people, must appear to be strict with the Chinese, and we suffer. On board there is not one sick person. (Quoted in Jaime Veneracion, "Rizal in San Francisco," *Manila Mail*, Oct. 30–Nov. 5, 1996)

After this experience, Rizal warned that America was not hospitable to Filipinos: "I'll not advise anyone to make this trip to America, for here they are crazy about quarantine, they have [a] severe customs inspection, imposing [duties] on anything."

After seven days in quarantine, Rizal was finally allowed to set foot in San Francisco, where he made a point of taking a room at the very prestigious and expensive Palace Hotel. A few days later, Rizal went by ferry to the inland Port of Stockton, where he would board a train for Sacramento and continue on to Reno, Salt Lake City, Chicago, and New York City. On his train ride across America, Rizal realized the enormous wealth, power, and imperialistic ambitions of the United States. In his essay "The Philippine Century," he predicted that American expansionism would extend across the Pacific to as far away as the Philippines.

Ten years later, on May 1, 1898, Rizal's nightmare became a reality when

Commodore George Dewey and the U.S. Navy's Third Asiatic Squadron steamed into Manila Bay and obliterated an antiquated Spanish naval fleet. The entire Spanish fleet of seven unarmored ships was destroyed, and 380 men were killed or wounded. The American fleet did not lose a single ship or crew member. That day marked the beginning of the United States as a world superpower, a position of power, wealth, and leadership that it has held since then.

Dewey was popularly believed to have just happened to be near the Philippines when the Spanish-American War broke out. President William McKinley even proclaimed publicly that he had had to consult a map to see where, exactly, the Philippines was located. McKinley knew, in fact, about the Navy's secret orders to Commodore Dewey to attack, but he told the American public that he had to get down on his knees and pray to God for guidance about what to do with the Philippines. Guided by "divine inspiration," McKinley claimed it was America's duty to "civilize" and "Christianize" the Philippines—never mind that it was already a predominantly Catholic country,

after 300 years of Spanish colonialism. With his conscience cleared, McKinley wrote his famous letter of "benevolent assimilation," outlining the official U.S. policy in the Philippines.

Filipinos did not concur with McKinley's vision. They declared their independence from the United States, and elected a congress and the republic's first president, Emilio Aguinaldo. At the time, Filipinos believed that the United States would not make the Philippines a colony, since it was scarcely a hundred years earlier that the United States had declared its own independence from British colonialism. But the United States formally claimed the Philippines as American territory in the 1898 Treaty of Paris. A few weeks later, American troops fired on Filipino troops at the outskirts of Manila, and the Filipino-American war began.

Instead of the quick and easy victory the Americans expected, the war dragged on for over three years as Filipinos carried

Dewey Monument, Union Square

out a protracted campaign of guerrilla warfare. In response to a Filipino victory in Balangiga, at Samar Province—in which a company of American soldiers was ambushed and nearly wiped out—the U.S. military intensified its battle tactics. Entire villages were burned and their inhabitants massacred, including women, children, and the elderly. It was at Samar that General "Hell Roaring" Jake Smith gave his famous order: "Kill and burn, kill and burn, the more you kill and the more you burn the more you please me." (Francisco 1987) When asked by a Marine major what he meant by this, Smith replied, "Kill everything over ten years old." A reporter described the consequences of Smith's operations: "The truth is, the struggle in Samar is one of extermination."

Not to be outdone, Major General J. Franklin Bell, in Batangas Province, carried out a scorched-earth policy and rounded up all Filipinos into hamlets surrounded by "free-fire zones." Philippine scholars argue that this was, in fact, a precursor to the Vietnam War. These brutal policies led to the deaths of hundreds of thousands of Filipinos, the majority of whom died from disease and starvation. Bell would later brag to a *New York Times* reporter that in Luzon alone over 600,000 Filipino died as a result of the war. Philippine nationalists give a higher figure and argue that this genocidal war led to the deaths of one million Filipinos.

San Francisco played a crucial role in this war of American imperialism. All the U.S. Army volunteers who fought in the war were recruited, assembled, and trained in San Francisco's Presidio. The Spanish-American War was so popular that Americans volunteered to fight in this war, and people from all over the country came to train in San Francisco. Newly trained soldiers boarded military transport ships at Fort Mason and steamed for the Philippines. After the war, the soldiers returned to the Presidio to receive their discharge papers. Wounded soldiers received medical care and were rehabilitated at the Letterman Army Hospital.

One of the most famous soldiers of the war would later become a local San Francisco hero. In 1902 Colonel Frederick Funston became a national hero when he captured the leader of the Philippine revolution, Emilio Aguinaldo. A few years later Funston endeared himself to law-and-order San Franciscans when he enforced martial law during the 1906 earthquake. Filipinos, however, remember him as someone who bragged about shooting Filipino prisoners of war and hanging Filipino civilians, and also as an anti-Catholic bigot who enjoyed desecrating churches. Today, part of Golden Gate National Park is named after him, as are two streets in San Francisco.

Not only was the Spanish-American War an imperialistic war to expand American capitalism, it was also a racist war. Americans went to the Philippines when Social Darwinism was at its height. Most American officers fighting in the war were veterans of Indian wars in America and saw themselves as fighting another Indian war. Described as "Injuns" and "savages," Filipinos were seen as being like Native Americans. Furthermore, because of their dark skin, Filipinos were compared to African Americans and called "niggers" and "brainless monkeys." These racist attitudes would later affect the way Americans at home perceived and treated Filipinos in the United States.

At the war's end, inhabitants of the Philippines became American colonial subjects. Officially, they were classified as American "nationals" and given the same legal status as Native Americans. For immigration purposes, this meant Filipinos were not aliens and could migrate freely into the United States. But they were also not American citizens and, thus, did not have the right to vote or to hold elected public office. In effect, America was simply allowing its colonial subjects visiting rights but no political participation rights.

The Birth of Manilatown

Filipinos first came to California in large numbers in the 1920s and 1930s, many having initially gone to Hawaii as labor recruits for the Hawaiian Sugar Planters Association. At the completion of their labor contracts, many Filipinos left Hawaii and emigrated to California, where wages and working conditions were slightly better.

Filipino family dining in Chinatown (c. 1943)

PHOTO COURTESY PACIFICO MORTEL

The majority of these early Filipino immigrants were single, able-bodied young men between the ages of eighteen and twenty-five. Coming mainly from the Ilocos region in Northern Luzon and from Cebu and Panay in the Visayan Islands, they immigrated for many reasons: economic opportunities, education, adventure, and to join relatives who made the journey earlier. San Francisco was their main port of entry (Filipinos also arrived through Los Angeles and Seattle). Upon arrival, the majority of Filipinos boarded high-priced taxis and went out to Stockton to work in the asparagus fields in the San Joaquin–Sacramento Valley.

Not all Filipinos, however, were farm workers. Men who remained in San Francisco formed a bachelor community called Manilatown, in a three-block radius around Kearny and Jackson Streets, next to Chinatown. At its height, over 10,000 residents, mostly Filipino bachelors, lived in Manilatown. A migrant labor community, they lived in residential hotels such as the International Hotel, the Palm Hotel, the Temple Hotel, the San Joaquin, the Stanford, and the Columbia Hotel. Some worked in restaurants as cooks and waiters and in hotels as bell-hops and elevator "boys." Others worked in the domestic service sector as house servants, cleaners, and chauffeurs. Still others started businesses that catered to a predominantly Filipino clientele. These businesses included pool halls, lunch counters, restaurants, coffee shops, cigar shops, barber shops, clothing and grocery stores, a photography studio, and gambling establishments.

Right in the middle of Manilatown was the New Luneta Café, a typical Filipino business. In front was a lunch counter that served Filipino food: chicken *adobo* (stew), *pancit* (noodles), and rice, the Filipino's staple. But behind the lunch counters was another business: tables that supported card games of rummy and poker. Gambling was one of the means by which some Filipinos supported themselves during the off-season. The pool halls and lunch counters also served as information centers and mailing addresses for migrant Filipino workers. Employment opportunities were posted on chalkboards with the names, addresses, and telephone numbers of prospective employers. It was a good source of information for finding one's relatives and friends: someone would inevitably know where a certain Filipino was living and working.

Manilatown was a community that provided temporary employment and supported Filipinos during the off-season, following work in the farms, fields, and salmon canneries. Ordinary San Franciscans avoided Manilatown and thought that the Filipinos living there were dangerous and socially undesirable. They were described as "trouble-making Filipinos" and "pickpockets." While the Hall of Justice and the police station were located only a block away from Manilatown, the police rarely shut down Manilatown's gambling operations, except for the carefully orchestrated police raids to calm the fears of City residents.

The Battle for the International Hotel

At the very heart of Manilatown was the International Hotel, a three-story, red-brick building at 848 Kearny Street, at the corner of Jackson. In the 1970s it also became the most famous residence of Filipinos. The I-Hotel symbolized the Filipino American struggle for identity, self-determination, and civil rights. It was a struggle that involved not only Filipinos but other Asian Americans, African Americans, Latin Americans, student activists, religious groups and organizations, gays and lesbians, leftists, and community activists.

The eviction was part of a larger development project occurring in the Bay Area. As early as 1946, corporate organizations proposed ambitious urban development projects. Organizations such as the Bay Area Council proposed the Bay Area Rapid Transit system, and the San Francisco Planning and Urban Renewal Association proposed neighborhood urban renewal by eliminating urban "blight" in the Western Division. Other proposals included building the Golden Gateway project, a series of freeways intersecting San Francisco—a project rejected by the City—and the Yerba Buena Center project, which, when completed, also displaced thousands of residents from the South of Market. By the late 1960s, as part of this Manhattanization of San Francisco, the expanding financial district was encroaching on Manilatown and neighboring Chinatown. In the autumn of 1968, Milton Meyer and Company, which owned the hotel, started sending eviction notices to the tenants of the I-Hotel. "To my mind," explained Walter Shorenstein, chairman of Milton Meyer, "I was getting rid of a slum." In response, the tenants organized the United Filipino Association (UFA) to battle the eviction.

Among the earliest Filipino activists working with the I-Hotel was Violeta Marasigan, then a recent graduate of San Francisco State College, who was hired as a social worker by the UFA as part of their Multi-Service Center: "When I started working with the old men, I saw that they were discriminated against in terms of their access to social services. A lot of them had been here for over thirty years, but they could still barely speak English or write." These manongs were mostly single retired farmworkers and seamen living on social security retirement benefits. Marasigan, known as "Bullet X" to her friends, discovered that they were not receiving their full benefits. "At that time, when the SSI benefits were around $200 a month for the maximum, Filipinos were only getting around $90 to around $130," recalled Marasigan. "None of the Filipinos knew that they were not getting the full benefits due to them." Marasigan accompanied the Filipinos to the SSI office and spoke with their caseworkers. "After that, everybody had their full SSI benefits."

The late sixties was the height of the antiwar movement and Third World student strikes at San Francisco State College and UC Berkeley. Student activists became among the strongest supporters of the I-Hotel. Emile De Guzman, a young Filipino student leader of the 1969 Third World Strike at Berkeley, had been working with Pete Velasco, Larry Itliong, Philip Vera Cruz, and other Filipino members of the United Farmworkers Union in Delano. Born and raised in San Francisco, De Guzman grew up visiting Manilatown with his father. When he heard about the eviction notices and the subsequent fire that killed three hotel tenants, he rallied other Berkeley students to protest the eviction: "I got really involved in the I-Hotel and organized students to go down there and picket outside Walter Shorenstein's office."

The International Hotel Tenants Association (ITHA) eventually replaced the UFA, and Filipino students activists like De Guzman assumed the leadership. It was through a coalition of students, tenants, and community activists that the ITHA was able to sign a three-year lease and avoid eviction. In order to avoid further public criticism of his role in the eviction, Shorenstein sold the hotel to the Four Seas Investment Corporation, a Hong Kong–based company that planned to demolish the building and replace it with further "commercial" development in the form of an underground parking garage.

It was not just Filipinos, however, who got involved in the I-Hotel struggle. Jean Ishibashi, a third-generation Japanese American born in Chicago, was pregnant at the time but still came to the I-Hotel protests. "For many decades, I carried my family's unspoken anger from eviction and internment," said Ishibashi. "When I learned that elderly Asians who were my father's age were being evicted, I identified with them, and that's why I showed up." For Ishibashi, the I-Hotel symbolized a time when "the Asian American community as a whole came together." It was mostly, however, the more progressive and left-leaning members of Asian America.

Elderly Chinese also resided in the I-Hotel. The Asian Community Center and the Chinese Progressive Association were located in the I-Hotel. Both organization strongly supported mainland China and Chairman Mao Zedong's Communist government, and this conflicted with the Chinatown leadership, which supported the Koumintang Government (KMT) in Taiwan. "This was also part of the continuing attacks against the I-Hotel," said De Guzman. "The Chinese leftist organizations would always show a lot of films about China."

Not surprisingly, Filipino activists at the I-Hotel shared the same political leanings as their Chinese neighbors. "During that time, Joe Diones was the manager of the I-Hotel," said Marasigan, herself an anti–martial law activist who would later be imprisoned by President Ferdinand Marcos. "He was a very good manager,

Sheriff Richard Hongisto after overseeing the evictions from the I-Hotel (1977)

Filipinos in San Francisco

you see, but he was also a card-bearing member of the Communist Party of the USA." The leftist *Kalayan* newspaper was also published at the I-Hotel, and its members would go on to form the *Katipunan ng mga Demoratikong Pilipino* (KDP), which became the largest Filipino socialist organization in America. With its left-leaning management and tenants, the red brick building quickly became known as "the Red Block."

African Americans and whites were among the supporters of the I-Hotel. The Rev. Jim Jones of the infamous People's Temple brought members of his congregation, mostly elderly African Americans, to the protests. "We even had a terrorist group that supported the I-Hotel," recalled the poet Al Robles. "The Weathermen group planted a bomb at the Herbst Theater, and they went on radio and said, 'We did this because the I-Hotel was being oppressed.'" The bomb did not explode, but upon hearing the news at the time, Robles looked out an I-Hotel window, saw hundreds of people marching and chanting, and said, "We don't even know who these guys are. What kind of *manongs* are these?"

The I-Hotel became a bastion of Asian American cultural expression. Formed by Asian Americans from the Bay Area, the Kearny Street Workshop (KSW) had an office on the first floor of the Hotel. Luis Syquia, a poet and activist of the I-Hotel struggles, explains, "The main focus, rationale, and philosophy behind the Kearny Street Workshop was to really reflect the communities that we came from, and also to contribute to those communities through our art." KSW brought together Chinese, Filipino, Japanese, and Korean artists and writers in one community. Rejecting the idea of "art for art's sake," Luis believed that "art was always a tool for social change." Some of KSW's members were artist Jim Dong, playwrights Lane Nishikawa and Norman Jayo, photographers Crystal Huie and Leny Limjoco, silk-screen artists Leland Wong and Nancy Hom (KSW's current director), and poets Al Robles, George Leong, Doug Yamamoto, Genny Lim, Russell Leong, Jeff Tagami, and Shirley Ancheta.

For Manilatown and its Filipino residents, the I-Hotel represented a life and community. Explained Robles, the unofficial "Zen master" of the Filipino community, "The I-Hotel was the life of the *manongs*, the life of the Filipinos. It was their heart, it was their poetry, it was their song." Robles, whose poetry was recently collected in *Rappin' with 10,000 Carabaos in the Dark* elaborated: "It wasn't only a hotel: it was a gathering place that brought them together. It was celebration; it was ritual. It was bringing back a life."

After battling eviction proceedings for over nine years, this community of *manongs* and poetry was brought to a violent end in the early morning hours of August 4, 1977. At around 4 a.m., over 300 riot-equipped police and sheriff's deputies cordoned off the surrounding streets, encircled the hotel, and began their assault on 3,000 community activists and protesters.

"The police came down Kearny Street, with horses and police cars—it was like the Roman legions," recalls De Guzman. The police did not go through the front door. Instead, they used extension ladders on fire trucks to climb up to the top floors and fight through a group of I-Hotel defenders. Sheriff Richard Hongisto, who had spent five days in jail for refusing to enforce the eviction court order, led the assault. Hongisto, who would run unsuccessfully for mayor in 1992, was featured in the pages of the *San Francisco Chronicle* and *San Francisco Examiner*, as he used a sledge hammer to break down tenants' doors.

De Guzman, then the president of the International Hotel Tenants Association, described what happened: "Once the police and sheriffs got into the building, they broke into the tenants' rooms. Then they started breaking things up, stealing, taking what the *manongs* had, broke the toilets—that way there were no toilet facilities," so the tenants could never return. The *Examiner* featured a photograph of De Guzman being dragged out by deputies in riot gear.

Meanwhile, in front of the hotel, over 2,000 community activists and protesters had locked arms in a nonviolent attempt to prevent the police from entering the building. Shouting "We won't move!" I-Hotel defenders lined up nine rows deep as the police started their frontal assault. "The police were brutalizing people outside in front of the hotel," said De Guzman. "They would run their

PHOTO COURTESY IAN MacTAGGART

I-Hotel activist supporting elderly tenant during eviction (1977)

horses up front and hit people with their clubs. They just tore people up, hitting them on the head, and jabbing them with nightsticks."

Escorted by two I-Hotel activists, Felix Ayson, a 79-year-old Filipino who could no longer walk or hear, was one of the last people to leave the I-Hotel. As he left with the assis-

Graffiti by Twist in the hole left by the I-Hotel eviction (1993)

PHOTO D. S. BLACK

tance of two hotel supporters, Ayson told an *Examiner* reporter: "I think my end is very near from this beautiful world."

The eviction of the International Hotel tenants made the national news and cost the City over $3 million and a lot of bad publicity. The eviction outraged the nation. Concerned over the forced eviction of poor elderly citizens, Senator Frank Church of the Senate's Committee on Aging sent a delegation to investigate the incident.

In 1997, nearly twenty years after the forced eviction, the City of San Francisco, with the help of federal funding, began the construction of a $20 million, 15-story, 104-unit building. After years of continued advocacy by I-Hotel community activists, this "New I-Hotel" will provide affordable housing for senior citizens, newly arrived immigrants, and low-income San Franciscans. The proposed building will also have a Filipino Community Center, Museum and Exhibition Hall, and a four-story St. Mary's Chinese Elementary School.

After the I-Hotel: South of Market and Daly City

While Manilatown was occupied mostly by Filipino bachelors and migrant workers, Filipino families lived mainly in the South of Market. The mass migration of Filipinos there occurred right after World War II, when Filipino men who served in the U.S. Army brought home "war brides," Filipino women they met and married while serving in the Philippines.

"I remember that there were lots of Filipinos living in the South of Market,"

Streets, and in the South Park area. Eventually, many of them moved farther out to the Fillmore and Mission districts, and to Daly City.

In 1965 the Immigration Reform Act was passed, which eliminated racially restrictive immigration quotas for Asians, and set a quota of 20,000 immigrants for the Philippines as well as every country in Asia. Intended primarily as a "family reunification" law for European families, it resulted in the unexpected immigration of thousands of Asians. Many more Filipino immigrants came to settle in the South of Market. By 1990, in fact, Filipinos constituted 30 percent of the area's population. As a result of this huge immigrant influx, St. Patrick's Catholic Church on Mission Street became predominantly Filipino, as did Bessie Carmichael Elementary School. Filipino organizations, such as the Caballeros de Dimas Alang, advocated for new retirement facilities for elderly Filipinos, and in 1979 the Dimas Alang House (named after José Rizal's pen name), a retirement home for Filipinos and other San Franciscans, was built with HUD funding. The surrounding streets were named after Filipino heroes: Lapu-Lapu, Bonifacio, Mabini, and Rizal—the only streets in San Francisco with Filipino names. To take care of the educational needs of newly arrived Filipino immigrants, the Filipino Educational Center was built and staffed by predominantly Filipino teachers.

"These days most of the Filipino immigrants are not even from Manila," explained M. C. Canlas, director of West Bay's Teen Center. "They're mostly from the province, especially Pangasinan, where I'm from." Canlas, who left his teaching job at the University of the Philippines in 1984 during the Marcos martial-law era, is one of many Filipino service providers who help keep the South of Market community healthy. Filipino youth participate in basketball games and tournaments, arts projects, festivals, and other productive activities. West Bay and other organizations help Filipinos find employment, housing, and medical services. South of Market is also alive with Filipino cultural and artistic expression. The Filipino American Arts Exposition hosts a parade on Market Street and a festival at the Yerba Buena Center. The walls of the Powell Street BART Station are filled with art work created by Filipino teenagers commissioned by the City.

Daly City, the new Filipinotown, is the capital of the Filipino American community. At 27 percent of the population (1990 census), Filipinos constitute the largest ethnic group in Daly City. It is home to the highest concentration of Filipinos in the United States. Here, Filipinos can pick up the *Manila Mail, Philippine News, Manila Bulletin,* and *Filipinas,* or they can watch Philippine cable and television broadcasts. The "capitol" of Filipinotown is Serramonte Mall, where nearly everyone you meet is Filipino and speaks Tagalog, Visayan, or Ilocano. Westlake Mall is another popular spot, and the location of an annual Filipino festival, in June. But it is the restaurants and nightclubs that really give the flavor and beat to Filipinotown: at Goldilocks, Three Bears, Manila Bay Express, Max's, and Manila Bay Cuisine you can eat chicken *adobo, pancit* noodles, beef *kare-kare* with *bagoong*, and, for dessert, *halo-halo* ice cream shakes and *turon* (fried bananas wrapped in crêpes). At restaurant/nightclubs such as Tito Rey's, Solita's, Manila Garden, and Pinay's you can dance to the latest hits from Manila.

Breaking the stereotype of complacent and apolitical Filipinos, Michael Guingona, a second-generation Filipino American, became Daly City's first Filipino mayor in 1995. Each summer a Filipino American festival is held at the Westlake Mall, which brings together thousands of Filipinos for a cultural celebration and feast.

It has been a long journey for Filipinos. But in spite of a history of imperialism, racism, exclusion, and forced eviction, they have endured. Today, Filipinos comprise the largest Asian American community in California. The community still faces some recurring problems stemming from white society's misunderstandings and misconceptions about the Filipino community. In San Francisco and the Bay Area, it is a healthy community that has reached a critical mass. Where it goes in the future is the exciting challenge.

Acknowledgments

I wish to thank Jovy Angat, Fred Basconcillo, M. C. Canlas, Felipe Daguro, Emile De Guzman, Rudy Delphino, Jean Ishibashi, Violeta "Bullet X" Marasigan, Pacifico Mortel, Al Robles, Bill Sorro, and Luis Syquia for their oral-history participation and comments on this paper.

References

Francisco, luzviminda. 1987. "The First Vietnam: The Philippine-American War, 1899–1902." In *The Phillippine Reader*. Edited by Daniel B. Shirmer and Stephen Rosskamm Shalom. Quezon City: Ken.

Mollenkopf, John. 1983. *The Contested City*. Princeton: Princeton University Press.

Tenant Power in San Francisco

by Randy Shaw

IT IS AUGUST 1977. Thousands of San Francisco Bay Area activists have jammed the streets in a final effort to stave off the eviction of elderly Filipino tenants at the International Hotel. The International Hotel has already become a symbol for the massive planned displacement of San Francisco's low-income residents, who stand in the way of expanded commercial and downtown development. The hotel's mysterious owner, the Hong Kong–based Four Seas Investment Company, has announced no plans for the site after eviction of the tenants and demolition of the hotel. Despite massive protests, San Francisco's liberal political leadership—from Mayor George Moscone to powerful Congressman Phil Burton—does not prevent the tenants' eviction. Two years later, Mayor Dianne Feinstein refuses to oppose the hotel's demolition, and the heart of a once-thriving Manilatown is leveled. (Curtis Choy's award-winning film, *The Fall of the I-Hotel*, is available on video.)

The ability of a rarely seen liquor magnate from Thailand to evict nearly a hundred elderly tenants, for no stated reason, perfectly captures the state of landlord-tenant relations in San Francisco in 1977. No laws stood in the way of landlord greed. San Francisco landlords could force long-term tenants to move simply by issuing an eviction notice and awaiting the sheriff's arrival. Landlords could raise rents as much and as often as the market could bear. The absence of any government regulation of rent increases or evictions enabled landlords to replace low-income and working-class tenants with those who could afford costly rents. This process of "gentrification" was fueled not only by the absence of government regulations, it was also encouraged by federal tax laws. All the funds spent renovating and gold-plating rental units for occupancy by higher-paying tenants could be deducted from a landlord's taxes as a business expense. Even better, residential landlords could deduct a pro-rated share of the building's cost on the theory that the value of a four-unit Victorian, like a piece of machinery, steadily decreases over time. This depreciation deduction, along with the mortgage interest tax break associated with real estate ownership, made residential real estate a popular tax shelter during an era when high incomes were still taxed at a 70 percent rate.

When the 1981 supply-side economics tax law reduced top personal income tax rates, real estate lobbyists obtained even greater benefits for their industry. The 1981 law allowed investors to deduct double the annual depreciation, so that the cost of purchasing a building could be written off in only fifteen years. These unprecedented incentives for real estate tax shelters intensified speculative pressures at a time when gentrification, displacement, and rising rents were already afflicting urban America. Investors' ability to deduct virtually the entire cost of being landlords and then profit quickly from rising real estate values had a particular impact on attractive cities like San Francisco. From 1982 to 1986, when a new tax law repealed the 1981 benefits, San Francisco tenants faced a housing market where rents were rising at unprecedented rates.

Government encouragement of real estate investment, speculation, and gentrification reflected the real estate industry's tremendous political power. This was particularly true in San Francisco, where tenants in 1977 had few allies. Mayor George Moscone had been swept into office by a tremendous grassroots campaign and had a long record as a liberal state legislator. However, he refused to anger his real estate backers, who included major contributors to the Democratic Party. Like his ally Mayor Willie Brown, Moscone symbolized San Francisco's liberal politicians: culturally tolerant, staunchly pro-labor and pro–civil rights, but supportive of poor people's interests only if they did not clash with the interests of the politicians' allies in the corporate and real estate sector. Because enacting laws to protect tenants necessarily restricted landlord power, San Francisco's liberal politicians wrung their hands over the I-Hotel eviction and other injustices to tenants, but refused to take action.

1978–1980: The Urban Crisis

As 1978 began, the I-Hotel evictions, rising rents, gentrification, and the rapid displacement of low-income people from neighborhoods were increasingly discussed as part of a broader urban crisis. While poverty, unemployment, and a host of related ills had long plagued urban America, what changed clearly in the 1970s was the transformation of previously undesirable real estate into venues for speculative investment. Like the I-Hotel tenants, people of color often occupied the rundown buildings and communities that were prime targets for landlord profiteering. The urban housing crisis thus fused those activists who were primarily focused on supporting struggles of people of color with those engaged with class and economic issues. As housing politics became a central arena for progressive political struggles, committed young activists with broad political-analysis skills came to be part of San Francisco's burgeoning tenant movement.

A spark was needed to ignite this budding political force, and it came from a surprising source: Howard Jarvis, a longtime landlord lobbyist and antitax activist. Jarvis's Proposition 13, on California's June 1978 ballot, is best known for ushering in a nationwide tax-cutting frenzy. While Proposition 13's tax-limitation provisions continue to damage the state's finances, the measure also created a groundswell of public support for laws restricting landlord power over tenants. How did a measure designed to benefit residential and commercial landlords galvanize tenants and lead to the widespread imposition of rent control? Blame landlord greed.

Because Proposition 13 significantly reduced property tax assessments, its supporters argued that tenants should vote for the measure so that they could share in their landlords' tax savings. However, after Proposition 13 passed, few tenants realized any savings. Angry at being deceived, tenants in many cities responded to Proposition 13's deliverance of huge tax rebates to landlords by going to the ballot to recover their fair share.

In San Francisco, tenant activists created a November 1978 ballot measure (Proposition U) that required landlords to rebate 100 percent of their Proposition 13 savings. While the Proposition U campaign was conceived and led by tenant activists, this nascent electoral effort drew strong support from the Catholic Archdiocese, as well as from labor and social justice activists previously uninvolved with tenant concerns. Mayor Moscone and his liberal allies maintained their refusal to challenge real estate power and refused to support the measure. (Harvey Milk was the only elected San Francisco official to endorse Proposition U.) Moscone's endorsement would have helped refute opposition claims that Proposition U was too "radical," and his failure to give Proposition U his stamp of approval likely affected the outcome. Despite this lack of political support, and being outspent twenty-five to one by landlords, Proposition U narrowly lost, fifty-three to forty-seven. The closeness of the race surprised experts and encouraged tenant leaders to explore a new ballot measure.

The 1978 election results foreshadowed three important developments. First, the I-Hotel struggle and rising real estate values had increased insecurity and hence militancy among tenants, particularly among seniors with a high voter turnout record. Second, the 1970s downtown high-rise boom was already changing the demographics of San Francisco's tenant population. As tenants became increasingly college educated and white-collar (and had higher incomes), the tenant vote increased as a percentage of the electorate. Third, the November 1978 ballot saw significantly increased public activism among San Francisco's gay and lesbian community. San Francisco had already become a gay Mecca, and activists had elected openly gay leader Harvey Milk to the Board of Supervisors in 1975. The statewide November 1978 ballot, however, included a measure (the Briggs Initiative, Proposition 6) that galvanized and substantially broadened gay and lesbian political activism. Proposition 6 would have barred gays and lesbians from teaching in public schools. Defeating the measure became a crusade for gay and lesbian activists, and San Francisco's "No on 6" campaign involved hundreds if not thousands of active volunteers. After the defeat of Proposition 6, many of these volunteers became involved with tenants rights. This transition was not surprising, because gay and lesbian activists were primarily tenants whose clubs and organizations reflected their progressive political sympathies. For gay and lesbian tenants of the late 1970s, San Francisco was a safe harbor; being priced out of their homes and forced to leave their city of refuge had particularly severe consequences.

While increased gentrification very likely made the emergence of a politically influential San Francisco tenant movement inevitable, Proposition 13 unquestionably advanced this process. It gave tenants the moral high ground necessary to justify government regulation of the long-inviolate King Real Estate.

After barely surviving Proposition U, San Francisco landlords needed to calm the waters so as not to jeopardize their continued ability to profit from an unregulated real estate market. This strategy was immediately and irrevocably sabotaged by one of San Francisco's leading apartment owners, Angelo Sangiacomo. Sangiacomo's vast holdings primarily housed older, middle-income, white tenants. This demographic group was not much in evidence at I-Hotel protests or the Proposition U campaign. Ignoring the broader political context, Sangiacomo chose a historical moment of rising tenant anger to impose huge rent increases on his tenants. In so doing, he came to be known—and by landlords scorned—as the man who brought rent control to the city.

While San Francisco's political leaders ignored the displacement of low-income tenants who were ethnic minorities, Sangiacomo's threat to quintessential Old San Franciscans drew widespread public rebuke. Sympathetic media focus on the plight of Sangiacomo's tenants effectively forced reluctant politicians to intervene on the tenants' behalf. While politicians fiddled, activists saw Sangiacomo's action as providing the opening for voter acceptance of dramatic new legal protections for tenants. Joined in the newly created San Franciscans for

Affordable Housing, tenant activists, labor unions, the Catholic Archdiocese, and gay and lesbian activists began gathering signatures for a comprehensive rent control and housing reform measure for the November 1979 ballot.

With Sangiacomo suddenly having made the dreaded words "rent control" thinkable, Mayor Dianne Feinstein, who assumed power following the November 1978 assassination of George Moscone, faced a choice. Feinstein was closely aligned with real estate interests and had few links to the progressive groups that had elected her predecessor. If Feinstein did nothing, she risked the emergence of a liberal challenger running on a housing crisis platform in the November 1979 mayoral election. Her inaction might also pave the way for SFAH's strong rent control initiative to win a sweeping victory. Rather than risk either possibility, Feinstein won legislative passage of a sixty-day prohibition on rent increases. After this moratorium expired, the city adopted a moderate Rent Stabilization Ordinance in June.

San Francisco's enactment of any form of rent control was considered by many to be astonishing. Landlords were furious, feeling that Feinstein should have weathered the storm and waited for the voters' verdict on SFAH's November ballot measure. SFAH also criticized Feinstein, seeing the city's adoption of weak rent control as a strategy to preempt their own comprehensive solution to the city's housing crisis. SFAH proceeded with their initiative, assuming that voters would recognize the need for stronger action. They were wrong, as became obvious after SFAH's Proposition R lost by a huge fifty-nine to forty-one margin in the November 1979 race. While the low-turnout election expanded the margin of defeat, it was clear that swing voters felt that Feinstein's rent law had addressed the problem and should be given time to work.

1980–1991: Rent Control Wars

Proposition R's staggering defeat changed the course of the San Francisco tenant movement. The election also revealed deep divisions among groups seemingly united in their agenda for attacking the urban crisis. The broad, diverse SFAH coalition initially splintered during the Proposition R campaign over a slow-growth measure (Proposition O) on the same ballot. SFAH's supporters in the building trades and janitors unions actively opposed the measure (their members built and cleaned office buildings) and diverted potential resources from Proposition R to the "No on O" effort. But SFAH's neighborhood activists and the *San Francisco Bay Guardian* strongly supported Proposition O, viewing "Manhattanization" as causing the housing crisis that Proposition R was designed to address. The result: organized labor left the San Francisco tenant movement after the election, and some unions, including the powerful building trades, came to actively oppose the tenant agenda.

Proposition R's urban crisis coalition also fell prey to bitter infighting between leaders of the city's tenant organizations and representatives of other groups. Tenant leaders complained that the broader coalition reduced their control over their own agenda; this tension was heightened when Proposition R's labor backers strongly opposed the slow-growth measure that tenant groups saw as critical to stemming rising rents. As internal bickering came to dominate Proposition R campaign meetings, many organizational representatives became tired of the infighting associated with the tenant campaigns. Proposition R's defeat led many organizations to return to working on their own specific agendas, having had their fill of tumultuous tenant politics.

Tenants won significant gains in 1979, in addition to rent control. The rising real estate values that spawned gentrification also created touristification in the form of the conversion of single-room-occupancy residential hotels (SROs) to tourist lodgings. From 1975 to 1979, thousands of SROs were converted or demolished, thus contributing to the exodus of poor and working people from the city. When the elderly tenants at the Tenderloin's Dalt Hotel faced the forced displacement from their homes in 1979, the massive shift in tenant consciousness, after the I-Hotel debacle only two years earlier, became clear. Where the earlier tragedy led to no official intervention, media outrage over the Dalt tenants forced politicians to act. A citywide moratorium on hotel conversions was imposed in 1979, which was followed by legislation in 1981 that, like the moderate rent control, had many loopholes but gave tenants unprecedented safeguards. The city's Residential Hotel Ordinance became an ongoing battleground, with tenants successfully strengthening the law with legislative reforms in 1985, 1987, and 1990. The Residential Hotel Ordinance is arguably the most successful land-use regulation in San Francisco history, having accomplished its goal of preserving the city's largest supply of low-cost housing. The law's broad political support is a legacy of the I-Hotel struggle.

As a result of divisions that emerged during the Proposition R campaign, San Francisco's tenant movement failed to become a broad-based vehicle for addressing the city's problems. Instead, Proposition R's defeat led many to return to nonhousing activism, while those activists still focused on the housing crisis established new tenant organizations.

The Catholic Archdiocese, which assisted Proposition R, continued its strong support for tenants in 1980 by creating a parish-based housing organization at Old St. Mary's Church. The Old St. Mary's Housing Committee brought white, middle-class, retired, and working people into active involvement in citywide tenant issues. The Tenderloin Housing Clinic was also formed in 1980 and joined with the recently created North of Market Planning Coalition to increase tenant activism in one of the city's poorest neighborhoods. The San Francisco chapter of the Gray Panthers began to focus extensively on tenant issues in 1980, and the San Francisco chapter of the New American Movement (NAM), a democratic-socialist organization, created a pro-tenant advocacy group called the Affordable Housing Alliance. NAM viewed the urban housing crisis as the central arena for progressive political struggle, and brought committed young activists with political experience to the city's tenant movement. The creation of these new tenant organizations in 1980, along with the San Francisco Tenants Union (founded in 1970), paved the way for increasing tenant activism.

As rents rose and gentrification and displacement worsened, tenant activists unified around a common goal: strengthening rent control. While Proposition R represented a comprehensive response to all aspects of city housing policy, since 1980 the tenant movement has been a series of campaigns designed to improve the very weak 1979 rent control ordinance. This exclusive focus on rent control had positive and negative implications. The 1979 laws clearly provided tenants with inadequate legal protections against eviction, and permitted automatic 7-percent annual rent raises, an amount well in excess of inflation. Moreover, San Francisco's rent control law allowed unlimited rent increases on vacant apartments. This gave landlords an economic incentive to evict, and meant that the housing stock would, as tenants vacated, become increasingly unaffordable. As a result, rent control on vacant apartments (that is, vacancy control) became the chief goal of tenant groups throughout the 1980s.

Tenants' exclusive focus on strengthening rent control, however, had a major downside: the movement became divorced from the larger urban crisis agenda. Tenant-landlord and rent control fights were no longer surrounded by discussions of class, economic unfairness, and redistribution of wealth. The broader context of rent control as akin to progressive taxation was replaced by debates that ignored tax benefits offered to landlords, their superior wealth, and the conflict between Democratic Party politicians who espoused Republican free-market principles when rent control was involved. The tenant movement was increasingly comprised of people whose involvement arose from negative personal experiences with their landlords, rather than from a broader political outlook. Progressive activists who came to tenant issues in response to an urban crisis were not drawn to tenant organizations whose only response to the crisis was stronger rent control. The highly politicized young activists of the 1960s and 1970s gave way, in the early 1980s, to what is commonly described as the most politically conservative generation of recent times. Economic problems from 1980–1983 made college students more job-conscious than political, and those affected were often the children of parents who come of age in the quiet 1950s and did not advocate activism. Activists may not view their actions as affected by demographic changes, but the decline in younger activists in the tenant movement through the 1980s was often beyond the individual organizations' control.

Exclusive focus on rent control also isolated the tenant movement from other progressive constituencies. For example, even though downtown Manhattanization fueled rising rents, tenant organizations in the 1980s were not involved in slow-growth campaigns. Nor were they involved in neighborhood rezoning battles, even though the downzoning of residential neighborhoods forestalled tenant displacement by commercial development. This isolation deprived the tenant movement of valuable political allies and limited activists' participation in rent control issues.

Through the 1980s, the negative impact of the tenant movement's narrow focus on rent control was masked by incremental successes in this arena. During the decade, tenants achieved a reduction in the annual rent increase from 7 to 4 percent, greater restrictions on evictions, and some curtailment of a landlord's ability to obtain rent increases above the automatic annual limit. Tenants also won Board of Supervisors' passage of the chief item on their agenda—vacancy control—only to have Mayor Feinstein, herself a landlord, twice veto it.

By 1986, tenant organizations saw themselves as a politically powerful constituency whose failure to obtain its main goal, vacancy control, was entirely attributable to an unsupportive mayor. The election of a pro-tenant mayor in November 1987 would remedy this. Tenants strongly backed candidate Art Agnos, who professed to support vacancy control. Soon after Agnos's landslide victory, however, the tenant movement's political isolation and weakness became evident. Agnos refused to move quickly on vacancy control and, instead, told tenants to sit down with their longtime adversaries (wealthy landlords) to resolve their differences. Fearful of disagreeing with the newly elected "pro-tenant" Agnos, tenant organizations capitulated to the mayor's demand. Thus began a four-year odyssey of tenant subservience to Agnos's political agenda. This submission was premised on the mistaken but widespread belief that Agnos would ensure city adoption of a vacancy control measure that would slow rising rents on much of the city's rental housing supply. (I discuss Agnos's relationship to the city's tenant movement in *The Activist's Handbook: A Primer for the 1990s and Beyond* (University of California Press).)

Why did tenant groups err in assuming that Agnos could ensure vacancy control? The answer appeared when Agnos's signature on vacancy control legislation in 1991 was immediately followed by a landlord-initiated referendum. The referendum showed that vacancy control had always depended upon winning a popular vote and could not be achieved simply by electing sympathetic politicians. While such politicians could raise funds to help the referendum campaign (Agnos broke his promise to do this), the tenant movement's achievement of its long-sought goal ultimately required a yes vote from a majority of the electorate. Winning this majority would require the type of broad-based progressive coalition that the tenant movement had abandoned, with its exclusive focus on rent control.

The tenant movement's electoral base in 1991 was also weakened by the evaporation of the underlying economic conditions that initially gave rise to demands for vacancy control. The 1986 federal tax reform measure repealed the generous real estate tax shelters created five years earlier and immediately reduced real estate values in San Francisco and throughout the country. As potential buyers seeking tax shelters suddenly disappeared, speculators holding properties when the law changed were unable to obtain the expected quick sale and profit, and faced foreclosure. The absence of buyers caused real estate values to plummet, and savings and loans to go bankrupt because of insolvent borrowers. The type of speculative gentrification schemes that had greatly increased rents in San Francisco and other cities steadily declined. The downturn of the real estate market contributed to and coincided with California's broader economic slowdown. As a result, the five-year period prior to San Francisco's 1991 vacancy control vote saw average rents on vacant units rise less dramatically than in the 1979–1985 period, and even less than would be permitted under the vacancy control ordinance.

Whether vacancy control could ever have prevailed at the polls is unclear; it is certain, however, that November 1991 was the worst of all possible times for a vacancy control election. In addition to the tenant movement's narrowed electoral base and the weakening pressure on rents, the lack of competing state or federal elections in November 1991 brought real estate money from throughout California into San Francisco's anti–vacancy control campaign. Landlords spent nearly $1 million defeating vacancy control, and these funds had the auxiliary benefit of electing the pro-landlord candidate Frank Jordan as mayor. Commentators saw San Francisco's 1991 election results as the demise of Agnos and the city's tenant movement. The experts were only half right.

In retrospect, the tenant movement's best opportunities for winning a vacancy control ballot measure occurred in 1986 or 1990, during electoral cycles that consistently produce particularly progressive voter turnouts. Even during these years, however, the fundamental flaw in a vacancy control electoral strategy would have emerged: vacant units do not vote. A political agenda that delivers no immediate benefits to voters, and that offers only the prospect of reward (that is, a voter who moves may pay a lower rent on the new home due to vacancy control), is always susceptible to defeat by a well-funded opposition campaign.

1992–1996: Old Strategies, New Victories

The twin defeats of Agnos and vacancy control forced tenant activists to reexamine their strategies, their tactics, and their movement. A consensus was reached that several years of exclusive focus on vacancy control had drained organizational energies and deterred the necessary infusion of new activists. A movement arising out of an urban-crisis political analysis had narrowed its focus to rent control and then to one specific reform, vacancy control. For several years, people interested in working on other tenant issues simply had no place to go.

Activists also recognized that the election results showed the weakness of the tenants' strategy of seeking to strengthen rent control by electing presumably pro-tenant politicians. Any significant rent control reform passed by the Board of Supervisors and signed by the mayor would always be subject to a popular vote; tenants had to focus on strengthening their own electoral base, not the politicians'.

With the opportunity for a new approach, a series of agenda-setting neighborhood conventions were scheduled in order to bring new ideas and activists into the tenant movement. The strategy: grassroots tenants rather than leaders would develop an agenda and recreate the broad-based, participatory focus of the movement's origins.

Each neighborhood convention was charged with selecting two priority issues for discussion at a city-wide tenant summit. The summit would decide if tenants should go forward with creating ballot initiatives for the November 1992 elections, and, if so, what the measures should include. A ballot initiative would break the movement's excessive and ultimately unproductive reliance on the legislative process and politicians to achieve results. It would also put movement back into the tenant movement and allow tenants themselves to frame their agendas, rather than force them to support measures watered down by their politician allies.

The initiative strategy had its detractors: they argued that, after the narrow loss of Proposition U in 1978, the four most recent rent control initiatives had suffered landslide defeats. Some felt that tenants should lay low after vacancy control's 1991 defeat and that a major setback in 1992 would destroy what was left of the movement's political credibility. Critics of the initiative strategy saw no prospect of tenants overcoming yet another high-budget landlord opposition campaign; their analysis failed to understand that the 1992 initiative would not be framed as a standard landlord-tenant battle but as a broad-based campaign for economic fairness.

The ballot measure that emerged from the 1992 convention process would have cut the automatic allowable rent increase in half, from 4 percent a year to 60 percent of inflation, which amounted to about 2 percent. The tenant movement's decade-long rent control focus was cast aside and replaced with an updated urban-crisis analysis: tenants were victims of a local version of Reagan-Bush trickle-down economics. The Clinton-Gore presidential ticket made economic unfairness a central theme in 1992, and San Francisco's tenant movement hitched its initiative, Proposition H, to this nationwide theme. (See *The Activist's Handbook* for a detailed account of the Proposition H campaign.)

The reintroduction of a class analysis into tenant politics enabled the movement to reconnect with other victims of top-down economic policies. The Proposition H campaign identified itself as a strategy concerned with several issues: helping low-income children, maintaining the well-being of people with AIDS, finding a way to keep seniors in their longtime homes, and preserving the city's racial and ethnic diversity. Liberal homeowners, who are the swing votes in San Francisco tenant ballot measures, finally had an initiative they could identify with. The reconnection of the tenant movement to broader progressive constituencies was essential for Proposition H to prevail.

Despite impressive endorsements from new constituencies, highly effective grassroots literature distribution, and the framing of the campaign as a referendum on Reaganomics, few experts thought Proposition H would prevail. "No on H" billboards and bus shelter signs flooded the city, and landlords outspent tenants $300,000 to $25,000. The alternative weeklies endorsed Proposition H but provided little coverage, and saw the campaign backers as hardworking but doomed to defeat.

Proposition H backers assumed that its appeal to the direct economic self-interest of voters would overcome the opposition's scare tactics. On election night, the assumption proved correct. Proposition H prevailed fifty-three to forty-seven, and ran over ten points ahead of prior tenant measures in the city's swing precincts. Since Proposition H took effect in December 1992, annual rent increases have been reduced from 4 percent to 1.9, 1.3, 1.1, and 1.0 percent. The revived tenant movement created a multimillion-dollar transfer of wealth from landlords to tenants.

The Proposition H campaign also accomplished its goal of creating new tenant leadership. Chief among new leaders was Ted Gullicksen of the San Francisco Tenants Union, who revived activism in what had become primarily a tenants' counseling organization. Gullicksen's commitment to aggressive, class-conscious politics helped lead the movement back to its roots. His involvement with Homes Not Jails, a squatters group, also fostered the reconnection between tenants organizations and young, more militant activists.

After Proposition H's victory, Gullicksen looked to the November 1994 ballot to remedy San Francisco rent control's biggest loophole: the exemption of owner-occupied buildings of four units or less. San Francisco's large supply of restored Victorian fourplexes and duplexes had long been attractive to both legitimate owner-occupants and profit-seeking speculators. The latter group could move a 25-percent owner or an owner's relatives into a small building and then exempt the remaining tenants from rent control. While many felt that attacking a loophole previously benefiting the popular "mom and pop" landlords could never prevail, Gullicksen argued that an initiative based on Proposition H's economic fairness rationale could win. He was right. In a victory as surprising as Proposition H, Gullicksen's Proposition I won narrowly in the November 1994 election. Landlords who raised $1.1 million to defeat vacancy control, and $300,000 to kill Proposition H, could only raise $80,000 against Proposition I (the large landlords already covered by rent control were not affected by Proposition I, and some felt they would be helped by subjecting sympathetic small landlords to the afflictions of rent regulation).

Thus three years after the defeat of vacancy control and the election of a pro-landlord mayor, the city's tenant movement won the two biggest victories of its history. Success was achieved by ignoring the legislative process and by tenants, not politicians, shaping their own agenda. Many activists wondered whether a strategy born from necessity (that is, a mayor who would veto any pro-tenant legislation made initiatives the only option) would continue in a different political environment. The 1995 election of the self-professed pro-tenant Willie Brown as mayor soon answered this question.

1996 to the Present: Dealing with Willie

During his thirty-year political career, San Francisco Mayor (and former California Assembly Speaker) Willie Brown was hardly an ally of tenants. This was true even when Brown's Assembly district was heavily tenant; Brown's only involvement in the tenant struggles of 1977–1995 was on the side of landlords opposing vacancy control.

Affordable housing late in the century

Brown's campaign for mayor aimed to compensate for his dubious record by actively courting the tenant vote. He acknowledged his past shortcomings and attributed them to his focus on state rather than local politics. To prove his commitment, Brown endorsed and mailed to voters a Tenants' Bill of Rights drafted by tenant advocates. The Bill of Rights provided specific commitments on virtually every item tenants sought. When Brown was challenged in a mayoral debate about his allegiances, he insisted he was for tenants. Brown split the tenant vote with a pro-tenant rival in the general election and had overwhelming support in his runoff against the landlord-backed incumbent. When Brown took office in January 1996, tenants felt they had a mayor who recognized the political, if not perhaps the equitable, value of supporting tenants' rights. Because Brown had adopted the tenants' agenda for 1996, tenant activists focused on enacting their platform. Brown proved quite willing to meet with tenants and consistently expressed support for the cause. When the mayor appointed a Rent Board sympathetic to tenants, activists were particularly encouraged.

Unfortunately, Brown's support for tenants quickly waned. The first item on the tenants' agenda, a measure that would reduce illegal owner move-in evictions, languished in committee at the Board of Supervisors. Brown had advised tenants to use a close political ally and appointee as the measure's sponsor, but he failed to intervene when the ally made a deal with landlords to delay the measure. Unwilling to repeat their experiences with former Mayor Agnos, tenant activists demanded that Brown use his admitted control over the board to promptly pass the measure. After agreeing to ensure passage, Brown subsequently flip-flopped and arranged a further delay. When the eviction-protection measure finally reached the Board in December 1996, Brown's two appointees cast the deciding votes to kill the legislation. As tenant leader Ted Gullicksen told the *San Francisco Chronicle*, Willie Brown "just led us down the road to slaughter."

Brown's abandonment of the tenant cause corresponded with the onset of a new wave of skyrocketing residential rents and property values. Fueled by the economic boom in neighboring Silicon Valley, San Francisco rents climbed 37 percent from February 1996 to February 1997. While existing tenants remained protected by rent control, average monthly rents on vacant apartments rose to $1,233 during this period, and to $1,724 for two-bedroom units. The steep rises showed no signs of abating through the end of the year.

Owner-occupancy evictions of seniors and other tenants living with below-market rents doubled in the year following Brown and the Board's rejection of legislative protection. As low-income people are forced out of the city, with the middle class soon to follow, the city's elected officials continue to maintain a "Don't Worry, Be Happy" attitude.

As the San Francisco tenant movement moves through its third decade, it remains the city's leading opposition to the final transformation of an economically diverse, primarily working-class town into a city for tourists and the economic elite. The median income for a single person in 1997 had already reached $45,000, and average single-family home prices exceeded $300,000.

Everyone concerned with reclaiming San Francisco has a stake in stemming this steadily upward altering of the city's economic base.

The Tenderloin
What Makes a Neighborhood

by Rob Waters and Wade Hudson

THEY GATHER ON THE JONES STREET sidewalk as they have every morning since St. Anthony's Dining Room first opened its doors almost fifty years ago. First in line are the disabled people in wheelchairs and on crutches, the families with children, the old people. After an hour, the line suddenly swells with hundreds of new arrivals, and soon it's wending its way around the corner onto Golden Gate Avenue, snaking past St. Boniface church, and rounding another corner to turn onto Leavenworth Street. As people enter the line, a young man wearing a St. Anthony's badge hands them cardboard numbers to reserve their places.

Until five years ago, the people in this line stood across the street from a barren parking lot strewn with litter and surrounded by graffitied brick walls. Today, a graceful eight-story cream and beige building rises on the site. A mounted security camera points down at the glass front door. Inside, just yards away from the densely packed line, in a courtyard ringed by ivy-covered walls and softened by ferns and flowering plants, a child with a mop of curly red hair climbs on a jungle gym across from an elderly couple sitting quietly on a bench.

Perhaps no corner in the Tenderloin better symbolizes what has—and has not—changed in this neighborhood over the past twenty years. One side seems almost like a time capsule, the site of an endlessly repeating ritual that's been acted out each day since St. Anthony's served its first meal in 1950. These days, the dining room's staff and volunteers are serving more meals than ever, nearly 2,000 hot lunches to some 1,200 people, most of them homeless or with incomes so low they can't afford their own food. They are people like Eugea Shaw, a 47-year-old African American who's lived or worked in the Tenderloin for nineteen years. Or "Granny Gear," as she gives her name, an unemployed former secretary and bartender who ate her first meal at St. Anthony's in 1970. Gear, 50 and nearly toothless, survives today on the $345 a month she gets from the city's General

Assistance program, and she lives in a small hotel room. Lately, she says, she's been eating at St. Anthony's every day. "I don't have a refrigerator," she explains, "so it's hard for me to make my food stamps last."

Across the street, the building at 111 Jones, built and run by an arm of the Catholic Church known as Mercy Services, is also a sanctuary for the poor, but the feeling could not be more different. The tasteful construction and quiet ambiance creates a sense of peace and serenity for the 108 families lucky enough to live there. "When you come inside this building," says resident Kira Slobodnik, "you forget about everything outside." Slobodnik, 62, and her husband fled the growing anti-Semitism of her native Ukraine and came to San Francisco in 1992. A university graduate and former Russian teacher in Kiev, Slobodnik shares her home with other immigrants and refugees from Russia, China, and Vietnam, along with a few native-born Americans such as longtime Tenderloin resident Joe Kaufman, a burly activist and poet who's been involved in community organizing campaigns since he moved to the Tenderloin in the late 1970s. More than 3,500 people applied to move into the building's 108 units before it opened in 1993. When a lottery was held to choose among the applicants, the Slobodniks and Kaufman hit their numbers. Eugea Upshaw, a regular diner and former employee of St. Anthony's Dining Room, did not.

The shifting fortunes of Kira Slobodnik, Joe Kaufman, and Eugea Upshaw illustrate the changes that have taken place in the Tenderloin and point up the challenges facing those who grapple with the seemingly intractable problems of poverty, housing, and jobs in America today. Impassioned activists, longtime Tenderloin residents, newly arrived immigrants, and caring providers of social services have spent the last two decades struggling to improve the community and to make it a more livable place. Their work, which reached its peak of potency in the mid-1980s, prevented the neighborhood from being devoured by forces of development and gentrification and preserved the Tenderloin as a low-income community.

But the limitations of their work are also clear. For every Kira Slobodnik and Joe Kaufman who managed to get a place in the sun in a building like 111 Jones, there are scores of Eugea Upshaws and Granny Gears who wait in soup lines for their meals and spend their nights in cheap welfare hotels or sleep in doorways on the street.

Tenderloin activists succeeded in awakening and mobilizing their community, but no neighborhood can make a revolution within its own borders. More than most neighborhoods, the Tenderloin is buffeted by developments across the ocean and policy shifts across the country. Even the lucky lottery winners who got into the oasis at 111 Jones Street may find their new residence to be less stable

Hungry San Franciscans stand in line on the south side of Golden Gate Avenue for a free meal at St. Anthony's Dining Room across from 111 Jones Street (right).

than they might have thought. The draconian changes made by Congress in its viciously misnamed "welfare reform" package may soon wipe out the meager incomes of many of the building's immigrants.

Tagged with the name "Tenderloin" decades ago because of its similarity to a New York neighborhood that was regarded as a choice assignment for corrupt cops, San Francisco's Tenderloin is a forty-block section of downtown that is home to some 20,000 people. It is San Francisco's most diverse and unusual neighborhood, and also one of its poorest. Southeast Asian refugees, African Americans, Latinos, Filipinos, and Russians all make their home in "the 'Loin." So do thousands of seniors and children.

Bordered by the theater district and Union Square on the east, and City Hall, the Opera House, Symphony Hall, and the glitzy new public library on the west, the Tenderloin has almost everything. High-priced condos on O'Farrell Street. Luxury hotels such as the St. Francis and the Clift. Top-flight restaurants such as Wolfgang Puck's Postrio. Street hookers by the dozens who work the busiest thoroughfares, tolerated by San Francisco juries that refuse to prosecute. Whorehouses posing as massage parlors and strip joints. Drug dealers selling illegal substances and liquor stores vending legal ones. Trendy dance clubs such as Club 181 that attract slumming movie stars like Michael Douglas, next to a liquor store where a customer was recently killed by a stray bullet. A Vietnamese nightclub busted with a stock of high-powered weapons in the basement, a few doors from a well-managed hotel that caters to European budget travelers. Residential hotels with rooms the size of a large closet, and studio and one-bedroom apartments where Southeast Asian families of four, five, six or more members crowd onto the mattresses that get stacked in the corner each morning.

Twenty years ago, buildings like 111 Jones Street, where Kira Slobodnik and Joe Kaufman live, didn't exist in the Tenderloin. In those days, the area was seen by most San Franciscans as the city's red-light district, a desolate wasteland of prostitutes, drug addicts, and criminals. Echoing and perpetuating the popular stereotype, the *San Francisco Examiner* called the neighborhood "Hell at your doorstep," and Supervisor Richard Hongisto described it as "a sleazy district that is . . . a disgrace to the city."

The truth, of course, is much more complicated. In the 1970s, the Tenderloin was perhaps the poorest district in the city, a neighborhood with a large concentration of low-income seniors, people with disabilities, and single drifters who floated in and out of the neighborhood's single-room hotels, eking out a living from casual labor or the meager stipends of the city's General Assistance program. Scores of business spaces sat vacant and boarded up. Its residents, for the most part, came in two shades, black and white, but its nighttime population swelled with thrill-seekers from throughout the Bay Area who came to the neighborhood to walk on the wild side and taste its illicit pleasures. It was—and still is—a neighborhood where violence flared frequently, especially if you were part of its drug scene: in 1976 the Tenderloin had 40 percent of the city's drug overdoses and a quarter of its homicides.

The Tenderloin was condemned by politicians and newspaper columnists, but ignored and neglected when it came to doling out city services. It was a neighborhood without the institutions and sense of cohesion that allow a community to define itself. Some people, including social service providers who worked there, thought that would never change. "The Tenderloin has no social structure of its own," said the Rev. Don Seaton in 1971, as he was leaving his post as the director of Central City Hospitality House, a neighborhood service agency. "It is not a community and never will be. It's impossible to organize the Tenderloin."

In less than ten years, Seaton's predictions would be proven wrong. By the end of the seventies, two simultaneous developments—the influx of thousands of Southeast Asian immigrants and a wave of neighborhood activism and community organizing—began to transform the Tenderloin into one of the most active neighborhoods in the city, a community with a growing sense of itself and its mission, and a growing determination to fight for its own survival as a neighborhood where low-income people could afford to live.

Up to that point, the Tenderloin had managed to escape the redevelopment bulldozers that had swallowed large chunks of the Western Addition in the 1950s and 1960s and were then engulfing the South of Market. But as the economy of America's favorite city became more and more dependent on tourism, the Tenderloin—with its central location, its proximity to the Union Square shopping and tourist district, and its large supply of residential hotels—began to look increasingly appealing to players, large and small, in the tourist trade.

The owners of the neighborhood's residential hotels saw that they could make far more money renting rooms by the night to bargain travelers than they could renting rooms by the month to seniors and poor people on low fixed

The Tenderloin. The Coral Sea is just two blocks down Turk Street from the Philip Burton Federal Office Building.

incomes. So a number of hotel owners began an often brutal effort to move permanent tenants out of their buildings and convert them into lodging for tourists. Unable to issue straight-out eviction notices to sitting tenants because of the city's rent laws, these owners found other ways of getting tenants to leave. They turned down the heat, cut off elevator service, and pulled chairs out of the lobby, trying to make tenants so uncomfortable that they would leave. Some offered bribes to tenants willing to move. Once the buildings were emptied, the owners slapped on coats of fresh paint, gussied up their lobbies, and glued Visa stickers to their front doors. The profits, by Tenderloin standards, were great: rooms that once brought in $180 a month now rent for $30 or $40 a night.

Then, in 1980, an even bigger threat emerged. That summer, three national hotel chains announced plans to develop luxury high-rise hotels in the Tenderloin. Taken together, the projects proposed by the Ramada, Hilton, and Holiday Inn would plant nearly 2,000 high-cost hotel rooms on the fragile eastern edge of the neighborhood, effectively linking them to the Powell Street tourist strip and Union Square.

Neighborhood residents and leaders in a newly emerging community organization, the North of Market Planning Coalition, saw these developments for the major threats that they were, and sprang into action. The Coalition had been founded in 1977 by representatives of social service agencies working in the neighborhood. But soon, with a staff of young organizers funded by VISTA (a federal program, sister to the Peace Corps, that sent volunteers to work in poor neighborhoods in the United States), the Coalition began to build up a membership base among neighborhood residents and to organize the neighborhood. Committees were formed to battle against the conversion of residential hotel units to tourist use, and also to resist the construction of the new hotels—or at least gain compensation for their effects on the neighborhood.

One of the people who enlisted in the fight against the hotels was Joe Kaufman, a disabled artist and poet who joined the Coalition after attending a community meeting. "I saw a sign in a laundromat on Eddy Street and decided to go to the meeting," Kaufman recalls. He had recently moved to the Tenderloin, after being forced out of his home in the Haight-Ashbury by a city-funded housing renovation program that pushed up neighborhood rents. "I got thrown out of the Haight and I wanted to be a part of improving a neighborhood. Now I was living in the Tenderloin and here was a way to fight back against the same kind of forces that pushed me out of the Haight and were now threatening the Tenderloin."

Kaufman and other neighborhood activists formed committees to wage the fight against hotel conversions and the luxury hotels. They organized demonstrations and lobbied members of the Board of Supervisors and Planning Commission. When the projects came up for discussion at public hearings, residents packed the meetings, cheering as activists like Kaufman and Jean Mellor denounced the hotels, and booing as hotel lawyers discoursed on the planning code. The neighborhood's new newspaper, the *Tenderloin Times*, devoted extensive coverage to the fight against the hotels and brought the issue to the attention of Tenderloin residents.

In the end, the community campaign was unable to block the luxury hotels outright, but it did extract millions of dollars from the developers, money that was used to subsidize low-cost housing and fund community projects. At virtually the same time, the battle against hotel conversions was meeting with partial success: neighborhood activists convinced the Board of Supervisors to pass a law banning the conversion of residential hotels to tourist use.

Both of these victories had significant flaws. By the time the anticonversion ordinance passed in 1981, hundreds of units had already been lost. And even after the law's passage, city officials charged with implementing its provisions did little at first to enforce it. With sustained pressure, however, the ordinance helped protect the neighborhood's fragile stock of affordable housing.

In a similar vein, the mitigation measures agreed to by the developers of the new luxury hotels were unprecedented locally and nationally. But the final accord was also a compromise, an accommodation to the power of the hotels and their allies in the pro-development administration of Mayor Dianne Feinstein. In truth, the neighborhood probably got as much out of the developers as it possibly could, given the political realities of the day. The hotel struggle established the Planning Coalition as a neighborhood power and laid the foundations for an even more important battle. At the same time, however, the process of community organizing, negotiation, and compromise—coupled with the neighborhood's dependence on paid organizers and outside funding—established a pattern that would ultimately contribute to the unraveling of the neighborhood's political strength.

When the dust finally cleared and the fight against the hotels was over, neighborhood activists realized that they couldn't keep fighting projects one by one; they needed a better way to safeguard the neighborhood against undesirable development. So the Planning Coalition drew up its own zoning plan for the neighborhood, calling for reduced building heights, fewer bars, and limits on commercial uses—and then convinced the city to implement most of it. Never again would high-rise projects be able to build in the neighborhood; heights in most areas were restricted to eighty feet.

In seeking to protect the neighborhood from encroaching development, the rezoning was largely successful. The central sections of the Tenderloin stayed off-limits to major development projects, and the restricted development potential helped restrain land costs and curb real estate speculation. Rezoning was a central part of a strategy to protect the neighborhood by gaining greater control over how land would be used, and who would get to use it. A second part of that strategy was for community agencies and nonprofit housing developers to buy key sites in the neighborhood. If, on every block that outside developers might covet, community-based groups owned a lot or a building, they would be able to block developers from assembling all the parcels they would need. And if these community agencies owned apartment buildings and residential hotels, they could provide the low-cost quality housing that the neighborhood desperately needed.

The first group to blaze the nonprofit housing trail was Reality House West, which had previously operated a drug rehabilitation program in the Western Addition. Seeking partly to provide housing for ex-convicts, Reality House bought the Cadillac Hotel, a once-venerable 160-unit hotel on Eddy Street that had fallen on hard times and was largely vacant. Leroy Looper, the director of Reality House, bought the building, renovated it, and operated it as low-cost housing for the poor. It quickly became one of the nerve centers of the neighborhood, its lobby and dining room the site of numerous, sometimes contentious, community meetings, its commercial storefronts rented to community agencies working to organize and improve the neighborhood.

A few years later, the Tenderloin Neighborhood Development Corporation picked up the effort, launched with money and energy from the Catholic Franciscan community that was active in the Tenderloin. The group began by buying four neighborhood buildings, which it envisioned turning into tenant-run cooperatives, where residents would decide for themselves how things should be run.

At the same moment that the Tenderloin was rousing itself politically and beginning to pull together as a neighborhood, dramatic events on the other side of the Pacific Ocean began to make ripples, then waves in the Tenderloin. Starting in the late 1970s and intensifying in the early 1980s, thousands of Southeast Asian refugees began arriving in the neighborhood. They were fleeing the violence and devastation of war, the squalor of overcrowded refugee camps, and the new communist regimes of Vietnam, Cambodia, and Laos. The Tenderloin, with its supply of comparatively cheap rental housing, became the principal settlement point of refugees landing in San Francisco.

This sudden influx of families and children made clearer than ever the critical lack of basic services for the residents of the Tenderloin. A concrete jungle with no parks, playgrounds, or greenery was now home to thousands of children. A community that had to depend for its grocery needs on corner stores with lots of liquor but little fresh food was now the home of large families, squeezed into studio and one-bedroom apartments, who wanted to buy fresh foods.

The dramatic demographic shift that took place in the neighborhood, along with the community's new focus on organizing, gave the neighborhood a stronger voice to advocate for itself, along with new resources to help meet its needs. One resource was the relative economic clout and entrepreneurial skill of the Southeast Asian community. Though most newly arriving Southeast Asians were desperately poor and had to depend on welfare benefits to survive, the Asian community's networks of mutual support allowed some families to open small markets where people could buy fresh vegetables, meat, and fruit, along with the specialty ingredients needed for Asian cooking. Today, there are a score of Asian-owned markets in the Tenderloin, and dozens of Vietnamese, Chinese and Cambodian restaurants.

The neighborhood's need for fresh produce was also addressed in another way when the American Friends Service Committee, a Quaker service organization, set up the Heart of the City Farmers Market in United Nations plaza on the edge of the Tenderloin. Today, after sixteen years, the market is still going strong, giving neighborhood residents a chance to buy fruits and vegetables—as well as live chickens and freshly caught fish—directly from farmers and producers.

Other community-based organizations were also looking around the neighborhood, finding major needs, and mobilizing to meet them. To serve the new population of children, for instance, neighborhood leaders and activists demanded a park. Boeddeker Park, named after the founder of St. Anthony's Dining Room, opened in 1985, but competition for its use soon made it a center of controversy. Since one overused park didn't come close to meeting the needs of the neighborhood for recreation space, neighborhood groups pushed the city to set up a children's playground, which opened in 1996 on Ellis Street.

When large numbers of homeless people began appearing on the streets of the neighborhood and at the offices of emergency service providers in late 1982, activists, social workers, and homeless people themselves began to mobilize and demand action from the city. Two ad hoc advocacy groups arose and took up the issue. One, the Central City Shelter Network, was a collection of agencies providing services to homeless people; the other was a group of homeless people that called themselves the Homeless Caucus. The *Tenderloin Times* began to report on the growing numbers of homeless people, the first media outlet in the city to do so, and made the issue into a crusade. Other media picked it up and the city began to respond, first by providing cots and money to local churches so they could set up shelters in their basements, and later by contracting with the owners of residential hotels in the Tenderloin, South of Market, and Mission districts, many of them dilapidated slum properties that community groups and the city had been trying to upgrade for years.

With the assistance of organizers from the Planning Coalition and other groups, the Caucus became the militant voice of the homeless, holding demonstrations outside the million-dollar house of Dianne Feinstein, staging sit-ins in the chambers of the Board of Supervisors. The Shelter Network, by contrast, was polite and reasonable; its members were soon filling most of the seats on the Mayor's Homeless Task Force—and getting most of the contracts to provide homeless services.

A crying need for mental health services that would be radically different from traditional models led to a community campaign for a client-run self-help program, where people in need or in crisis could get nonmedical services and human support from trained volunteers from the community, rather then detached mental health professionals. The campaign was championed by the *Tenderloin Times*, which ran numerous articles on the subject and sponsored community forums that brought health commissioners and other media to the neighborhood to hear from residents and advocates. These concerted efforts led the Health Department to allocate a half-million dollars to set up the Tenderloin Self-Help Center. The contract to run the center was awarded to Central City Hospitality House, which still runs the program.

Neighborhood arts and cultural organizations also took root and flourished. Arts programs based at the Cadillac Hotel, and especially at Hospitality House, nurtured artistic talents, provided workshop space, and organized exhibitions that enabled the work of neighborhood artists to reach a wider public. Two theater groups sprang up in the neighborhood, producing plays with neighborhood actors, and attracting city-wide audiences; one group, the Exit Theater, continues today. The 509 Cultural Center was born as a performance space for local musicians and a meeting and gathering place where neighborhood residents could share artistic and political ideas and visions. Murals were painted on public walls around the neighborhood.

The success of these efforts to create a sense of community and to enhance the neighborhood's political power had four key elements. One was the drive and enthusiasm of residents determined to change their neighborhood. They joined the Planning Coalition in droves and ran spirited campaigns to be elected by fellow members to the group's board of directors. At its peak in the mid-1980s, the Coalition had a dues-paying membership of around 500 people.

Another was the large number of activists and professionals who chose to work in the neighborhood. These community workers, a mix of young organizers and people with technical skills and training in city planning, housing development, and newspaper publishing, provided important leadership and savvy to the neighborhood's battle for survival.

A third was the community's multilingual newspaper, the *Tenderloin Times*, which consistently investigated and broke important stories that were picked up by the city's mainstream media. The paper—which from 1985 on was published in Vietnamese, Cambodian, and Laotian as well as English—was one of the few community organizations that maintained connections with the different ethnic groups in this increasingly diverse neighborhood.

Finally, the infusion of substantial funds from local foundations and charities associated with the Franciscan order helped sustain all of these neighborhood projects, allowing them to hire staffs to carry out their work.

The activism of neighborhood residents seeking to protect their community made the Planning Coalition and the neighborhood a force to be reckoned with. But, in the end, it also empowered a new set of deal makers and service providers, the skilled professionals who, for the most part, actually negotiated on behalf of the neighborhood with would-be builders and city officials, or ran those programs funded by the city or private foundations.

Some neighborhood residents seemed instinctively to understand this process. Darwin Dias, an activist and Coalition member active in the campaign to fight the hotels, criticized the luxury-hotel settlement as "chump change." And indeed, if you compare the enduring value of the three hotels, and their permanent, physical presence in the neighborhood, with the fifteen-year life of the payments the developers had to make, it's hard to disagree. Even worse was the neighborhood's inability to secure jobs for Tenderloin residents. Though the developers agreed, as a condition of their building permits, to make strong efforts to hire residents, very few of the hundreds of jobs created at the three hotels were given to neighborhood folks.

Another resident, Don Davis, was even more critical of the professional activists who worked for community organizations like the Planning Coalition and the *Tenderloin Times*. Davis railed against them as "carpetbaggers" and charged that they took jobs that should have gone to low-income people. He argued that the neighborhood would be better off if poor people led the resistance. Davis, who survived by scavenging items from financial district garbage bins and selling them at flea markets, was often seen on picket lines, where his shouting could be heard from blocks away. His style was disruptive and his attacks were often brutal and personal, but his accusations contained a kernel of truth.

As the 1990s opened in the Tenderloin, several factors conspired to chip away at the gains of the previous decade and to increase the pressure and tension that festered in the neighborhood. On the street, crack cocaine replaced heroin as the drug of choice, adding a harder, more desperate, and more violent edge to the neighborhood's drug culture and bringing what the Rev. Cecil Williams of Glide Memorial Church called "the stench of death" to the neighborhood and to Boeddeker Park, across the street from his famous church. The community's long and successful campaign to build this park was badly marred by its slow metamorphosis into a hangout for drinkers and a haven for drug deals, where sellers and buyers from all over town could come to do their business. The Southeast Asian children and seniors who had come to the park in its early days now stayed away, and the park became the province of African Americans. These changes in the park, along with the fear of crime, heightened racial tensions that had long existed in the neighborhood.

Crime, of course, had long been one of the neighborhood's biggest problems and most contentious issues. It was compounded by the city's unwritten policy of allowing the Tenderloin to function as a containment zone where drug dealing, prostitution, and public drinking could occur with relatively little interference, and where liquor stores, massage parlors, and strip joints were licensed in greater numbers than any other part of the city. Beyond a general agreement in the neighborhood that more cops walking Tenderloin beats would be good, there was little consensus

Boeddeker Park at Turk and Mason in the Tenderloin, with the Hilton looming in the background

about how to tackle crime. Some in the neighborhood argued for a stronger police presence, for sharp crackdowns on drug sales and prostitution, and for greater limits on the number of agencies serving homeless people or those with drug and alcohol problems. Others were more concerned with police harassment of the homeless, and wanted to see more, not fewer, services for people needing substance-abuse treatment. Virtually alone among Tenderloin agencies, Glide tried to reach out to the neighborhood's African American crack users and draw them into recovery. Through it all, the police department failed to deliver in any significant way on its frequently repeated promise to get cops out of their patrol cars and onto the street, walking beats. Increasingly, neighborhood agencies operated more on their own. As the nineties wore on, the relative cohesion that had existed in the eighties weakened. In the eighties, community organizing and increased media focus on the Tenderloin had shone a spotlight on the neighborhood and enabled it to demand and actually procure increased city funding for desperately needed services and housing. But as bigger pots of money began to flow to nonprofit agencies in the neighborhood, those agencies and their directors became the neighborhood's most powerful players. Unlike groups such as the Planning Coalition, which had an elected board of directors composed largely of neighborhood residents, the agencies were essentially unaccountable to anyone.

As the power and influence of the agencies grew, the strength of organizers and advocates declined. In the 1990s, the North of Market Planning Coalition lurched from crisis to crisis, losing its funding and laying off all or most of its staff several times. As it sought to survive, it became increasingly driven by the search for funds and the interests of its funders, rather than the goals and desires of neighborhood residents. It received funding from the new luxury hotels in the neighborhood, held meetings in conference rooms donated by its former adversary, the Hilton Hotel, and placed the hotel's public relations director on its executive committee. Under this new direction, the Coalition actively recruited as members large numbers of condo owners and refused to oppose a proposed Business Investment District that would have given the wealthiest property owners, rather than elected officials, the power to collect revenue and administer services, including security.

The *Tenderloin Times*, which had always been dependent on outside funding, lost most of its foundation support and failed in its efforts to achieve a greater level of self-sufficiency from advertising and commercial activities. Then, in the early nineties, financial mismanagement brought crisis to Central City Hospitality House, the agency that founded and published the *Times*. Its board of directors opted to shut down the paper and lay off its by then miniscule staff to save money for its direct services it was providing to the homeless.

The Tenderloin Self-Help Center, conceived through a community-based process, moved away from its original vision under the management of Hospitality House. When it opened, the center operated as an autonomous, client-directed center, with minimal supervision from Hospitality House. Clients participated in open community meetings to establish policies for the Center and to elect leaders who met regularly with staff. But not long after opening, Hospitality House fired the Center's director and dismantled its internal democratic structure. Though the Center has retained its nonmedical approach, the concept of client power has faded.

In retrospect, the organizers and advocates who placed the Tenderloin on the city's political map made several mistakes that contributed to the decline in the neighborhood's power. They failed to develop an economic strategy that would allow them to maintain their work after the inevitable occurred and foundations decided to shift their funding elsewhere. They also failed in many cases to nurture and develop indigenous neighborhood leadership that could continue their work when they decided to move on. Few organizers and agency heads gave much attention to truly empowering low-income residents of the neighborhood. And even the groups that did so, seemed to move away from that ideal in the 1990s.

The Tenderloin Neighborhood Development Corporation stopped trying to develop tenant self-management in its buildings and opted instead to become good, nonprofit landlords of safe, affordable, and well-maintained buildings.

The Planning Coalition failed to maintain its early levels of neighborhood involvement and participation in board elections. To Garth Ferguson, a longtime Tenderloin activist and homeless advocate who has been a board member of the Coalition, this shift in focus helped bring about the organization's demise. "What I liked about the Coalition in the early days was that it really seemed to want to hear what people wanted and to help them get it," says Ferguson. "It responded to its constituents and it helped turn people into leaders. Losing that has been its downfall—people became elitist instead of empowering others."

Today, the Joe Kaufmans of the neighborhood will find no flyers in laundromats inviting them to meetings, and no copies of the *Tenderloin Times* stacked in apartment-house lobbies or newsstands. The Planning Coalition has laid off its entire staff. A number of neighborhood leaders, former allies, are now bitter enemies. Serious racial divisions afflict the community.

One source of that friction is visible at the corner of Golden Gate and Jones, where Granny Gear and Eugea Upshaw stand in line at St. Anthony's, across from 111 Jones. In many ways, that building, and other nonprofit housing in the neighborhood, is a product of the community mobilization of the 1980s. Neighborhood activists put nonprofit housing on the agenda as a way to house the Tenderloin's poor, and to ensure that they would continue to be able to live in their neighborhood. Yet few previous residents of the Tenderloin actually live in the 108 units at 111 Jones, and only three African American families. The same is true of a new building developed by Network Ministries on Ellis Street.

The agencies that developed these buildings point out that because they were using government funds to buy the land and construct the buildings, they could not restrict the applicants to neighborhood residents, nor could they establish quotas to ensure that the racial breakdown of the building reflected that of the neighborhood. Their only option was to run a lottery, open to all who earned enough money to afford to pay the rents—around $375 for a one-bedroom apartment—but not so high as to be above official definitions of low income. The result is a strange twist on gentrification: people who get General Assistance can't afford to live there, but people getting higher federal disability benefits can.

These nonprofit developers were faced with a decision: they could play by government rules and provide housing mostly for immigrants, most of whom had not lived in the Tenderloin and had not been part of the neighborhood's struggles, or they could refuse and not build any housing at all. Given these choices, their decision is certainly defensible, but it plays into racial division and perpetuates troublesome notions about the deserving and the undeserving poor.

In the Tenderloin, Southeast Asian families with children are seen as deserving, and a number of agencies are working effectively on their behalf. The Bay Area Women's and Children's Center, for instance, has led the crucial and successful fight to establish a Tenderloin grade school, a campaign that received a great deal of favorable media attention. But efforts to start up a drop-in center for crack-addicted women with children, primarily African Americans, has met with fierce opposition from other Tenderloin groups fearful that such a program would bring more drug addicts into the neighborhood.

Not long ago, such disputes would have been hashed out within the neighborhood. The Planning Coalition would have discussed it in a board meeting; the *Tenderloin Times* would have covered the debate in a story. But today there is no community-wide forum, no group that can really perform the function of bringing neighborhood groups and people together to discuss ideas and conflicts. Instead, there is an increasing sense of competition and infighting among neighborhood organizations, along with a sense of dread about what the new welfare cuts will do to the Tenderloin.

But beyond the neighborhood's own mistakes and failings, it is suffering from forces that are well beyond its control. Local activists can never make real progress toward reducing poverty until there is a political movement capable of demanding fundamental change and action at the federal level. As long as the federal government consciously creates and perpetuates widespread poverty and unemployment in the name of fighting inflation, neighborhoods such as the Tenderloin will continue to be swamped with a tide of poverty-related human misery.

The Tenderloin is not alone. Similar forms of deterioration can be seen in neighborhoods across the country. The prosperity of the nineties mostly benefits the already wealthy, and the ascendancy of the New Democrats has seemingly blocked effective federal action on behalf of the poor. What's left to too many poor people is what was left to Eugea Upshaw and the 3,500 other people who applied for an apartment at 111 Jones: a thirty-five-to-one shot in a lottery.

Despite the setbacks that have befallen the Tenderloin in recent years, and despite the growing tension, a number of organizations continue to do critical work and to reap results. The Coalition on Homelessness and the housing development group that it spawned, the Community Housing Partnership, have bought and renovated three buildings where more than 200 formerly homeless people now live and work. The Partnership set up a training program to teach people construction and building maintenance skills and has a construction arm that employs eighteen people to do renovation and maintenance work on buildings owned by nonprofit housing groups all over the city. The campaign for a Tenderloin grade school has borne fruit, and in 1998 the neighborhood's first ever public school is scheduled to open. The building will be much more than just a school, it will be a twenty-four-hour community center that will also house a variety of community programs and services.

The gains of the 1980s, combined with this ongoing community work, give the Tenderloin a structure and organizational base that it did not have twenty years ago. If the neighborhood can recapture the activism that it was once known for, and begin to make links with other groups around the city and country that are attempting to change policies on the federal level, the Tenderloin's next decade might be a brighter one.

Call Any Vegetable
The Politics of Food in San Francisco

by Jesse Drew

Gone are the days when the corner grocer bought fresh fruits and vegetables from the local farmer, and was limited to a selection of the produce ripening at the moment in local fields.
> —J. J. Rodale, whole foods pioneer and longtime advocate of organic farming techniques

Since we're neighbors, let's be friends!
> —Safeway jingle, 1980s

STROLL DOWN THE AISLES of some of the larger Bay Area supermarkets. Bags and boxes of various brands of granola loom over you, nestled among the Sugar Frosted Flakes and Cap'n Crunch. Wheat and whole-grain breads stretch many chariots long before you. Soy milk beckons to you from vacuum-packed cartons. Clear acrylic plastic bins of bulk beans, grains, pastas, and dried fruits and nuts stand gleaming before you. Freshly misted organic fruits and vegetables, from avocados to zucchini, glisten under the fluorescent lights.

This supermarket landscape seems common enough today, but a generation ago it would have appeared only in a mirage. Go back a few decades in the Bay Area and your supermarket stroll would have been different. The kinds of breads available were mostly white. Bulk grains or beans? No such thing. Organic anything? Unheard of. Granola? A radical plot to destroy the constitution of America's young. Instead, you would have found aisles and aisles of highly processed foods, often created more in the laboratory than the kitchen, and possessing little nutritional value.

San Francisco has always been famous for its restaurants and gastronomical diversity. But in the city known nationally for "Rice-a-Roni the San Francisco Treat," there was little indication that the City by the Bay would become a center for the organic whole foods movement. The rejection of the processed, junk-food American cuisine would occur alongside the development of a new radical consciousness in the 1960s. To the growing ranks of political activists and countercultural converts, the unhealthy and synthetic processed American cuisine was beginning to be perceived as part and parcel of a political-economic system that was increasingly viewed as racist, imperialist, and dominated by corporate greed. America, under the banner of Coca-Cola and the Hamburger, was fighting a war against the civil rights movement at home and against Third World independence movements abroad. The image of the pig became the metaphor for everything wrong about America, a gluttonous monster gobbling everything in sight. But within the belly of this fast-food beast arose a movement that saw the fight against war and injustice as linked to a fight for better quality food at cheaper prices. San Francisco would emerge as a primary center and spiritual home of this new food consciousness. From the anti-HUAC riots of 1960 to the Diggers movement, to the Summer of Love, to the radical political movements of the late sixties and early seventies, the Bay Area has often been at the forefront of challenges to conformity and the status quo. These radical social movements generated a wide, rapidly growing countercultural environment that quickly moved beyond any single focal point of dissension, to develop a broad critique of everyday life. Breakfast, lunch, and dinner are, of course, integral parts of everyday existence.

The questions of who controls what we eat, and who gets to eat in the first place, were central aspects of the politics of the sixties and seventies. Alongside food conspiracies, food co-ops, and baking and warehousing collectives arose projects whose aim was to feed the people, to ensure food for those shoved aside from the American dinner table. From the Diggers' free food ritual in the Haight-Ashbury to the Black Panther Party's "breakfast for children" programs, the question of food became a matter of fierce political struggle, resulting in jailings, beatings, and even deaths. It would be a mistake, therefore, to view these developing movements for healthy food through the lens of 1990s lifestyle thinking as merely the result of individualistic consumer choices. The notion of "we are what we eat" was strongly linked to the body politic of the sixties and seventies, as integral to the fight for social justice.

> Most of the fresh vegetables once seen in a local market are there no longer, because they cannot be shipped without spoiling, so the farmer does not plant them. Where, then, do the 4,500 new items on the grocery shelves come from? Those 4,500 new products are being manufactured, not grown. . . .
>
> —J. J. Rodale

The desire to eat purer and healthier foods certainly did not start in the sixties. The aversion to processed foods dates from the last century when new flour-

Old Produce Market (c. 1956). As much as 20 percent of the produce passing through this area rotted before it could be distributed, which fueled city plans to move it southward to its current site on the Islais Creek wetlands landfill east of Bayshore Blvd.

milling mechanisms were invented, making flour whiter but removing the nutritious germ, oil, and husk. The modern canning industry developed as well, enabling canned goods production to develop on an industrial scale. Modern food-processing techniques, industrialization, and the decline of farming removed many Americans from direct sources of foods. Early critics of industrialization saw this as a threat to the health of the nation and argued that people should strive to eat pure foods. In the early nineteenth century, Sylvester Graham (inventor of the graham cracker) marketed his brown crackers as an antidote to the new popular white flour. Dr. Kellogg (inventor of the corn flake), made a breakfast product based on Graham's "granula," made from pieces of graham crackers, later renaming it "granola" to avoid trademark infringement.

Advances in transportation systems and refrigeration technologies enabled a truly national system of food preparation and distribution to emerge. Food factories arose alongside the increasing consolidation of all basic industries by corporate conglomerates, producing food assembly-line style, regardless of the result-ing loss of nutritional value or flavor. The rise of corporate agriculture in the thir-ties led to increased use of chemical fertilizers and the abandonment of tradition-al family farm patterns of crop rotation and manure spreading.

Despite the criticisms of modern food production, most Americans were infatuated by the love affair between technology and modernity. Bolstered by an expanding advertising industry, packaged, processed, and refined foods were per-ceived as clean, modern, and convenient. Most people were not aware that much of this food had been stripped of vitamins, minerals, and fiber content, or that much of the price consumers paid went to packaging and advertising costs. Food with a well-known label on it—Wonderbread, Ritz Crackers, Maxwell House—was what was welcomed into the American pantry.

World War II caused a momentary lapse in corporate food production for the consumer market, leading to the popularization of victory gardens, small home vegetable plots intended to aid the war effort. In San Francisco alone, there were as many as 70,000 such home gardens. Shortages of food during the war led some to look for other ways of procuring food for urban populations. In San Francisco, this effort led to the creation of the San Francisco Farmer's Market.

The San Francisco Farmer's Market

> This little lesson in primitive economics started San Franciscans thinking. It was about an age-old question: Who's getting all the money between the producer and the con-sumer? They reasoned that something must be wrong with our system of food distrib-ution when they paid such high prices in the city, while within a radius of 35 miles the farmers couldn't give their crops away.
>
> —John G. Brucato, creator of the San Francisco Farmer's Market

The head of the San Francisco Victory Garden Council, John G. Brucato, became concerned after hearing about large amounts of fresh fruits and vegetables going to waste in nearby farmlands, which were mostly small family farms run by European immigrants. Consumers were continuing to pay high prices for produce in the city, but nearby farmers were receiving much less from canneries and wholesalers. Brucato decided to help consumers make a direct connection with the farmers and to inform the public about farm surpluses. As Brucato explains (*The Farmer Comes to Town*, San Francisco: Burke, 1947):

> Hungry San Franciscans, resentful of the high prices for fruit and vegetables in retail stores, could then pool their cars and go directly to the farmer. In many cases, they would do the actual picking, settle on a fair price, and drive home loaded with food. Frequently they would can the fruit on a community basis.

The city dweller benefited and the farmer was grateful for any outlet for his surplus crop.

The consumer-farmer exchange was so successful that another bigger, bolder plan was hatched whereby farmers would come to town with produce and sell directly to the city people. A 72,000-square-foot vacant lot at the corner of Market Street and Duboce Avenue was chosen. On opening day, August 12, 1943, the lot was jammed with over 1,000 buyers, and dozens of farmers' trucks with fresh produce. By the third day, an estimated 50,000 people had walked off with produce from over one hundred farmers' trucks. A great success, the Farmer's Market opened the eyes of many people to the wisdom of organizing alternative means of procuring foods. It also educated the public to the inevitable conflict arising from tampering with the lucrative business arrangement enjoyed by big wholesale grocer operations. Farmers reported being intercepted on the roads by men offering them cash to turn around and go home, and various state and city officials tried to find ways of shutting the market down.

The Farmer Still Comes to Town

The original Farmer's Market is still alive and well in San Francisco. In 1944 the market relocated from Market and Duboce to city-owned land on Alemany and San Bruno. In 1945, after many attempts by large retailers to eliminate the market, the voters of San Francisco voted seven to one to set up a permanent Farmer's Market owned and operated by the city. Now, on a typical Saturday morning, over one hundred farmers come to the market to sell their home-grown produce to thousands of San Franciscans. The Farmer's Market inspects county agricultural records to ensure that the sellers are actual farmers and are not simply re-selling produce bought elsewhere. This arrangement gives city people access to cheap, fresh produce and allows farmers to cut out the middleman. It also allows the farmers to sell produce that is rejected by wholesalers as irregular or misshapen. Thus food that would have gone to waste can be purchased by consumers at cheap prices.

A newer market was founded in the mid-eighties to serve the inner-city neighborhood of the Tenderloin. The Heart of the City Farmers Market was set up with the help of the American Friends Service Committee to provide cheap and fresh produce to an area generally lacking large produce markets (though rich in vendors of alcohol). The market sells vegetables, fruits, fish, and other items to a largely Southeast Asian population. The Heart of the City Farmers Market makes a great difference to the many elderly people who live in the Tenderloin and to people who rely on public transportation, as the city-owned market is not easy to get to.

Heart of the City Farmers Market, open Wednesdays and Sundays
in U.N. Plaza in the Civic Center

These markets are constantly battling against the relentless encroachment of San Francisco's powerful real estate interests. The San Francisco Farmer's Market, whose site was once at the foot of a barren and out-of-the-way hillside, now finds itself ringed by newly built condominiums. The Heart of the City Farmers Market is increasingly out of favor with downtown interests who feel that working-class Tenderloin residents crowding around fish and produce vendors is not consistent with their vision of gentrification.

On the other hand, there is one market in San Francisco that does have the blessing of downtown. At the Embarcadero Ferry Plaza there is a Farmer's Market run by the San Francisco Public Market Collaborative, a private organization composed mainly of real estate, architectural, and restaurant interests. Their market is geared toward upscale patrons who find such small open markets to be charming accompaniments to nearby expensive hotels and restaurants. Their goal is to use the market as a model for a permanent, high-quality, discriminating market, one that would add to the ambiance of the area and boost real estate values as well.

Commercial interests wish us to buy and eat certain foods. Highly refined foods keep better than do natural foods; they are easier to store and ship.
　　　　　　　　—Adele Davis, *Let's Eat Right to Stay Fit* (1954)

Many backyard agricultural activities shriveled in the consumer frenzy of the postwar years, when Mom was recruited out of the war industries and sent to the kitchens and supermarkets to stock up on an ever-exploding market of new processed foods. The space age brought an abundance of new food concepts from corporate America, from the ubiquitous TV dinner to the phosphorescent orange glass of Tang, "the drink of the astronauts." Many even believed that in the future the modern cuisine would consist of a food pill and a glass of water. But a rumbling had begun to be heard in the belly of America.

The beginnings of the great refusal of All-American cuisine lay in the social upheavals of the sixties, in which San Francisco played a major role. Many forces converged to produce this refusal:

(1) The realization dawned that despite our reputation as the wealthiest nation on earth, many of our citizens still went hungry. This was brought to the attention of many by the 1962 publication of Michael Harrington's *The Other America*. America's notorious food-wasting sharply contrasted with the mid-sixties famine in Biafra and other war- and poverty-wracked nations, situations brought into American homes by the mass media.

(2) The revelation that America's food sources were saturated with fungicides, chemical fertilizers, and pesticides provoked widespread fear, particularly after the 1962 publication of Rachel Carson's *The Silent Spring*. Many questioned the basic assumption that science and technology were beneficial to food production, while some were inspired to reevaluate traditional techniques of agricultural production.

(3) The anticolonial awakening of Third World countries and the rise of nationalist consciousness among people of color in the United States created a surge of interest in cuisines from underdeveloped nations, whose foods often have greater nutritional value and better flavor at less cost. Third World staples like beans and rice, curries, tofu, millet, bean sprouts, whole grains, and raw vegetables began to take their place in the kitchens of San Francisco's communes, collectives, and group households. In some of these, chopsticks began to displace the knife and fork as the culinary tool of choice. Added to this consciousness about food consumption was the rediscovery of alternative methods of agriculture, and in particular the nonexploitative and more earth-friendly horticulture of Native American and Asian cultures.

(4) Corporate greed was made all-too-obvious in the struggle between the

field workers who harvest America's food and giant agribusiness corporations like Tenneco and Dow Chemical. The struggle of César Chavez and the United Farmworkers Union in the 1960s to improve basic working conditions in the rich agricultural valleys of California reminded city-dwellers where their food came from. The UFW helped dispel the popular, bucolic myth of the small family farmer and unveiled the grim reality of the factories in the field.

(5) A growing movement for vegetarianism was sparked by new understanding about the sentient nature of animals and by growing concern that eating meat was generally unhealthy. Frances Moore Lappé's *Diet for a Small Planet* (1971) pointed out the link between Western meat-eating and the waste of land and grain associated with it.

These factors helped to forge an implicit unity concerning the politics of food and the right to eat nutritiously at an affordable price. By distributing food for free and by organizing food co-ops, thousands of San Franciscans contributed to building an alternative to white-bread America.

The Diggers

In the mid-sixties, before the hippies came along, the Diggers emerged in the Haight-Ashbury. Inspired by a philosophy of social anarchism and direct action (they took their name from radicals in the English Revolution), the Diggers attempted to create the conditions for a new society by acting out that idealized society. Through their combination of guerrilla theater and political agitation, they sought to create a university of the streets and to erase the boundary between life and art. They creatively attacked the institution of money, opening a series of free stores where you could walk out with whatever you chose. The Diggers were famous for their free-food program, which operated every afternoon in the Golden Gate Park Panhandle. There they erected a giant wooden frame, the Free Frame of Reference, which they placed around their makeshift kitchen, allowing rush-hour commuters to view their art. The Diggers helped feed the thousands of young people who poured into the Haight-Ashbury to make it a central gathering place of America's alienated youth.

The free-food program was dependent on whatever the Diggers could scrounge up to cook. Normally, that meant gleaning old but edible vegetables from the downtown Produce Market (later destroyed by the Golden Gateway redevelopment project) and creating innovative meals from discarded produce. And sometimes wholesalers and businesses would donate their surplus. To a great extent, the Diggers depended on the surplus generated by the booming economy of the mid-sixties. In an era before garage sales, the image of preparing and serving a free meal from the discarded waste of the marketplace set an inspiring example of rejection of the rampant consumerism and wastefulness evident in American life. Recovering wasted produce and buying bulk quantities of dried goods such as rice and beans showed people ways to eat good food on little money. The example of the Diggers encouraged other free-food programs, notably the Black Panther breakfast programs in San Francisco and other cities.

The Digger philosophy gave a radical foundation to the exploding countercultural movement. By then, hundreds of group households, urban communes, and collectives were hip to buying fresh produce from the markets and buying in bulk. Free-meal programs for the swelling thousands of people became increasingly untenable, which led to looking for ways to institutionalize bulk buying. These new ideas took shape in the creation of the San Francisco Food Conspiracy.

The Food Conspiracy

Many houses belong to one of the Food Conspiracies. The conspiracies are groups of people in different neighborhoods who get healthy food for the cheapest prices possible. There are conspiracies all over the city, including ten in the Haight. Each house does some work, and this breaks down the servant-master trip of grocery stores.
—San Francisco Good Times (July 18, 1972)

The San Francisco Food Conspiracy was a loose federation of autonomous buying clubs based either on neighborhood or political affiliations. Household representatives would meet to discuss and take orders on quantities and varieties of produce and bulk items. If there were ten households in the buying group, for example, each household might order ten pounds of brown rice, so an order of a single hundred-pound sack of rice could be placed. Or several households might agree to split a case of bananas. The orders were taken, money exchanged, and then the buying club coordinator placed the order. Volunteers picked up the food and brought it back to a central location in the neighborhood, where members either picked up their order or had it delivered.

There were hundreds of such clubs in San Francisco by the early 1970s, in the Haight-Ashbury, the Western Addition, Noe Valley, and many other neighborhoods. For many conspiracy members, it would be the first time they sampled such fare as brown rice, bulgur, garbanzo beans, tofu, and whole-grain flours. For many others, it marked the discovery of delicious fresh vegetables, in contrast to the canned or frozen ones they had pushed around their plates as children.

The building of food conspiracies were, at their core, political acts. Such conspiratorial activities were often used as ways to organize neighborhoods against price-gouging supermarkets and to raise consciousness about the irrationality of the profit system. The Black Panther Party used their food co-op to agitate for more independent economic activity on the part of the African American community. Food conspiracies grew rapidly all over the United States, and in many cities the range of ordering included nonfood items such as tools, farm equipment, and even tractors.

But the food-buying club model was very time-consuming and depended on volunteer labor. People grew weary of working so much to stock their kitchens. Activists felt that such buying clubs discriminated against full-time workers with kids, who might not have time to go to a buying meeting, run down to the Wholesale Produce Terminal (the edge-of-town replacement for the old downtown Produce Market), or break down food orders. New models for serving people were being looked at and discussed.

The People's Food System

Many of the core members of the local food-buying clubs began to discuss the feasibility of abandoning the food conspiracy model and opening up storefronts instead. These co-op stores first appeared in the mid-seventies and soon sprouted all over town. These included Seeds of Life (Semillas de Vida) on 24th Street, the Rainbow Grocery on 16th Street in the Mission, the Haight Store, and the Good Life Grocery on Potrero Hill. By and large, the stores were run by worker-owned collectives, with workers who rotated jobs within the stores and used some form of profit-sharing for payment. They featured boxes of organic vegetables, wooden bins of bulk beans, grains, and dry goods, large plastic buckets of honeys, oils, and nut butters, and perhaps a section for whole-wheat breads and other baked goods.

The stores provided visibility for the political and social concerns of the collective members and allowed them to earn a living from productive, nonexploitative work. Jobs were offered to people in dire need of employment, such as recently paroled prisoners and refugees from Central America. Although some people were critical of the abandonment of the food conspiracy principle that all must perform work to reap the benefits of cooperative buying, the food stores were successful in spreading the benefits of cheap and healthy eating to poor and working people.

The bulk of these food stores came together to form the People's Food System. A formal network of stores provided economic and logistical advantages as well as greater political influence for activists trying to make the link between radical social change and what people eat. *Turnover*, the magazine of the People's Food System, illustrated the symbiosis of politics and food in its many issues. Issue

20, for example, had articles on food production in Cuba (in English and Spanish), facts behind the fiber fad, information on the Nestlé boycott, and an article on tofu.

With a network of stores, other collectives came into being to support the growing distribution system. People's Bakery and Uprisings Bakery baked the bread, Merry Milk and Red Star Cheese provided the dairy, Veritable Vegetable provided the vegetables, and People's Warehouse handled the central warehousing tasks. The People's Food System, by the late 1970s, was employing hundreds of people, and feeding thousands cheap, nutritious food while promoting the benefits of collective work, not-for-profit economics, and radical social change.

From Patty Hearst to Dan White

Thanks to a series of sometimes horrible events, the politics of food remained a central focus for the Bay Area during the mid-seventies. The Symbionese Liberation Army kidnapped Hearst heiress Patty Hearst and demanded that the Hearsts deliver one million dollars in food to poor people, including those in San Francisco's Fillmore District, in exchange for their kidnapped daughter. Thirty thousand people showed up to collect the food that the Hearsts supplied. Ronald Reagan was incensed: "It's just too bad we can't have an epidemic of botulism. . . . There is a characteristic on the part of the people that they want something for nothing." On the other hand, the SLA complained that "Instead of $70.00 worth of top quality food, the people have gotten $8.00 worth of mediocre food. Instead of fresh meat, half the people received one chicken. Many stood in long, cold lines for only a bag full of cabbages, while others stood in line and got nothing at all." Patty Hearst agreed with her captors: "It sounds like most of the food is of low quality. No one received any beef or lamb, and it certainly didn't sound like the kind of food our family is used to eating."

Another underground guerrilla group, the New World Liberation Front, began a campaign of bombings of Safeway supermarkets, demanding better food at cheaper cost. Doggie Diner, the once ubiquitous hot dog stand (with the large sculpture of a dachshund that appears to be choking to death) was bombed at least once. McDonald's, when it first attempted to raise its golden arches on Haight Street, was picketed for many months, before being firebombed. In the jungles of Guyana, Jim Jones of People's Temple murdered hundreds of his followers with a deadly batch of Kool-Aid. And in the murder trial of Dan White, the assassin of San Francisco Mayor George Moscone and Supervisor Harvey Milk, the jury agreed that Dan had eaten too many Twinkies and drunk too much

Coke, and was therefore not entirely responsible for his murderous actions. The largest riot in San Francisco history followed his slap on the wrist.

Shoot-out at the People's Warehouse

The People's Food System was not just a network of food stores. Its members saw it as an organization dedicated to radical social change, mostly agreeing on the importance of democratic procedure in running a collective organization. The People's Food System also attracted people who were interested in using it for their own ends. One such group was Tribal Thumb, a small collective of people who were connected to an eatery called Wellsprings Reunion, located in the South of Market area. The leader of the group, Earl Satcher, was a saxophone-playing ex-convict whom many people saw as the cult leader of the Wellsprings group. Tribal Thumb and a few allies in Veritable Vegetables were accused of intimidating members and trying to take over the People's Food System. The dispute escalated into threats of violence and led to several secret meetings of the People's Food System to discuss what actions should be taken. An emergency meeting was held on April 26, 1977, at the People's Warehouse space. Called to discuss the expulsion of members deemed disruptive to the organization, the meeting degenerated into a hostile confrontation between opposing sides. Tribal Thumb members and their allies (including two Dobermans) were in the parking lot, reportedly intimidating and threatening Food System representatives against voting for the expulsion of disruptive members. During the break, gunfire broke out in the parking lot, leaving ex–San Quentin 6 member Willie Tate critically wounded. Tribal Thumb leader Earl Satcher was shot dead. Although the shock of the gunfight soon wore off, the Food System began to succumb to larger changes.

The Inner Sunset Collective during their grand opening in 1975

By the end of the 1970s, a distinct change could be discerned in the super-markets and groceries of the Bay Area. Items formerly found only in co-ops or health food stores were appearing on the shelves. Large numbers of people sought out healthy alternatives to the plastic American food fare as whole foods entered the mainstream. Cheez Whiz and Tang made way for rennetless, low-fat cheddar and organic apple cider. Reaganism and a resurgent right wing prompted many of the workers in the Food System to put their political energies elsewhere, such as in the growing antinuclear movement and in Central America solidarity work. Long hours for low pay also began to take their toll on Food System members. Most stores quietly disappeared, although a few hung on for quite a while. Today, the glowing exception to the demise of the People's Food System is the newly expanded Rainbow Grocery on Folsom Street.

Let Them Eat Organic, Sprouted, Whole Wheat Baguettes!

When pesticides get banned we're safe up north,
we just sell them to those other countries,
soon there's lots of exotic deformed babies,
somehow that's not our fault.

—"A Growing Boy Needs His Lunch," sung by Jello Biafra, The Dead Kennedy's lead singer, who ran for Mayor of San Francisco with the slogan "There's always room for Jello!"

A generation of people have grown up taking for granted gastronomical phenom-enon such as organic vegetables, tofu, soy milk, granola, and the panoply of whole foods. Vegetarianism and macrobiotics, not long ago considered bizarre and extreme to most Americans, are now run-of-the-mill. You can ask for a vegetari-an meal on an airline without batting an eye. Many Chinese restaurants have abandoned monosodium glutamate (MSG). Mexican restaurants offer whole-wheat and spinach tortillas with tofu and vegetable fillings. Candlestick Park (now corporate-sponsored 3Com Park) offers tofu dogs to sports fans. Not even in their wildest dreams could the whole-foods pioneers of the 1960s have imag-ined the success of their proselytizing. California cuisine, the breakaway diet of health-conscious yuppies (who have the disposable income for high-end designer foods) owes its existence to the food consciousness of the 1960s. So, too, do the brave souls of Food Not Bombs, who keep the Digger ethic alive by ladling out hot soup to the homeless, despite police harassment. Even the popularity of super-store warehouse buying owes much to the example of bulk buying set by food co-ops. Farmer's markets in San Francisco are more popular than ever, not only with health-conscious produce consumers but also with immigrants from Southeast Asia and Latin America, where open-air markets are a way of life.

Rainbow Grocery, one of the last remnants of the original People's Food System, in its new digs at 13th and Folsom Streets

Still, as we approach the end of the century, the quality and affordability of food is as much an issue for most people as it was one hundred years ago. The gap between rich and poor has widened considerably, so healthy food, like so much else necessary to a good life, remains out of reach for many. Many co-ops and health food establishments have lost sight of the original goal of keeping nutritious food affordable, concentrating somewhat lopsidedly on stocking expensive and exotic health food items.

New kinds of disasters arise as food production becomes increasingly global, regulations are weakened, and corporations cut corners to harvest greater profits. To make food more durable and transportable, manufacturers want to submit food to nuclear irradiation, despite the health concerns of many. The dairy industry wants farmers to use rBST, the bovine milk stimulant, to squeeze more milk from the dairy herd. Victorious in winning American acceptance of the pink, juiceless, plastic tomato, agribusiness continues its crusade to make vegetables and fruit even more tasteless but easier to transport. The spread of mad cow disease in Europe and repeated instances of E. coli contamination in the United States remind us that the politics of food is far from over.

San Francisco takes its food seriously. After all, this is the city that has more restaurants per capita than any other in the United States. In the quest for nutritious food and equitable distribution, thousands of San Franciscans have mobilized to develop creative and alternative ways of procuring this most basic human need. As the century ends, San Franciscans show no sign of letting up in the battle against corporate cuisine. New efforts to shorten the distance between farm and city are under way. Community-sponsored agriculture, whereby small organic farmers sell shares of their farms in exchange for a share of the annual harvest, are increasingly popular. Urban gardens bloom in every neighborhood and in many schoolyards, where teachers try to stress the importance of both nutrition and respect for the land. San Francisco shows no sign of relinquishing its reputation as a city with an appetite for social change and a hunger for a wholesome and ecologically sound diet.

Food Not Bombs serves free vegetarian fare in the Civic Center and has endured several hundred arrests during the past decade for allegedly lacking the necessary permits.

Seeing the Trees Through the Forest
Oaks and History in the Presidio

by Pete Holloran

HERE IN AN ANONYMOUS CORNER of the Presidio of San Francisco a forgotten cemetery lies buried beneath the sand. No signs memorialize the dead. The most obvious evidence of past human occupation are the discarded bricks and twisted metal that mark this as one of the Presidio's many landfills. As gophers and wind redistribute the sand across the surface of the landfill, fast-growing native plants colonize the open sand.

In the mid-1880s the Marine Hospital began using the sand dunes behind its building as a cemetery to bury seamen who had died at the hospital. By 1896, more than two hundred sailors had been buried beneath "hummocks of half-tamed sand dunes." The sandy graves were marked with slight wooden crosses and covered with native dune wildflowers, including California poppies and baby blue eyes. (Maniery 1994)

By 1912, the cemetery was no longer in active use, though the headstones remained. For the next few decades its history is obscured. By the mid-1950s, though, the Army began dumping construction debris on top of the cemetery without removing all the bodies. Bulldozers later covered the debris with sand, which was eventually colonized by a few species of native wildflowers.

Who is responsible for protecting this complex landscape? Since 1994, when the Army transferred the Presidio to the National Park Service, this little patch of sand, brick, and bones has become contested terrain. According to park guidelines, there are two kinds of protected resources: natural resources and cultural resources. The park's resource management staff is divided along the same fault line into different divisions. As our understanding of the land improves, though, this division of the world into nature and culture is becoming obsolete.

The air above the landfill always vibrates with hummingbirds. Their green irides-cent feathers flash in the sunlight; the scolding is incessant. I'm accustomed to hearing their constant chatter in my backyard far from any natural area, but I sel-dom catch more than a fleeting glimpse. Here I can watch them speed about in pursuit of nectar and partners. I once saw one chase away a red-tailed hawk many times its size.

Not far from the edge of the landfill are a few precious coast live oaks, potent symbols of life and renewal. When the winter rains come, new leaves emerge and catkins release their pollen to the wind. Later, as spring nears, endosperm fills the bulging acorns. The hummingbirds come then too and engage in dazzling courtship displays, building nests in the oaks as early as February.

To the indigenous peoples of the San Francisco peninsula, the coast live oak was more than a symbol; it was perhaps the single most important plant species. They ate acorns, created bowls and utensils from the wood, and started fires with the bark and wood. Medicinal remedies were prepared from oak bark and leaves. (Bocek 1984)

Countless other organisms are equally dependent on coast live oak wood-lands, which harbor more wildlife than any other terrestrial plant community in this region. Coast live oaks are host to many species of small moths, for example. (De Benedictis et al. 1990) These moths and other invertebrates found on the tree feed a wide variety of birds, including Hutton's vireo, which is so dependent on the oak that it has been described as "the spirit of the live oak tree." (Davis 1995) This songbird about the size of your palm—not much bigger than a hummingbird—flits methodically around the oak canopy snapping up caterpillars, weevils, and count-less other insects. Its hanging nests, woven from lichens, leaves, and strips of bark and held together with spider silk, can be found in the Presidio's oak woodlands. But vireo numbers have dramatically declined throughout San Francisco and the Bay Area as oak woodlands have been destroyed by development.

This decline may have begun as early as the late eighteenth century when the first Europeans arrived and began cutting Presidio woodlands to supply fire-wood for a growing population. To them, the oaks were almost an afterthought. On a spring day in 1776 one of the first Europeans to see this land worried more about the lack of tall trees for timber. "There is not a tree on all those hills," Father Pedro Font wrote, "though the oaks and other trees along the road are not very far away." (Bolton 1931) Like the California Indians they displaced, the Spanish and *mestizo* (people of mixed Spanish/Indian descent from Mexico) sol-diers depended on the surrounding land for food, clean water, and shelter. They brought cattle to graze the grasslands, cleared other areas for vegetable gardens,

PHOTO COURTESY GREG GAAR COLLECTION

Presidio and Golden Gate (c. 1870s). Crissy Field wetlands are visible on the bayshore.

and harvested firewood from the oak groves.

By the time the U.S. Army took over the Presidio in 1846, the landscape had been so altered that few trees remained. With the ability to resprout vigorously, oaks had survived periodic fires and occasional wood harvesting by California Indians, but the garrison's growing needs eventually depleted the woodlands. "In providing fuel for the use of troops," one resident wrote in 1859, "the thickets of scrub oaks in the [Presidio] Reserve [have] been destroyed." He added that "there is scarcely a tree left for ornament or use." The troops had to switch to coal for cooking and heating. (Thompson n.d.)

An oak branch carved into the shape of a bowl is a cultural resource; the tree it came from and all its progeny are natural resources. To some cultural resource advocates, the importance of these oaks to indigenous people becomes significant only when artifacts are involved. Others feel that coast live oaks should be honored in all their complexity and not just when they become utensils.

To many, the Presidio's oak groves are cause for hope, but as Francis Bacon reminded us, hope is a good breakfast but a poor supper. Waiting for hope's harvest is a good way to go hungry. The oak grove evokes decades of failed harvests, a visible reminder of what has been lost, of tragedies whose scars are still visible on the land. To this urban dweller teetering here at the end of the twentieth century and its ecological catastrophes, coast live oaks are powerful indigenous symbols of hope and history—of culture and nature. But their native land is divided.

Seeing the Trees Through the Forest   335

As natural resources in a national park, mature oaks are protected; their future is more or less secure. But what of the acorns that find themselves just beyond an area designated as "natural"? Will they find a place to put down roots and raise a family of hummingbirds? Within the confines of this national park, not all oak seedlings are welcome.

The Presidio faces many pressures as part of the most visited national park in the country, including congressional demands that it become self-sufficient within fifteen years or be sold. (Holloran 1996) The fate of its buildings are hotly contested. From an oak's point of view, though, the most important debate is over the future of the 780 acres of open space.

Of these 780 acres, the park has designated only 145 acres as protected natural areas; an additional 100 acres may be available for eventual restoration. The rest are "cultural landscapes." These landscapes include parade grounds, ballfields, an airfield, a golf course, and more than 300 acres of trees planted by the Army. Because of their age, most of these features are considered protected cultural resources.

But what happens when there is a conflict between the conservation of natural and cultural resources? As defined by the National Park Service, cultural landscapes are nearly always the victor. The hegemony of cultural landscapes begins with their very definition: any evidence of "the interaction of people and place over time" can become part of the cultural landscape. Its components can include "topography, vegetation, structures, circulation networks, land-use patterns, building clusters, and small-scale features such as signs and flagpoles." (Golden Gate National Recreation Area 1994) So defined, natural processes become just another layer on a landscape defined by its human characteristics; nature is subsumed by culture.

As we imagine the future of the Presidio landscape, are we compelled to repeat the errors of the Army and other residents simply because those errors were committed in the "historic" past, i.e., more than fifty years ago? If the Army filled a tidal marsh wetland to build an airfield, should we restore the historic wetland or rebuild the historic airfield? If the Army dumped toxic material into a landfill, should it be removed or left in the environment as evidence of the Army's construction practices? If the Army planted thousands of trees among the dunes and grasslands, should we restore the indigenous native plant communities or the historic plantings, when the trees begin to die?

The park finds itself in such odd situations because of its attempt to impose fixed temporal boundaries on landscapes, which by their very nature change over time. It is impossible to arrest the evolution of a landscape. It is also impossible to restore landscape features to a particular moment in time; the replica will always be different, a creature of its creators and a captive of its past. As one historian said of a mountain range in Oregon, "No one can restore the Blues back to their original state; however, we can restore the Blues back to an inevitably altered, but not inevitably impoverished, biota—by giving up our ideals of maximum efficiency and commodity production, and substituting other ideals which allow for complexity, diversity, and uncertainty." (Langston 1995)

The historic ideals that transformed the Presidio landscape also need to be updated, just as other military values have been modified (ending racial segregation and the all-male military are two obvious examples of changing military values). The complex Presidio landscapes will be revealed best by an approach that values diversity over narrow interpretations of history. By treating the Presidio primarily as a cultural landscape, we privilege the victor's version of history: a civilizing force tamed the wild landscape. This interpretative framework is no longer in favor in most disciplines, but its legacy remains apparent in park publications about the Presidio's natural landscape.

Consider a different narrative of the Presidio's history. A few remnant natural areas, including several oak groves, withstood the massive disturbance of more than two centuries of continuous military occupation. Native plant communities survived twenty decades of live-ammunition drills, grazing, and firewood cutting, but not without some losses. At least eighty-four native plant species, for example, have been eliminated from the Presidio, nearly a quarter of its original species diversity. Some conservation biologists predict further losses since only a tenth of the Presidio's area is set aside as protected natural areas. According to a famous model of biogeography, a ninety-percent reduction in area leads to a fifty-percent decline in species diversity. If this model holds true for the Presidio, an additional eighty locally uncommon species—an additional quarter—may be lost in the future if its natural areas are not reconnected and expanded. (Vasey 1997)

Most readers are familiar with these two types of stories about the transformation of natural landscapes by their human inhabitants. In the archetypal version of these narratives of decline, the fall from original grace was precipitated by the bite of an apple, not the felling of an oak. But by focusing on discontinuities— the disappearance of pristine Nature and its transformation into an ordered human landscape—we misunderstand the dynamic nature of human history and biological systems. (Cronon 1995) Different cultures have occupied this corner of the San Francisco peninsula, and created a succession of landscapes, each dependent on the previous for its fundamental components. (Flores 1994) Where is nature then? It is all around; the landscapes are saturated with it. The boundaries between nature and culture are as gray as summer fog.

The Presidio's western cliffs have a timeless quality about them. They appear unmoved by the ocean crashing around them. Geological time is quite different from ours; in a staring match, humans blink before rocks do. Ten thousand years ago, a wink to a rock but an eternity to humans, the cliffs were more than thirty miles from the ocean. Sea level was approximately 100 meters below its present level. At the time of the last glacial maximum, the Sacramento–San Joaquin River flowed through the Golden Gate and emptied into the ocean beyond the Farallones. The land was probably covered with massive sand dunes far more extensive than the enormous dunes that so impressed early visitors. San Francisco Bay was not a bay but a complex of river valleys. (Atwater et al. 1977; Wells 1995)

As the climate warmed, sea level rose at a fairly rapid rate for several thousand years. Around eight thousand years ago, San Francisco Bay was reborn— these drastic sea-level changes have flooded the region at least four times, each time recreating the bay. Tidal marshes developed along its fringes, including the northern edge of the Presidio. These marshes, among the most productive ecosystems in California, nourished vast numbers of wildlife. Invertebrates fed in the mudflats and marshes, sharks and fish gobbled up invertebrates, birds feasted on both. There was room in the food web for grizzly bears and wolves. In the marshes farther southeast in what is now Montgomery Street downtown, an early resident of San Francisco would "watch bears, wolves and coyotes quarreling over their prey." (Richardson n.d.) Other early visitors were astonished by the flocks of birds that settled into the marshes, so numerous that they darkened the sky as they landed.

The most abundant evidence of human habitation on the Presidio, not surprisingly, is from the tidal marshes along the bayshore. Midden sites there date from more than a thousand years ago; earlier evidence of human habitation of the Presidio may have been inundated by the rising sea. The bones reveal that the local inhabitants used numerous birds and mammals as well as nearly thirty fish and shark species.

The indigenous inhabitants of San Francisco used more than 150 different plant species in addition to dozens of animal species to provide for their needs. (Bocek 1984) Thoughtful management by the Yelamu* helped foster the abundant

---

* The descendants of the indigenous people of the Bay Area call themselves Ohlone, and their preference should be paramount. Following the careful scholarship of Randall Milliken, I use Yelamu here to refer to the approximately 160 people who inhabited several villages in the area now known as San Francisco. (Milliken 1995) They shared many close linguistic and cultural affinities with other indigenous peoples around San Francisco Bay, the Santa Cruz peninsula, and Monterey Bay. I use the term Ohlone when referring to this larger cultural and linguistic group.

Soldiers carry out artillery maneuvers on eastern edge of today's Crissy Field (c. 1876).

and diverse native plant communities on which they depended. Willows, for example, needed pruning to encourage the straight young poles preferred by basketweavers. Fire was perhaps their most potent management tool, as it prevented shrub encroachment on grasslands rich in edible bulbs and kept the landscape open for deer. (Anderson 1993) One visitor recorded fires while camping near Mission Dolores in late October 1816. "All night," he wrote, "great fires burned on the land at the back of the harbor; the natives are in the habit of burning the grass, to further its growth." (Chamisso 1936)

Centuries of such management had a dramatic effect on the landscape, but the changes were not immediately apparent to the Europeans who first visited Yelamu territory. The bounty of this managed landscape was currency in the first recorded exchange of gifts between the Spanish visitors and the Yelamu. On a March day in 1776 two Yelamu men visited the Spanish camp at Mountain Lake and brought firewood, probably harvested from live oaks. (Bolton 1931)

A few days later, when Juan Agustín Bautista de Anza selected a site for the future presidio, or fort, he chose an open mesa with dramatic views in all directions. He was witnessing an inhabited landscape, kept open by the Yelamu to meet their need for diverse natural products. Without their fires, the flower-studded grasslands noted by Anza and his associates probably would have reverted to dense maritime chaparral dominated by ceanothus, blackberry, and poison oak.

Several centuries without fire have enabled these scrub species to dominate the western bluffs of the Presidio, but when Father Pedro Font walked around the area with Anza during the spring of 1776, he recorded a "very open" mesa studded with "an abundance of wild violets." Font had marveled at the plentiful wildflowers near his campsite on the shore of Mountain Lake. "There are yerba buena and so many lilies," he wrote, "that I had them almost inside my tent." (Bolton 1931)

This mesa of superlatives was the result of centuries of interaction between powerful natural and cultural processes. The deer and elk, the wind and fog, the willow pruning and fire starting—all had contributed to the "very green and flower-covered" mesa encountered by Font. (Bolton 1931) The panoramic views that Font considered so breathtaking are now blocked by buildings and trees.

A few months after Font and Anza departed, two Franciscan priests arrived in San Francisco to establish a mission and presidio. They traveled with a group of fourteen soldiers, seven settlers, an unknown number of women and children, and thirteen young Indian servants, including a California Indian from Monterey who spoke a language similar to the local people's. (Milliken 1995) Traditional narratives of the Presidio glide over the cultural complexity of this moment of contact between peoples. According to the standard narrative, the sprawling Spanish empire engulfed all in its path, transforming the land and eliminating its native peoples forever; there is little evidence of indigenous people but graves, place names, and a few survivors.

Recent scholarship, in contrast, has emphasized the complexity of this period, "the time of little choice" for the indigenous people. The Spanish were actually in the minority, accompanied by *mestizo* and *criollo* (people of Spanish heritage born in Mexico) soldiers and settlers and indigenous Americans from other parts of Alta and Baja California. Even the pottery they brought with them displayed evidence of two centuries of cultural evolution in the Americas. (Department of the Army et al. 1996)

At first the Yelamu welcomed the newcomers with gifts gathered from the landscape. "They continued to visit us frequently," Father Francisco Palóu wrote of these early days, "bringing us presents of small value, principally shellfish and grass seeds." (Milliken 1995) It wasn't long, though, before the Yelamu did not conform to Spanish expectations for a conquered people. Less than six months after Palóu arrived in Yelamu territory, the hostilities began. All the eyewitness accounts of this time, though, were written by the ultimate victors, in this case Father Palóu:

> In the last visits which they made in early December they began to disgrace themselves, now by thefts, now by firing an arrow close to the corporal of the guard,

and again by trying to kiss the wife of a soldier, as well as by threatening to fire an arrow at the neophyte from the mission of Carmelo who was at this mission.

A few days later Spanish soldiers sought out and killed one of the Yelamu men who had threatened to fire an arrow. (Milliken 1995) Within just six months the visitors had demonstrated their superior firepower, and that they would use it in ways quite out of proportion to the original perceived offense.

To Yelamu youth, the material goods and military prowess of the Spanish must have been exciting and worthy of close study. Curious young men were among the first to embrace some aspects of mission culture. Almost exactly a year after the Franciscans arrived, they baptized three young men, including twenty-year-old Chamis, who, like the other two, had lost his father years before. Ten months later Chamis married the fourteen-year-old Paszém in the first Christian marriage ritual to take place in the Bay Area. (Milliken 1995) These details are important because the Yelamu and other California Indians of the period finally have names and lives of their own—fathers, mothers, birthplaces, tribal affinities, weddings, births, and deaths. Palóu, Font, and other Spanish chroniclers are well known, but Randall Milliken's careful work with mission records provides important context for understanding this time of initial contact between cultures and the tremendous social upheaval that followed. (Milliken 1995)

Within a few years, social relations had become quite complex among the Spanish fathers, *mestizo* soldiers and settlers, Baja Californians, recently converted Christian Indians, and those who remained outside the mission system. Some settlers coerced indigenous people into providing free labor. The mission fathers

PHOTO COURTESY GREG GAAR COLLECTION

Crissy Field wetlands (c. 1890s)

and soldiers would occasionally protect the local villagers from such depredations; at other times they would sponsor the coercion themselves. The development of an incipient agricultural economy was at the root of most conflict. Cattle owned by settlers would eat crops planted by Indians; cattle owned by Indians would trample fields planted by other Indians. But in perhaps the greatest transformation of the local food economy, the settlers' cattle and row-crop agriculture had appropriated the land that had produced the huge variety of native plants on which the indigenous people had depended. In 1782, for example, less than six years after the Santa Clara mission was established, there were reports that cattle had dramatically altered the landscape:

> They will have to rely for their food on the herbs and acorns they pick in the woods—just as they used to do before we came. This source of food supply, we might add, is now scarcer than it used to be, owing to the cattle; and many a time the pagans living in the direction of the pueblo have complained to us about it. (Milliken 1995)

The complex interaction between nature and culture that had shaped the northern San Francisco landscape for at least a thousand years—and probably much longer—had been completely transformed in less than a decade.

To the Yelamu, the landscape of the northern edge of the San Francisco peninsula was a storehouse of natural products; to the Spanish and later occupants, the Presidio's landscape was a barren, harsh place. "The view of the Bay is fine from the high hills," remarked one visitor during the mid-nineteenth century, "but every thing looks dirty and sandy; you cannot [avoid] the impression that it is a mean country." (Thompson n.d.)

It depends on your perspective, though. Early residents of San Francisco viewed the Presidio in a very different light. In May 1850 an *Alta California* reporter wrote a glowing report of the spring wildflowers: "The surface of the hills present at the present time a most refreshing appearance, covered with verdure and brilliant with the various tints of the wild flowers, with which they are studded in all directions." By the late 1860s and early 1870s the Presidio grounds were so attractive to outsiders that a movement developed among San Francisco residents to acquire the Presidio for public use, either as a park or for development. (Thompson n.d.) In 1870, for example, the Board of Supervisors unanimously passed a resolution asking Congress to allow the city to use the land as a park. "It is claimed," one reporter wrote, "that this tract is the most attractive spot for a park on the peninsula, and that much of the land is well-watered and susceptible to cultivation." (Carter 1871)

Rebuffed by Congress, the city decided that a thousand acres of western sand dunes should be transformed into the city's main park. A young surveyor then working for the Army stepped in as Golden Gate Park's first superintendent. By 1874, four years after becoming superintendent, William Hammond Hall and his workers had planted nearly 60,000 trees and shrubs in the sand dunes and grasslands of the park and its eastern extension, the Panhandle. (Clary 1980)

By the early 1880s there was considerable interest in landscaping the Presidio using similar techniques. In March 1883 Major W. A. Jones proposed a massive tree planting program in his "Plan for the Cultivation of Trees Upon the Presidio Reservation." Major Jones began with an appeal to the example of the "successful operation at the Golden Gate Park of San Francisco" as a model tree nursery operation. (Jones 1883)

Much of the appeal of the Presidio landscape, Jones realized, was due to its proximity to "a great and growing city." San Francisco would watch very closely what the Army did to the landscape. "The eyes of people of culture are upon us," he warned, and "if it be worth while to plant trees on the Reservation at all, they should be planted effectively, and not dumped into the ground by the thousand, at random." (Jones 1883)

Like many of his contemporaries, Major Jones did not place much value on the indigenous landscape. The sand dunes and dusty grasslands that turned brown every summer may have appeared glorious to wandering reporters in May, but they did not conform to others' expectations of what park lands should look like. The tidal marshes that played such a central role in the Yelamu economy seemed waste-lands to Jones and the residents of late-nineteenth-century San Francisco. "The main idea," Jones wrote, "is to crown the ridges, border the boundary fences, and cover the areas of sand and marsh waste with a forest that will generally seem con-tinuous, and thus appear immensely larger than it really is." This well-ordered human landscape would accentuate the difference between post and city. "In order to make the contrast from the city seem as great as possible, and indirectly accen-tuate the idea of the power of the Government," he wrote, "I have surrounded all the entrances with dense masses of wood." (Jones 1883) To Jones, the planted for-est's appearance was paramount. He recognized the scenic importance of Presidio vistas and planned to leave the valleys unchanged and the views from grassy sum-mits such as Inspiration Point unobstructed.

Three years later, after Jones had been transferred from the Presidio, the first mass tree planting took place on the first celebration of Arbor Day in California. Adolph Sutro, who had paid hundreds of unemployed workers to plant trees over large portions of San Francisco, donated 3,000 trees to the post. By 1892, six years later, Army officials would boast that 329,975 trees had been planted to date—the first major landscaping effort ever undertaken by the Army. (Thompson n.d.) Major Jones's warning regarding planting thousands of trees at random went largely unheeded.

Several critics were quick to raise objections to this massive tree planting effort. In 1892 post commander Colonel William Montrose Graham derided the tree planting for taking up 400 acres that could be used for training exercises. In language eerily prescient of present-day issues regarding public parks, Graham also objected to "the dense thickets that are being formed, which makes shelters and secure hiding places for the tramps that infest the reservation." (Thompson n.d.) A few years later Colonel Graham raised strenuous objections to additional tree plantings. He stridently opposed a plan to plant 60,000 Monterey pines in 40 acres along the southwest border because the growing garrison would eventually require those lands for training purposes. "It is urgently recommended," he wrote in one scathing letter, "that the planting of more trees be prohibited by the proper military authorities." He was overruled and the massive plantings proceeded. (Thompson n.d.)

Presidio neighbors objected to the fast-growing eucalyptus trees that blocked their views. They did not appreciate the Army's desire to accentuate the boundary between post and city. "The Government made a mistake when it planted eucalyptus trees along the southern boundary of the Presidio reservation," a journalist reported in the April 1895 of the *San Francisco Real Estate Circular*. "In spite of protests from property-owners," the Army insisted on keeping what the reporter called "an eyesore and interceptors of the finest view in the country."

By 1901 the Army realized that it needed to develop "a systematic and permanent plan of improvement" for the Presidio landscape rather than the haphazard approach that had characterized previous efforts. The Army asked for expert advice from the U.S. Forest Service, then in its early years. The forester found that the 420 acres of plantings were too crowded and required extensive thinning. The Army agreed that plantings had been carried out without a plan in the past and announced their intention to manage the forest more intensively. (Thompson n.d.)

In 1902 Jones himself commented on how the tree plantings had developed in the nearly twenty years since he wrote his proposal. The architect of the Presidio forest recommended extensive tree removal to allow "the handsomest specimens a good chance to develop and also to make room for trees of different form and shades of foliage." He had developed an appreciation for the scenic and natural beauty of the Presidio and recommended removing trees in some areas to plant lupines and other wildflowers. In a striking admission, he suggested that the Army should "leave the sand dune just as it is." (Thompson n.d.)

Despite many initiatives and plans by various Army officers, the Presidio forest developed haphazardly and without an overall design. Various advisers had recommended removal of thousands of trees, but only a fraction had been thinned. However it developed, though, the Presidio forest had become a dominant feature of the Presidio landscape. To many, the mature tree plantings had considerable aesthetic and scenic value. In 1970, when the Army removed 340 trees for new construction, protests by neighbors reached the newspapers. Civic groups took pride in the trees and sponsored additional tree plantings over the years. In 1972, for example, the Boy Scouts planted 1,200 trees; when these died, they planted 250 more. (Thompson n.d.)

Others have explicitly rejected such tree plantings as intrusive and unnecessary. To plant a tree can be an exemplary act, but planting the wrong tree in the wrong place can have disastrous consequences. The famous photographer Ansel Adams grew up along the southern border of the Presidio and cherished the coast live oaks along Lobos Creek. As a child he "explored every foot," he later remembered, and cherished the "rampant and fragrant" spring wildflowers. In 1910, an eight-year-old Adams was devastated by the "ruthless damage" caused when "the Army Corps of Engineers, for unimaginable reasons, decided to clear out the [coast live] oaks and brush." (Adams et al. 1985) Decades later, Adams railed against tree plantings in the nearby Marin Headlands by Boy Scouts. "I cannot think of a more tasteless undertaking than to plant trees in a naturally treeless area, and to impose an interpretation of natural beauty on a great landscape that is charged with beauty and wonder, and the excellence of eternity." (Williams 1991)

Attitudes about the Presidio's indigenous landscape have changed over the years. For several thousand years indigenous peoples depended on the landscape for all their needs and managed it for diversity. For a hundred years—a relatively short time—another attitude held sway. According to this view, the barren landscape required radical transformation; the wastes were to be cloaked in evergreen trees. Cultural attitudes toward the land have evolved, though, and for many visitors biological diversity is once again a paramount value.

Tree plantings may have suited human needs for a few decades, but they exacted a terrible price on biological diversity. To the Xerces blue butterfly (*Glaucopsyche xerces*), the trees became their coffin in the first documented extinction of a butterfly in North America. The demise of the Xerces blue began during the rapid growth of San Francisco in the 1860s and 1870s as its sand dune habitat was converted to housing and farms. As early as 1875 Hans Behr, a local entomologist and early member of the California Academy of Sciences, was predicting its demise. "*Glaucopsyche xerces* is now extinct," he told a friend. "The locality where it

588

Lobos Creek (right) and the sand-filled valley that was the last home to the Xerces blue butterfly (*Glaucopsyche xerces*) before its extinction in the 1940s (photo looking east, c. 1900)

used to be found is converted to building lots, and between German chickens and Irish hogs no insect can exist besides louse and flea." (Pyle et al. 1981) By the time of his death in 1904, though, naturalists had rediscovered the butterfly on the Presidio in the sand dunes north of Lobos Creek. But its habitat was drastically reduced by the growth of Monterey pine and cypress trees planted by the Army; it was last seen in the early 1940s.

Some biologists bristle when the Presidio's tree plantations are referred to as a forest. To them, forests are natural ecosystems that harbor tremendous biological diversity. At the Presidio, it's true that the understory does not harbor much diversity. As the trees grew, native plant communities with more than a hundred species were replaced by a single-species canopy under which only a few weedy species could survive. The tree plantings also expanded beyond their original boundaries; eucalyptus and pine trees produced thousands of saplings that made further incursions into neighboring native plant communities. As they aged, the plantings acquired slightly more complexity and became habitat for several bird species, including nesting red-tailed and red-shouldered hawks. Overall diversity, though, is much lower than in native plant communities, particularly coast live oak woodlands.

By 1994, when the post became a national park, the Presidio forest was a wreck. Huge patches of invasive weeds choked the understory and thousands of old and weakened trees had become hazards. Winter storms in December 1995 sent hundreds of trees crashing to the ground. The park was closed for several days as emergency crews repaired damage to infrastructure and buildings that may have exceeded several million dollars. Deferred maintenance and haphazard planting had contributed to a forest that was on the edge of collapse.

A series of forest management plans—four since 1980, and another in the works as I write—have attempted to address the forest's problems. In recent plans, the park considers the forest first and foremost as a significant cultural resource worthy of restoration. In a recent study, the park identified the tree plantings as a "contributing" resource to the former post's status as a National Historic Landmark—along with 477 buildings, 11 sites, 166 structures, and 8 objects. (GGNRA 1993) The authors concluded that "the afforestation of the Presidio . . . ranks as a monumental undertaking and as one of the Army's most impressive accomplishments in the area of landscape planning. The Presidio clearly stands apart from all other military installations in the nation as a pioneer in landscape architecture on a massive scale." Whether you consider the tree plantings impressive or not, there are problems in determining their significance. After all, as the authors of a Presidio history suggested in their epigraph, "Significance, like beauty, is in the eye of the beholder." (Thompson et al. 1992)

The park decided that the Presidio's "period of significant historical development" covered the years from 1776 to 1945. "Contributing resources in the district," they concluded, "therefore are comprised of all buildings, structures, objects, and other landscape features that possess historical integrity reflecting their character during one or more of these periods." (GGNRA 1993) With a few strokes of the word processor, they established the hegemony of a particular interpretation of history. The natural and cultural landscapes of other organisms— native flora and fauna, the Yelamu—are allowed to remain, but only where military history has not deposited its detritus. To the winner go the spoils; this fascination with artifact privileges the landscape created by those with the most grandiose plans of domination and power.

For the moment, let's agree with the park service that the hundreds of acres of tree plantings are historically significant and illustrate the evolution of cultural values. As with any project involving a cultural landscape, the next stage is the most critical: what sort of treatment does this particular cultural landscape deserve?

In its previous forest management plans, the park has advocated replanting the Presidio forest as the trees grow old. An aerial photograph of the forest from the 1930s would guide the restoration effort. This privileged document would determine future land-use decisions—where trees would be replanted and where native vegetation would be restored. The complex landscape would become fixed in time, its spatial outlines determined forever by a snapshot of how the landscape looked at an arbitrary point in time.

National guidelines for historic preservation, though, suggest that this treatment is not entirely justified. They set forth several conditions for restoration: "when the property's . . . historical significance during a particular time outweighs the potential loss of extant materials, features, spaces, and finishes that characterize other historical periods; when there is substantial physical and documentary evidence for the work; and when contemporary alterations and additions are not planned." (Department of the Interior 1992) None of these conditions appears to be met. The problem is not so much with the idea of cultural landscapes, but with its rigid application to the evolution of the Presidio landscape.

Conflicts between advocates for natural and cultural resources occasionally arise in other parks, acknowledges Nora Mitchell, director of the park service's Olmsted Center for Landscape Preservation. Mitchell attempts to find a compromise, emphasizing that landscapes themselves are dynamic. A park's mission, she argues, is to retain—but not replicate in detail—the distinctive features of landscapes. The analysis of historic landscapes and their significance is an important endeavor, but those findings should inform decisions rather than provide a straitjacket. At a recent talk, a park superintendent asked Mitchell if landscape preservation necessitates repeating the mistakes of the past. In her diplomatic answer she said that the best information about the past doesn't necessarily tell you what actions make sense for the future. Her motto could be summed up as "respect for the past, flexibility for the future." (Mitchell 1997)

Others in the field have come to the same conclusion. An author of an article on the treatment of historic plant material acknowledged that while we should "strive to retain extant historic plant material as a record of our past and replace missing features in-kind, there may be times when the particular conditions of a historic landscape or specific historic plant may warrant an alternative solution." (Meier 1992) What sort of alternatives exist for the future of the Presidio forest?

Diversity should be the paramount value—not the historic legacy of domination. The biological diversity of the Presidio would be enhanced by reconnecting fragmented natural areas and expanding rare plant habitat where feasible. Decades of change have made some areas less amenable to native plant restoration. Large areas along the ridges—probably several hundred acres in extent—would be prime candidates for forest restoration. A variety of evergreen tree

View of the Presidio and the Golden Gate (1920s)

species, including coast live oaks and other natives, should be planted instead of the narrow range of species now found in the forest. This general approach is more rational than accepting as gospel the haphazard planting scheme that was carried out in fits and starts up to the 1930s. With diversity in mind rather than an aerial photograph at hand, all the present-day values of the Presidio forest would be retained and enhanced. It would provide better habitat, more recreational opportunities, and additional scenic and aesthetic features.

Some challenge such proposals to restore the Presidio forest as ahistorical, but it is no more anachronistic than other examples where changing values have forced us to make changes. We do not honor landfills; we remove them. We do not valorize genocide; we need to talk about the lingering effects of the U.S. military on the indigenous peoples of California, the Philippines, and other lands where soldiers from the Presidio have fought. We provide acres of parking lots and a few square feet for bikes, although these innovations weren't necessary until the nonhistoric, postwar period.

The central paradox of the Presidio is its transformation from military post to national park, from a culture of domination to a landscape of freedom. There is a glaring need for park service publications to be more honest about the Army's legacy. While writing several interpretative pieces for the park as a volunteer, I was admonished to avoid any comments about the Army that could be perceived as negative. It is dishonest, though, to be silent about the Army's complex impacts on the land and its people. The Army was not an exemplary steward of the Presidio landscape. Just last month, after spending tens of millions to investigate its own toxic landfills, they recommended spending just $1.5 million on toxic cleanup—and $34.5 million to monitor the contamination they had left behind. It is true that the Presidio has become an important refuge for biodiversity, but this is due to the Army's neglect rather than any environmental program. Indeed, its active environmental program—a massive tree planting effort—contributed to the widespread decline of biodiversity.

The interaction of nature and culture on this corner of the San Francisco peninsula has been exceedingly complex for centuries; its future promises to be even more complicated. To coast live oaks and hummingbirds, our deliberations about the meaning of history are critically important. Should the Presidio forest be replicated, acre for acre and tree for tree, the web of life will unravel a little more, and acorns will find few places to put down roots. If our plans for the future of the Presidio forest are informed by diversity as well as history, the oaks will return in greater and greater numbers.

In a forgotten little corner of the Presidio, not far from a cemetery buried beneath a landfill, oak saplings strain for the light beneath fifty-year-old pine trees. Most eventually die for lack of light, but a few struggle on. Next winter, after one of the pines gives up under the strain of a December storm, will the park plant another pine destined to shade out the oak saplings? Will a narrow vision of what a forest should look like cut short the life of a young oak tree? Our answer to these questions will reveal much about our hope for the future and our fascination with the past. But sometimes, by listening to coast live oaks and vireos, we can learn much about the many hidden dimensions of our multistoried history.

References

Adams, Ansel, with Mary Street Alinder. 1985. *Ansel Adams: An Autobiography.* Boston, MA: Little, Brown.

Anderson, Kat. 1993. "Native Californians as Ancient and Contemporary Cultivators." In *Before the Wilderness: Environmental Management by Native Californians.* T. Blackburn and K. Anderson, eds. Menlo Park, Calif.: Ballena Press.

Atwater, Brian F., Charles W. Hedel, and Edward J. Helley. 1977. *Late Quaternary Depositional History, Holocene Sea-Level Changes, and Vertical Crustal Movement, Southern San Francisco Bay, California.* Washington, D.C.: U.S. Geological Survey Professional Paper 1014.

Bocek, Barbara R. 1984. "Ethnobotany of Costanoan Indians, California, Based on Collections by John P. Harrington." *Economic Botany* 38: 240–255.

Bolton, Herbert Eugene. Ed. 1931. *Font's Complete Diary.* Berkeley: University of California Press.

Carter, Charles D. 1871. *San Francisco Real Estate Circular* 5:2.

Chamisso, Adelbert von. 1936. *A Sojourn at San Francisco Bay, 1816.* San Francisco: The Book Club of California.

Clary, Raymond H. 1980. *The Making of Golden Gate Park: The Early Years: 1865–1906.* San Francisco: California Living Books.

Cronon, William. 1995. "The Trouble with Wilderness; or, Getting Back to the Wrong Nature." In *Uncommon Ground: Toward Reinventing Nature.* W. Cronon, ed. New York: W. W. Norton.

Davis, Jeff N. 1995. "Hutton's Vireo (*Vireo huttoni*)." In *The Birds of North America,* No. 189. A. Poole and F. Gill, eds. Washington, D.C.: The Academy of Natural Sciences, Philadelphia & The American Ornithologists' Union.

De Benedictis, J. A., D. L. Wagner, and J. B. Whitfield. 1990. "Larval Hosts of Microlepidoptera of the San Bruno Mountains, California." *Atala* 16:14–18.

Department of the Army and the U.S. Army Corps of Engineers. 1996. *The Archeology of the Presidio of San Francisco.* San Francisco.

Department of the Interior. 1992. *The Secretary of the Interior's Standard for the Treatment of Historic Properties.* Washington, D.C.

Flores, Dan. 1994. "Place: An Argument for Bioregional History." *Environmental History Review* 18:1–18.

Golden Gate National Recreation Area. 1993. *Presidio of San Francisco, National Register of Historic Places Registration Forms.* San Francisco.

Golden Gate National Recreation Area. 1994. *Final General Management Plan Amendment, Presidio of San Francisco.* San Francisco.

Holloran, Peter. 1996. "The Greening of the Golden Gate: Community-based Restoration at the Presidio of San Francisco." *Restoration & Management Notes* 14:112–123.

Jones, W. A. 1883. *Plan for the Cultivation of Trees Upon the Presidio Reservation.* Copy in Bancroft Library, University of California at Berkeley.

Langston, Nancy. 1995. *Forest Dreams, Forest Nightmares: The Paradox of Old Growth in the Inland West.* Seattle, WA: University of Washington Press.

Maniery, Mary L. 1994. *Summary of the San Francisco Marine Hospital Cemetery, Presidio of San Francisco, California.* Unpublished report for U.S. Army Corps of Engineers and Jones & Stokes Associates.

Meier, Lauren. 1992. "The Treatment of Historic Plant Material." *The Public Garden* (April).

Milliken, Randall. 1995. *A Time of Little Choice: The Disintegration of Tribal Culture in the San Francisco Bay Area, 1769–1810.* Menlo Park, CA: Ballena Press.

Mitchell, Nora. 1997. "Protecting Landscapes: Contributions from Landscape Preservation to Management of Parks & Reserves." Presentation at George Wright Society, 9th Conference on Research & Resource Management, Albuquerque, New Mexico, March 17–21, 1997.

Pyle, R. M., M. Bentzien, and P. Opler. 1981. "Insect Conservation." *Annual Review of Entomology* 26:233–258.

Richardson, Steve. n.d. "The Days of the Dons." In *San Francisco Memoirs, 1835–1851: Eyewitness Accounts of the Birth of a City.* M. E. Barker, ed. San Francisco: Londonborn.

Thompson, Erwin N. n.d. "The Presidio Forest" (draft). Published in 1997 as a chapter in his *Defender of the Gate: The Presidio of San Francisco, a History from 1846 to 1995.* San Francisco: Golden Gate National Recreation Area.

Thompson, Erwin N., and Sally B. Woodbridge. 1992. *Special History Study: Presidio of San Francisco: An Outline of Its Evolution as a U.S. Army Post, 1847–1990.* Denver, CO: Golden Gate National Recreation Area.

Vasey, Mike. 1997. "Baseline Inventory of Terrestrial Vegetation on Natural Lands of the Presidio of San Francisco, California." Unpublished draft report available from Golden Gate National Recreation Area, San Francisco.

Wells, Lisa E. 1995. "Environmental Setting and Quaternary History of the San Francisco Estuary." In *Recent Geologic Studies in the San Francisco Bay Area.* E. M. Sanginés, D. W. Anderson, and A. B. Buising, eds. Pacific section, Society of Economic Paleontologists and Mineralogists.

Williams, Ted. 1991. "Don't Worry, Plant a Tree." *Audubon* (May).

About the Contributors

Nicholson Baker is the author of four novels—*The Mezzanine, Room Temperature, Vox,* and *The Fermata*—and two works of nonfiction, *U and I* and *The Size of Thoughts*. He lives in Berkeley with his wife and two children.

Gray Brechin is a doctoral candidate in the University of California, Berkeley, Geography Department. A former San Francisco journalist, he is the author of numerous articles on the environment and architectural history. His *Farewell, Promised Land: Waking from the California Dream* (with Robert Dawson) and *Imperial San Francisco: Urban Power, Earthly Ruin* will be published by the University of California Press.

James Brook is a poet and translator living in San Francisco. He has translated works by Guy Debord, Victor Serge, Benjamin Péret, Gellu Naum, Alberto Savinio, and others. He edited, with Iain Boal, *Resisting the Virtual Life: The Culture and Politics of Information*.

Chris Carlsson, co-founded *Processed World* magazine (1981–1993) and edited the anthology *Bad Attitude*. He will release in 1998 *Shaping San Francisco*, a multimedia, digital companion to *Reclaiming San Francisco*, which will be available as a CD-ROM and as free public kiosks around San Francisco. In spite of his longstanding hostility to religion, he attends Critical Mass on the last Friday of every month, a San Francisco ritual he helped begin in 1992.

Jon Christensen is editor of *Great Basin*, a quarterly of journalism, literature, and art. He also writes for *The New York Times, Pacific News Service, High Country News,* and other publications. He is working on a book about the Great Basin for the University of Nevada Press. He lives with his family in Carson City, Nevada.

Timothy W. Drescher has been a community mural activist for over twenty-five years. He was a member of PLACA and one of the organizers of the *ILWU Mural-sculpture* in San Francisco. Former editor of *Community Murals Magazine*, he is the author of *San Francisco Murals: Community Creates Its Muse 1914–1994*. He teaches in the Interdisciplinary Humanities Department at San Francisco State University.

Jesse Drew is a videomaker, writer, and activist living in San Francisco. He once stopped a busload of Republican Convention delegates by sticking a potato in the tailpipe of the diesel engine, and thus truly appreciates the power of our vegetable friends.

Ann Garrison is a San Francisco writer. She has written for *The San Francisco Examiner, The San Jose Mercury News, San Francisco Focus, Macworld, Macweek, Cable in the Classroom, Interactions,* KQED-FM, and NBC News.

Juan Felipe Herrera, marauder poet and co-founder of Manikrudo Spoken Word Ensemble, lives and works in Fresno, California. His most recent book is *Mayan Drifter: Chicano Poet in the Lowlands of America.*

Pete Holloran is a volunteer with the Golden Gate National Recreation Area and president of the Yerba Buena chapter of the California Native Plant Society. Trained as a historian, he helped edit the papers of Martin Luther King, Jr., at Stanford University from 1985 to 1997.

Wade Hudson was an editor of the *Tenderloin Times* in the 1980s. Today, Hudson, a community organizer and writer who still lives in the Tenderloin, is a part-time cab driver, coordinator of the Economic Security Project, and author of *Economic Security for All: How to End Poverty in the United States.*

Anthony W. Lee is an Assistant Professor of Art History at the University of Texas at Dallas and the author of *Painting on the Left: Diego Rivera, Radical Politics, and San Francisco's Public Murals.*

Tommy L. Lott currently teaches philosophy at the University of Missouri, St. Louis. He has written two books, *Like Rum in the Punch: Alain Locke and the Theory of African American Culture* and *The Invention of Race.* He is also the editor of *Subjugation and Bondage: Critical Essays on Slavery and Social Philosophy,* and co-editor with John P. Pittman of the *Blackwell Companion to African American Philosophy, 1999.*

Bernie Lubell is an artist whose interactive installations have evolved from his graduate studies in psychology, which he interrupted twenty-seven years ago to come to San Francisco. Lubell has shown work in the Bay Area and Los Angeles.

Juliet Flower MacCannell, Professor Emerita of the University of California, Irvine, is a writer and artist whose current projects include *Things to Come: The Hysteric's Guide to the Future Female Subject* and further San Francisco collaborations with Bernie Lubell and Dean MacCannell. Her best-known books are *The Regime of the Brother, Figuring Lacan,* and *Thinking Bodies.* She was Artist in Residence, Headlands Center for the Arts in 1993.

Dean MacCannell is a San Francisco-based writer who has recently turned to performance and installation work. He teaches in the Department of Environmental Design and Landscape Architecture at the University of California, Davis. Recent books include *The Tourist: A New Theory of the Leisure Class* and *Empty Meeting Grounds.* His work has been featured on PBS and BBC.

Marina McDougall is an independent curator who has worked with the Exploratorium in San Francisco and the Museum of Jurassic Technology in Los Angeles. Her short films *A Monumental Landscape*, *If You Lived Here, You'd Be Home by Now*, and the forthcoming *Concrete Trilogy* explore the urban landscape.

Hope Mitnick practices architecture, designs museum exhibits, and creates sets for films located in San Francisco.

Nancy J. Peters is editor-in-chief of City Lights Books. She is the co-author, with Lawrence Ferlinghetti, of *The Literary World of San Francisco: A Pictorial History of Its Beginnings to the Present Day* and editor of *War After War* and the *City Lights Review*.

Gayle S. Rubin is an anthropologist who teaches women's studies at the University of California at Santa Cruz. She is writing a book on San Francisco's gay male leather community. A collection of her essays on feminism, sexuality, gender, and politics will be published by the University of California Press.

Susan Schwartzenberg is a photographer who has exhibited her work internationally. Her recent book *Cento: A Market Street Journal* was commissioned by the San Francisco Art Commission. She is Director of Media at the Exploratorium in San Francisco.

Randy Shaw is the Director of the Tenderloin Housing Clinic and author of *The Activist's Handbook: A Primer for the 1990s and Beyond*. See his "Ask the Activist" column at http://www.igc.org/activist. His e-mail address is thc@igc.apc.org.

Georgia Smith lived and worked in San Francisco for many years, producing public television documentaries and news. Her first piece of writing for the theater, *Salon Viardot*, was recently produced in San Francisco. She lives in Paris.

James Sobredo has a Ph.D. from UC Berkeley and is currently an assistant professor in his specialty, Asian-American Studies, at Cal State University, Northridge.

Richard A. Walker is Professor and Chair of Geography at the University of California, Berkeley, where he has taught since 1975. He has written on a wide range of topics in economic and urban geography, as well as environmental policy, philosophy, and California studies. He is co-author, with Michael Storper, of *The Capitalist Imperative: Territory, Technology and Industrial Growth* and, with Andrew Sayer, of *The New Social Economy: Reworking the Division of Labor*. He is at work on a book on the economic, political, and cultural geography of the San Francisco Bay Area.

Rob Waters was editor of the *Tenderloin Times* in the 1980s. Today, Waters writes on health, family, and social issues for *Health* magazine and other publications, and teaches journalism at San Francisco State University.

SHAPING San Francisco
An Interactive Multimedia Excavation of
the Lost History of San Francisco

SAN FRANCISCO HISTORY—
LIKE YOU'VE NEVER SEEN IT BEFORE!

SHAPING San Francisco

(CD-ROM for Windows 3.x, 95, NT)

"Due to its content alone, it is one of the most impressive and continually intriguing CD-ROMs ever produced... *Shaping San Francisco* is truly a magnificent achievement, ... an attempt to make good on the promises of multimedia that were so exciting five years ago."

—*Microtimes*, May 1998

"Unlike most CD-ROMs, with their bland [writing], seemingly lifted from encyclopedic micro-essays, *Shaping San Francisco*'s text is engaging, intellectual and lengthy."   —*S.F. Bay Guardian*, January 14, 1998

"*Shaping San Francisco* is a history of the city—with a distinctively activist bent. *Shaping San Francisco* doesn't ignore the city's beauty... [but] it is not the usual cable car and sourdough view..."

—*San Francisco Chronicle*, January 20, 1998

Available for $35 plus $5 S/H by mail from City Lights Mail Order **OR** Shaping San Francisco, 1095 Market Street, Suite 210, San Francisco, CA 94103, or call (415) 626-2060. Order by credit card by phone: 1-888-425-7737 or on the internet from AK Press (www.akpress.org)

CITY LIGHTS PUBLICATIONS

CITY LIGHTS REVIEW #4: Literature / Politics / Ecology
Cocteau, Jean. THE WHITE BOOK (LE LIVRE BLANC)
Cornford, Adam. ANIMATIONS
Cortázar, Julio. SAVE TWILIGHT
Corso, Gregory. GASOLINE
Cuadros, Gil. CITY OF GOD
Daumal, René. THE POWERS OF THE WORD
David-Neel, Alexandra. SECRET ORAL TEACHINGS IN TIBETAN BUDDHIST
    SECTS
Deleuze, Gilles. SPINOZA: Practical Philosophy
Dick, Leslie. KICKING
Dick, Leslie. WITHOUT FALLING
di Prima, Diane. PIECES OF A SONG: Selected Poems
Doolittle, Hilda (H.D.). NOTES ON THOUGHT & VISION
Ducornet, Rikki. ENTERING FIRE
Eberhardt, Isabelle. DEPARTURES: Selected Writings
Eberhardt, Isabelle. THE OBLIVION SEEKERS
Eidus, Janice. VITO LOVES GERALDINE
Fenollosa, Ernest. CHINESE WRITTEN CHARACTER AS A MEDIUM FOR
    POETRY
Ferlinghetti, L. ed. CITY LIGHTS POCKET POETS ANTHOLOGY
Ferlinghetti, L., ed. ENDS & BEGINNINGS (City Lights Review #6)
Ferlinghetti, L. PICTURES OF THE GONE WORLD
Finley, Karen. SHOCK TREATMENT
Ford, Charles Henri. OUT OF THE LABYRINTH: Selected Poems
Franzen, Cola, transl. POEMS OF ARAB ANDALUSIA
García Lorca, Federico. BARBAROUS NIGHTS: Legends & Plays
García Lorca, Federico. ODE TO WALT WHITMAN & OTHER POEMS
García Lorca, Federico. POEM OF THE DEEP SONG
Garon, Paul. BLUES & THE POETIC SPIRIT
Gil de Biedma, Jaime. LONGING: SELECTED POEMS
Ginsberg, Allen. THE FALL OF AMERICA
Ginsberg, Allen. HOWL & OTHER POEMS
Ginsberg, Allen. KADDISH & OTHER POEMS
Ginsberg, Allen. MIND BREATHS
Ginsberg, Allen. PLANET NEWS
Ginsberg, Allen. PLUTONIAN ODE
Ginsberg, Allen. REALITY SANDWICHES
Goethe, J. W. von. TALES FOR TRANSFORMATION
Gómez-Peña, Guillermo. THE NEW WORLD BORDER

Harryman, Carla. THERE NEVER WAS A ROSE WITHOUT A THORN
Heider, Ulrike. ANARCHISM: Left Right & Green
Herron, Don. THE DASHIELL HAMMETT TOUR: A Guidebook
Higman, Perry, tr. LOVE POEMS FROM SPAIN AND SPANISH AMERICA
Jaffe, Harold. EROS: ANTI-EROS
Jenkins, Edith. AGAINST A FIELD SINISTER
Katzenberger, Elaine, ed. FIRST WORLD, HA HA HA!: The Zapatista Challenge
Kerouac, Jack. BOOK OF DREAMS
Kerouac, Jack. POMES ALL SIZES
Kerouac, Jack. SCATTERED POEMS
Kerouac, Jack. SCRIPTURE OF THE GOLDEN ETERNITY
Lacarrière, Jacques. THE GNOSTICS
La Duke, Betty. COMPAÑERAS
La Loca. ADVENTURES ON THE ISLE OF ADOLESCENCE
Lamantia, Philip. BED OF SPHINXES: SELECTED POEMS
Lamantia, Philip. MEADOWLARK WEST
Laughlin, James. SELECTED POEMS: 1935–1985
Laure. THE COLLECTED WRITINGS
Le Brun, Annie. SADE: On the Brink of the Abyss
Mackey, Nathaniel. SCHOOL OF UDHRA
Masereel, Frans. PASSIONATE JOURNEY
Mayakovsky, Vladimir. LISTEN! EARLY POEMS
Morgan, William. BEAT GENERATION IN NEW YORK
Mrabet, Mohammed. THE BOY WHO SET THE FIRE
Mrabet, Mohammed. THE LEMON
Mrabet, Mohammed. LOVE WITH A FEW HAIRS
Mrabet, Mohammed. M'HASHISH
Murguía, A. & B. Paschke, eds. VOLCAN: Poems from Central America
Murillo, Rosario. ANGEL IN THE DELUGE
Nadir, Shams. THE ASTROLABE OF THE SEA
Parenti, Michael. AGAINST EMPIRE
Parenti, Michael. BLACKSHIRTS & REDS
Parenti, Michael. DIRTY TRUTHS
Pasolini, Pier Paolo. ROMAN POEMS
Pessoa, Fernando. ALWAYS ASTONISHED
Peters, Nancy J., ed. WAR AFTER WAR (City Lights Review #5)
Poe, Edgar Allan. THE UNKNOWN POE
Porta, Antonio. KISSES FROM ANOTHER DREAM
Prévert, Jacques. PAROLES
Purdy, James. THE CANDLES OF YOUR EYES

Purdy, James. GARMENTS THE LIVING WEAR
Purdy, James. IN A SHALLOW GRAVE
Purdy, James. OUT WITH THE STARS
Rachlin, Nahid. THE HEART'S DESIRE
Rachlin, Nahid. MARRIED TO A STRANGER
Rachlin, Nahid. VEILS: SHORT STORIES
Reed, Jeremy. DELIRIUM: An Interpretation of Arthur Rimbaud
Reed, Jeremy. RED-HAIRED ANDROID
Rey Rosa, Rodrigo. THE BEGGAR'S KNIFE
Rey Rosa, Rodrigo. DUST ON HER TONGUE
Rigaud, Milo. SECRETS OF VOODOO
Ross, Dorien. RETURNING TO A
Ruy Sánchez, Alberto. MOGADOR
Saadawi, Nawal El. MEMOIRS OF A WOMAN DOCTOR
Sawyer-Lauçanno, Christopher. THE CONTINUAL PILGRIMAGE: American
      Writers in Paris 1944-1960
Sawyer-Lauçanno, Christopher, transl. THE DESTRUCTION OF THE JAGUAR
Scholder, Amy, ed. CRITICAL CONDITION: Women on the Edge of Violence
Sclauzero, Mariarosa. MARLENE
Serge, Victor. RESISTANCE
Shepard, Sam. MOTEL CHRONICLES
Shepard, Sam. FOOL FOR LOVE & THE SAD LAMENT OF PECOS BILL
Smith, Michael. IT A COME
Snyder, Gary. THE OLD WAYS
Solnit, Rebecca. SECRET EXHIBITION: Six California Artists
Sussler, Betsy, ed. BOMB: INTERVIEWS
Takahashi, Mutsuo. SLEEPING SINNING FALLING
Turyn, Anne, ed. TOP TOP STORIES
Tutuola, Amos. SIMBI & THE SATYR OF THE DARK JUNGLE
Ullman, Ellen. CLOSE TO THE MACHINE: Technophilia and Its Discontents
Valaoritis, Nanos. MY AFTERLIFE GUARANTEED
VandenBroeck, André. BREAKING THROUGH
Vega, Janine Pommy. TRACKING THE SERPENT
Veltri, George. NICE BOY
Waldman, Anne. FAST SPEAKING WOMAN
Wilson, Colin. POETRY AND MYSTICISM
Wilson, Peter Lamborn. PLOUGHING THE CLOUDS
Wilson, Peter Lamborn. SACRED DRIFT
Wynne, John. THE OTHER WORLD
Zamora, Daisy. RIVERBED OF MEMORY

San Francisco peninsula as portrayed in the U.S. Coast Survey Map of 1869,
with 1990s neighborhood names superimposed